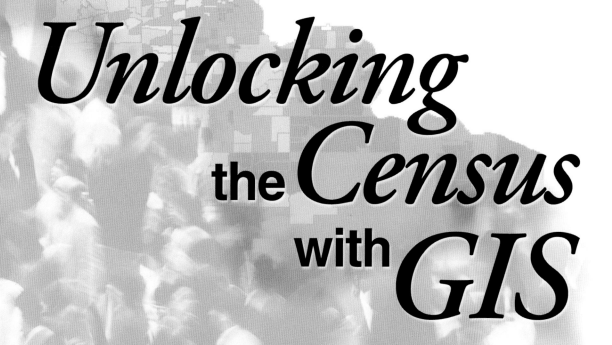

Unlocking
the *Census*
with *GIS*

Alan Peters and Heather MacDonald

ESRI Press
REDLANDS, CALIFORNIA

First printing June 2004.
Printed in the United States of America.

Library of Congress Cataloging-in-Publication Data
Peters, Alan H.
Unlocking the Census with GIS / Alan Peters and Heather MacDonald.
     p. cm.
   Includes bibliographical references and index.
   ISBN 1-58948-113-5 (pbk. : alk. paper)
   1. United States-Census-Handbooks, manuals, etc. 2. Geographic information systems-Handbooks, manuals, etc.
   3. United States-Population-Statistics-Data processing. 4. United States-Economic conditions-Statistics-Data
   processing. 5. Housing-United States-Statistics-Data processing. 6. United States-Census, 22nd, 2000.
   I. MacDonald, Heather I. (Heather Isabella), 1960- II. Title.
   HA37.U55P48 2004
   317.3--dc22   2004012552

Published by ESRI, 380 New York Street, Redlands, California 92373-8100.

Books from ESRI Press are available to resellers worldwide through Independent Publishers Group (IPG).
For information on volume discounts, or to place an order, call IPG at 1-800-888-4741 in the United States,
or at 312-337-0747 outside the United States.

Contents

List of maps

List of tables

This book is aimed at professionals and students who would like to make more effective use of census data in their work. Our book assumes no prior knowledge of the census or other official data sources and only the barest of acquaintance with geographic information systems (GIS). However, even if readers don't have access to GIS, the book should still be useful because most of it explains the organization and content of the census. Since access to census data is increasingly Web-based, readers will get the most benefit from this book if they have an Internet connection handy. For some of the material, an understanding of basic statistical analyses will be helpful, particularly with parts of chapters 1, 4, and 6.

We planned this book initially as a short guide to the 2000 Census of Population and Housing; however, the project soon developed into something much more comprehensive. The book's main focus remains the 2000 Census, but we now also deal (though in much less detail) with earlier Censuses of Population and Housing, the TIGER/Line® mapping system, the Economic Census, the American Community Survey, and a range of other related data sources. One of the central themes of the book is how GIS can be used to simplify access to and analysis of data that is presented in a fundamentally spatial format. GIS software is now much more widely available than it was just a few years ago; it is also now much easier to use. With this in mind we designed the book focusing on ways in which novice users of both GIS and the census could use GIS technology to improve their understanding of the census.

In each chapter, readers will find sidebars; in most cases they cover interesting facts about the census or a data source. There are also separate text boxes where we deal with more complex issues than those in the main text. At the end of chapters 3 through 6 we include applied examples of census analysis. We have endeavored to choose examples that show important principles at work or techniques that have broad applicability to census use. These examples are hypothetical, created by us to illustrate practical applications. They do not reflect actual decision-making processes in actual agencies.

The first chapter of the book is an organizational and conceptual introduction to the Census of Population and Housing. The focus here is on the questionnaires, census geography, the organization of data output, the reliability of the data, and the American Community Survey. Since most other official data sources rely on organizational concepts similar to those used in the Census of Population, much of the material in this chapter has applicability to a wide range of data.

Chapter 2 is a hands-on explanation of how to acquire census data and census maps, and then connect the two. A detailed tutorial on using American FactFinder, the Census Bureau's main Web-based data access tool, as well as guidelines on using databases to manage and link census data are included in this chapter. A detailed description of the Census Bureau's TIGER/ Line mapping system and a section on accessing other official maps useful to urban analysts are also included.

Chapter 3 explains the demographic and social variables in the Census of Population and Housing and then briefly summarizes the vast array of other official and semi-official data sources related to these topics. The two examples developed in this chapter deal with two challenges (and opportunities) raised by the spatial analysis of secondary data. The first shows readers how to deal with changes to census geography and concepts to do analyses over time, and the second suggests a method of defining coherent "neighborhoods" (and determining whether they exist).

Chapter 4 looks at the economic variables in the Census of Population and Housing and then discusses the Economic Census and the various economic data sources published by the Census Bureau, the Bureau of Labor Statistics, and the Bureau of Economic Analysis that are commonly used by analysts at the local level (i.e., programs such as County Business Patterns and ES202). The first applied example at the end of the chapter shows how a variety of census data formats can be combined to analyze concentrations of poverty and to identify locations of opportunity. The second shows how to deal with the data holes created by the application of nondisclosure rules to local economic data, and then goes on to construct a local employment multiplier.

Chapter 5 examines the housing data collected in the Census of Population and Housing (much of which will soon be collected annually in the American Community Survey instead of in decennial censuses). Other sources of housing data collected by the Census Bureau and the Department of Housing and Urban Development, other federal and state agencies, and private organizations are explained. The first example in this chapter demonstrates how the spatial analysis of census data can be used to determine target locations for new housing development, focusing on strategies to update information that is often fairly dated by the time the census is released. The second example shows how other data sources that provide more detail on specific housing characteristics (such as the American Housing Survey) can be combined with census data to answer specific questions (in this instance, about housing quality).

Chapter 6 covers transportation. We begin by looking at the transportation variables in the Census of Population and Housing, then describe the two data products derived from the census that also provide information not available anywhere else: the Public Use Microdata Sample (PUMS) and the Census Transportation Planning Package (CTPP). Both of these are widely used by transportation professionals. This chapter also covers various other transportation data sources. The first applied example shows how microdata can be used to develop estimates of modal choice and how confidence intervals can be constructed for these estimates. The second example shows how journey-to-work data can be used to examine the effectiveness of an employment policy experiment aimed at increasing localized labor demand in a metropolitan area.

Finally, chapter 7 is a brief introduction to the issues involved in disseminating the results of census analyses. After an introductory discussion of the potential that GIS holds to democratize access to data in local communities, the chapter continues with an evaluation of alternative data dissemination strategies.

At first encounter, the census can seem a dauntingly large and complex beast. It is not always clear what data can be used to answer the particular question at hand, and often key pieces of data are not collected in the decennial census. The Census Bureau has tried to ease these problems with their wonderfully rich and helpful Web site at *www.census.gov*. The bureau also publishes a large number of documents indispensable to census data analysis. However, navigating around these resources can itself be intimidating and confusing. We hope that this guide to the census and related data sources will demystify the choices and suggest practical solutions to many of the dilemmas users of secondary data face. We also hope that by focusing on GIS as an enabling technology for data acquisition and analysis, we will encourage faster, more efficient, and most importantly, more meaningful analyses using census data.

Although both of us had substantial experience using census data to analyze urban and regional problems when we began this project, writing this book has also been a learning experience for us. Mostly, these lessons have been very positive and have further convinced us of the untapped potential the data has to diagnose urban problems, to inform policy or investment decisions, and to evaluate the consequences of those decisions. The next decade will bring significant changes in the way we collect and organize information about people and how they live, work, and travel. Annual (rather than decennial) updates to this information, as well as improved timeliness, will significantly increase its usefulness for urban analysts. We suspect this will also make census-based spatial analysis a more central and indispensable professional skill—not just for planners, but for all those involved in improving urban life.

Alan Peters
Heather MacDonald

Acknowledgments

Without countless other people this book would not exist. We are particularly grateful to ESRI for supporting this book and to Christian Harder, publisher of ESRI Press, and our editor, Dave Boyles, for moving the book from a rough idea to completion. We also thank Savitri Brant, who designed the book and cover; Tiffany Wilkerson, who did the copyediting; Edith M. Punt, who did the cartographic review; and Cliff Crabbe, who supervised print production.

Our knowledge of and experience with the census has developed over many years of research and consulting. Nearly every project we have worked on has brought its own census data challenges. Staff at the Census Bureau, the Bureau of Labor Statistics, and the Bureau of Transportation Statistics have always been ready with help, advice, and common sense. For this book in particular we are immensely grateful for the help and guidance given by the wonderfully knowledgeable people on the Census Bureau staff. Over the years we have also been helped, nudged, prompted, and guided by the staff at the Government Documents Library at the University of Iowa and at the Employment Statistics Bureau of Iowa Workforce Development. When learning about map data, the Iowa Geological Survey Bureau (IGSB) was almost always the place where we started. At IGSB, Jim Giglierano deserves special mention for his help and patience. The IGSB provided some of the orthophotography and other map data we used in the book. Jason Siebrecht, the GIS coordinator for Linn County, Iowa, also provided photography, and we are grateful to him.

In our home department, the Graduate Program in Urban and Regional Planning at the University of Iowa, John Fuller has always been a helpful resource. John, a professor specializing in transportation regulation, has an uncannily consistent ability to know what data you need (even before you do) and then find it. He helped greatly with chapter 6, and we thank him. We also thank Paul Hanley, who contributed material to chapter 6. David Connolly, a graduate student and research assistant, did an excellent job of fact-checking and made many helpful suggestions for restructuring earlier drafts of the book. Thanks also to Xiaobei Chen for the design of the ESRI® ArcIMS® site we discuss in chapter 7. The graduate planning students we have taught over the years were the real source of our idea for this book, which we conceived as both a guide to beginning users and a helpful resource for those who have called on us for advice many years after graduating.

Try as we may, there are bound to be errors in a book such as this. For these errors we apologize to our readers. The errors are ours and not the fault of any of those who helped us.

Chapter 1

The *census:*
An *introduction*

At the beginning of the last century, most U.S. households contained seven or more people. By 1950, most households contained two people.

In 1950, people living alone accounted for less than one out of ten households (9.5 percent). By 2000, more than one out of four households, about 26 percent, consisted of a person living alone.

Women headed one out of five households in 1970, but thirty years later they headed one out of every three households.

In 1950, about 78 percent of households were made up of married couples; in 2000, married couples represented only about half of all households (nearly 52 percent). During that same period, other types of family households (men and women living with family members but with no spouse) grew from 11.3 percent of all households to 16.4 percent.

Nearly half of all family households headed by a man with no spouse, and nearly three out of ten of family households headed by a woman with no spouse, had children under 18 in 2000 (compared to one in five for male-headed and about one in three female-headed households in 1950) (Hobbs and Stoops 2002, chapter 5).

Underlying this brief synopsis is an array of dramatic social and economic changes that have occurred over the past century—different mores regarding divorce and children born outside marriage, new economic opportunities for women, changed responsibility for elderly parents, and a housing market more accommodating to individuals living alone. Talk-show hosts and politicians may see in these numbers yet another indicator of the decline of U.S. standards of morality; others may applaud the decline of the "married majority" and the expansion of individual choice that these changing demographics indicate.

Regardless of one's personal attitudes, understanding changes in household structure (along with changes in the population, housing stock, commuting patterns, and economy) is the starting place for responding to the new challenges and opportunities they present. A recent cover story in *Business Week* proclaims the latest round of social revolution: "Unmarried America: say goodbye to the traditional family. Here's how the new demographics will change business and society" (Conlin 2003, 106). The tax and pension penalties that unmarried people bear are the focus of the article; similar points could be made about job structure, health care, and housing. Governments, firms, and social organizations ignore changing social and economic structure at their peril.

As the source of the data quoted above, the U.S. census plays an essential role in charting and analyzing these changes. Exponential improvements in computer hardware and software over the past decades have enabled a wider range of analysts (even those with quite limited technical ability) to answer the questions that should shape intelligent public policy. While many types of researchers may make use of the census (from market researchers to investment analysts to presidential candidates), we focus here on researchers with a primarily urban and regional focus. For this group of users, the spatial analysis capabilities we have at the beginning of the twenty-first century offer an exciting way to enrich our understanding of the implications of the bald numbers in the census files.

This book focuses on the research needs of a broadly defined group of "urban analysts"—city planners, community development organizations, real estate development firms, economic development specialists, transportation planners and engineers, property appraisers, and social service providers. We assume readers are well acquainted with the substantive challenges entailed in analyzing cities and regions and have a basic level of familiarity with widely used computer programs such as spreadsheets and general-purpose databases. We assume readers have little or no familiarity with census data or GIS software, although we do not provide a manual for any particular GIS software package. Rather, we aim to provide the beginning or intermediate census user with the principles, skills, and techniques needed to locate, download, and analyze available data using any one of a number of GIS packages on the market. We expect the reader will consult the manual for the particular package used to find out how to create a thematic map, perform a travel-demand analysis, and so on. Our book, we hope, will answer all the essential questions a researcher may have about how to link census and other urban or regional data to any particular GIS package, how to design analyses to answer specific questions, and how to interpret the results.

This chapter introduces the key principles and concepts underlying the U.S. census. The remainder of this section defines the census and explains how it has evolved in the United States since it was first conducted in 1790. The role of GIS in census-based analyses is outlined. The second section describes the decennial census (the Census of Population and Housing) and explains why and how it has evolved to the present. In this section we discuss the major way the decennial census will change in the next decade as the American Community Survey (ACS) is phased in to replace the so-called "long form"—the detailed demographic, economic, and housing questions asked of a sample of U.S. households. We address the issues raised by sampling, rather than enumerating, all these detailed characteristics. Finally, we discuss the accuracy of the data.

The third section of the chapter covers the basic concepts users should grasp to use the data appropriately. Census geography and geographic summary levels are explained. These concepts are the basis for the description of the geographic hierarchy and the FIPS (Federal Information Processing Standards) numbering system with which all spatial analysts work. The organization of summary files, tables, and variables is explained next. Finally, the major census data products are described. This section aims to demystify the initially confusing (but quite logically structured) array of data types confronting a new user. Where appropriate, we refer the reader to the detailed technical documentation provided by the Census Bureau.

What is "the census"?

"The census" is actually many different censuses and various related surveys. So what is a census? The word "census" comes to us from the Latin *censere* (or in English to *assess*) and originally referred to the enumeration and registration of people and property, often for the purpose of taxation. In its more modern sense (which entered the English language only in the middle eighteenth century) a "census" is usually understood to be an enumeration—that is, a count of everybody or everything. The Census of Population and Housing, the particular census that many professionals mean when they use the word "census," does include a 100 percent count of a population and housing. Surveys, which provide most of the information in the Census of Population and Housing, are usually understood to rely on a sample of people or households or businesses or whatever. New users may wonder whether the census would be better if none of it was based on a sample; the intuition here is that counting everything is surely better than counting only some things.

In fact, most demographers argue that a properly defined survey may give *more* accurate information than a full enumeration would. The Census Bureau, the agency responsible for conducting the Census of Population and Housing and various related surveys, uses surveys both because they are often more accurate than full enumerations, and also because they are much cheaper. However, the Census Bureau also continues to enumerate the population because, in January 1999, the Supreme Court ruled that Section 195 of Title 13 of the U.S. Code precludes the use of statistical sampling to produce congressional apportionment counts.[1] Sampling is however legal for other (nonapportionment) purposes, including redistricting.

What is a 100 percent count (a full enumeration) of the population? Does the Census Bureau ever miss people in its decennial Census of Population and Housing? In other words, is the 100 percent count really 100 percent? Are all homeless people counted? Are illegal immigrants ever missed? And what about those people who, for whatever reason, prefer to have no contact with government? In fact, it is likely that the census fails to count millions of people. Moreover, not all those missed are homeless, illegal immigrants, or radical libertarians. So a 100 percent census

[1]Title 13 of the U.S. Code specifies the powers and duties of the Census Bureau, the basic procedures of the census, and the sort of data that may be collected.

does not necessarily cover 100 percent of people—this is why surveys may be more accurate than censuses. Using statistical techniques, samples can be designed to deal explicitly with the problem of hard-to-count populations. Fortunately we have a *fairly* good idea of how many people have been missed, what they look like, and where they live. But *fairly* good is far from complete information. We have better data on how many African-Americans are missed than, say, how many illegal immigrants are missed. And counts of the homeless population are, in most cases, little better than broad estimates. So the Census of Population and Housing is not quite as complete as many would like to believe. But in many cases it provides us with the best data there is on people in the United States. Moreover, the data has status in law. The process of apportioning the 435 seats in the House of Representatives to the fifty states, mandated by Article 1 Section 2 of the U.S. Constitution and undertaken every ten years, is based on the portion of the nation's population in each state as measured by the decennial census.[2]

The census population numbers are also used to

- determine many other state and local political districts;
- distribute federal funds to states and local areas, state funds to local areas, and federal, state, and local funds to individual neighborhoods (around $283 billion is distributed annually this way from the federal government alone); and
- evaluate many federal, state, and local programs.

Regardless of its flaws, the census has enormous importance in the daily lives of state and local planners, government officials, and most land-development professionals.

The Economic Census is the other major census program in the United States (we discuss the Economic Census in more detail in chapter 4). It is conducted every half-decade, in years ending in two and seven (e.g., 1992, 1997, 2002). Again, much of this "census" information actually relies on surveys. Both federal and state governments also conduct a number of independent surveys and censuses (County Business Patterns, Current Population Survey, ES202, and so on). In the subject-area chapters that follow, we point readers to a variety of related data sources. The discussion in this chapter focuses on the broad organization of the Census of Population and Housing. A large amount of other official data follows the general organizational structure of the Census of Population and Housing.

GIS and the census

At its simplest, a geographic information system (GIS) is a database manager connected to another software program that is able to draw maps digitally. Queries of the database can be shown using maps. So if we wanted to know which counties in New Jersey had a population of more than a million people, we would query an appropriate state or national database (usually derived from the Census of Population and Housing), and the GIS would then be instructed to draw a map indicating which counties met this criterion and which did not.

GIS software has been around since the 1970s, but it is only over the past decade that GIS has become broadly institutionalized in local government, urban planning, and other land

[2]Each state is assigned one representative, and the remaining 385 seats are distributed according to population.

professions (for simplicity, we will refer to this group of users as urban researchers). Technical users with interests in the census have used GIS since the technology surfaced in order to help make sense of the huge amount of information provided by the census. Over the past half decade, the number of people using GIS has dramatically increased due to changes in the technology. GIS has become both more powerful and easier to use, and the connection between GIS software and census data is now straightforward.

In fact, since the 1990 Census, a GIS has been an all but necessary tool for any significant census analysis. Census data can now be incorporated into a GIS, with minimal preprocessing. And a GIS will allow the connection of this data to other data sources in a way that traditional databases and statistical software do not. For instance, if you were to analyze how school children's travel time would change with rural school district consolidation, it would be necessary to combine demographic information on school districts (available from the Census of Population and Housing) with the location of schools (possibly from a text-based database of school street addresses that would then be geocoded—in others words, turned into a map). Travel times for individual children to proposed consolidated schools could then be computed and compared to current commuting times.

Admittedly, census data can be used by researchers without computers or any knowledge of GIS. It is possible to go to the census books in so-called "depository" libraries[3] and, provided you understand the rudiments of census geography and the variables, look up data the old-fashioned way. However, computers allow much faster, easier access to data. Thousands, if not millions, of pieces of data may be downloaded at one time into one of a variety of user-friendly file formats that make the data relatively easy to use and analyze. Doing this by hand would take months, if not years. GIS makes the acquisition and analysis of data much faster. Since the census is organized and published around defined spatial units—what we call "census geography," which includes states, counties, cities, tracts, and blocks—the built-in spatial analysis capabilities of a GIS make analyzing census data that much more intuitive and powerful. Many of the ancillary census products, such as TIGER/Line geographic data and the Census Transportation Planning Package (CTPP) journey-to-work data, are most useful when used within a GIS framework. So although you need not know GIS to use the census, a GIS will greatly simplify (and in some instances, make practically possible) more advanced analyses of census data.

The Census of Population and Housing

The U.S. Constitution mandates that the Census of Population and Housing be undertaken every ten years to apportion seats in the House of Representatives. Over the years the census has grown in size and function, collecting an increasingly wide range of data on the U.S. public.[4] Costs have also increased. In 1790 the census cost $44,377 and counted 3,929,214 people. In 2000 the census cost $4.5 billion and counted 281,421,906 people. Staff (enumerators) have also increased, from 650 in 1790 to over a half million in 2000. Although the U.S. census may

[3]Depository libraries (often at larger state universities) are designated by the Census Bureau as storekeepers (the Federal Depository Library Program). There are about fourteen hundred depository libraries in the nation, at least one in each congressional district. The libraries keep copies of most federal publications.
[4]For a complete description of the changes to the questions asked, see U.S. Census Bureau (2002a). The chapters that follow discuss recent changes.

Table 1.1 Summary of questions asked	
100 percent Short Form	
Name	Race
Household relationships	Hispanic origin
Sex	Tenure (home owned or rented)
Age	
Sample long form	
Population	**Housing**
Social characteristics	Physical characteristics
Marital status	Units in structure
Place of birth, citizenship, and year of entry	Year structure built
School enrollment and educational attainment	Number of rooms
Ancestry	Year moved into residence
Residence five years ago	Plumbing and kitchen facilities
Language spoken at home and ability to speak English	Telephone
Veteran status, disability	Vehicles available
Grandparents as caregivers	Heating fuel
Economic characteristics	Farm residence
Labor force status	Financial characteristics
Place of work and journey to work	Value of house or monthly rent paid
Occupation, industry, and class of worker	Utilities, mortgage, taxes, insurance, etc.
Work status in 1999	
Income in 1999	

Source: Adapted from U.S. Census Bureau (2002b) at www.census.gov/mso/www/c2000basics/00Basics.pdf.

not be the modern world's oldest (the eleventh century Domesday book is arguably the oldest; England's Board of Trade conducted local censuses in the American colonies beginning in the early 1600s, and Sweden conducted a full national census in 1749), it is the world's oldest continuous national census.

The census questionnaire

There are actually two questionnaires: the 100 percent short form questionnaire (which satisfies the legal requirements of apportionment) and the long form questionnaire completed by a sample of people and households. Nationwide, about one in six households receives the long form, but the rate varies considerably depending on the size of the area. In smaller areas the rate may be as high as one in two, while in densely populated areas it may be as low as one in eight.

Table 1.1 summarizes the questions asked in the short and long forms. The actual short form questionnaire for Census 2000 is shown in box 1.1, and the long form questionnaire is shown

[4]For a complete description of the changing questions asked, see U.S. Census Bureau (2002a). The chapters that follow discuss recent changes.

in the appendix. Before actually using census variables, it is always a good idea to look at the questions asked to generate those variables. Both the short and the long forms were printed in six languages in 2000 (English, Chinese, Korean, Spanish, Tagalog, and Vietnamese). Non-English forms could be requested in advance.

The questionnaire has changed over time. The Census Bureau has documented most of these changes and differences in instructions given to census enumerators in a wonderful historical publication, *Measuring America: The decennial census from 1790 to 2000* (U.S. Census Bureau 2002a).

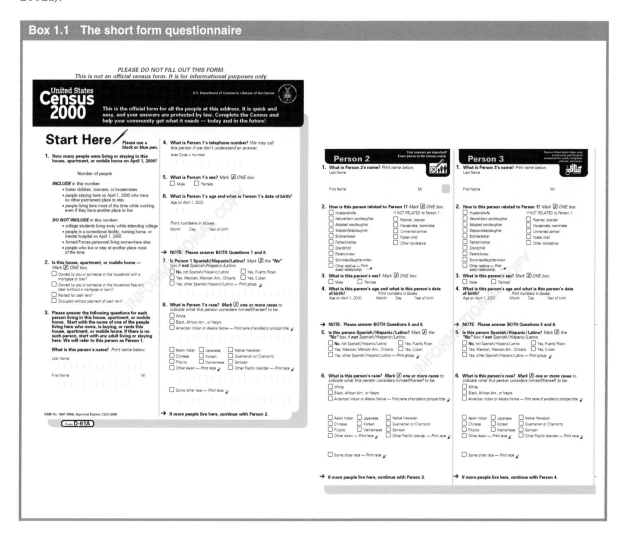

Box 1.1   The short form questionnaire

Box 1.1   The short form questionnaire (continued)

Unlocking the census with GIS

Person 4

Information about children helps your community plan for child care, education, and recreation.

1. What is Person 4's name? *Print name below.*
Last Name

First Name   MI

2. How is this person related to Person 1? *Mark ☒ ONE box.*
- ☐ Husband/wife
- ☐ Natural-born son/daughter
- ☐ Adopted son/daughter
- ☐ Stepson/stepdaughter
- ☐ Brother/sister
- ☐ Father/mother
- ☐ Grandchild
- ☐ Parent-in-law
- ☐ Son-in-law/daughter-in-law
- ☐ Other relative — *Print exact relationship.*

If NOT RELATED to Person 1:
- ☐ Roomer, boarder
- ☐ Housemate, roommate
- ☐ Unmarried partner
- ☐ Foster child
- ☐ Other nonrelative

3. What is this person's sex? *Mark ☒ ONE box.*
- ☐ Male
- ☐ Female

4. What is this person's age and what is this person's date of birth? *Print numbers in boxes.*
Age on April 1, 2000   Month   Day   Year of birth

→ NOTE: Please answer BOTH Questions 5 and 6.

5. Is this person Spanish/Hispanic/Latino? *Mark ☒ the "No" box if not Spanish/Hispanic/Latino.*
- ☐ No, not Spanish/Hispanic/Latino
- ☐ Yes, Mexican, Mexican Am., Chicano
- ☐ Yes, Puerto Rican
- ☐ Yes, Cuban
- ☐ Yes, other Spanish/Hispanic/Latino — *Print group.*

6. What is this person's race? *Mark ☒ one or more races to indicate what this person considers himself/herself to be.*
- ☐ White
- ☐ Black, African Am., or Negro
- ☐ American Indian or Alaska Native — *Print name of enrolled or principal tribe.*

- ☐ Asian Indian
- ☐ Chinese
- ☐ Filipino
- ☐ Other Asian — *Print race.*
- ☐ Japanese
- ☐ Korean
- ☐ Vietnamese
- ☐ Native Hawaiian
- ☐ Guamanian or Chamorro
- ☐ Samoan
- ☐ Other Pacific Islander — *Print race.*

- ☐ Some other race — *Print race.*

→ If more people live here, continue with Person 5.

Person 5

Knowing about age, race, and sex helps your community better meet the needs of everyone.

1. What is Person 5's name? *Print name below.*
Last Name

First Name   MI

2. How is this person related to Person 1? *Mark ☒ ONE box.*
- ☐ Husband/wife
- ☐ Natural-born son/daughter
- ☐ Adopted son/daughter
- ☐ Stepson/stepdaughter
- ☐ Brother/sister
- ☐ Father/mother
- ☐ Grandchild
- ☐ Parent-in-law
- ☐ Son-in-law/daughter-in-law
- ☐ Other relative — *Print exact relationship.*

If NOT RELATED to Person 1:
- ☐ Roomer, boarder
- ☐ Housemate, roommate
- ☐ Unmarried partner
- ☐ Foster child
- ☐ Other nonrelative

3. What is this person's sex? *Mark ☒ ONE box.*
- ☐ Male
- ☐ Female

4. What is this person's age and what is this person's date of birth? *Print numbers in boxes.*
Age on April 1, 2000   Month   Day   Year of birth

→ NOTE: Please answer BOTH Questions 5 and 6.

5. Is this person Spanish/Hispanic/Latino? *Mark ☒ the "No" box if not Spanish/Hispanic/Latino.*
- ☐ No, not Spanish/Hispanic/Latino
- ☐ Yes, Mexican, Mexican Am., Chicano
- ☐ Yes, Puerto Rican
- ☐ Yes, Cuban
- ☐ Yes, other Spanish/Hispanic/Latino — *Print group.*

6. What is this person's race? *Mark ☒ one or more races to indicate what this person considers himself/herself to be.*
- ☐ White
- ☐ Black, African Am., or Negro
- ☐ American Indian or Alaska Native — *Print name of enrolled or principal tribe.*

- ☐ Asian Indian
- ☐ Chinese
- ☐ Filipino
- ☐ Other Asian — *Print race.*
- ☐ Japanese
- ☐ Korean
- ☐ Vietnamese
- ☐ Native Hawaiian
- ☐ Guamanian or Chamorro
- ☐ Samoan
- ☐ Other Pacific Islander — *Print race.*

- ☐ Some other race — *Print race.*

→ If more people live here, continue with Person 6.

Person 6

Your answers help your community plan for the future.

1. What is Person 6's name? *Print name below.*
Last Name

First Name   MI

2. How is this person related to Person 1? *Mark ☒ ONE box.*
- ☐ Husband/wife
- ☐ Natural-born son/daughter
- ☐ Adopted son/daughter
- ☐ Stepson/stepdaughter
- ☐ Brother/sister
- ☐ Father/mother
- ☐ Grandchild
- ☐ Parent-in-law
- ☐ Son-in-law/daughter-in-law
- ☐ Other relative — *Print exact relationship.*

If NOT RELATED to Person 1:
- ☐ Roomer, boarder
- ☐ Housemate, roommate
- ☐ Unmarried partner
- ☐ Foster child
- ☐ Other nonrelative

3. What is this person's sex? *Mark ☒ ONE box.*
- ☐ Male
- ☐ Female

4. What is this person's age and what is this person's date of birth? *Print numbers in boxes.*
Age on April 1, 2000   Month   Day   Year of birth

→ NOTE: Please answer BOTH Questions 5 and 6.

5. Is this person Spanish/Hispanic/Latino? *Mark ☒ the "No" box if not Spanish/Hispanic/Latino.*
- ☐ No, not Spanish/Hispanic/Latino
- ☐ Yes, Mexican, Mexican Am., Chicano
- ☐ Yes, Puerto Rican
- ☐ Yes, Cuban
- ☐ Yes, other Spanish/Hispanic/Latino — *Print group.*

6. What is this person's race? *Mark ☒ one or more races to indicate what this person considers himself/herself to be.*
- ☐ White
- ☐ Black, African Am., or Negro
- ☐ American Indian or Alaska Native — *Print name of enrolled or principal tribe.*

- ☐ Asian Indian
- ☐ Chinese
- ☐ Filipino
- ☐ Other Asian — *Print race.*
- ☐ Japanese
- ☐ Korean
- ☐ Vietnamese
- ☐ Native Hawaiian
- ☐ Guamanian or Chamorro
- ☐ Samoan
- ☐ Other Pacific Islander — *Print race.*

- ☐ Some other race — *Print race.*

→ If more people live here, list their names on the back of this page in the spaces provided.

Form D-61A

Please turn to go to last page.

Persons 7 – 12

If you didn't have room to list everyone who lives in this house or apartment, please list the others below. You may be contacted by the Census Bureau for the same information about these people.

Person 7 — Last Name

First Name   MI

Person 8 — Last Name

First Name   MI

Person 9 — Last Name

First Name   MI

Person 10 — Last Name

First Name   MI

Person 11 — Last Name

First Name   MI

Person 12 — Last Name

First Name   MI

FOR OFFICE USE ONLY

A. JIC1   B. JIC2   C. JIC3   D. JIC4

The Census Bureau estimates that, for the average household, this form will take about 10 minutes to complete, including the time for reviewing the instructions and answers. Comments about the estimate should be directed to the Associate Director for Finance and Administration, Attn: Paperwork Reduction Project 0607-0856, Room 3104, Federal Building 3, Bureau of the Census, Washington, DC 20233.

Respondents are not required to respond to any information collection unless it displays a valid approval number from the Office of Management and Budget.

Thank you for completing your official U.S. Census 2000 form.

The "Informational Copy" shows the content of the United States Census 2000 "short" form questionnaire. Each household will receive either a short form (100-percent questions) or a long form (100-percent and sample questions). The short form questionnaire contains 6 population questions and 1 housing question. On average, about 5 in every 6 households will receive the short form. The content of the forms resulted from reviewing the 1990 census data, consulting with federal and non-federal data users, and conducting tests.

For additional information about Census 2000, visit our website at www.census.gov or write to the Director, Bureau of the Census, Washington, DC 20233.

If you need help completing this form, *call 1-800-XXX-XXXX between 8:00 a.m. and 9:00 p.m., 7 days a week. The telephone call is free.*

TDD — *Telephone display device for the hearing impaired. Call 1-800-XXX-XXXX between 8:00 a.m. and 9:00 p.m., 7 days a week. The telephone call is free.*

¿NECESITA AYUDA? *Si usted necesita ayuda para completar este cuestionario llame al 1-800-XXX-XXXX entre las 8:00 a.m. y las 9:00 p.m., 7 días a la semana. La llamada telefónica es gratis.*

There is a formal process to decide what questions are to be asked in any census; this naturally involves the Census Bureau, plus the Office of Management and Budget (OMB), the U.S. Congress, and census users around the country. Deciding what questions to ask involves balancing the federal government's need for information about its citizens with citizens' right to privacy. Generally speaking, for a question to be included, there must be some specific federal need for the data (data must be mandated, or required, by law or by the Constitution). Due concern must be given to the intrusiveness of questions. Continuity is also important; ideally, census questions should remain as constant as possible across censuses to enable historical comparisons. However, legal, social, or economic changes may require new sorts of data or new ways of measuring the same characteristics.

After the 1990 Census, the Census Bureau and the Office of Management and Budget (OMB) organized a review to determine what subjects to include in Census 2000. Federal agencies were asked to identify all legal mandates. The needs of a wide range of nonfederal users (state and local governments, community organizations, business, academics, religious groups, and the general public) were also surveyed. Various standing advisory committees, expert panels, users' groups, and so on were also consulted.

Two tests of proposed census content were then undertaken: the 1996 National Content Survey (also known as the U.S. Census 2000 Test) and the 1996 Race and Ethnic Targeted Test (also known as the 1996 Census Survey). Focus groups made comments on questionnaire design and content. Cognitive research was also undertaken, evaluating, among other things, behavioral responses to alternative visual designs of the proposed census. Some of this research is available at *www.census.gov/srd/www/byyear.html* (or search the U.S. Census Bureau home page by typing in "content determination"). One result was that both the short and the long forms had fewer subjects in 2000 than in 1990.

The Census Bureau submitted subjects planned for inclusion in Census 2000 to Congress on March 31, 1997, and the planned questions on March 30, 1998. Questions were then submitted to the OMB on June 30, 1998. The OMB has the statutory responsibility to ensure that questions meet essential data needs and that the time burden of filling out a questionnaire is kept to a minimum. For details on the full process, see U.S. Census Bureau (2002a).

Nevertheless, important changes were made to the 2000 questionnaire.[5] The change that has received the most public attention concerns race. The "race" question has undergone constant modification since the earliest days of the census. Respondents in 2000 were allowed to select one *or more* racial categories to describe their racial identity, or they could write in a

[5]For a detailed description of changes between the 1990 and 2000 questionnaire, see *Major differences in subject-matter content between the 1990 and 2000 Census questionnaire* at *www.census.gov/population/www/cen2000/90vs00.html*.

specific racial identification. In 1990 only one race category per respondent was allowed (this is explained in more detail in chapter 3). Other significant changes included a new question about grandparents as caregivers, a new definition of disabilities, and the elimination of a question about sewage disposal. Several questions were also moved from the short to the long form.

Many of the changes to the questionnaire reflect social shifts in U.S. society and law. Consider the case of the head-of-household in married-couple households. In 1970, the head-of-household was the person considered head by the household itself; but if a married woman was living with her husband, the husband was always defined as the head to simplify tabulations (Myers 1992, 51). By 1980 this was untenable. In the 1980 Census, the "head-of-household" terminology was replaced by "householder," and wives in married-couple households could be designated as the householder. Since the characteristics of the householder are, in some instances, assigned to the household, this complicated the identification of trends from previous censuses. Wives tend to be younger than their husbands, so this change may have resulted in an underestimation of the age of householders.

While there is a formal administrative process to determine the questions included in each census, external political voices also influence the process. In the buildup to the 1990 Census, many social researchers argued that it was important to ask questions about respondents' sexual behavior. Sexually transmitted diseases, particularly AIDS, had become a major public policy concern. There were, of course, good reasons not to ask such questions in the 1990 Census: for one the questions would be highly intrusive, which is why questions about sexual behavior had never been asked before. Because of privacy issues, a number of senators and congressional representatives were vehemently opposed to the questions, and they were never included in the 1990 Census questionnaire. However, the 2000 Census included a question about "unmarried partners" in nonfamily households, and same-sex unmarried partner households are now shown in the tables (see box 3.4, chapter 3).

Questions about religion have never been asked in the U.S. Census. However, they are common census questions in other countries; although religious classification in these countries is sometimes resisted in creative ways. In 2001, Statistics Canada reported that "[a]n astonishing 20,000 Canadians declared themselves to be followers of the religion of Jedi, the guardians of peace and justice in the Star Wars flicks" (Canada.com 2003). Canadians were outdone by the Australians and the British (at 70,000 and 400,000 followers of Jedi, respectively). A Canadian man circulated an e-mail encouraging people to identify themselves as followers of Jedi. He said the Jedi membership drive was his way of "thumbing his nose at the government for asking what he feels is an inappropriate question. 'My religion is my issue, not the government's'" (Canada.com 2003).

Changes to the census questionnaire, although undertaken in a formal administrative manner, nevertheless reflect political pressures on the Census Bureau, current federal and national policy concerns, and current social mores. The Census of Population and Housing is not a neutral and objective numerical description of the U.S. public. The census is also, in part, a political document reflecting current political, policy, social, and moral concerns. Nothing illustrates this better than the history of how questions about race and ethnicity have changed over time.

> In the 1870 Census, the first census conducted after the abolition of slavery, the instructions to marshals (enumerators) read as follows:
>
> "*Color*—It must not be assumed that, where nothing is written in this column, "White" is to be understood. The column is always to be filled. Be particularly careful in reporting the class *Mulatto*. The word is here generic and includes quadroons, octoroons, and all persons having any perceptible trace of African blood. Important scientific results depend upon the correct determination of this class in schedules 1 and 2" (U.S. Census Bureau 2002a, 14).
>
> As in previous censuses, "Indians" (Native Americans) were not to be recorded on the schedule of population unless they were taxed (although marshals were, for the first time, encouraged to record nontaxed "Indians" living off reservations). In 1880, a separate schedule was developed to enumerate "Indians" living on reservations. By 1900, the instructions had been purged of detailed definitions of types of "mulattos" and instead read as follows, reflecting the immigration (and integration of Native Americans) that had occurred in the previous two decades:
>
> "Column 5. Color or race. Write 'W' for white; 'B' for black (negro or negro descent); 'Ch' for Chinese; 'Jp' for Japanese, and 'In' for Indian, as the case may be" (U.S. Census Bureau 2002a, 36).

Another example is worth considering here. In the early 1990s, a few politicians argued that the traditional census had become a huge invasion of personal privacy and suggested the questionnaire be replaced by a new form, which was the size of a postcard. Obviously such a small form would mean that the vast majority of questions in the current census would have to be removed. This initiative got nowhere. Nevertheless, the Constitution mandates only the counting of people; it does not mandate the gathering of other census data.

The American Community Survey

One of the major problems faced by users of detailed demographic, economic, and housing data from the decennial census has been how to update estimates in the later years of each decade. There is usually a two- to three-year lag in the release of sample data, and by the end of the period analysts are relying on data that is ten or twelve years old. In 1996, the Census Bureau began a new initiative that may resolve the problem by the end of this decade, assuming full congressional funding is provided. The American Community Survey (ACS) will be conducted annually for a sample of approximately 3,000,000 households (plus 36,000 households in Puerto Rico and 2.5 percent of the group quarters population). Once it is fully phased in, the ACS will provide the equivalent of long-form census data annually (U.S. Census Bureau 2003e, 3). A decennial census will still be conducted, but this will consist of the short form only. The sample will be drawn from every county, Native American Tribal Area, and Hawaiian Home Land, and although the sample size will not be equivalent to the approximately 17 percent sample on which the long form is based, preliminary evaluations suggest that sampling error will be only slightly increased for most places (Griffin and Obenski 2002, 27). Data from large jurisdictions (more than 65,000 people) will be available after the first year the ACS is fully implemented. For smaller jurisdictions (more than 20,000 people), a three-year average will provide an equivalent sample to that of the long form, and for places with less than 20,000 people, a five-year average will provide the equivalent. Assuming the ACS is fully implemented on schedule in July 2005, the equivalent of long-form data will be available for every location by 2010, eliminating the need for a long-form questionnaire for the decennial census. Updated data will be available annually from that point on. This will significantly enhance the census's usefulness for local planning efforts and overcome one of the major problems that data users have faced until this point.

While the ACS is intended to collect the same level of detail as the long-form census data, and at the level of statistical reliability, there are some important differences between the ACS and the current long form.

The ACS will be a rolling survey with four three-month survey cycles each year: A skilled core staff will be available to do follow-up phone and in-person interviews with nonrespondents during each cycle, rather than the much larger temporary staff of enumerators the decennial census relies on. So, it is possible that ACS data will be higher quality with less nonsampling error. Imputation rates (the amount of data for items with no response that is imputed; imputation rates are discussed in the following section of this chapter) were compared for the 2000 Supplemental Survey and the Census 2000 long form. Preliminary comparison suggests that improved follow-up for the Supplemental Survey resulted in significantly lower imputation rates for key population items (gender, race, age, household relationship, and Hispanic origin) (Griffin and Obenski 2002, 20). No similar comparisons are yet available for nonresponses by households (as opposed to nonresponses on particular questions), but these may be higher because the decennial census allows enumerators to collect information from neighbors if a household cannot be contacted, while the ACS requires data be obtained from a household member (Griffin and Obenski 2002, 17).

The ACS will use a different definition of "place of residence": The decennial census defines "place of residence" as the place people live the majority of the year. Instead, the ACS will define "place of residence" as the place people live when surveyed, as long as they have lived there, or plan to live there, for two months or more. This will affect local population counts during each decade. (The decennial census will continue to enumerate people using the traditional definition of "usual place of residence.") "Snowbirds" who spend winter in a southern location will now be counted at their winter home if surveyed during winter and at their summer home if surveyed during summer; the other home would be counted as vacant. College students, traditionally counted at the place they attend college rather than their parents' home, may instead be counted at their parents' home if surveyed over the summer months (U.S. Census Bureau 2003e).

This change is likely to improve the accuracy of long-form census data because it will now include seasonal residents, which should provide a more accurate picture of the "typical" population in a place. However, it will affect the comparability of several long-form census variables between 2000 and 2010. For instance, we may see sharp increases in the number of occupied manufactured homes and apartments in so-called "snowbird" destinations, fewer cost-burdened young adult renters in college towns, and so on. Using two different definitions of the population base—one in the decennial enumeration and one in the ACS—will raise new questions about the methods used to weight sample respondents. However, the change will improve our ability to understand regular seasonal migration and the impact this has on local demographics, economies, and housing markets.

The ACS will provide annual data on population characteristics: This should improve the population estimates the Census Bureau produces in years between censuses (discussed in chapter 3). More precise data on international and internal migration, fertility differences, housing characteristics, seasonal residence, and racial characteristics, has the potential to significantly improve population estimates. By mid-2003, three Supplemental Surveys had been completed (from 2000 to 2002) and data had been released for several metropolitan areas and counties with populations over 65,000. While the coverage is not complete, the data provides a useful update for those areas, although it is not broken down at smaller geographic levels.

Annual Public Use Microdata Sample (PUMS) data, one of the few census resources that provides data by individuals rather than by geographic units (described in detail in chapters 3 and 6), will be available based on the ACS for geographic areas of 100,000 people or more. Other questions, such as how base tables, derived reports, and analytic reports will be produced and disseminated, are still being discussed. The ACS Web site *(www.census.gov/acs/www)* will provide more information as it becomes available.

Improved timeliness will involve tradeoffs: The small increase in sampling error overall will affect smaller places and some data items more than others. Sampling error is the inaccuracy that results from using a sample to represent the characteristics of a population—in general, the smaller the sample as a proportion of the population, the larger the sampling error may be (this is discussed in greater detail in the following section of this chapter). Sampling error is typically measured by the coefficient of variance (CV). For places with fewer than 20,000 people (most census tracts, small cities and towns, and many rural counties), ACS estimates are anticipated to have CVs approximately one third higher than the CVs for the decennial long form (Griffin and Obenski 2002, 29). Timeliness may offset some of the losses in accuracy. Overall, data quality will improve more for larger places (more than 65,000 people) than for smaller places because of timeliness and lower nonsampling error. Differences in the time period over which data is collected will raise some dilemmas. When establishing fair market rents, for instance, should the Department of Housing and Urban Development (HUD) use the most recent data for larger places and five-year averages for small places, which may bias the estimate of rents in small places downward? Or, should it ignore the most recent available data and use five-year averages for every place to ensure consistency (U.S. Department of Housing and Urban Development 2002a, vi)?

A second issue is that sampling error may increase more for some population groups than for others, because rates of response to mailback surveys differ dramatically among racial and ethnic groups. The ACS will only sample nonrespondents for follow-up at a rate of one-in-three, instead of following up on every nonrespondent as in the decennial census. This problem is being addressed in the redesign of the sampling procedure, based on experience with the Supplemental Surveys and the ACS test sites, to attain a more uniform sampling error across demographic groups (Griffin and Obenski 2002, 29).

A less tractable problem is raised by differences in sampling error for different data items. Some items are correlated—they have responses that we would expect to cluster within the same household (such as reported race, ancestry, or language spoken at home). Consequently, a sample will include fewer independent observations and have a higher sampling error for those items. For instance, if most Laotian households are not included in the sample, the number of Laotian individuals in that location will be underestimated by a wider margin than, for instance, the number of employed individuals, an item less likely to be correlated within households.

Data on housing vacancy rates suffers from a related problem. Because vacant units will only be identified from the one-in-three sample selected for in-person follow-up from addresses with no response, vacant units will be undersampled compared to occupied housing units and those items based on vacant units (asking price if rented, type of unit, and so on) will have a higher CV (Griffin and Obenski 2002, 28).

Another tradeoff is that the ACS data will not be released for areas smaller than census tracts. Block group data on gross rents, linguistic isolation, or people with disabilities, for instance, may be important for many local planning applications. This is especially the case in rural areas, where counties may contain only one tract, and block groups may provide a more appropriate delineation of service areas. Block and block group data will still be released for items in the enumeration, but analysts will lose an important level of spatial detail.

Sampling error

The population characteristics shown in some census data products do not necessarily match those of other data products. For instance, the total population of people 65 years and older shown in Summary File 1 for Dane County, Wisconsin, may be different than the total for the same location from the Public Use Microdata Sample (described in more detail in chapters 3 and 6). Why are they different if they come from the same census? Census data products based on the long form are generated from samples and are not exact representations of the characteristics of the total population. The sample-based data is obtained from one-in-six housing units on average. In other words, a single household was providing answers for five other households. The accuracy of the population estimate depends in part on how typical the people within the sampled housing units are to those within the geographic area. A complex weighting scheme is used by the bureau to improve estimates of the population characteristics, but small discrepancies are unavoidable.

Differences between the 100 percent count data and the sample data arise for two reasons: sampling and nonsampling errors. They have different causes and can be controlled to a different extent. Sampling errors occur simply because not every household is being asked to respond. Sampled households may not be representative of all households. For example, if sampling is based on the "luck of the draw," then all the households within the sample may have incomes lower than the average for all households (the "true" mean). We use the concepts of sampling error to estimate these effects for any sample by calculating confidence intervals. This is explained in box 1.2.

Unlike sampling error, nonsampling error is the result of the data collection, processing, and reporting stages. Nonsampling error has two components: nonrandom nonsampling error and random nonsampling errors.

- Nonrandom errors bias the results consistently in a positive or negative direction. For example, if householders constantly understate their age (or overstate the value of their home), then the results of the sample will have a negative (or positive) nonsampling error.
- Random nonsampling errors do not bias the sample in one direction or the other but (in theory) cancel each other out. For example, if people round their commuting time to the nearest five-minute interval, the errors of the higher estimates will cancel the errors of the lower estimates within the sample. Random nonsampling errors increase the variability of the sampled responses. However, the increase in variability caused by random nonsampling errors can be mathematically estimated as part of the sampling error calculations.

The accuracy of the data: The address list, the undercount, and adjustments to the census

Since 1970, households with city-style street addresses have received their census questionnaire by mail. For this system of delivery to work comprehensively, the Census Bureau must have an up-to-date accurate address list for the entire country. For 2000, the quality of the address list depended on the Local Update of Census Addresses (LUCA) program. The bureau worked with local governments to update the street address database—cities and counties should have the best information because in almost all places they control both the road development and

Box 1.2   Sampling error, standard error, and confidence intervals

Imagine drawing all possible samples from the same population of households: the average income of each is likely to differ slightly from the "true" average income of the population, but the average income of all samples will be the same as the "true" average. Each sample would have a sample error: the measure of how far it deviates (or varies) from this "true" average (mean). Of course, we could only calculate this precisely if we knew the "true" mean, but we can estimate sample error based on the proportion of the total population in the sample. For small populations, we would need a larger proportionate sample to ensure the same level of sample error as we would get with a much smaller proportionate sample of a large population. This is why households in very small places are oversampled (at a rate of about one-in-two) compared to households in large places (which are sampled at a rate of one-in-eight). Sample error is zero when the "sample" includes the total population.

Standard errors are estimated based on sample errors. The standard error measures the variation among estimates of the "true" mean from all possible samples. It provides an estimate of how much any particular sample's mean is likely to differ from the "true" mean; in practical terms, it allows us to say things like: "the average income of households in place *x* is $35,000, plus or minus $2,000." The Census Bureau calculates unadjusted standard errors for each variable in each data product; these are shown in the technical documentation for each product. Together with

sampling rates (the percent of the population in the sample) and design factors (the ratio of the estimated standard error to the standard error of a simple random sample), also provided in the technical documentation, standard errors can be calculated for each data item. A detailed example of the calculation is shown in chapter 6.

The main purpose of calculating standard errors is to construct a confidence interval around estimates—the "plus or minus $2,000" mentioned above. A confidence interval is the range within which we can expect the average value of a characteristic (calculated over all possible samples) to fall with a specific level of probability. Thus, if the above estimate of "plus or minus $2,000" was based on a 95 percent confidence interval, we could say with a 95 percent probability of confidence that the income range $33,000 and $37,000 includes the average estimate from all possible samples (in practical terms, the "true" mean). As the reader may remember from elementary statistics classes, standard errors are related to the "normal curve" (assuming the variable is normally distributed). For an interval ranging one standard error above and below the estimated (sample) mean, we could say with a 68 percent probability of confidence that the interval includes the average estimate from all possible samples; for an interval from 1.645 times the standard error above and below the sample mean, we could say this with 90 percent confidence; and for an interval of two standard errors on either side of the sample mean, we could say this with 95 percent confidence.

address designation processes. The U.S. Postal Service validated addresses and identified missing addresses. New addresses were then added to the TIGER/Line system, the central street address database (TIGER/Line is described in greater detail in chapter 2). In some cases, census enumerators also went door-to-door looking for living quarters not in the address file. As a result, more than four-fifths of households received a questionnaire by mail. Households living in areas that did not have city-style street addresses (this includes much of the rural United States) had their questionnaires delivered directly (U.S. Census Bureau 2000a).

The questionnaires were delivered on March 13–15, 2000, and follow-up postcards were sent out to remind those who had not completed their questionnaires to do so and thank those that had. Finally census enumerators telephoned or visited those households that did not complete the form. The final response rate on the short form was 67 percent, better than the 1990 Census's 65 percent and considerably better than the expected rate of 62 percent. Things were not quite so good for the long form—the expected response rate was 60 percent, the actual rate 54 percent (U.S. General Accounting Office 2000).

Just how accurate are the resulting numbers? Inaccuracy derives from a number of sources. Respondents may lie or guess, census workers may make clerical or computational errors (these fall into the category of nonsampling error), and potential methodological problems with the way the Census Bureau deals with incomplete and contradictory questionnaire responses exist. With data from the long form, there is also sampling error (explained above).

From a policy point of view, the "undercount"—the failure to count some of the population—is the major problem. The undercount is divided into

- the "sheer undercount," the failure to count people who live in the nation; and
- the "differential undercount," when some groups are undercounted more than others.

For instance, young black males may be undercounted more than young white males, middle-aged people may be undercounted less than people in their twenties, and renters may be undercounted more than owners. The worrying aspect is that some places have a higher proportion of those groups likely to be undercounted (compare Detroit, Michigan, which has a very large African-American population, with Des Moines, Iowa, which has a small African-American population). Since political representation and a considerable amount of federal money is distributed according to census population counts, cities with high proportions of people likely to be undercounted usually lobby the Census Bureau and Department of Commerce to have their populations adjusted upward (and bring legal suits when lobbying fails) (Cantwell, Hogan, and Styles 2003). Unfortunately, it is also true that even if a city knew that its population had been counted perfectly, it would still be in that city's interest to claim that its population had been undercounted.

City planners are often responsible for spearheading local responses to a potential or suspected undercount. Estimating the size of the undercount is entirely feasible—the methods to do this are well-established though clearly are not 100 percent accurate. Two different methods are used in the United States:

- demographic analysis
- special post-census surveys (in 1990 and 2000)

Demographic analysis uses records of births, deaths, migration, Medicare enrollment, estimates of legal but unrecorded emigration, and estimates of illegal immigration to estimate how many persons (by age, sex, and race) should have been counted in the census. The method is entirely separate from the census count itself, and thus provides an independent evaluation of the completeness of census coverage. To be useful, the method relies on accurate and complete administrative records. Unfortunately, emigration is poorly recorded in the United States, and illegal immigration has increased over the past few decades. Procedures have to be developed to fill these data holes before a demographic analysis can provide valid numbers (U.S. Census Bureau 2001).[6] In 2000, these procedures were the source of some concern.

Demographic analysis indicates that the undercount has declined significantly over the past sixty years, down from 5.4 percent in 1940 to 1.2 percent in 1980, up slightly in 1990 to 1.8 percent, followed by a massive drop in 2000 to 0.1 percent (see table 1.2). Historically, the undercount of African-Americans is much greater than that of non-African-Americans, and the undercount of males (white and African-American) much greater than that of females. The age pattern of the undercount for African-American males is particularly interesting. In 2000, African-American males 10 to 17 years of age were slightly overcounted (-1.9 percent undercount). But the undercount shoots up for 18- to 29-year-olds (5.7 percent) and is even greater for 30- to 49-year-olds (9.9 percent). It is adult African-American males under 50 who are most likely to be missed, although African-American households are being counted adequately (U.S. Census Bureau 2001).

In 1990 the post-census survey was called the Post-Enumeration Survey (or PES). PES used a dual-system estimator to calculate the number of persons missed by the census. This method is akin to the tagging (or "capture-recapture") techniques often used to estimate animal populations in the wild. Essentially, the method tries to locate the same individual twice. Statistical methods allow the success rate of these attempts to be converted into an estimate of the total population.

Table 1.2 Estimated net census undercount by race and sex, 1940–2000							
	1940	1950	1960	1970	1980	1990	2000
Total	5.4	4.1	3.1	2.7	1.2	1.8	0.1
African-American, male	10.9	9.7	8.8	9.1	7.5	8.5	8.1
African-American, female	6.0	5.4	4.4	4.0	1.7	3.0	3.1
Non-African-American, male	5.2	3.8	2.9	2.7	1.5	2.0	1.6
Non-African-American, female	4.9	3.7	2.4	1.7	0.1	0.3	0.5

Source: For 1940 through 1990, see Robinson et al. (1993). For 2000, see U.S. Census Bureau (2002c, table 1). Note that the latter document also gives figures for demographic analysis of the 1990 Census; these are slightly different from those reported here. See also U.S. General Accounting Office (1998, table II.2).

[6]There are a few nations that measure population not using a census or sampling but using national population registers of births, deaths, marriages, divorces, moves, and so on. This requires considerable oversight of a nation's citizenry (Lavin 1996). Demographic analysis parallels this method.

The estimated 1990 undercount according to the PES was 1.6 percent, compared to 1.8 percent from the demographic analysis. Like demographic analysis, PES showed a very high undercount for non-Hispanic African-Americans (4.6 percent using PES). It also shows high undercount for Hispanic (5 percent using PES) and Native Americans living on reservations (12.2 percent using PES) (U.S. Census Bureau 2003b, table 1). The estimated undercount for non-Hispanic whites was 0.7 percent.

For Census 2000 two separate series based on a post-enumeration survey were released: the Accuracy and Coverage Evaluation (ACE) estimates. ACE Revision II provides the best estimates (U.S. Census Bureau 2003b). The first version of ACE estimates indicated a largish undercount (1.2 percent), but demographic analysis indicated a tiny undercount (the final revised estimate was 0.12 percent). After some investigation, it emerged that there were substantial methodological problems with ACE I. ACE Revision II tries to solve as many of these problems as is feasible. The final net undercount Revision II estimate for the total U.S. population is -0.5 percent; in other words, there was a slight overcount. The upshot is that the original census count was 281,421,906, but the final revised demographic estimate was 281,759,858. The estimate from ACE Revision I was over 284.5 million, but from Revision II (and with adjustment for correlation bias) it was a mere 280,090,250 (U.S. Census Bureau 2002c). These are huge swings in estimation (a range of 4.5 million people). Ignoring the estimates with obvious methodological flaws, the revised demographic analysis suggests the census undercounted 337,952 people, while ACE Revision II suggests that the census found 1,331,656 more than there really were (a range of about 1.7 million people).

Which estimate is right? How could there be such huge swings in the Post-Enumeration Survey? And, more to the point, how could the population be overcounted? There are few simple answers to these questions, and the reader is encouraged to read the detailed material put out by the Census Bureau on these issues (U.S. Census Bureau 2001; 2002c; 2003b). As a general matter though it is unclear which estimate (of the actual census count, the revised demographic analysis, and ACE Revision II) is correct. Fortunately, all three are, by historical standards anyway, fairly close. Keep in mind that the ACE Revision II estimate of a -0.49 percent undercount has a standard error of 0.2; so if we chose a 95 percent confidence interval it would mean that the true undercount estimate is likely to fall in the range of -.09 percent (-.49 + .2 + .2) to -.89 percent (-.49 - .2 - .2).

The simple fact is that counting the U.S. population is a dauntingly difficult task—there were methodological problems with the census count, with the demographic analysis, and with ACE. There is little reason to prefer one set of the three revised sets of results over another. Thus the Census Bureau decided not to adjust the final census count for 2000 up or down based on the results of demographic analysis or ACE. In 1990 there also was no adjustment, although at that time there were better methodological grounds for adjustment.

There were a number of reasons for the swings in the ACE estimates; an important one is the existence of "duplicates." For instance, households with teenagers away at college may indicate

Table 1.3 Net undercount for various demographic groups, 2000 and 1990 (percent)				
	2000 ACE Revision II		**1990 PES**	
	Estimate	**Standard error**	**Estimate**	**Standard error**
Total	-0.49	0.20	1.61	0.20
Race/origin:				
Non-Hispanic white	-1.31	0.20	0.68	0.22
Non-Hispanic African-American	1.84	0.43	4.57	0.55
Hispanic	0.71	0.44	4.99	0.82
Hawaiian and Pacific Islander	2.12	2.73	2.36	1.39
Non-Hispanic Asian	-0.75	0.68	2.36	1.39
Native American on reservation	-0.88	1.53	12.22	5.29
Native American off reservation	0.62	1.35	0.68	0.22
Tenure				
Owner	-1.25	0.20	0.04	0.21
Nonowner	1.14	0.36	4.51	0.43
Age and sex				
0–9	-0.46	0.33	3.18	0.29
10–17	-1.32	0.41	3.18	0.29
18–29 male	1.12	0.63	3.30	0.54
18–29 female	-1.39	0.52	2.83	0.47
30–49 male	2.01	0.25	1.89	0.32
30–49 female	-0.60	0.25	0.88	0.25
50+ male	-0.80	0.27	-0.59	0.34
50+ female	-2.53	0.27	-1.24	0.29

Souce: This table has been adapted from U.S. Census Bureau (2003b, table 1). Note: Negative numbers indicate an overcount.

those children still living at home, but those same teenagers may also be counted in college dormitories or apartments. In fact, 19-year-olds were one of the most overcounted age groups in Census 2000. In other cases, a vacant housing unit may be misclassified as occupied, and households and persons may then be "imputed" (a process by which missing records for house-holds, families, and persons are created by the Census Bureau) to that housing unit. There were also problems in the LUCA street address program that may have resulted in the duplication of some housing units. The swing in the ACE and ACE Revision II estimates is in large part the result of better methodologies to control for duplicates in Revision II (U.S. Census Bureau 2002d).

Before moving on it is worth having a more detailed look at the undercount in 1990 and 2000 for some important demographic groups (see table 1.3). Notice that the undercount (posi-tive or negative) was often statistically insignificant (for instance, the ACE Revision II estimates for Native Americans, and Hawaiians and Pacific Islanders). The differential in undercount between owners and renters has worsened since 1990, as has the undercount of all adult males younger than 50. Unsurprisingly, the net undercount varies by state. Fortunately, in most states with a positive undercount, the difference between the census count and the ACE Revision II estimate was smaller than the ACE Revision II standard error. For instance, California has a census count of 33,871,648 persons but ACE Revision II estimated the population at 33,915,728. However, the standard error of that estimate was 87,146, indicating that the census count was not statistically different from the ACE estimate (U.S. Census Bureau 2003c, table 1).

Using the Census of Population and Housing

In this section we cover three important issues necessary to understanding and using the census: census geography, the tables and variables, and the publication schedule. Of these, census geography is the most complex.

Census geography and summary levels

The census is organized around geographical units for which data is summarized. For the vast majority of census publications, it is impossible to get information on individuals. Title 13 guarantees the confidentiality of answers to the census questionnaire:

- Employees of the Census Bureau must take an oath of confidentiality.
- There is security for completed census questionnaires.
- There are detailed disclosure-avoidance programs implemented by the bureau to ensure that tabulations do not allow the identification of specific persons or households.

Thus the data must be *aggregated,* in other words, summed or averaged over a particular geographical area. So we usually talk of data for a particular *summary* level, meaning data at a specified level of geographical aggregation. Some of these geographical regions or units exist independently of the census such as cities (towns, villages, and so on), counties or their equivalents, states (and similar areas such as the District of Columbia and outlying territories like the U.S. Virgin Islands and Guam), or the United States as a whole. These are *governmental units.* There are also *statistical units,* things like blocks, block groups, tracts, urbanized areas, metropolitan areas, census regions, and census divisions. Statistical units are created by the Census Bureau and do not exist as independent governmental units. Most people intuitively understand what a governmental unit is—it's the statistical units that cause trouble. The focus of the following discussion is on the statistical units.

The main geographical hierarchy[7]

Table 1.4 summarizes the main geographical hierarchy. In the discussion that follows, government and statistical units are printed in bold type when they are introduced.

Although census questionnaires are assembled by actual street addresses, the lowest level of tabulated census geography is the block. A **census block** is usually defined by roads, though it may also be bounded by rivers, streams, railroad tracks, invisible boundaries such as city or

[7]This discussion of census geography units is based explicitly on U.S. Census Bureau (2003a, appendix A, and 2003d, chapter four).

Table 1.4   **The main census geography hierarchy**
United States
Region
Division
State (includes District of Columbia, Puerto Rico, and four Island Areas[a])
County
County subdivision
Place
Census tract
Block group
Census block
Note: [a]American Samoa, Guam, the Commonwealth of the Northern Marina Islands, and the Virgin Islands of the United States.

county limits, or even imaginary extensions of roads. In a typical city with a grid road structure, four intersecting streets delimit the boundaries of a block. In fact it is the centerline (an imaginary line in the center of all public roads) of those four intersecting streets that define the block. Blocks typically have a population of about 85 people. In rural areas, blocks may contain an area of many square miles. For Census 2000, blocks were completely renumbered using four-digit codes, for instance "4000" (in 1990, blocks were identified using a three- or four-digit code, the first three digits being numbers, the last being an alphabetic suffix). The treatment of water areas was changed between 1990 and 2000. In 1990 all water areas in a block group (see below) were given a single block number ending in "99." In 2000, a water area completely in a land block was given the same number as the land block, but if the water area touches two or more blocks then the water area gets its own code.

Comparatively little census information is made available for blocks—only the information on the short form. One reason for this is the confidentially requirement of all census data. No data may be made public that would allow users to identify individuals, individual families, or households—the long-form sample data would, in some cases, allow individual households or persons to be identified at the block level. Another important reason is that long-form-derived data would have very large sampling errors at the block level.

Blocks are then assembled into **block groups.** A block group with the identification number "4" will include all blocks with numbers between "4000" and "4999." Obviously, blocks cannot cross block group boundaries. Most block groups were designated locally as part of the Census Bureau's Participant Statistical Areas Program. The Census Bureau undertook the designation only where state, local, or tribal authorities declined to, or where potential local participants could not be found. Block groups range from 600 to 3,000 people, but the bureau considers a population of 1,500 the optimum (1,000 for Native American reservations). Block groups (the lowest level for which sample data is available) are then assembled into **census tracts.** Block groups cannot cross tract boundaries. Tracts are delineated locally wherever possible. Tracts are meant to be fairly homogenous and permanent areas with similar demographic and economic characteristics and living conditions. In other words, they are intended to resemble something approximating small neighborhoods. The area covered by tracts depends on population density. Population size usually ranges between 1,500 and 8,000 with an optimum size of 4,000 (2,500 in Native American reservations and island areas). Counties with fewer people than this have a single census tract (tracts do not cross county lines). In 1990, some counties had tracts and others had block numbering areas (BNAs). For 2000, all BNAs were replaced with tracts. Blocks, block groups, and census tracts are assigned FIPS codes that are unique within each county. When appended to the state and county FIPS codes, each has a unique number. FIPS codes are explained in more detail later in this section.

As places grow, roads are built, new blocks are created, and new block groups and tracts defined (and the opposite may be true in declining communities). Thus block, block group, and tract boundaries may change from census to census, making some historical comparisons in fast-growing areas tricky, to say the very least. From an analytic point of view, this is most often a problem at the tract level where over a decade there may be a considerable redefinition of tracts (this issue is dealt with in some detail in chapter 3).

Tracts are part of **counties** or **county equivalents,** and counties compose **states.** Each county has a unique five-digit FIPS code made up of a three-digit county code and a two-digit state code. A full listing of state and county FIPS codes is given in appendix A of U.S. Census Bureau (2003d). Few counties change boundaries between censuses, but enough do that users doing county analyses should consult the Census Bureau publication *Significant changes to counties and county equivalent entities: 1970–present* (*www.census.gov/geo/www/tiger/ctychng.html*). States almost never change their boundaries, and if they do it is almost always in ways that are insignificant from the point of view of census analysis.

There are many different types of "county equivalents." In Louisiana, **parishes** have the functions that counties do in most other states. Alaska has no counties; the statistically equivalent areas are **organized boroughs** (these are governmental units) and **census areas** (these are statistical units designated cooperatively by the Census Bureau and the state of Alaska). In Maryland, Missouri, Nevada, and Virginia there are **incorporated places** (cities) that are independent of any counties. For the purpose of the census, they perform the same functions and are treated as county equivalents. They are known as **independent cities.** Confusingly, some data tabulations on independent cities are given at the county summary level and some at the place summary level. The District of Columbia is treated as both a state-equivalent and a county-equivalent unit.

County subdivisions fall into three main categories: **minor civil divisions** (MCDs), **census county divisions** (CCDs), and **unorganized territories.** Twenty-eight states have MCDs; the legal status of MCDs varies considerably across those states.[8] In some states, MCDs can include places (cities), but in others all places are their own MCDs. In twelve states,[9] MCDs have much the same legal functions as incorporated places (cities)—in these states the Census Bureau tabulations for places includes MCDs. In ten states with MCDs, portions of some counties are not covered by MCDs—these are called **unorganized territories.** States without MCDs have CCDs;

[8]They are variously known within states as American Indian Reservations, assessment districts, boroughs, charter townships, election districts, election precincts, gores, grants, locations, magisterial districts, parish governing authority districts, plantations, precincts, purchases, road districts, supervisor's districts, towns, or townships.
[9]Connecticut, Maine, Massachusetts, Michigan, Minnesota, New Hampshire, New Jersey, New York, Pennsylvania, Rhode Island, Vermont, and Wisconsin.

unlike MCDs (which are governmental units of census geography), CCDs are statistical units determined by the Census Bureau in cooperation with state and local governments. Finally, in Alaska, **census subareas** are statistical divisions of boroughs and census areas.

States are then organized into **divisions**, and divisions into **regions.** These are defined in table 1.5.

Region	Division	Constituent states
Northeast	New England	Maine, New Hampshire, Vermont, Massachusetts, Rhode Island, Connecticut
	Middle Atlantic	New York, New Jersey, Pennsylvania
Midwest	East North Central	Ohio, Indiana, Illinois, Michigan, Wisconsin
	West North Central	Minnesota, Iowa, Missouri, North Dakota, South Dakota, Nebraska, Kansas
South	South Atlantic	Delaware, Maryland, District of Columbia, Virginia, West Virginia, North Carolina, South Carolina, Georgia, Florida
	East South Central	Kentucky, Tennessee, Alabama, Mississippi
	West South Central	Arkansas, Louisiana, Oklahoma, Texas
West	Mountain	Montana, Wyoming, Colorado, New Mexico, Arizona, Utah, Nevada, Idaho
	Pacific	Washington, Oregon, California, Alaska, Hawaii

Table 1.5 Regions and divisions

The main geographical unit hierarchy and the associated FIPS number system

Each state has a two-digit code number—technically its FIPS (Federal Information Processing Standards) code.[10] Iowa, for instance, has the FIPS code "19," Illinois the code "17." Each county in each state will have a three-digit county code. Our home county is Johnson County, Iowa. Its code is "103." Thus Johnson County, Iowa, is uniquely defined by the FIPS code "19103." In Illinois the county code "103" refers to Lee County. To uniquely identify Lee County, the five-digit state and county FIPS code must be used: "17103."

Each tract in the United States is uniquely identified by the state and county codes plus a further six-digit tract code, the last two digits working as implied decimal places. The first tract of Dane County, Wisconsin, has the code "000100" (sometimes the code will be given as "1.00") (see figure 1.1). Thus the full identification of this tract is "55025000100." The most northeasterly tract of Dane County is "011800" (or "118.00"). Its full code is "55025011800." A tract that has been divided up into multiple tracts over time will usually have numbers in the decimal place positions of the tract code. This is the case for tracts "120.01" and "120.02" in Dane County ("55025012001" and "55025012002").

Individual tracts are then divided into block groups and block groups into blocks. The most northeasterly tract in Dane County, "55025011800," has three block groups, "1," "2," and "3." This provides the full block group code: "550250118001," "550250118002," and

[10]FIPS codes are a standardized numeric or alphabetic code issued by the National Institute of Standards and Technology (NIST).

"550250118003." The most northeasterly of these three is "550250118002." This block group consists of sixty-four blocks, the lowest level of census geography. Each block is identified with an additional three numbers. Thus the first block is "550250118002000" and so on. As we noted before, the unit identification system is hierarchical—we start with a state and then move down from there.

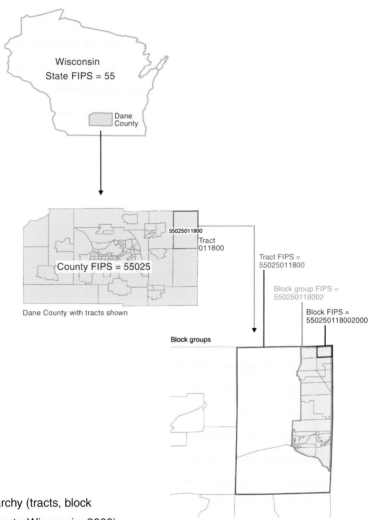

Figure 1.1 FIPS code hierarchy (tracts, block groups, and blocks, Dane County, Wisconsin, 2000).

The basic census hierarchy for Puerto Rico and U.S. indigenous people

Unfortunately, there are a vast number of other units of census geography beyond the basic hierarchy described above. Puerto Rico and the census units for U.S. indigenous people pose some special problems.

- **American Indian areas:** Here the hierarchy goes **tribal block group** → **tribal census tract** → **tribal subdivision** → **American Indian reservation (federal)** or **off-reservation trust land** or **Oklahoma tribal statistical area** (OTSA). In some instances there is an alternative hierarchy: tribal block group → tribal census tract → **tribal designated statistical area** (TDSA) or **American Indian reservation (state)** or **state designated American Indian statistical area** (SDAISA).
- American Indian Reservations are lands where the federal government has—by treaty, statute, or court order—recognized that Native American tribes have primary governmental authority. Common names for reservations are: colonies, communities, pueblos, rancherias, ranches, reservations, reserves, tribal towns, and tribal villages. Reservations may cross county and state lines.
- TDSAs are statistical units for recognized tribes that do not have a reservation or off-reservation trust land.
- OTSAs are statistical units for tribes in Oklahoma that formerly had a reservation in the state but no longer do.
- A state reservation is land held in trust by a state for a particular tribe.
- SDAISAs are statistical entities for state-recognized Native American tribes that do not have a state recognized reservation.
- **Alaska native areas:** Here the hierarchy goes block group → tract → **Alaska native village statistical area** (ANVSA) → **Alaska native regional corporation** (ANRC). Twelve ANRCs cover all of Alaska, except for the Annette Island Reserve, which is a Native American reservation. A thirteenth corporation covers Alaska natives not living in Alaska and not identifying with any of the other twelve ANRCs. ANVSAs are the settled portions of Alaska native villages—this unit aids in the presentation of data but has little meaning on the ground since native villages often have no determinate boundary.
- **Hawaiian Home Lands:** Here the hierarchy goes block group → tract → **Hawaiian Home Lands** (HHL). This is a new unit for Census 2000 and includes land held in trust for native Hawaiians by the state of Hawaii.
- In Puerto Rico, the **municipio** is treated as the equivalent of a county in the United States. The municipio is then divided into **barrios** or **barrio-pueblos,** and barrio-pueblos and some barrios are divided into **subbarios.** Puerto Rico has no incorporated places—instead the Census Bureau designates the **zona urbana,** essentially the governmental center of each municipio, and **comunidades,** or other urban areas.

The units described in this section are, like all units of the census hierarchy, composed of blocks.

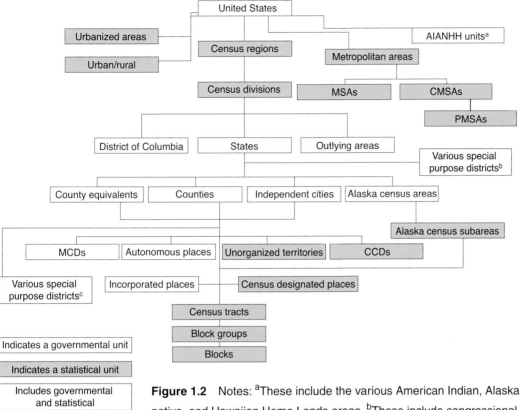

Figure 1.2 Notes: [a]These include the various American Indian, Alaska native, and Hawaiian Home Lands areas. [b]These include congressional districts, state legislative districts, school districts, urban growth areas, and Alaska native regional corporations. [c]These include voting districts and Traffic Analysis Zones.

The extended census geography hierarchy

The main hierarchy does not cover a wide range of geographical units crucial to the work of urban land professionals. Figure 1.2 summarizes the most important elements in the extended hierarchy. Note again that blocks are the "building blocks" of all higher levels of census geography.

Cities, towns, villages, boroughs, etc.: These are all **places.** Places have a special assigned five-digit FIPS code based on the alphabetical order of the place's name within a state. There are three main categories of place: **incorporated places, census designated places** (CDP), and **consolidated cities.** None of these crosses state lines, but they may cross county lines.

Incorporated places are cities, towns, and so on that have legal existence according to the laws of their states. This usually means they have defined governmental functions. However, there are various naming complications across states. Towns in New England, New York, and Wisconsin, and boroughs in New York are treated as MCDs; they are not treated as incorporated places. As we indicated earlier, boroughs in Alaska are treated as county equivalents. Maryland, Missouri,

Nevada, and Virginia have independent cities that are not part of any county; nevertheless these are treated by the Census Bureau as counties (and also as county subdivisions and places).

CDPs are statistical units (they have no legal status outside of the census) for built-up areas with dense population settlement that have not incorporated (in other words, are not recognized as a city, town, or village by state law). CDPs are designated by the Census Bureau in cooperation with local officials. Note that for 2000 there were no minimum size thresholds for CDPs (though there were in previous censuses). From 1950 through 1970, CDPs were called "unincorporated."

Consolidated cities are places where the legal functions of an incorporated place (city, town, and so on) have merged with its county or MCD but where the county or MCD continues to have a separate legal status. In the data hierarchy, data for a consolidated city will be shown at the county or MCD level (depending on the nature of the consolidation). In some consolidated cities there may be semi-independent places. In some tabulations, data for consolidated cities is not provided. Rather, each semi-independent place will have its own data record. Data for what is known as the **consolidated city (balance)** will also be provided; the balance will be the numbers for the entire consolidated city minus the numbers for its semi-independent places.

Metropolitan areas: A **metropolitan area** (MA) is a county or set of counties with a population over 100,000 (75,000 in New England), and a central city population of at least 50,000. Outlying counties are included in a particular MA if enough workers in the adjacent counties commute to the center county for work—in other words, the outlying counties should be functionally integrated with the central county. The outlying counties must also meet additional criteria of population density, urban population, and population growth. The population of the MA is then divided into those **living inside the central city** and those **outside the central city.**

MAs are then categorized into three further units: **metropolitan statistical areas** (MSAs), **primary metropolitan statistical areas** (PMSAs), or **consolidated metropolitan statistical areas** (CMSAs). Think of an MSA as an independent MA, in other words, an MA not functionally linked to any other MA (although two independent MSAs may still be contiguous). CMSAs are interconnected groups of MAs, akin to a conurbation. The individual MAs in a CMSA are then called PMSAs, not MSAs.

Note that in New England, MAs consist of sets of cities and county subdivisions rather than counties. However, New England also has an alternative county-based definition of MSAs called **New England county metropolitan areas** (NECMAs). The main frame of map 1.1 shows all MSAs, CMSAs, and PMSAs in the United States and the smaller detailed frame shows those (with names) for parts of Illinois, Indiana, and Wisconsin. Table 1.6 lists all CMSAs as of 1990. There is a four-digit FIPS code to identify each MA and in the case of a PMSA a further code to identify the CMSA to which it belongs.

Urban/rural and urbanized areas: People and housing units in **urbanized areas** (UA) and **urban clusters** (UC) are classified **urban.** Rural areas include people and territory outside of UAs and UCs. UAs and UCs are densely settled areas defined as sets of

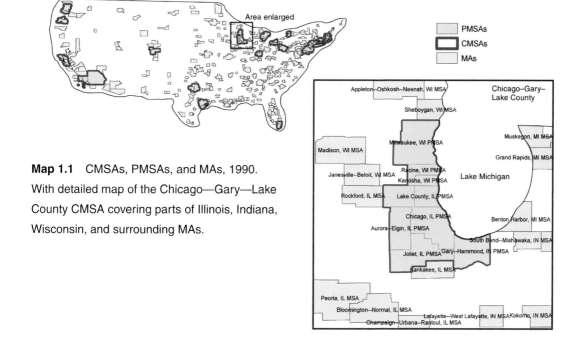

Map 1.1 CMSAs, PMSAs, and MAs, 1990. With detailed map of the Chicago—Gary—Lake County CMSA covering parts of Illinois, Indiana, Wisconsin, and surrounding MAs.

- blocks or block groups with at least 1,000 persons per square mile
- surrounding blocks or block groups with 500 persons per square mile
- less densely settled blocks or block groups that nevertheless form connections across more densely populated blocks and block groups

A place, an MCD, a county and, most confusingly to new users of the census, a metropolitan area, may include both urban and rural areas. Technically a UC is a densely settled territory with a population between 2,500 and 50,000 while a UA has more than 50,000 people. Practically then, "urban" will include densely settled places with a population greater than 2,500 and rural will include (besides agricultural areas and open country) places—cities, towns, villages, and so on—with less than 2,500 people.

The definition of a UA changed markedly between 1990 and 2000. A UA or UC may contain more than one place. The dominant place in a UA is called the **urban area central place.** A place may also be partly within and partly outside an urban area, in which case it is referred to as an **extended place.**

Purpose-defined districts: Census data is tabulated for several other kinds of districts:

- **School districts:** Each school district has a five-digit code unique within a state. Three types of school district are recognized: elementary, secondary, and unified.
- **State legislative districts:** These are the districts represented in the upper and lower houses of state assemblies.
- **Voting districts:** This covers the election districts, precincts, wards, and so on used by state, local, and tribal government for elections.

Table 1.6 CMSAs in 1990	
Boston–Lawrence–Salem, MA–NH	Los Angeles–Anaheim–Riverside, CA
Buffalo–Niagara Falls, NY	Miami–Fort Lauderdale, FL
Chicago–Gary–Lake County, IL–IN–WI	Milwaukee–Racine, WI
Cincinnati–Hamilton, OH–KY–IN	New York–Northern New Jersey–Long Island, NY–NJ–CT
Cleveland–Akron–Lorain, OH	Philadelphia–Wilmington–Trenton, PA–NJ-DE–MD
Dallas–Fort Worth, TX	Pittsburgh–Beaver Valley, PA
Denver–Boulder, CO	Portland–Vancouver, OR–WA
Detroit–Ann Arbor, MI	Providence–Pawtucket–Fall River, RI–MA
Hartford–New Britain–Middletown, CT	San Francisco–Oakland–San Jose, CA
Houston–Galveston–Brazoria, TX	Seattle–Tacoma, WA

- **ZIP Code tabulation areas (ZCTA™):** These are areas that approximate the areas covered by the U.S. Postal Service's five-digit or three-digit ZIP Code. ZCTA-based tabulations replace ZIP Code tabulation provided in the 1990 and earlier censuses.
- **Traffic Analysis Zone (TAZ):** These are areas created by local transportation officials (those in metropolitan planning organizations, or MPOs) and are used for specialized tabulations of journey-to-work, place-of-work, and traffic-flow data. The data is published as part of the Census Transportation Planning Package (CTPP). Each TAZ has a six-character code that uniquely identifies it within a county. TAZs and the CTPP are described more fully in chapter 6.

Beyond these there are a number of other specialized areas that are either limited to particular areas of the country (such as **urban growth areas** in Oregon) or are associated with particular data sources (such as **Public Use Microdata Areas,** or PUMAs). Some of these will be discussed in the more detailed chapters that follow.

Summary level and tabulated data

Almost all census data is aggregated to a particular geographical scale, the "summary level," each with its own code. If we wanted data summed to the state level, we would need summary level "040" data. County level data is "050." Tract data is "140." Table 1.7 provides the most important summary level codes for urban land professionals.

Notice the difference between level "080" and level "140." If we wanted tract data for Dane County, Wisconsin, and we decided to download using the "140" summary level, we would get data on all tracts in the county. If we selected multiple counties, or even multiple states, then we would get tract information for all counties and states selected, organized by county. But if we downloaded using "080," the data would be organized differently. Tracts would be organized into the places in which they exist and those places would be organized into the county subdivisions

Table 1.7 Selected summary level codes	
Summary level code	**Geographical element**
010	United states
020	Region
030	Division
040	State
050	State-county
060	State-county-county subdivision
070	State-county-county subdivision-place/remainder
080	State-county-county subdivision-place/remainder-census tract
090	State-county-county subdivision-place/remainder-census tract-urban/rural-block group
140	State-county-census tract
150	State-county-census tract-block group
160	State-place
170	State-consolidated city
390	State-MSA/CMSA
391	State-MSA/CMSA-central city
850	Five-digit ZCTA
Note: These are only the most commonly used summary level codes. See U.S. Census Bureau (2003a, chapter 4) for a full set of codes.	

in which they exist. Tracts not in places would be categorized into the remainder (the nonplace part) of the county subdivision.

For those who plan to download and use the raw data tables provided by the Census Bureau (see chapter 2 for details), it is absolutely crucial to become familiar with the summary level code system. The codes will be necessary to extract information from the tables.

Data variables and data tables

The census is distributed as a series of data tables (sometimes called matrices) and associated data variables. Each summary file (in fact, each data product) has technical documentation in which tables and variables are described. For instance, chapter 5 of Summary File 3's technical documentation describes the available tables, and chapter 7 of the documentation lists the variables and their constituent data dictionary reference names (U.S. Census Bureau 2003a).

Counts for each of these subvariables are shown for a particular summary level. To find out the percentage of African-Americans in a particular geographic area, variable "P006003" would need to be divided by variable "P006001."

"Table P6: Race," part of the basic population tables based on the population (not a sample), is made up of eight subvariables, each with its own data dictionary reference name:

Total	P006001
White alone	P006002
Black or African-American alone	P006003
American Indian and Alaska Native alone	P006004
Asian alone	P006005
Native Hawaiian and other Pacific Islander alone	P006006
Some other race alone	P006007
Two races or more	P006008

"Table H79: Aggregate value (dollars) for all owner-occupied housing units by units in structure" shows not a count for each subvariable, but the total value of all homes in each category. It has eight constituent subvariables:

Aggregate value	H079001
1, detached	H079002
1, attached	H079003
2	H079004
3 or 4	H079005
5 or more	H079006
Mobile home	H079007
Boat, RV, van, etc.	H079008

To obtain the average value of mobile homes, for instance, the aggregate value for H079007 would be divided by the number of owner-occupied mobile homes (from "Table H32: Tenure by Units in Structure").

The system of tables and variables may seem very complex to new users of the census, but with a little practice the system is quite straightforward. Following two simple principles will simplify the process:

- First, choose a table making sure you understand the universe from which the table is drawn and the levels of geographic aggregation at which the table is available (for Summary File 3 this information will be provided in U.S. Census Bureau 2003a, chapter 5).
- Find out the constituent data dictionary reference names of the constituent variables (for Summary File 3 this will be provided in U.S. Census Bureau 2003a, chapter 7).

Census data products

The Census Bureau produces a number of standard data products commonly used by urban land professionals. These are listed in table 1.8. This data is available on computer tapes, CD–ROM, and on the Web. Acquiring census data for analysis in a GIS is discussed in detail in chapter 2.

Table 1.8 Major census data tabulations	
Name of product	Variables, lowest level of geography
100 percent data	
Redistricting Data Summary File	Population counts, blocks
Demographic Profile	Selected population and housing characteristics, tracts
Congressional District Demographic Profile	Selected population and housing characteristics, congressional districts
Summary File 1 (SF1)	Counts and cross tabulations on short-form questions, blocks
Summary File 2 (SF2)	Similar to SF1, but with detailed breakdowns by race, Hispanic origin, and American Indian, Alaska Native tribes, tracts
Sample data	
Demographic Profile	Selected population and housing characteristics, tracts
Congressional District Demographic Profile	Selected population and housing characteristics, congressional districts
Summary File 3 (SF3)	Social, economic, and housing characteristics, block group/tracts
Summary File 4 (SF4)	Similar to SF3, but with detailed breakdowns by race, Hispanic origin, and American Indian, Alaska Native tribes, tracts
Public Use Microdata Samples (PUMS)	Raw long-form data but with confidentiality screening. One percent sample for the nation, states, and some substate areas, 5 percent sample for state and substate areas. One percent Super Public Use Microdata Areas (Super-PUMAs), 5 percent PUMAs

There are also "special reports" put out by the Census Bureau (such as *Demographic trends in the 20th century* or *Racial and ethnic residential segregation in the United States: 1980–2000*) and various shorter "census briefs" (such as *The black population: 2000,* or *The 65 years and over population, 2000).* The advantage of these publications is that analysis has already been performed on the raw census numbers. You do not have to do the work yourself. However, these publications usually present data at a broad geographical scale, not the scale most relevant to the needs of urban analysts. Box 1.3 lists the full set of briefs and special reports available at the time of writing.

The Census Bureau also produces various specialized data publications that combine information from the Census of Population and Housing, the Economic Census, and various other sources. These include the following:

- *Census Transportation Planning Package (CTPP).* The Census 2000 version of the CTPP was not ready at the time of writing (the Census Bureau was experiencing difficulty compiling that data), but the 1990 version was available. The CTPP is used in an economic example

At the time of publication, the following briefs and special reports had been published:

Briefs:

1. *Overview of race and Hispanic origin* (C2KBR/01-1)
2. *Population change and distribution: 1990–2000* (C2KBR/01-2)
3. *The Hispanic population* (C2KBR/01-3)
4. *Race and Hispanic or Latino origin by age and sex for the United States: 2000* (PHC-T-8)
5. *The white population: 2000* (C2KBR/01-4)
6. *The black population: 2000* (C2KBR/01-5)
7. *The two or more races population: 2000* (C2KBR/01-6)
8. *Congressional apportionment* (C2KBR/01-7)
9. *Households and families: 2000* (C2KBR/01-8)
10. *Multigenerational households for the United States, states, and for Puerto Rico: 2000* (PHC-T-17)
11. *Gender: 2000* (C2KBR/01-9)
12. *Male-female ratio by race alone or in combination and Hispanic or Latino origin in the United States: 2000* (PHC-T-11)
13. *The 65 years and over population: 2000* (C2KBR/01-10)
14. *Population and ranking tables of the older population for the United States, states, Puerto Rico, places of 100,000 or more population, and counties* (PHC-T-13)
15. *The United States in international context: 2000* (C2KBR/01-11)
16. *Age: 2000* (C2KBR/01-12)
17. *Housing characteristics: 2000* (C2KBR/01-13)
18. *The Native Hawaiian and other Pacific Islander population: 2000* (C2KBR/01-14)
19. *The American Indian and Alaska Native population: 2000* (C2KBR/01-15)
20. *American Indian and Alaska Native tribes for the United States, regions, divisions, and states* (PHC-T-18)
21. *The Asian population: 2000* (C2KBR/01-16)
22. *Disability status: 2000* (C2KBR-17)
23. *Employment status: 2000* (C2KBR-18)
24. *Employment status of the population in households for the United States, states, counties, places, and for Puerto Rico: 2000* (PHC-T-28)
25. *Poverty: 1999* (C2KBR-19)
26. *Home values: 2000* (C2KBR-20)
27. *Housing costs of renters: 2000* (C2KBR-21)
28. *Veterans: 2000* (C2KBR-22)
29. *The Arab population: 2000* (C2KBR-23)
30. *Educational attainment: 2000* (C2KBR-24)
31. *Occupations: 2000* (C2KBR-25)

32. *School enrollment: 2000* (C2KBR-26)

33. *Housing costs of homeowners: 2000* (C2KBR-27)

34. *Geographical mobility: 1995 to 2000* (C2KBR-28)

35. *Language use and English-speaking ability: 2000* (C2KBR-29)

36. *Summary tables on language use and English ability: 2000* (PHC-T-20)

37. *Marital status: 2000* (C2KBR-30)

38. *Marital status for the population 15 years and over for the United States, regions, states, Puerto Rico and metropolitan areas: 2000* (PHC-T-27)

39. *Grandparents living with grandchildren: 2000* (C2KBR-31)

40. *Structural and occupancy characteristics of housing: 2000* (C2KBR-32)

Special reports:

1. *Mapping Census 2000: The geography of U.S. diversity* (CENSR/01-1)

2. *Emergency and transitional shelter population: 2000* (CENSR/01-2)

3. *Population in emergency and transitional shelters* (PHC-T-12)

4. *Racial and ethnic residential segregation in the United States: 1980–2000* (CENSR-3)

5. *Demographic trends in the 20th century* (CENSR-4)

6. *Married-couple and unmarried-partner households: 2000* (CENSR-5)

7. *Hispanic origin and race of coupled households* (PHC-T-19)

8. *Adopted children and stepchildren: 2000* (CENSR-6RV) and (PHC-T-21)

9. *Domestic migration across regions, divisions, and states: 1995 to 2000* (CENSR-7)

10. *State-to-state migration flows: 1995 to 2000* (CENSR-8)

11. *Migration for the population 5 years and over for the United States, regions, states, counties, New England minor civil divisions, metropolitan areas, and Puerto Rico: 2000* (PHC-T-22)

12. *Migration and geographic mobility in metropolitan and nonmetropolitan America: 1995 to 2000* (CENSR-9)

13 *Internal migration of the older population: 1995 to 2000* (CENSR-10)

14. *Migration by sex and age for the population 5 years and over for the United States, regions, states, and Puerto Rico: 2000* (PHC-T-23)

15. *Migration of natives and the foreign born: 1995 to 2000* (CENSR-11)

16. *Migration by nativity for the population 5 years and over for the United States and states: 2000* (PHC-T-24)

17. *Migration of the young, single, and college educated: 1995 to 2000* (CENSR-12)

18. *Migration by race and Hispanic origin: 1995 to 2000* (CENSR-13)

19. *Migration by race and Hispanic origin for the population 5 years and over for the United States, regions, states, and Puerto Rico: 2000* (PHC-T-25)

All of these are available at *landview.census.gov/population/www/cen2000/briefs.html*

in chapter 4 and is discussed in a transportation context in chapter 6. The CTPP data is distributed on CD–ROM and also on the Web.

- *Statistical abstract of the United States.* This publication is produced annually and includes data from the Census of Population and Housing, various updates to that census, the Economic Census, and various other official data sources. The data is best at the national and state levels. It is produced as a paper publication, as a CD–ROM, and is available on the Web.
- *State and metropolitan area data book.* This is also produced annually and includes data from the Census of Population and Housing, the Economic Census, and various surveys and updates. It is produced annually and is available on CD–ROM and the Web.
- *City and county data book.* This is produced annually and includes data from the Census of Population and Housing, the Economic Census, and various surveys and updates. It is produced annually and is available on CD–ROM and the Web. Data is provided for larger cities and counties.
- *TIGER/Line system.* This is the Census Bureau's main mapping database. It is described in detail in chapter 2.

Almost all of this data can be downloaded from the Web (there are complete instructions in chapter 2), or users may order CD–ROMs or DVDs directly from the Census Bureau. Depository libraries will usually have all the necessary information in electronic format.

Organization of the rest of the book

Chapter 2 is a hands-on discussion of downloading Census of Population and Housing data, and the ways that data can be brought into a GIS—it assumes almost no knowledge of the census beyond topics covered in this chapter. It also assumes very limited knowledge of GIS. The chapter is considerably more introductory than the ones that follow. Before more complex census analyses can be attempted, users should become familiar with the basic methods of data acquisition.

The four chapters following chapter 2 focus on particular sets of data. In each of these chapters we describe the relevant variables included in the decennial and other censuses, consider supplementary sources that can be used to extend or update analyses, and develop a few practical examples of analyses using census data and sometimes other sources. The discussion of particular examples is intended to clarify general principles of data access and use. Examples were chosen to illustrate typical methods of dealing with the major challenges census-based spatial analyses pose.

Chapter 3 looks at demographic and social data, perhaps the most commonly used census data. Chapter 4 examines the economic and occupation data in the Census of Population and Housing and also describes the Economic Census and various related economic data sources. Chapter 5 covers housing and community development data. Chapter 6 focuses on travel and commuting data, particularly the Public Use Microdata Sample (PUMS) and the Census Transportation Planning Package (CTPP).

Chapter 7 considers distribution strategies, particularly using the Web as a way of providing clients and the public easy access to information.

Chapter **2**

Downloading
the **data** and the **maps**

This chapter deals with a set of closely related hands-on issues. We begin by discussing how to access workable census maps in a GIS. Then we move on to acquiring digital census data and connecting the maps to that data. Following this is a short and generic primer on analyzing map-based data using selections and overlays. The final section covers other sorts of official maps that urban land professionals often use. This chapter is introductory and assumes little previous knowledge of a GIS. Readers who know how to download and integrate data with maps can safely move on to chapter 3. Our aim in this chapter is not to provide point-and-click exercises but to supply readers new to using the census in a GIS environment with various strategies for acquiring maps and data. We emphasize the variety of methods available to acquire maps and data, and the advantages and disadvantages of each of these.

Downloading and translating the TIGER/Line maps

The Census Bureau's main mapping system is published as TIGER/Line files. TIGER is an acronym that stands for Topologically Integrated Geographic Encoding and Referencing system. Unfortunately, these files are in raw text format, so in order to be useful in a particular GIS program the TIGER/Line files must be translated into a file format understandable by that GIS. (The organization of the raw data files is discussed in box 2.1.) Until quite recently this was a far from simple task, but over the past few years technological changes have made the use of TIGER/Line files much simpler. For instance, the distribution of TIGER/Line files on the Web has meant that it is much easier to keep up with the most current TIGER/Line edition (previously one had to wait for the postal delivery of CD–ROMS). Also, translation software has become faster, much less bug-ridden, more efficient, and less expensive. Plus, there are more translation options than there used to be. Best of all, already translated TIGER/Line files are available free on the Web. However, these improvements mean that users have more choices and thus need to be able to make more informed decisions about TIGER/Line data. In this section, we will describe various strategies for acquiring usable TIGER/Line files.

At the broadest level the main decisions are (1) whether you want to spend money on map acquisition and (2) whether your organization will translate internally or download or buy files that have already been translated. To get hold of usable digital maps, you will need to choose among four different strategies.

1. Download the files from the census site and then translate them using a (free or nearly free) translation utility.

The raw TIGER/Line files are available at *www.census.gov/geo/www/tiger/index.html*. This site not only includes the latest TIGER/Line files but also older versions, in particular the 1992 version that provides a link between 1980 and 1990 census geography. The site also includes metadata for various versions of the TIGER/Line system. As of this writing, the most recent published files are for 2002 (if you need specific TIGER/Line files from the 1990s, contact the Census Bureau or your local metropolitan planning organization (MPO)). After selecting this data source (*www.census.gov/geo/www/tiger/tiger2002/tgr2002.html*), select a particular state and then a county. In this chapter's examples, we will use maps and data for Dane County, Wisconsin, home to the state's capital, Madison. Wisconsin has the state FIPS code 55, and Dane County has the FIPS code 025 (FIPS codes can be found in U.S. Census Bureau 2003d, appendix A). The TIGER/Line file we will need to download is "tgr55025.zip." Data must be downloaded one county at a time. Since the files are zipped, you will need unzipping software to use them. Most computer users have a copy of WinZip® or its equivalent. However, if you are unzipping TIGER/Line files for multiple counties, it is worth downloading and installing the ExtractNow zip utility. It is fast and will allow you to extract multiple archives with one button click. Once unzipped you will usually have sixteen files per county; in this case, the files are: TGR55025.RT1 through TGR55025.RT8 and TGR55025.RTA, .RTC, .RTH, .RTI, .RTP, .RTR, .RTS, .RTT, and .RTZ. The content of these files is described in box 2.1.

The next step is to translate these files into a standard GIS format. Some translation utilities come free with GIS software. The ArcToolbox™ tool, part of the ArcGIS® suite, contains a built-in TIGER-to-Coverage Wizard; this will convert TIGER/Line files into ESRI's coverage format (and ArcToolbox wizards will translate them into geodatabase and shapefile formats). While useful for parcel mapping, this translation wizard is not particularly helpful for analysis using census geographic units.[1] Considerable additional work will be necessary to make the resulting files useful in a census analysis setting. Caliper™ GIS products (Maptitude®, TransCAD®) come with very good built-in translation facilities. Moreover, both of these products also read from and write to a wide variety of standard GIS file formats, including ESRI shapefiles and MapInfo® format .mif files.

[1]The AML script TIGERTOOL will translate for pre-8.x versions of ArcInfo™ software. The script is available at arcscripts.esri.com. If you use the ArcToolbox or AML™ tool you may find the TIGER® Census Data Interpreter, also available at the ArcScripts site, invaluable. This provides aliases to field names and links to a table of CFCC codes (see box 2.1 on CFCC codes).

The raw TIGER/Line files are extracts from the census TIGER database and are available for all counties and statistically equivalent areas in the United States.

There are also files for Puerto Rico and the Island Areas. The raw post-Census 2000 TIGER/Line data for each county consists of the following files.

Table 2.1 Individual TIGER/Line Record Types and files			
File type	**Record contents**	**Example of file**	**Comments**
Record Type 1	Complete chain basic data record	TGR55025.RT1	This provides a single unique record for each complete chain, including *x* and *y* coordinates for start and end points.
Record Type 2	Complete chain shape coordinates	TGR55025.RT2	When Record Type 1 is not a straight line, these will provide shaping points, essentially a series of *x* and *y* coordinates.
Record Type 4	Index to alternate feature identifiers	TGR55025.RT4	Alternative names for complete chains.
Record Type 5	Complete chain feature identifiers	TGR55025.RT5	List of unique names for all complete chains.
Record Type 6	Additional address range and ZIP Code data	TGR55025.RT6	
Record Type 7	Landmark features	TGR55025.RT7	Area and point landmark features.
Record Type 8	Polygons linked to area landmarks	TGR55025.RT8	
Record Type A	Polygon geographic entity codes: current geography	TGR55025.RTA	Full geography description for each polygon.
Record Type B	Polygon geographic entity codes: corrections	TGR55025.RTB	
Record Type E	Polygon geographic entity codes: economic census	TGR55025.RTE	
Record Type H	TIGER/Line ID history	TGR55025.RTH	Provides the geographic identity codes used in the economic census.
Record Type I	Link between complete chains and polygons	TGR55025.RTI	This links Record Type 1 to Record Type P, in other words, the complete chains to polygon internal points.
Record Type P	Polygon internal point	TGR55025.RTP	
Record Type R	TIGER/Line ID record number range	TGR55025.RTR	
Record Type S	Polygon geographic entity codes: Census 2000	TGR55025.RTS	
Record Type T	TIGER zero-cell ID	TGR55025.RTT	
Record Type U	TIGER/Line ID overpass/ underpass identification	TGR55025.RTU	
Record Type Z	ZIP+4 Codes	TGR55025.RTZ	

Note that Record Types 4, 6, 7, 8, B, E, U, and Z may be left out of a county's data if the data contained in these records is not appropriate for that county. Each file, or Record Type, is a text file that can be read directly in a text editor such as WordPad. Each record in each file is a nondelimited line of text. Thus the first record (the first line) of a Record Type 1 county file may read:

"11102 49453252 B   A41
55550250250850008500   01270001270010911091   -89836264+42999997-
89838575+42998886"
and another record:
"11102 49467030 AS Rosa   Rd   A41   15   99   14
9800005370553705   55550250254800048000   4800048000000020100020110322003
-89478432+43066868 -89478432+43066002."

To understand what this means, users must (1) understand something of TIGER topology, (2) have the data dictionary for Record Type 1 files, (3) understand census geography, and finally (4) understand the feature coding system (Census Feature Class Codes or CFCCs). TIGER/Line Technical Documentation 2002 (U.S. Census Bureau 2003d) has a complete discussion of these topics. Chapter 1 has a discussion of TIGER topology; chapter 3 describes CFCCs; chapter 4 is a summary of census geography; and chapter 6 provides the data dictionaries for each Record Type. What follows is an abbreviated discussion of three of these topics (we will assume readers covered census geography in the first chapter of this book).

TIGER/Line topology

Topology describes how in some mapping systems (systems that use topological data models) points are used to define lines, and lines are used to define polygons. The details of topology are well beyond this book; nevertheless, it is important to have some idea of TIGER/Line topology to understand and use the data better.

TIGER/Line consists of six basic spatial objects, four of these being topological, and two not:[1]

1. Node—topological: A node is the junction of two or more chains or the end point of a chain. Think of a node as the beginning point or end point of a line segment. In figure 2.1, each arrow is defined by a node at the beginning (the end tip of the arrow) and one at the end (the front tip of the arrow). Essentially, the end and front tips of each arrow are nodes.

2. Complete chain—topological: Think of a complete chain as a line segment with start and end nodes. It may also have shape points if the line is not straight. A complete chain will also explicitly reference left and right polygons; in other words, the chain acts as a border between two units of census geography and will indicate explicitly which

[1] This description is taken and modified from U.S. Census Bureau (2003d, 1.5–1.8).

census polygon is on the left of the chain and which census polygon is on the right. In figure 2.1 each arrow represents one complete chain.

3. Network chain—topological: Think of this as a chain or line segment with beginning and end nodes but no right and left polygons. In other words, these are lines that are not used to define census geography. Network chains may define things like pipelines, creeks, and so on.

4. GT Polygon—topological: These are elementary polygons and are both complete and exclusive. They are complete in that they completely cover a surface, and they are exclusive in the sense that they have no overlap. Think here of a map of all tracts in the United States. There is no overlap between tracts, and all the tracts together (plus a polygon representing the area outside the United States) cover the entire surface. Figure 2.2 covers the same surface areas as figure 2.1. But the various GT Polygons are now visible, though only GT Polygon A has its complete boundary visible. Notice that various complete chains may penetrate a GT Polygon (in this example, Lakeview Knoll and Valley View Knoll and a third unnamed cul-de-sac), but still not define the GT Polygon's boundary.

5. Entity point—nontopological: A point for identifying point features or polygon

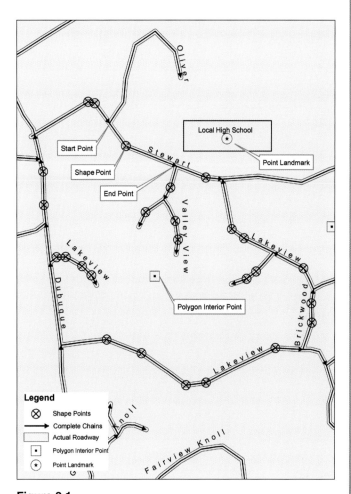

Figure 2.1

features that have been collapsed to a point. Entity points are used to represent things such as towers, buildings, buoys, and so on.

6. Shape point—nontopological: These define the line segments in chains and are mainly used to represent the curvature of geographic features. For instance, in figure 2.1, the single complete chain that is Lakeview Knoll from Dubuque Street through to Brickwood Knoll has a total of five shape points.

43

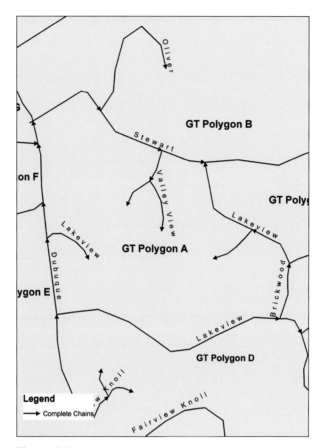

Figure 2.2

Record Type data dictionaries

The data dictionary for each Record Type defines how the text TIGER/Line should be read by a database. In this section we will focus on the Record Type 1 file—the other Record Types work in much the same way. The data dictionary for the Record Type 1 files (this is also called the Complete Chain Basic Data Record) is as follows:

Table 2.2 Data dictionary for TIGER/Line files Record Type 1					
Field	**Type**	**Beg**	**End**	**Len**	**Description**
RT	A	1	1	1	Record type
VERSION	N	2	5	4	Version number
TLID	N	6	15	10	TIGER/Line, permanent 1-cell number
SIDE1	N	16	16	1	Single-side source code
SOURCE	A	17	17	1	Linear segment source code
FEDIRP	A	18	19	2	Feature direction, prefix

FENAME	A	20	49	30	Feature name
FETYPE	A	50	53	4	Feature type
FEDIRS	A	54	55	2	Feature direction, suffix
CFCC	A	56	58	3	Census Feature Class Code
FRADDL	A	59	69	11	Start address, left
TOADDL	A	70	80	11	End address, left
FRADDR	A	81	91	11	Start address, right
TOADDR	A	92	102	11	End address, right
FRIADDL	A	103	103	1	Start imputed address flag, left
TOIADDL	A	104	104	1	End imputed address flag, left
FRIADDR	A	105	105	1	Start imputed address flag, right
TOIADDR	A	106	106	1	End imputed address flag, right
ZIPL	N	107	111	5	ZIP Code, left
ZIPR	N	112	116	5	ZIP Code, right
AIANHHFPL	N	117	121	5	FIPS 55 code (American Indian/ Alaska Native area/Hawaiian Home Land) 2000 left
AIANHHFPR	N	122	126	5	FIPS 55 Code (American Indian/ Alaska Native area/Hawaiian) 2000 right
AIHHTLIL	A	127	127	1	American Indian/Hawaiian Home Land trust land indicator, 2000 left
AIHHTLIR	A	128	128	1	American Indian/Hawaiian Home Land trust land indicator, 2000 right
CENSUS1	A	129	129	1	Census use 1
CENSUS2	A	130	130	1	Census use 2
STATEL	N	131	132	2	FIPS state code, 2000 left
STATER	N	133	134	2	FIPS state code, 2000 right
COUNTYL	N	135	137	3	FIPS county code, 2000 left
COUNTYR	N	138	140	3	FIPS county code, 2000 right
COUSUBL	N	141	145	5	FIPS 55 code (county subdivision), 2000 left
COUSUBR	N	146	150	5	FIPS 55 code (county subdivision), 2000 right
SUBMCDL	N	151	155	5	FIPS 55 code (subbarrio), 2000 left
SUBMCDR	N	156	160	5	FIPS 55 code (subbarrio), 2000 right
PLACEL	N	161	165	5	FIPS 55 code (place/CDP), 2000 left
PLACER	N	166	170	5	FIPS 55 code (place/CDP), 2000 right
TRACTL	N	171	176	6	Census tract, 2000 left
TRACTR	N	177	182	6	Census tract, 2000 right
BLOCKL	N	183	186	4	Census block Number, 2000 left
BLOCKR	N	187	190	4	Census block Number, 2000 right
FRLONG	N	191	200	10	Start longitude
FRLAT	N	201	209	9	Start latitude
TOLONG	N	210	219	10	End longitude
TOLAT	N	220	229	9	End latitude

The heading "Type" indicates whether the field is alphanumeric (A) or numeric (N), "Beg" indicates where in the text string the field begins, "End" indicates where it ends, and "Len" shows how many characters of the string compose the field. The first line (or record) in the file "TGR55025.RT1" is:

"11102##49453252#B###A41##55550250250850008500##################################0127000127001091109I#-89836264+42999997-89838575+42998886."

This is the same record we used at the beginning of this box, but here we have replaced blank characters or spaces (which indicate no data) with "#" so that it is easy for readers to count characters. Thus, for this complete chain the Record Type is "1," the Version Number is "1102." The TIGER/Line identification number is "49453252". This complete chain is missing street address data, but the chain is in Wisconsin (characters 131 and 132 are "55" indicating state FIPS 55, Wisconsin, is on the left of the chain. Characters 133 and 134 are also "55" indicating that state 55 is on the right side of the chain as well). Characters 135–137 are "025" and so are characters 138–140, indicating that county "025" (Dane County) is on either side of this chain. Tract 012700 is on the left and right side of this chain, and block "1091" is also on the left and right side of this chain. The chain begins at a longitude of -89°83'62.64 and a latitude of +42°99'99.97 and ends at longitude -89°83'85.75 and latitude +42°99'88.86. These are unprojected coordinates although the TIGER/Line system actually begins life using a projected coordinate system (mainly the Universal Transverse Mercator or UTM projection).

We do not cover the data dictionaries for the other record types; they are available in the TIGER/Line technical documentation. A TIGER/Line conversion program converts the text-based information in the various Record Type files into one of the standard map file formats used by GIS software.

Census Feature Class Codes (CFCCs)

The feature codes allow users to identify individual features. Sometimes this is crucial for analyses. Feature Class A consists of roads. CFCC A11 to A18 are primary highways with limited access. For instance, an A11 is a "primary road with limited access or interstate highway, unseparated," while an A14 is a "primary road with limited access or interstate highway, unseparated, with rail line in center." A21 to A28 are primary roads without limited access, A41 to A48 are local neighborhood and rural roads, A62 consists of traffic circles, A65 ferry crossings, and so on. The full list is available in U.S. Census Bureau (2003d, chapter 3).

Class B consists of railroads, Class C miscellaneous ground transportation, (C10 are pipelines, C31 aerial tramways, monorails, or ski lifts), and Class D are landmarks. For instance, D10 are military installations, D23 trailer courts or mobile home parks, D24 marinas. Custodial facilities are listed under D30 to D37, educational and religious institutions D40 to D44, transportation terminals D50 to D57, employment centers D60 to D66, towers D70 to D71, open space D80 to D85, and so-called special purpose landmarks D91 to D96 (for instance D94 are police stations).

Physical features are categorized in Class E (for instance E21 is a ridge line, E23 a named island), Class F covers so-called nonvisible features, Class H hydrography (water), Class P provisional features, and Class X features yet to be classified.

If you needed to know the income and racial characteristics of those living next to highways in a particular county, you would have to translate TIGER/Line files for road and blocks groups (if that was your unit of analysis) and download block group data. You would then select the roads that are highways (A11 to A18 and possibly a few other related codes) and find those block groups that intersect, in some way, with those selected road types. You could then identify the racial and income characteristics of people living in those selected block groups.

Further notes on usage

The post-Census 2000 TIGER/Line files added four new files: Record Types B, E, T, and U. Record Type 3 contained the 1990 geographic entity codes—essentially the 1990 census geography. Type 9 provided a link between the so-called Key Geographic Location (KGL) building with its own ZIP+4 Code and an actual street address. This information has been suppressed for confidentiality reasons. Notice also that the post-2000 files

have other important changes. Some field names have changed and the structure of some Record Types has also been changed. The technical documentation has a full listing of these changes.

TIGER/Line, like any large data set, is subject to error. Some of that error is the simple result of human and processing mistakes. A road may be missing or misidentified. Fortunately, there are active data quality control programs aimed at correcting these sorts of errors. In fast-growing areas, the TIGER/Line system will always be missing the most recent developments on the ground.

Over and above issues of simple error and the impossibility of being entirely up-to-date, there are a range of more complex data accuracy issues. Suppose we do have a particular TIGER/Line segment representing a particular length of roadway; just how spatially accurate is that representation? Is the length and shape of the feature and the relative position of the road feature accurately represented by the map? (This type of accuracy is sometimes referred to as "ground truth.") And how correct is the attribute data (CFCC codes, etc.) describing that segment?

The positional accuracy (essentially how well the position of features on the ground is represented by the position of features on the map) of the TIGER/Line data is not good. Where the data is derived from 1:100,000 scale maps from the U.S. Geological Survey (USGS), TIGER/Line meets the National Map Accuracy Standards (167 feet), although the Census Bureau will not specify the accuracy of field updates to the data.

ESRI and third-party translation extensions are available from the ESRI scripting Web site (ArcScripts at *arcscripts.esri.com*) for download. TIGER® Reader, available at this site, is simple to use and powerful (note that it works on post-1997 files but generates errors on 2002 and

Box 2.2   Installing TIGER Reader and using it to translate raw TIGER/Line files into useful shapefiles

Download the TIGER Reader from the Arc-Scripts site *arcscripts.esri.com.* The downloaded file will be in zip format. Unzip it; the result will be a file called "tiger.avx." The suffix .avx indicates it is an ArcView™ extension written in the macro language Avenue. After making sure that ArcView is not running, the unzipped file should then be copied to the "C:\ESRI\AV_GIS30\ARCVIEW\ EXT32" folder. Now open ArcView 3.x, go to **File,** then **Extensions** and select the TIGER Reader. This will add a new icon to the ArcView toolbar; click it. After agreeing to the licensing arrange-ments, you will be asked to select the Record Type 1 file. This is the .RT1 file we unzipped (for Dane County, Wisconsin, "TGR55025.RT1"). Navi-gate to the place that you unzipped your TIGER/Line files and select this file. You will then be asked what census feature classes you want to translate (blocks, block groups, tracts, streets, and so on). Feature classes will be translated into shapefile for-mat, one shapefile for each feature class. Note that this translator will generate errors on pre-1997 and some post-2000 TIGER/Line files.

later translations). Unfortunately, it is written in the Avenue™ scripting language and so will only work for versions of ArcView up to 3.x. It won't work in ArcGIS. Users with ArcView 3.x will have to download the compiled script and install it in the correct directory before actually translating. Box 2.2 describes the process involved.

The advantage of this strategy is the low cost and the ability to keep translated files as up-to-date as the published raw TIGER/Line files (this is an important consideration in fast-growing areas with frequent changes in features). The main disadvantages of this strategy are that the translation software may not always directly provide the output needed, and that TIGER/Line files must be downloaded, unzipped, and translated one county at a time. For instance, suppose we wanted a map of all tracts in Texas. With most of this translation software, each county's tracts would be translated into a separate tract file (the actual translation processing can usu-ally be done in a single batch). Given that Texas has 254 counties, 254 different maps would result, one for each county. All of these 254 would then have to be processed (joined) into a single map layer or feature class. In ArcView 3.x and ArcGIS the GeoProcessing Wizard (use the Merge function) will do the necessary work, although the process of joining 254 shapefiles together is very slow and errors are easy to make.

2. Download the files from the census site and then translate them using an advanced translation utility.

The advantages here are the ability to keep translated files as up-to-date as the published raw TIGER/Line files and the ability to process a feature class for multiple counties into a single resulting file. The only disadvantage is the small cost involved. However, if you or your agency converts TIGER/Line files frequently, this method is likely to save money even in the short term. TGR2SHP is an excellent and relatively inexpensive piece of software that converts

TIGER/Line files to shapefile format. TGR2MIF will convert to the MapInfo .mif format. The software is available for purchase and download from *www.gistools.com*. Both these programs install in the standard Microsoft® Windows® manner. TGR2SHP may be added to ArcToolbox as a custom .exe thus integrating the software nicely into the ArcGIS environment. Box 2.3 describes the use of this software.

Box 2.3   Using TGR2SHP to translate raw TIGER/Line files into useful shapefiles

This is our preferred method. The software is inexpensive, fast, copes with various versions of TIGER/Line files, and will merge data for multiple counties into one file.

You will need to purchase, download, and install the software. Then download the TIGER/Line files for a county or for multiple counties (a major advantage of TGR2SHP is that it is able to translate a feature class for multiple counties into single shapefiles). Run the software. Navigate to the Record Type 1 files or to the original unzipped files. The latter option will allow you to skip unzipping manually. All data files should be in the same directory. The TIGER/Line version screen will appear (figure 2.3).

Press the **Edit** button and you will see the feature class window. Select the feature classes you would like translated—in this case we have selected tracts and blocks. Click **OK** and then press the **Go** button. The output window will appear (figure 2.4).

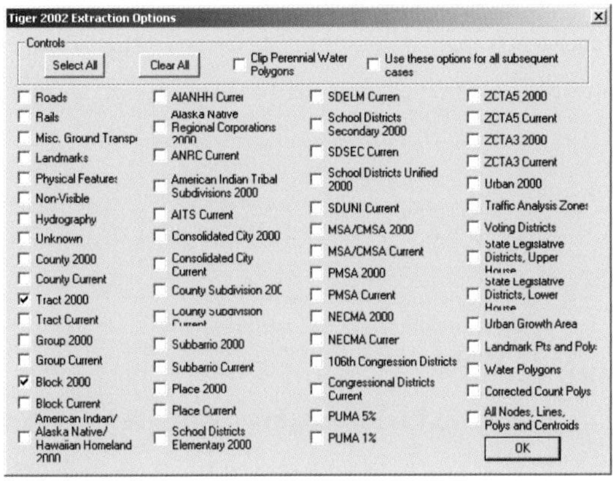

The **Organize by Theme and Merge** option in the Output Organization Options frame will allow you to merge a single feature class over multiple counties. The result will be a single shapefile that covers multiple counties, obviating the need to do any further geoprocessing to combine counties together (figure 2.5).

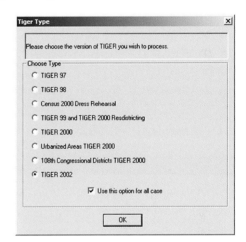

Figure 2.3

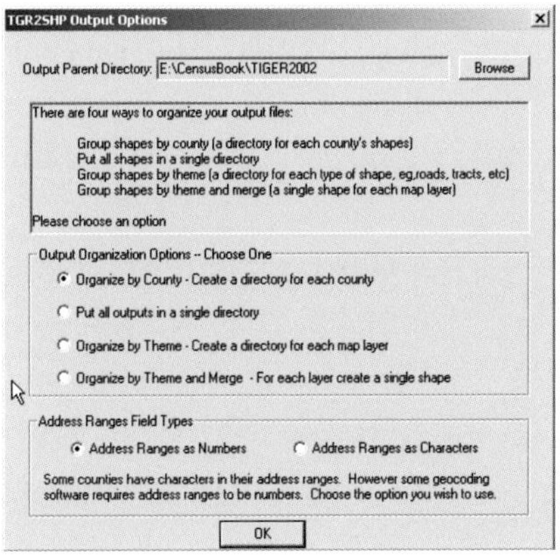

Figure 2.4

Figure 2.5

Other good translation utilities exist. For instance, the Universal TIGER Translator from International Computer Works (a replacement for the earlier TMT) allows advanced translation into MapInfo formats (*www.icwmaps.com*).

3. Download already translated and processed files from the Web.

TIGER/Line files already processed into shapefiles are available free from the Geography Network℠. Other versions, merged from counties to the state level, are available from the Maps and Cartographic Resources page of the Census Bureau's Web site (*www.census.gov/geo/www/maps*). The advantages here are that the translation and processing work have already been done, and they are free. Moreover, in the case of data downloaded from ESRI, the files have been processed in such a way that they are particularly easy to connect to census data files. We use this acquisition strategy all the time. The main disadvantage of this strategy is that you will not have immediate access to updates of the TIGER/Line files. Also, when using the Geography Network, data must be downloaded one county at a time. Thus for multicounty analyses the data must be joined. If you have downloaded shapefiles from the ESRI data site, ArcView 3.x and the ArcGIS GeoProcessing Wizard (use the Merge function) will do the necessary joining, though the process can be very slow. A number of other sites also allow downloading of translated TIGER/Line files, usually in shapefile or MapInfo .mif format. If you download from the Maps and Cartographic Resources page of the census site, you will not have access to block data or to any features that are not also part of standard census geography, such as streets and water features.

For very simple access to the TIGER/Line files, you can use the Internet Servers functionality in ArcMap™ to log onto the Geography Network. Click on the **Add Data** tool in ArcMap, choose **Add Internet Server,** type in *www.geographynetwork.com* as the URL. This will provide you with a new Internet server, *www.geographynetwork.com.* Double-click on the server, and the various services available at this site will appear. Choose "Census_TIGER2000." The data will be symbolized already, but you will not be able to download the data locally, making analysis cumbersome and in some cases impossible.

4. Buy fully processed files from a vendor.

Again, there are a number of vendors selling fully processed files and many consultants will provide tailor-made files for your needs. The vendor (or consultant) you choose will partly be determined by the GIS software you use and partly by your mapping needs and GIS abilities. The disadvantage of this method is cost. The advantage is that besides being translated, the maps will have been symbolized already and will be easy to use in a GIS. Often census data will have

The Geography Network provides access to a massive range of maps and also some useful data. Go to *www.geographynetwork.com*. Finding the TIGER/Line data can be a little difficult. Selecting **Data,** then **Downloadable Data Census 2000 TIGER/Line Data** will take you to the ESRI data server at *www.esri.com/data/download/census2000_tigerline/index.html*. Metadata is available on this page, as well as the links to the processed TIGER/Line files. Download TIGER/Line Data in shapefile format; you can choose multiple data layers for a single county or a single data layer for multiple counties. In other words, you could choose to download streets, blocks, tracts, places, and so on for a single county, or streets or blocks (not both) for multiple counties in a state.

A single zip format file will be delivered to you per download. This will need to be unzipped, and then each county or feature class you downloaded will need to be unzipped again. After unzipping, you will have as many shapefiles as counties or feature classes you downloaded. In this example, we will download 1990 and 2000 census tracts (figure 2.6).

After unzipping, the feature layers will be usable in most GIS programs. The "readme.html" page that accompanies the zips contains some basic metadata and links to additional metadata.

On opening the two layers, and symbolizing them appropriately, the analyst will be able to identify immediately the tract changes between 1990 and 2000 (figure 2.7, next page).

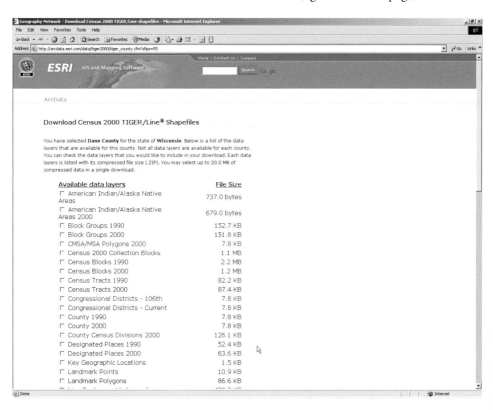

Figure 2.6

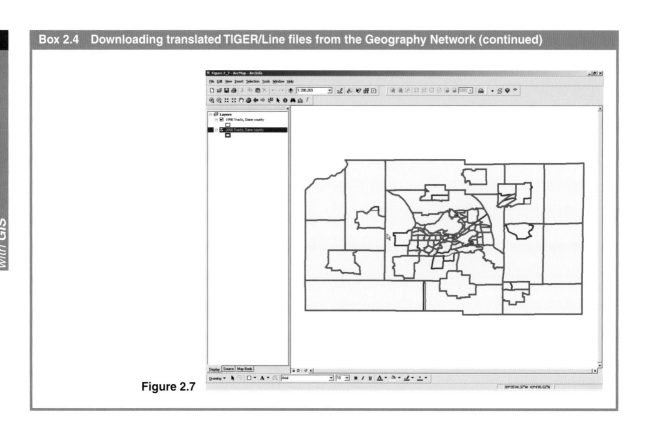

Figure 2.7

been attached to the maps, eliminating the need to download and preprocess the data, or to build a connection between the processed census data and the maps. The user is paying for the preprocessing and ease of use. For those using ArcGIS, ESRI has a particularly well-developed standardized product here, MapData.

Downloading census data

As with the downloading of TIGER/Line maps, acquiring census data has become much simpler over the past decade. But choices have to be made about the best way to acquire data. We will briefly describe some of these choices and illustrate downloading using various methods. In the following section of the chapter, this data will be attached to the map we downloaded in the previous section.

1. Using traditional mainframe computer resources.

Traditionally, any major census analysis would require mainframe computer work. Statistical programs such as SAS or SPSS would be used to analyze the locally downloaded data or would be used to run analyses on the mainframe itself. This is much less common today as there are simpler personal-computer-based data access methods. Nevertheless, for large multistate analyses a mainframe computer is still very useful.

2. Using the FactFinder tool to download data from the Web.

At the other end of the scale is American FactFinder, a new Web-based tool used by the Census Bureau to provide census data on the Web. It answers many of the criticisms of the bureau's earlier attempts at Web-based data acquisition. For all but the most complex analyses, American FactFinder will do the job. Moreover, it's free and relatively fast. Box 2.5 provides a fairly comprehensive tutorial on using American FactFinder to download census data. For complex data needs, various FactFinder-based downloads could be combined using database software.

Box 2.5   A FactFinder tutorial

American FactFinder's home page is at *factfinder. census.gov/home/saff/main.html?_lang=en*. You can also go to *www.census.gov*, the census home page, and choose FactFinder. The FactFinder home page consists of information and links to important census information such as census metadata. There is

a section of the page, "About this data set," which has links to very useful descriptions of both the decennial census and the economic census. However, if you want to download data, click on the **Data Sets** menu item on the main page (figure 2.8).

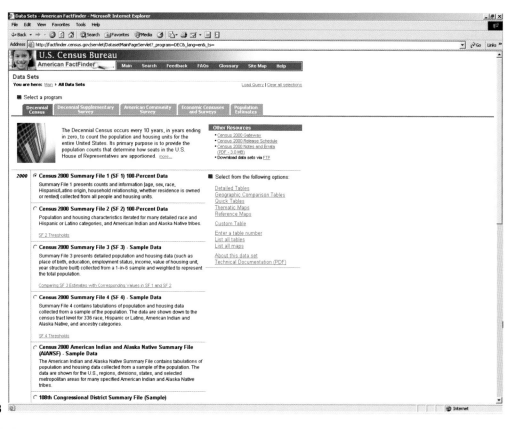

Figure 2.8

Box 2.5   A FactFinder tutorial (continued)

Various year 2000 data sets are available as well as STF1 and STF3 from 1990. Downloading is remarkably simple. Select a data set—in this case we select Census 2000 Summary File 1 (SF1), and we are presented with a menu of choices (figure 2.9).

Select SF3 and the same menu appears. For quick maps produced on the Web itself, select the **Thematic Maps** option. These maps are not particularly useful if you need to do more complex analyses, want to download data, or want to have control over map output. Nevertheless, these Web maps are an extremely convenient way of doing fast simple analyses of census data. In this example we choose **Thematic Maps,** under geographic types select **State,** then select the state we are interested in (in this case Wisconsin), then click **Next** (if we clicked on the **Map** button at this stage, all we would see is a map of Wisconsin), and then select a variable. In this example

we choose "TM-P031 Percent of persons who are foreign born, 2000." Click on **Show Results,** and the map is produced (figure 2.10).

The results for Wisconsin are shown by county; once the map is generated we could change that by selecting some other geography in the drop down list box on the top left-hand side of the screen. In fact, a range of other units of census geography is available to us; in this case, county subdivision, census tract, urban area, 106th Congressional district, and five-digit ZIP Code Tabulation Area are available. We then choose **census tracts.** The Web-mapping service will allow users to zoom right down to the street level, or to zoom to a particular address (or longitude/latitude) that is typed in. Clicking the **Identify** tool just above the top of the map window will give you basic information about any county (tract, urban area, and so on) in the map window that you click on.

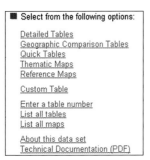

Figure 2.9

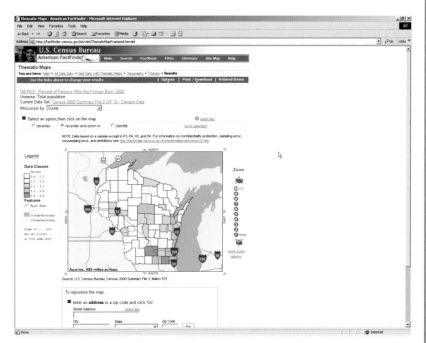

Figure 2.10

Box 2.5 A FactFinder tutorial (continued)

Above the map window is a horizontal menu bar, one of whose titles is **Options.** Under **Options** is the **Title** menu item that allows you to add a title to the map; a **Features** menu item allows you to display further features (such as roads and rivers) with the map. The **Boundaries** item allows label placement on the map, and the **Data Classes** item allows control of legends (or symbology). The **Related** items menu title provides a very useful page listing data sets and variables related to the variable you are currently mapping.

You can also save the map and the legend as images and then use these images in other documents such as word-processing files or your own HTML pages. In the map window and then in the legend window, right-click and select **Save Picture As,** provide a name in the dialog box, and the map and legend will be saved as .gif files. However, you will have difficulty using these maps in a GIS program. Instead, on the menu bar select the **Print/ Download** title and then the **Download** item.

This will open a download window (figure 2.11). You have the option of downloading in two database- compatible formats: Microsoft Excel format or a comma delimited text format. An Excel file will need to be exported into another format in order to be used by ArcGIS (we suggest Microsoft Access .mdb format) and many other GIS systems. Comma delimited files will require a small amount of preprocessing to maximize ease of use in ArcGIS, although the comma delimited text files can be opened directly by ArcGIS (the issues to be aware of are discussed in some detail later in this box). In this example we will choose to download comma delimited files. You will also be asked whether you want descriptive data ele-

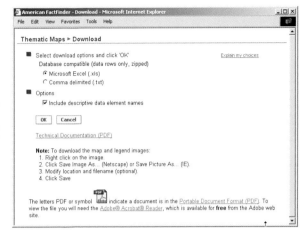

Figure 2.11

ment names. If you want to work with this data in a database or GIS, do not select the option to include descriptive names. These will confuse almost all databases. The download file will be in zip format and by default will be called "output. zip." Once the files have been unzipped, you will see that you have actually downloaded four text files:

- "readme_dec_2000_sf3.txt"
- "tm_dec_3000_st3_u_meta.txt"
- "tm_readme.txt"
- "tm_dec_2000_sf3_u_data.txt"

If you had decided to download in Excel format we would get the same four files except that "tm_dec_2000_sf3_u_data.txt" would be replaced by "tm_dec_2000_sf3_u_data.xls." This is the file that holds the actual census data. For detailed information about the variables, however, you will need to download the technical documentation.

A fragment of the resulting Microsoft Excel file is shown in figure 2.12 (next page). In this instance, we downloaded the descriptive titles so as to make the data easier to understand (remember that they

Box 2.5 A FactFinder tutorial (continued)

will have to be removed before bringing them into a GIS). Column H is variable "P021001," the universe, and column I is variable "P021013," the count of foreign-born. Column J or the "Class" field refers to the legend in the original map and is described in "tm_dec_3000_st3_u_meta.txt." The content of that file reads:

	A	B	C	D	E	F	End Review	H	I	J	K
1	GEO_ID	GEO_NA	GEOCOM	STATE	COUNTY	TRACT	MAP_DA	P021001	P021013	CLASS	
2	Geographi	Geograph	GEOCOM	STATE	COUNTY	TRACT	Percent of	Total	Total	Class	
3	14000US	Census	00	55	077	990200	0.6	2387	14	1	
4	14000US	Census	00	55	059	000800	12.5	2594	325	3	
5	14000US	Census	00	55	079	009600	8	2962	238	3	
6	14000US	Census	00	55	075	960900	1.4	2790	38	1	
7	14000US	Census	00	55	053	960500	2.3	4727	108	1	
8	14000US	Census	00	55	057	990302	2.4	1164	28	1	
9	14000US	Census	00	55	057	990301	2.4	1634	40	1	
10	14000US	Census	00	55	079	016400	39.4	5180	2041	5	
11	14000US	Census	00	55	079	120100	4.2	7855	328	2	
12	14000US	Census	00	55	117	000300	4.2	6662	283	2	
13	14000US	Census	00	55	039	040200	3	3226	98	1	
14	14000US	Census	00	55	027	961300	1.7	5040	86	1	
15	14000US	Census	00	55	139	001700	1.7	4707	82	1	
16	14000US	Census	00	55	099	970100	0.6	2938	19	1	

Figure 2.12

Theme Name—TM-P031. Percent of Persons Who Are Foreign Born: 2000
Universe—Total population
Data set—Census 2000 Summary File 3 (SF 3)—Sample Data
Unit—Percent
Formula—(P021013 / P021001) x 100
Classification Type—Natural Breaks
Class Breaks
Class 1—0.0–3.0
Class 2—3.1–7.5
Class 3—7.6–14.6
Class 4—15.3–25.7
Class 5—28.3–59.1

With regard to figure 2.12, notice too that the state FIPS code (the "STATE" field), county FIPS code, and tract FIPS code are all in separate columns (or fields). This will make our job of connecting this data to the maps we downloaded in the first section of this chapter that much more difficult.

Downloading census variables

Most users will want to download from many tables at a time and get all the variables available in those tables. Often, you may want to download for levels of census geography not available in the mapping tool. In this case you must select the file you want to generate data from, the census geography you want (block groups, counties, tracts, and so on), the area (state and possibly county and tract) you want data for, and the variables you need. Next, you will need to decide how you want to download the assembled data. We will download data on foreign-born residents for Dane County, Wisconsin, at the tract level.

On the main FactFinder page, choose **Data Sets;** since we want detailed population characteristics, we choose "Census 2000 Summary File 4 (SF 4)—Sample Data." On the menu that appears to the right of this choice, select **Detailed Tables.** We are then taken to the Select Geography page. Under geographic type, select **Census Tract,** which is listed under "State" and "County." What this means is that we will have to select a state and a single county and then download data for tracts in that county. Notice that the lowest level of geography available to us is the **Block Group.** This is because we are dealing with detailed population characteristics from the sample portion of the census. If we wanted data from the 100 percent portion of the census, we would choose Summary File

Box 2.5   A FactFinder tutorial (continued)

1—this is data (though only for a few variables) right down to the block level. We are then asked to select from a state (in this case Wisconsin) and then a county (in this case Dane). We are then asked what tract we want to download—the top option is **All Census Tracts.** Select this, click the **Add** button, and then the **Next** button.

At this point we select the variables we want to download (using the **Add** button). In this case we will download two variables, "P21 Place of birth by citizenship status" and "P22 Year of entry for the foreign born population." Click the **Show Results** button. The resulting page, formatted for presentation in a Web browser, is useful in previewing the data (figure 2.13). Printing a copy of this page can also aid data analysis undertaken at some future time.

Select **Print/Download** and then **Download** from the horizontal menu near the top of the page.

You will be presented with a wide range of download choices; avoid downloading in anything but database friendly Excel or comma delimited format. In this case choose "comma delimited" as the download format, and make sure you do *not* check "Include descriptive data element names." The zip file you will download consists of four files, two read me files, and two data files. As before, the data files can be opened in ArcMap (or Microsoft Excel, Microsoft Access, and most other database programs)—use the **Add Data** button in ArcMap. In ArcMap right-click on this newly imported data layer and select **Open.** The data table will show in a new window. In this example we now have information on two variable sets: P21 and P22 (figure 2.14, next page).

Notice that, as before, there is a field "GEO_ID" that identifies each tract. The "SUMLEVEL" field identifies the census geography of the

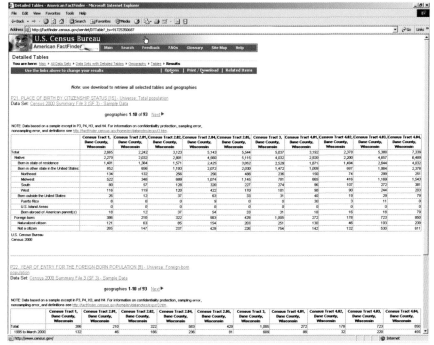

Figure 2.13

Box 2.5 A FactFinder tutorial (continued)

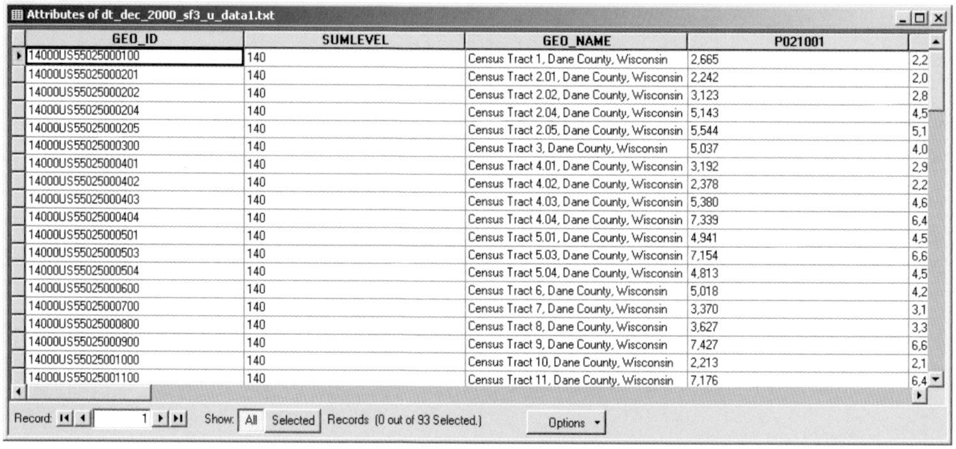

GEO_ID	SUMLEVEL	GEO_NAME	P021001	
14000US55025000100	140	Census Tract 1, Dane County, Wisconsin	2,665	2,2
14000US55025000201	140	Census Tract 2.01, Dane County, Wisconsin	2,242	2,0
14000US55025000202	140	Census Tract 2.02, Dane County, Wisconsin	3,123	2,8
14000US55025000204	140	Census Tract 2.04, Dane County, Wisconsin	5,143	4,5
14000US55025000205	140	Census Tract 2.05, Dane County, Wisconsin	5,544	5,1
14000US55025000300	140	Census Tract 3, Dane County, Wisconsin	5,037	4,0
14000US55025000401	140	Census Tract 4.01, Dane County, Wisconsin	3,192	2,9
14000US55025000402	140	Census Tract 4.02, Dane County, Wisconsin	2,378	2,2
14000US55025000403	140	Census Tract 4.03, Dane County, Wisconsin	5,380	4,6
14000US55025000404	140	Census Tract 4.04, Dane County, Wisconsin	7,339	6,4
14000US55025000501	140	Census Tract 5.01, Dane County, Wisconsin	4,941	4,5
14000US55025000503	140	Census Tract 5.03, Dane County, Wisconsin	7,154	6,6
14000US55025000504	140	Census Tract 5.04, Dane County, Wisconsin	4,813	4,5
14000US55025000600	140	Census Tract 6, Dane County, Wisconsin	5,018	4,2
14000US55025000700	140	Census Tract 7, Dane County, Wisconsin	3,370	3,1
14000US55025000800	140	Census Tract 8, Dane County, Wisconsin	3,627	3,3
14000US55025000900	140	Census Tract 9, Dane County, Wisconsin	7,427	6,6
14000US55025001000	140	Census Tract 10, Dane County, Wisconsin	2,213	2,1
14000US55025001100	140	Census Tract 11, Dane County, Wisconsin	7,176	6,4

Figure 2.14

data—in this case "140" or "tracts." The first of the downloaded fields "P021001" is also visible in the image. What does "P021001" mean? It is one of the variables that is part of the "P21" set. If you feel unsure about the detailed descriptions of any variable, you should always refer to the technical documentation. But for quick reference, the HTML version of the data that you downloaded is very useful. In this case, looking back at the HTML version, "P021001" is the total for the universe, in this case the population of each tract. "P021002" is the native-born population in each tract, and so on. Another quick way of keeping handy a description of all variables is to download an Excel version of the data (but now making sure to check "Include descriptive data element names") along with the comma delimited download. The Excel file will contain the necessary variable descriptions (akin to those in table 2.3).

FactFinder also allows you to download 1990 Census data using the same method. Keep in mind, however, that some variable names have changed, and that lower level census boundaries have also changed. For instance, the Census 2000 P21 table is the equivalent of the Census 1990 P37 table; the Census 2000 P22 table is the equivalent of the Census 1990 P36 table. Moreover, in 1990, Dane County had 89 tracts, but in 2000 it had 93. Before you can compare the foreign-born population in the 1990 tracts with that in the 2000 tracts, you need to be able to make the two sets of tract definitions roughly equivalent. The chapter that follows covers the techniques you need to know to get spatial equivalence between the 1990 and 2000 tract definitions.

There is one particularly big annoyance in the nonmapping section of FactFinder. As a result of the way in which census data is organized, the choice of higher level geography determines what lower level geography is available for download. For instance, to download tract data, you must first choose a state and then a county. In most instances, we can only download tracts within the chosen county. Thus if you want to get tract data for multiple counties, you must choose the first county for which you need data, then select and add the tracts in that county, then choose the second county, then select and add the tracts in

Box 2.5   A FactFinder tutorial (continued)

| Table 2.3   Downloaded census variables and their description ||
Variable name	Description
SUMLEVEL	Geographic summary level
GEO_NAME	Geography
P021001	Total population: Total
P021002	Total population: Native
P021003	Total population: Native; Born in state of residence
P021004	Total population: Native; Born in other state in the United States
P021005	Total population: Native; Born in other state in the United States; Northeast
P021006	Total population: Native; Born in other state in the United States; Midwest
P021007	Total population: Native; Born in other state in the United States; South
P021008	Total population: Native; Born in other state in the United States; West
P021009	Total population: Native; Born outside the United States
P021010	Total population: Native; Born outside the United States; Puerto Rico
P021011	Total population: Native; Born outside the United States; U.S. Island Areas
P021012	Total population: Native; Born outside the United States; Born abroad of American parent(s)
P021013	Total population: Foreign-born
P021014	Total population: Foreign-born; Naturalized citizen
P021015	Total population: Foreign-born; Not a citizen
P022001	Foreign-born population: Total
P022002	Foreign-born population: Year of entry 1995 to March 2000
P022003	Foreign-born population: Year of entry 1990 to 1994
P022004	Foreign-born population: Year of entry 1985 to 1989
P022005	Foreign-born population: Year of entry 1980 to 1984
P022006	Foreign-born population: Year of entry 1975 to 1979
P022007	Foreign-born population: Year of entry 1970 to 1974
P022008	Foreign-born population: Year of entry 1965 to 1969
P022009	Foreign-born population: Year of entry before 1965

that second county, and so on. If you need tract information on hundreds of counties, this will be a very slow procedure. In a similar manner, if you need block group data for multiple tracts, then you must choose individual tracts and download the block groups of those. On the whole, if you need data at a refined geographic scale for a large area (such as an entire state) then you may want to consider one of the other download strategies described in this chapter.

What format to use—Microsoft Excel or comma delimited?

Understanding more about your download choices will help reduce data frustrations during the data analysis phase.

Box 2.5 A FactFinder tutorial (continued)

Unlocking the census with GIS

- Many will prefer to download in Excel format because they are used to working with spreadsheets. Spreadsheets are particularly good at on-the-fly creation of new variables and so on. But it is crucial to remember that the resulting Excel spreadsheet should continue to look like a database table if it is going to be used in a GIS. In other words, all data must be in a single set of contiguous rows and columns. But even keeping this in mind, you will still be faced with the problem of translating your Excel file into something usable by a GIS.

  One possibility is to export your Excel file into Access .mdb format. DBMS/Copy is a particular useful piece of software for this task (*www.dataflux.com/dbms*). Another possibility is to open Access and use the **Import External Data** tool. *This tool will not work correctly if you still have a second row of descriptive headings in your Excel spreadsheet.* Also, if you create any new fields in the Excel file, make sure the field names are compliant with Access requirements for field names.

  Some will prefer to export the Excel data to dBase format. The major issues here are making sure that any changes to the original data are *correctly, explicitly, and manually formatted* (as text or numbers) and that the "database" range name includes any expanded set of fields.

- The main advantage of the comma delimited format is that it can be read directly by ArcMap. The problem here is that, in some instances, ArcMap will, in the importation process, treat numbers as text. This can create huge headaches later on. It is much better

to use DBMS/Copy or Access to import the delimited text file into an .mdb table. In Access you will use the **Get External Data** tool to perform the import.

There are two very important issues to keep in mind here. In the **Get External Data** tool, make sure to check the **First Row Contains Field Names** checkbox (since that is how the data has been downloaded from FactFinder), and also make sure to click on the **Advanced** button and then for each number field define the Data Type as "Double" (or any other appropriate number data type). If you do not do this, numbers will be read as text and make future analysis very troublesome. But all geographic identifiers (particularly the field "GEO_ID") must be left as "Text" data types. As before, if you downloaded the comma delimited text file with descriptive data names, you will have difficulty completing this process.

Other data resources in FactFinder

FactFinder provides access to a range of data beyond the 1990 and 2000 Censuses. The Data Sets section also provides direct online access to the Economic Census, the Decennial Supplementary Survey, American Community Survey, and Population estimates. Downloading this data involves a similar procedure to that used for the census. The Reference Shelf section of FactFinder provides access to historical and international data and comparisons, special reports, and technical briefs. There are also links to the *City and County Data Book* and the *State and Metropolitan Area Data Book,* both broad and useful sources of data for these units of geography (data comes not

Box 2.5   A FactFinder tutorial (continued)

only from the Census of Population and Housing, but also from the Economic Census and various other official data sources, including data on crime and health). There are links to the *U.S. Abstract of Statistics, U.S. Statistics in Brief,* and individual state data centers, among others. In most cases, however, downloading these other data sources in a format useable in a database or GIS is difficult if not impossible. However, all the data sources have information on ordering database-friendly versions of the data on CD–ROM.

3. Downloading free, already processed census data.

ESRI and Geography Network provide some data for download using the same method as described above in the discussion of downloading TIGER/Line files. The data has been preprocessed to allow quick connection to the maps downloaded from the Geography Network. The advantages here are no cost and ease of use. The disadvantage is that only some data is available (Summary File 1 and the 2000 Redistricting Data).

Many states maintain state data libraries (often held in one of the state universities) that allow already preprocessed data to be downloaded in a variety of well-known formats. This data will almost always be more extensive than that available from the Geography Network. Using a Web search engine, search under the state's name, the word "census data," and the name of the particular data file, for instance, "Indiana census data sf3." Data will usually be delivered in Microsoft Excel, Microsoft Access format, or dBase formats. Usually, this downloaded data will need some further processing to connect it with the downloaded and translated TIGER/Line maps.

4. Assembling and using the census data tables.

This is an alternative to the first option. It requires users be comfortable with personal database managers such as Microsoft Access. The process here is fairly complex, but once it has been learned is easy to apply to any census data needs. Box 2.6 describes the general procedures involved. The advantages of this method are that it's free and you end the process with complete data in a single database. The disadvantage is the complexity of compiling the database.

5. Using desktop census acquisition software.

For those intimidated by option four, an alternative is to buy software that will automatically (or nearly automatically) create the database for you. SF3toTable is the best census acquisition software we have seen. It is available from *www.gistools.com* in two versions: a cheaper standard version that will create one state's data at a time, and a considerably more expensive professional version that will do multiple states and has fewer restrictions on the distribution of the resulting tables. The advantages are as for option four above but without the need to know much about databases or follow complex instructions.

It would be useful to do this if you wanted information for an entire state; if you're dealing with only a few counties, metropolitan areas, or other single units, the FactFinder access tool is much faster and simpler. Detailed instructions for downloading ASCII text data files and importing them into several database programs can be found at *www.census.gov/support/SF1ASCII.html.*

However, the instructions are stronger on detail than they are on overview. Understanding a few principles will make this easier for users new to database files:

- The database structure file (SF1 or SF3) is a template; it contains the field (variable) headings and characteristics, but no data. The data is in seventy-six text files that must be downloaded, unzipped, renamed, and imported into the appropriate part of the database structure table.

- Each of the seventy-six data files includes a segment of tables; for instance, if you're interested in tables P6, P7, P20, and P146A-P146I, you'll need to download st00001.uf3, st00002.uf3, st000011.uf3, and st000012.uf3. The content of the text files is shown in the technical documentation section Data Records and Segmentation of the "read me" file found at *www2.census.gov/census_2000/datasets/Summary_File_3.*

- The data text files include no geographic identifiers; these are located in a separate file (for example, Iowa's geographic identifier file is iageo.uf3) that must be linked to the data files in Microsoft Access.

- The data files created in this way include every available geography and every variable

within the segment; for practical purposes, you will need to run a query to extract the variables at the geographic level you are interested in.

Step one: Assemble the files

Download the Summary File 3 template file from *www.census.gov/support/2000/SF3* in the database format you plan to use; for this example, we will be using Microsoft Access 2002.

Download the data files you need (for example, ia00003.uf3.zip), including the geographic identifier file (iageo.uf3.zip). Unzip them. Go to the DOS command prompt, find the directory you have unzipped the files to, and rename the .uf3 files as text files so the database program you're using will recognize them (**rename ia00003.uf3 ia00003.txt**).

Step two: Import the text data files into Microsoft Access

Refer to the instructions on importing text data files into Microsoft Access at *www.census.gov/support/SF1ASCII.html.*

Importing the text files into an existing table (the template file) is preferable. Choose the appropriate table (for example, SF30003 for ia00003.txt) from the template file.

Step three: Add geographic identifiers to the data file

Open the geographic identifiers table (for example, iageo.txt) in Microsoft Access and link it to each of the data files you have created. Refer to the instructions for linking tables in Microsoft Access at *www.census.gov/support/SF1ASCII.html.*

Resist the urge to link data tables to one another at this point; remember, these files contain every data item for every geographic level, and linked tables will be very unwieldy.

Step four: Choose the variables and geographic summary level of interest using a database query

Refer to the instructions for querying and saving results of a query to a table in Microsoft Access at *www.census.gov/support/SF1ASCII.html*.

At this point, choose the summary level you are interested in (for example, SUMLEV = 140 will give you counties and census tracts), and choose the geographic identifiers for that summary level (COUNTY and TRACT will give you the FIPS codes for each). A list of summary levels can be found in chapter 4 (Summary Level Sequence Chart) of the Technical Documentation for the summary file you are using. If you're assembling county level data, take note of the Geographic Component column on the left of the table. If you want data for whole counties only (rather than data broken down by geographic components of counties, such as urban vs. rural area) choose SUMLEV = 050 and GEOCOMP = 00.

You will also want to choose the variables you're interested in at this point so that the file you create with the query is manageable. You could choose variables from several different data files.

When you are done, export the table to the format you will be working with. This is a lot of work, but once the data is downloaded the original database can be queried to extract new combinations of variables at different spatial scales.

6. Using a census data service.

There are many providers of packaged census data and consultants who will customize census data products. This is similar to the fourth strategy described in the section on acquiring TIGER/Line maps above. It has the same advantages and disadvantages. If you have bought fully preprocessed TIGER/Line files from a vendor or consultant, then it is likely that census data can also be provided, either as part of the TIGER/Line package or as an add-on.

Connecting TIGER/Line derived maps to census data and displaying results

The third step consists of using maps to make sense of the census data. In most cases this means that the data and maps will have to be "joined." "Joined" is in quotes because "join" is a keyword in the database language (Structured Query Language or SQL, pronounced "sequel") most GIS programs speak. Technically a "join" connects a set of data fields in one database table to another set in another table. Obviously if one has paid for fully processed TIGER/Line files with associated data then no join should be necessary. In all other cases, users will need to "join" their maps to their data manually. The choices here will be determined by the map and data

Box 2.7   Using SF3toTable

SF3toTable is a wonderfully simple and fast way to access census data sets. There are five steps involved.

1. Download the state data files. Go to FactFinder, select **Reference Shelf,** then **Other Useful Data and Statistics,** then **FTP.** This will take you to the ftp download site. Select **Census_2000_ Datasets,** then **Summary File 3,** then select a state. Download the file named "all_state_name. zip" (for Wisconsin the file is called "all_Wisconsin.zip") and unzip it. The file is large, so make sure you have plenty of disk space.

2. Run the software and select the data files. Click the **Add Item** button and navigate to the folder where you have unzipped the downloaded census file. The file you will need is called "state_abbreviation geo_uf3.zip." For Wisconsin it is "wigeo_uf3.zip."

3. Choose the data tables you want to extract.

4. Choose the geography level of the output.

5. Select an output file. This file will be in either dBase or comma delimited format. The dBase format will be most useful for your needs. The resulting table will have a key field formatted like "STFID" and so may need no further processing before being joined to the map.

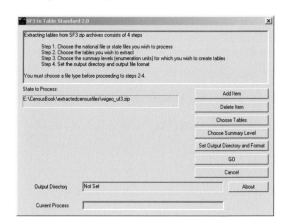

Figure 2.15

choices made, and by the computer abilities of the user. For neophytes this can be the most difficult part of the process.

In this section we will start with the simplest join scenario and focus on the most important principles of the join. At this point we will have most of the tools that will allow us to move onto more complex joins.

1. The simplest "join"—compliant key fields already established in both data sets.

At this stage we have downloaded a tract map for Dane County, Wisconsin, and we have also downloaded census data at the tract level for the state. The trick now is to pull these two together. Since both were downloaded from the Geography Network, both files have been pre-processed to make joining easy.

The central concept is the "key" or "key field." Each database table should have a field (or column) of data that uniquely identifies each row or record in some useful manner. This field is the "key field." The key field can be called anything though it is fairly common to call it "key."

The key field will usually consist of numbers, usually FIPS codes. However, these numbers will be formatted as text, and this should be immediately clear because they will be left justified (as is all text in most databases and spreadsheets), not right justified (common for numbers). This has important consequences for how the key field may be used. In a database or spreadsheet, the number "100" added to the number "333" will yield the arithmetic result "433." However, if the numbers are formatted as text, an arithmetic operation is impossible. The text operator closest to the arithmetic "and" or "+" is "&" or "ampersand." In this case "100 & 333" yields "100333," and "333 & 100" yields "333100." As a general rule you will want to steer clear of arithmetic operators when dealing with key fields. Text and logical operators will do all the work that is necessary.

In the following case, both map and data have key fields organized in exactly the same way (figure 2.16). We have opened the attribute table of the map (tgr55025tr00) and the data file (tgr55000sf1trt). Notice that the data file has 1,333 records (see very bottom of figure), the number of tracts in all of Wisconsin. The map file has only 93 records (the number isn't visible in the image)—these are the tracts in Dane County. The key field in both tables is "STFID."

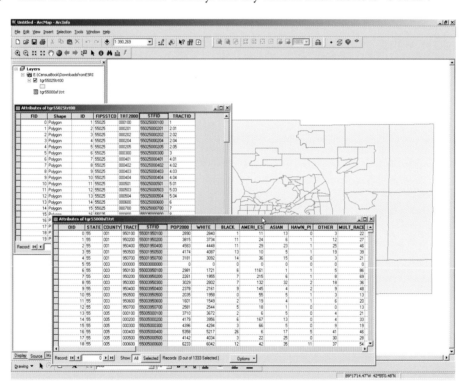

Figure 2.16

No further alterations to the key fields are necessary. All that is required is that the data be joined. In ArcGIS this is a simple matter. Right-click on the map you want to attach the data to, click on **Joins and Relates,** then **Joins,** and then select the proper join information, as in figure 2.17. The Join Data window allows the user to specify the key fields in each of the two tables

being joined together. In this case we will be joining data to the map. The map will determine the data records in the final joined table. Thus, in this example, the final joined table will have 93 records, not 1,333. If we joined the map to the data, we would end up with 1,333 records in the resulting table.

The result will be a combined table with data fields from both of the original tables (figure 2.18). Notice the new field names. They are made up of three elements: the originating table name, a period, and the name of the field in the originating table. Thus the field "STFID" in the originating map table "tgr55025trt00" becomes "STFID.tgr55025trt00" in the joined table. But the field "STFID" in the data table "'tgr55000sf1trt" becomes "tgr55000sf1trt.STFID" in the joined table. The joined table will have all the fields of both originating tables. It is possible to make this join permanent by exporting it to a new shapefile or to a geodatabase. Right-click on the now joined feature class and select **Data,** then **Export Data.** This will create a new shapefile (or new geodatabase feature class) with a data table consisting of the combined data.

Figure 2.17

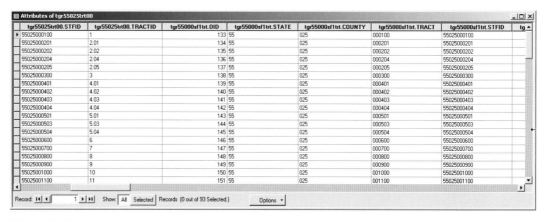

Figure 2.18

Note that some translation programs (TGR2SHP for instance) will also produce a compliant "STFID" field in output maps. In these cases the join remains as we have described in this section.

2. More complex joins—using ArcGIS to create key fields from census geography.

In many cases where data and maps are downloaded from different sites or are processed using different software, some preprocessing is going to be necessary in order to perform a join. Usually this will mean making the key field in one of the two tables compliant with the key field in the other. In the following example, we will use the data table downloaded from FactFinder and a map file translated from raw TIGER/Line files using the TGR2SHP software. As we noted earlier, TGR2SHP produces map layers or feature classes with compliant "STFID" fields. However, the data downloaded from FactFinder does not. Looking at figure 2.19, the first record of the table is a summary for Wisconsin. All the other records are tracts in Dane County. With the exception of the first record, the first field "GEO_ID" contains the full tract FIPS code. It's buried in the last eleven characters of each record, so we will need to extract these characters and put them into a new field we will call "STFID."

GEO_ID	SUMLEVEL	GEO_NAME	P021001	P021002	P021(
04000US55	040	Wisconsin	5,363,675	5,169,924	3,939,488
14000US55025000100	140	Census Tract 1, Dane County, Wisconsin	2,665	2,279	1,401
14000US55025000201	140	Census Tract 2.01, Dane County, Wisconsin	2,242	2,032	1,364
14000US55025000202	140	Census Tract 2.02, Dane County, Wisconsin	3,123	2,801	1,571
14000US55025000204	140	Census Tract 2.04, Dane County, Wisconsin	5,143	4,560	2,425
14000US55025000205	140	Census Tract 2.05, Dane County, Wisconsin	5,544	5,115	3,052
14000US55025000300	140	Census Tract 3, Dane County, Wisconsin	5,037	4,032	2,529
14000US55025000401	140	Census Tract 4.01, Dane County, Wisconsin	3,192	2,920	1,871
14000US55025000402	140	Census Tract 4.02, Dane County, Wisconsin	2,378	2,200	1,494
14000US55025000403	140	Census Tract 4.03, Dane County, Wisconsin	5,380	4,657	2,644
14000US55025000404	140	Census Tract 4.04, Dane County, Wisconsin	7,339	6,489	4,032
14000US55025000501	140	Census Tract 5.01, Dane County, Wisconsin	4,941	4,592	3,138
14000US55025000503	140	Census Tract 5.03, Dane County, Wisconsin	7,154	6,695	4,291
14000US55025000504	140	Census Tract 5.04, Dane County, Wisconsin	4,813	4,555	3,046
14000US55025000600	140	Census Tract 6, Dane County, Wisconsin	5,018	4,248	2,398
14000US55025000700	140	Census Tract 7, Dane County, Wisconsin	3,370	3,176	1,841
14000US55025000800	140	Census Tract 8, Dane County, Wisconsin	3,627	3,384	1,732
14000US55025000900	140	Census Tract 9, Dane County, Wisconsin	7,427	6,649	3,597
14000US55025001000	140	Census Tract 10, Dane County, Wisconsin	2,213	2,153	1,349

Figure 2.19

In order to get the data table ready for the join, take the following steps:

a. Convert the text file to database format. One option is to import the .txt data into Access and then open the resulting table in ArcMap. Another option is to add the .txt data file to your map document, then in the table of contents right-click on the data file and select **Open** to open the attribute table window. Click the **Options** button, select **Export** and export the file to dBase format. The second option can sometimes result in numbers being treated as text.

b. Create a new field in the now open dBase table. Add the new dBase file to your map document; open the attribute table window and select **Options** and **Add Field.** In the Add Field dialog, type in the field information. As with all key fields, the field should be formatted for text. It will need to contain exactly eleven characters, and for convenience we have called it "STFID." The new field will be added to the end of your data table.

Figure 2.20

c.   Fill the contents of the new field. Right-click on the heading of the new "STFID" field, and select **Calculate Values.** This will open the Field Calculator dialog. In the calculator textbox type: "Right ([GEO_ID], 11)." You could also generate this expression using the built-in string functions. This expression does the following: for each record in the "STFID" field, it displays the right-most eleven characters of whatever is in the "GEO_ID" field. The result is an "STFID" field that works in exactly the same way as the key we described in 1 above. You are now ready to make the join as we did before.

Why not do this preprocessing in a spreadsheet? Many inexperienced users feel much more comfortable using a spreadsheet than manipulating databases. While this is entirely feasible, the spreadsheet format, flexible and useful as it is, holds special traps for new GIS users. The best reason for doing the work in ArcGIS is that it is likely to result in the fewest mistakes. If you have data that is best analyzed in a spreadsheet, then by all means use one. But if you need to do GIS-based analyses, then you should get used to the idea of using structured database tables

---

Using a spreadsheet to generate a key field

Microsoft Excel or Corel® QuattroPro-2® could also be used to generate the "STFID" key from "GEO_ID." In this case, the data should be downloaded from FactFinder in Excel format rather than comma delimited format. Create a new column in the down-loaded spreadsheet and label it "STFID." In the first data row (the second row) in that column type in the function cell equation: "=RIGHT(A2, 11)." Copy this cell equation down to the last row of the data. If the field "GEO_ID" is not in column "A," then the equation should be changed appropriately. You must then manually format the new "STFID" column as text.

Once created you will need to get this data into a GIS. If you are using ArcGIS, then the worksheet should be saved in dBase format. Saving a spreadsheet in dBase format not only creates a new .dbf file but also creates in the original spreadsheet a range name called "Database." To avoid potential problems, make sure that the worksheet to be saved in dBase format has no extraneous numbers.

to store and manipulate your data. In the long run this will save you an enormous amount of time and energy. Although we recommend otherwise, we understand that many users will still prefer to use spreadsheets to do the preprocessing needed for a join; so we give an example using Microsoft Excel functions in the sidebar on the previous page.

Sometimes constructing key fields requires even more complex functions. For instance, state, county, and tract FIPS codes may be in three separate fields. Or FIPS codes may be nonstandard, for instance "55.025.10200." While these problems can be resolved in a spreadsheet (or, using SQL™, in a database), the VBScript functions built into ArcGIS provide a simple and consistent way of dealing with the likely problems involved in constructing key fields. For those with no programming skills, there will be a learning curve. Getting hold of a VBScript manual should help, although with a little practice a lot can be accomplished without referring to a manual. Most of the functions and operators you will need are text-based, significantly reducing the amount you need to learn. Box 2.8 takes you through some of the text and logical operators and functions most useful to constructing key fields for census geography and provides examples of how they can be used. Of course you could do this work in a spreadsheet using the built-in text and logical functions (the previous cautions about spreadsheets still apply). Or you could perform it directly in a database manager using SQL.

Box 2.8 Using text and logical operators in Visual Basic® to generate key fields

Fortunately, it is necessary to know only a little about text operators and decision structures in VBScript to generate successful census geography key fields. We will cover six types of operations.

1. **Concatenation.** If, in a table, we had a column called STATE containing the state FIPS code for each record, another called COUNTY with the county FIPS code, and another called TRACT with the tract FIPS code, we could create another column or field called, say, FULLFIPS. In the attribute table window, right-click on the new field, select **Field Calculator,** click on **Advanced,** and in the text box labeled "Pre-Logic VBA Script Code" type:

    x = STATE & COUNTY & TRACT

and then in the bottom text box (it should be labeled "FULLFIPS =") type in:

    x

This means that the variable "x" will be equal to the concatenation of STATE, COUNTY, and TRACT, and that the column called "FULLFIPS" will be made equal to "x" (see figure 2.21). If we were doing this for tracts in Johnson County, Iowa, this would take the state code for each record, "19," add to that the county code "103," and then add to that the various four- or six-digit tract codes, thus giving "191030001," "191030002," "191030003," and so on. Concatenate joins text pieces together—it does not add then arithmetically.

Figure 2.21

2. **Right**(string, length). This function returns a certain number of the right-hand side characters of a piece of text. The parameter "string" refers to the original piece of text, and "length" refers to the number of characters on the right that should be returned. So if we had a variable (or column in a data table) called COUNTYFIPS that included both state and county FIPS, for instance, "19103," "19104," "19105," and so on, and we merely wanted the county FIPS number, we would use the following code:

NewCOUNTYFIPS = Right(COUNTYFIPS, 3)

NewCOUNTYFIPS would then return "103," "104," "105," and so on. If the length parameter was changed to four, the function would return "9103," "9104," "9105," and so on. Notice that because this is a simple function it does not require use of the Advanced window in the Field Calculator. If you were to use the Advanced window, then in the "Pre-logic section" of the Field Calculator you would type: "x = Right(COUNTYFIPS, 3)" and in the bottom text box type "x."

3. **Left**(string, length). This function works just like the right function, except that it extracts characters from the left. Thus, using the example above, if we wanted to extract the state FIPS code from the combined state and county COUNTYFIPS, we would use the following code:

NewSTATEFIPS = Left (COUNTYFIPS, 2)

NewSTATEFIPS would then equal "19," "19," "19," and so on.

4. **Mid**(string, start, [length]). This will extract characters from the middle of a piece of text. Using the "start" parameter, you indicate where the extraction should start in the original piece of text, and the length parameter indicates how many characters from that start position to extract. Thus if we had a column (called FIPS) in a table which contained the full state, county, and tract FIPS, and we wanted to extract only the county FIPS and put that into another column called STATEFIPS, we would use the following code:

"STATEFIPS = Mid(FIPS, 3, 3)"

Thus from the text "191030001," it would extract "103." However, the statement "STATEFIPS = Mid(FIPS, 3, 4)" would incorrectly extract "1030."

5. **Len**(string). This measures the length of a piece of text. Thus "x = Len(COUNTYFIPS)" would consistently return the number "5" to

x, while "x = Len(NewSTATEFIPS)" would consistently return the number "2" to the variable x.

6. **If … Then.** This decision structure is very useful. Suppose again, that we are dealing with data for Johnson County, Iowa, from the 1990 Census. There is a column with the state FIPS code "STATE," one for the county FIPS code "COUNTY," and one for the tract FIPS code "TRACT." The problem is that some of the tract codes are four-digit (e.g., "0001"), and some are six-digit (e.g., "000301"). We want to develop a standardized tract FIPS code for a key field. It should include state, county, and tract FIPS, but where the tract FIPS is only four characters long, an additional "00" should be added to the resulting code. Thus we want tract "0001" to become "19103000100." But where tract FIPS are six characters, no extra 0s will be added. Create a new text field called "STFIP." Right-click on the new field, click on **Advanced** and in the "Pre-Logic" section of the Field Calculator type:

```
If Len(TRACT) = 6 Then
    x = STATE & COUNTY & TRACT
Else
    x = STATE & COUNTY & TRACT &
"00"
End If
```
In the bottom text box type:
```
x
```

As a general matter "If…Then" decision structures can take a number of forms:

```
If <some condition> Then
    <some calculation>
End If

If <some condition> Then
    <some calculation>
Else
        <in all circumstances not meeting that
condition, perform some other calculation>
End If

If <some condition> Then
    <some calculation>
ElseIf <some other condition> Then
    <some other calculation>
End If

If <some condition> Then
    <some calculation>
ElseIf <some other condition> Then
    <some other calculation>
Else
        <in all circumstances not meeting the pre-
vious conditions, perform some other calculation>
End If
```

Their various functions can be used together to solve most problems. For instance, in some older data, tract FIPS codes are formatted "19.103.0001" and sometimes "19.103.000601" depending on whether we are dealing with four-digit or six-digit tract codes. In other words, periods separate the three levels of census geography and tracts are sometimes four-digit and sometimes six-digit. If the original tract field were called "KEY" then the code would read:

```
state = Left ( [KEY] , 2)
county = Mid ( [KEY], 4, 3 )

If Len ( [KEY] ) = 15 Then
  tract = Right ( [KEY], 6 )
Else
  tract = Right ( [KEY], 4 )
  tract = tract & "00"
End If
```

name = state & county & tract

In the bottom text box type: name

Both the original field and the new field (called "KEYFIELD") are visible in figure 2.22.

Shape*	RECORD_ID	KEY	KEYFIELD
Polygon	1	19.103.0001	19103000100
Polygon	2	19.103.0002	19103000200
Polygon	3	19.103.000301	19103030100
Polygon	4	19.103.000302	19103030200
Polygon	5	19.103.0004	19103000400
Polygon	6	19.103.0005	19103000500
Polygon	7	19.103.0006	19103000600
Polygon	8	19.103.0007	19103000700
Polygon	9	19.103.0008	19103000800
Polygon	10	19.103.0009	19103000900
Polygon	11	19.103.0010	19103001000
Polygon	12	19.103.0011	19103001100
Polygon	13	19.103.0012	19103001200
Polygon	14	19.103.0013	19103001300
Polygon	15	19.103.0014	19103001400
Polygon	16	19.103.0015	19103001500
Polygon	17	19.103.0016	19103001600
Polygon	18	19.103.0017	19103001700
Polygon	19	19.103.0018	19103001800

Figure 2.22

Making analytical sense of the joined data

There is a wide range of ways of using maps and data analytically. The simplest of these involve making thematic overlays; essentially this involves coloring geographic units on the map to represent specific data values. More complex analyses will usually also involve queries. This section is not designed to teach users how to create thematic maps or undertake queries; our aim is merely to illustrate how the joined data can be used to perform spatial analyses.

Where do those of recent foreign origin live in Dane County? We will undertake the analysis at the tract level. We described the download of the necessary maps in box 2.4, the download of the necessary data in box 2.5, and the method used to join them together in the previous section. Having joined the data, we are now ready to make the maps. Before proceeding, it will be convenient to export our join into a new shapefile or geodatabase. At this point we need to calculate the percentage of foreign born. Referring back to table 2.3, we need to divide variable "P021013" by "P021001," that is, the foreign born by the total population.

We need to create a new field in the data table to hold our percentage calculation. We will call the field "FOREIGNP" and make it a "float" type (in the Attributes window of the shapefile, click the **Options** button and then select **New Field**). The Field Calculator can then be used to divide "P021013" by "P021001" and put the result into "FOREIGNP" (right-click on the field "FOREIGNP," select **Calculate Values** to turn on the Field Calculator). If there is a problem with the Field Calculator's ability to calculate a value, it probably is a result of the original comma delimited data file being opened directly in ArcMap instead of going through the intermediate translation to Access format or the failure to make sure that all number fields in the translation were actually treated as numbers and not text (see box 2.5 for details). In both cases, variables that should be treated as numbers are treated as text, and therefore numeric operations such as division are impossible. Thus "P021013" cannot be divided by "P021001." One solution is to go back and fix the data; another is to use some VBScript in the Field Calculator to solve the problem (see sidebar next page).

Using VBScript to convert text to numbers

The VBScript techniques needed to convert text to numbers in a field are fairly straightforward and have wide applicability. Right-click on the field "FOREIGNP," select **Calculate Values** to turn on the Field Calculator and then type in the following VBScript in the Advanced section of the Field Calculator:

```
x = Format ( [P021001] )
y = Format ( [P021013] )
If y > 0 Then
   z =  y / x
End If
```

Then make ForeignP = z in the lower box in the Field Calculator. Run the script and the proportion will be calculated. A few comments about the script: (1) the "Format" function will turn text into numbers, allowing calculations to be run; (2) the "If...Then" structure is necessary to avoid dividing into a zero. This script is only necessary if you have not imported the data correctly.

If you chose to download the census data as Excel files, then of course you could create the new fields in Excel and then import the result into Access, or export from Excel into dBase format.

0.00 to 3.2%
3.9 to 7.9%
8.3 to 13.4%
14.5 to 24.4%
59.1%

Map 2.1   Percentage by census tract of foreign born, Dane County, Wisconsin, 2000.

Once this has been achieved we are able to symbolize our map. The result, using natural breaks to define the legend, is map 2.1 (previous page). As we suspected, Dane County's foreign-born population is concentrated in the downtown areas of Madison, the state capital anchored in the middle of the county.

Other major sources of digital maps

Thus far we have discussed the acquisition of both digital maps (or more correctly map "layers" or "feature classes") and data from the census, how to connect the two, and finally how to use a GIS to begin symbolizing the connected data. The digital maps we have discussed thus far are all from the TIGER/Line system produced by the Census Bureau. Needless to say, various other branches of the federal government publish digital maps that are very useful to urban analysts. In this section we focus on three major categories of maps: orthophotographs, digital line graphs, and digital elevation models. At the end of this section we describe other useful map sources.

Including aerial photography and elevation maps

The utility and aesthetic quality of maps can often be improved by including a photographic base-layer, a shaded elevation base-layer, or some sort of a schematic base-layer. Base-layers often allow public audiences with little knowledge of mapping to orient themselves within a particular map, because such layers provide visual and topographic markers to the public. Base-layers can help the mapmaker convey information. Moreover, the aerial photographs, elevation models, schematic terrain maps, and the related maps we will discuss in this section are helpful to a range of urban analyses:

- They are often used to correct, edit, and update TIGER/Line-derived maps (most ortho-photos have considerably better ground truth than TIGER/Line files). Aerial photographs in particular are often more recent and more precise than TIGER/Line maps. The photographs may include roads and other features not yet in the TIGER/Line system. The photographs may then be used to digitize new road segments and other visible features.
- They can be used to analyze land-cover change or vegetative change. This usually involves comparing photographs (often infrared ones) for two time periods and using changes in color values of the photograph for the same piece of land to estimate likely land-cover or vegetative change. This technique may be used to analyze and estimate the loss of trees in an area or change in habitat for some species.
- Along similar lines, it is possible to show long-term land-use change and its effect on the environment. For instance, growth in impermeable surfaces such as parking lots may be measured in this way.
- Defining sensitive natural areas or pinpointing areas prone to erosion will require aerial photography and elevation models.

- Finally, creating three-dimensional visualizations of terrain from elevation models can be very useful in: (1) understanding the impact of proposed development on the landscape; (2) analyzing watersheds; (3) finding the optimal location of mobile-phone towers; or (4) analyzing the aesthetic consequences of proposed large billboards, large buildings, and so on.

Nevertheless, it is important to keep in mind that photographic, elevation, or topographic base-layers are not always appropriate and sometimes may even confuse the map's message. A rule of thumb is that if the purpose of your map is to convey thematic information organized by territory—for instance, the prevalence of vacant homes by block group, the percentage of minorities by census tract, or poverty rates by county—then photographic, elevation, and topographic base layers will tend to detract from your map rather than add to it.

Orthophotographs

Aerial photographs come in many forms. To be used as a map layer (or feature class) in a GIS, all photographs must be orthogonally rectified and must have coordinate information. Orthogonal rectification of a photograph corrects the terrain distortions that occur with any photograph of the earth's surface. The coordinate system information connects the orthogonally rectified space covered by the photograph to the space covered by your other maps. Orthophotographs—that is, orthogonally rectified photographs—are widely available in digital format so it is usually unnecessary to go through the process of manual rectification (although that process has become a lot simpler; see the Georeferencing toolbar in ArcGIS). However, to use an orthophotograph, you must know something of its coordinate systems. In most cases, when orthophotos are downloaded or delivered on CD–ROM, there will be an associated text file or HTML file describing the photo's "metadata." As you will remember, metadata is data about data; in a GIS this is usually information about how and when the map layer was developed and the map layer's coordinate system. This information can be of enormous benefit when a photographic base-layer you have downloaded mysteriously fails to show on your computer screen. In almost all cases this will mean that there is some coordinate system conflict, most likely that you are missing coordinate information for the orthophotograph.

Orthophotographs are usually distributed in some type of image format, most often TIFF (.tif), JPEG (.jpg), IMAGINE (.img) or MrSID® (.sid) formats. Coordinate information will either be held in the header information of the image file itself (as with a GeoTIFF) or will be held in a separate text file called a "world file." The world file has a peculiar naming convention: if the photographic image is in a file called "photo.tif," the associated world file will be in a text file called "photo.tfw." Likewise, if the photo file was called "photo.jpg," the world file would be "photo.jgw." If called "photo.sid," the world file would be called "photo.sdw." The image file and its associated world file must always be in the same folder for the GIS software to find and use the world file. The result is that you will usually need to download not just the image file containing the orthophotograph, but also an associated world file. If you don't, you will not be

Source: U.S. Geological Survey

Figure 2.23   Digital orthophoto quadrangle (DOQ) image, Cedar Rapids, Iowa.

able to overlay TIGER/Line derived maps layers, such as streets and water features, on top of the photos.

Orthophotos are downloadable free from some sources, but you should expect to pay for good images. The following is a brief description of the main sources of orthophotographs:

- The U.S. Geological Survey (USGS) has a near complete set of photo images for the continental United States. There are 7.5-minute (i.e., 7.5 minutes of longitude by 7.5 minutes of latitude) photos that cover the size of a standard "quad" or quadrangle (these are sometimes referred to as full-quad photos). The 3.75-minute photos are the size of a quarter of a standard quad (sometimes referred to as quarter-quads). Both the 7.5- and 3.75-minute quads are referred to as digital orthophoto quadrangles or DOQs. Before you request a particular DOQ you will need to know for which quadrangle you need an image. Go to *edc.usgs. gov/products/aerial/doq.htm*l for help on finding the right quadrangle and ordering (the page also has links to useful background information). For all states in the continental United States the photos are in the Universal Transverse Mercator (UTM) projection and use the 1983 North American Datum (or NAD 83) or the 1927 North American Datum (NAD 27). A particular UTM Zone is also specified. For instance, Johnson County, Iowa, is Zone 15 North. These images have a resolution of one meter (just over a yard) per pixel, meaning that each dot in the image represents 1x1 meters on the ground. DOQs can be in gray-scale or color—a 3.75-minute gray-scale image will usually be about forty to forty-five megabytes,

Figure 2.24   Infrared photo, Cedar Rapids, Iowa.

a color image of the same as much as three times this. Figure 2.23 is a fragment from a 1992 one-meter resolution DOQ covering part of downtown Cedar Rapids, Iowa.

Images based on the USGS orthophotographs can be downloaded from *www.terraserver. com*. The advantage of the TerraServer download, besides that of low cost, is that various download resolutions are possible, from sixteen meters to one meter. The main problem is that only small land areas can be downloaded at one-meter resolution. Thus, if you wanted to download a one-meter resolution photo for anything but a very small area, multiple images (and their world files) would have to be downloaded and then stitched together (the Image Analysis extension to ArcGIS is very useful for stitching—use the Mosaic functionality; you could also use the Mosaic function in Spatial Analyst). This is a time-consuming process and it's easy to make errors.

State geological survey bureaus also keep orthophotos. Sometimes it is possible to download one-meter quad-sized orthophotos free from these state sites (often these will be the same images as those available from the USGS). Moreover, state geological survey bureaus often run their own image programs; if they do you may find much more recent images than are available through the USGS. For instance, in cooperation with Iowa cities and counties, the Iowa Geological Survey Bureau undertook, in 2002, a one-meter resolution infrared photo inventory for the entire state. This imagery is a full decade more recent than the state's gray-scale photography. Figure 2.24 covers the same area as figure 2.23 and is also

Figure 2.25   High-resolution photo, Cedar Rapids, Iowa.

at one-meter resolution, but it is based on the 2002 infrared photography. The USGS Web site has links to all state geological bureaus.

- Many densely populated cities and counties are "flown" (jargon meaning "developing an orthophotographic inventory") every few years. Until quite recently the end product of this would be thousands of photographs printed on photographic paper. Now, however, city and county orthophotographs are much more likely to be distributed digitally. The main advantages here are: (1) the photographs are often much more recent that the USGS photographs; and (2) they tend to be at a much greater resolution than the USGS photography. It is now quite common for cities and counties to use one-foot resolution or even six-inch resolution photography. The result is dramatically better images, allowing detailed digitization of things like building footprints (essentially the perimeter of a building's foundation), sidewalks, and even some flora. Users should remember, however, that the quality improvements of high-resolution photography will not be visible on maps drawn at larger scales. High-resolution photographs attached to maps of a county will thus serve no useful purpose and will severely drain computer resources. Figure 2.25 covers a portion of the area visible in figures 2.23 and 2.24, but it is based on recent county photography at one-foot resolution.

    City and county photography will usually be held by the local assessor or by the GIS/information systems department. If a city or county has a GIS coordinator, this is the person to contact first. Local photography is sometimes published using non-UTM coordinate systems. It is important to make sure that you are provided not only with the images themselves but also the necessary metadata.

Some bigger cities and counties distribute photography on their mapping Web servers. Suitably configured Web browsers can access this information, as can specialized, and somewhat easier to use, GIS-based Web browsers.[2] In some cases it is possible to connect ArcGIS directly to the mapping server and thus to view and analyze images directly in ArcMap. To do this you must know the address of the city's or county's Web service (it will look something like a Web page address). Then go to ArcCatalog™, select **Internet Servers,** then **Add Internet Server,** and then type in the address of the service.

- It is also possible to buy custom photography for almost any place in the world. For small areas, satellite-derived imagery has mostly replaced airplane-derived imagery. The advantages here are that the photos will be recent and their resolution can be custom defined (better than six inches is possible). The main disadvantages are cost and the time taken to process the imagery.

Orthophotographs can help bring maps alive for the public. They provide convenient reference markers allowing nonmap users to feel much more comfortable with map-based information. In some instances they make maps look more aesthetically pleasing. But photographs can also provide information to the map analyst. They contain information on things that we seldom include in standard vector GIS data, things like building footprints, land cover, vegetation, and so on. As we indicated earlier, with the right GIS tools huge amounts of information can be extracted from standard orthographic images. They can be used to generate maps of impermeable surfaces such as parking lots, land-use change, vegetative change, and habitat loss and are an important element in determining land areas in need of protection.

There are, however, some dangers to using imagery. New users should keep the following in mind. The coordinate system of the images you use will determine the coordinate system of the maps that you produce. Most GIS programs will change the coordinate system of vector data on the fly. But it takes too many computer resources to do this for images. So it is usual practice to make sure the image is in the desired coordinate system (if it is not, translate it appropriately) and then have the software program and computer handle on-the-fly coordinate translations of the vector data. In fact, it is often wise to make sure that all data for all layers, both images and vector, are in the same coordinate system *prior* to the production and analysis of maps. This way computer processing resources are preserved.

Also make sure you are using a consistent datum. A few years ago students of ours were preparing maps for a public meeting on road surface run-off and the periodic flooding of a neighborhood creek. The final maps were produced in a hurry and were not checked. In the public presentation an audience member stood up and pointed out that the creek appeared to be on the wrong side of the road. It was. The creek layer was derived from an orthophotograph using the 1927 datum, whereas all the other data was in NAD 83. This had caused the creek to

---

[2]For instance, the ArcExplorer™ data viewer is a lightweight and free GIS data viewer. To download, go to *www.esri.com/software/arcexplorer/aedownload.html.*

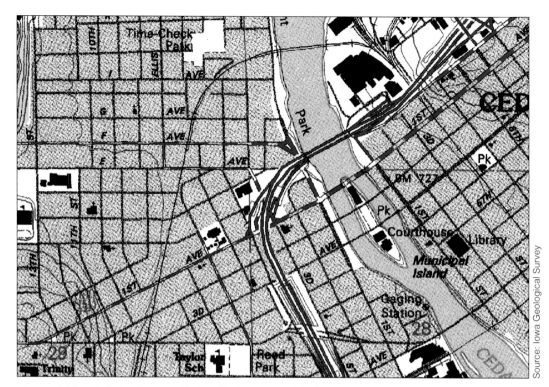

Figure 2.26   Digital raster graphic (DRG), Cedar Rapids, Iowa.

shift northward and westward on the map. Needless to say, this glitch undermined the students' authority and thus every policy suggestion they made. It is surprising how much imagery is still distributed using the NAD 27 (or the North American Datum of 1927). Overlaying one layer in UTM NAD 27 on some other in NAD 83 will show a spatially significant shift. Users should always check metadata and then make sure to use a consistent coordinate system and datum. Note also that TIGER/Line data is distributed using NAD 83 and uses a geographic (or unprojected) coordinate system. If using a DOQ base layer, most GIS programs will project TIGER/Line-derived map layers into UTM on the fly.

Digital raster graphics (DRGs) and digital line graphs (DLGs)

DRGs are scanned images of a standard series USGS topographic map. Go to *topomaps.usgs. gov/drg* for the DRG home page. Detailed background information on DRGs is to be found at *topomaps.usgs.gov/drg/drg_overview.html.* As with DOQs, 7.5- minute DRGs will need to be purchased (there is no 3.75-minute series), unless your state geological survey bureau has them available for free download. The 1:24,000 scale maps provide a ground resolution of eight feet or 2.44 meters (in other words one pixel of the image is equal to eight feet on the ground). As with DOQs, TerraServer also allows downloads at its Web site, but high-resolution images will be for very small areas. An image for a larger area will thus have to be stitched from many small-area images.

In our experience, DRGs are particularly useful in getting a nonmapping audience to locate itself and then understand the information being presented on a map. But they also provide important land-cover, contour, and land-feature information that is useful to urban analysts. Figure 2.26 shows a small fragment of a 7.5-minute DRG image. Like orthophotos, DRGs have other uses beyond that of providing informational base-layers. DRGs include information on water bodies, vegetation, elevation contours, roads, points of interest, and so on. Figure 2.26 is a fragment of a DRG covering the same area as figures 2.23 and 2.24.

The coordinate system cautions we gave for orthophotographs apply as much here. DRG images are published in UTM using either the 1927 or the 1983 datum. Check the metadata of the file to find out which. Because DRGs are images, they have associated world files or world file headers. As with orthophotos, world file information is crucial if you are planning to use a DRG as a base-layer in a map.

DLGs are an alternative to DRGs. These are vector files (they are not images) and include much of the same information that is in a DRG: the Public Lands Survey System (PLSS), boundaries, transportation, water features, elevation contours, manmade features, and vegetative cover. For some analyses, DLGs may be easier to work with than DRGs. The 7.5-minute DLGs correspond to 1:20,000, 1:24,000, and 1:25,000 topological maps. Most are in UTM, but some are in the State Plane coordinate system. Both NAD 27 and NAD 83 are used. Intermediate- and small-scale maps are also available. They are available for purchase at *edc.usgs.gov/products/map/dlg.html* for background and metadata information. Go to *edc.usgs.gov/geodata* for download information. Actual download occurs at GeoCommunity, a third-party service provider at *data.geocomm.com/dem.* Downloads are free or fee-based depending on the level of service required. The files are published in the federal government's SDTS (Spatial Data Transfer Standard) format and must be translated into some other format in order to be viewed in most commercial GIS programs. For those using ESRI products, ArcToolbox includes a translator.

Digital elevation models (DEMs)

DEMs are considerably more complex feature classes than images or DLGs, and to use them effectively requires more advanced GIS skills. DEMs contain detailed elevation data. Information about downloading is at *edc.usgs.gov/geodata.* Files are downloaded from the GeoCommunity at *data.geocomm.com/dem* and from some state geological survey bureaus. Of the available DEMs, the 7.5-minute (or 1:24,000) are the most useful (again these cover a full quadrangle). Like DLGs, DEMs are published in the federal government's SDTS (Spatial Data Transfer Standard) format and must be translated into some other format in order to be viewed in most commercial GIS programs. Commonly, DEMs will be translated into ESRI's GRID format. DEMs translated into GRIDs (we will call them DEM-derived GRIDs to be clear) can provide very useful information to both map users and viewers. Figure 2.27 shows a fragment of DEM information for the same area as the earlier orthophotographs and DRG. The deep bluish color indicates the lowest lying areas and deep green the highest.

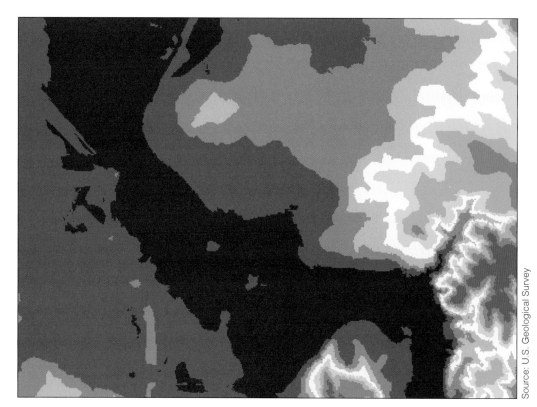

Figure 2.27   Digital elevation model (DEM) image, Cedar Rapids, Iowa.

Once in GRID format, DEMs can be translated into a full three-dimensional terrain model, such as a triangulated irregular network (TIN), or into a three-dimensional shape-file. Terrain models are extraordinarily useful. Use them to visualize the impact of proposed development on the landscape, to find the optimal location of mobile-phone towers, or to visualize the aesthetic consequences of proposed large buildings, billboards, and so on. In ArcGIS you will need the 3D Analyst™ extension to undertake these analyses.

DEMs are typically published by the USGS in UTM NAD 83, though some still use the 1927 datum. Ground coordinates (the *x* and *y* coordinates) are thus in meters. In most cases the *z* or height axis will also be in meters, but in a few cases it will be in feet. You will need to check the DEM's metadata. Having consistent units for *x, y,* and *z* axes will greatly aid the manipulation of the DEM.

At its simplest, the DEM-derived GRID can be used to provide a base layer in a map. Symbolized appropriately, this base layer will give a strong visual sense of topography. Most GIS programs allow not only various elevations to be presented in various colors, but also allow for shadowing, thus re-enforcing the visual sense of height. Again this will tend to aid the public's understanding of other information presented in the maps.

However, providing a visual aid to the understanding of topography is not the central purpose of DEMs. DEMs enable the calculation of slope, viewsheds, watersheds, and so on, all important information for urban land professionals. For instance, "sensitive natural area" ordinances commonly define what land in a community is subject to erosion, in order to protect that land. Erosion is usually a result of the slope of the land, its vegetation coverage, and its soil type. Slope will be calculated directly from a DEM. Vegetation will either be derived from aerial photography (infrared photography can be particularly useful here) or from land cover map layers (these are usually available from state geological survey bureaus). Soil type maps (and surficial geology) are also available from state geological survey bureaus.

Local government is another important source of elevation data. Cities and counties that have been flown for orthophotographs in the recent past may have ordered a very high-resolution elevation model at the same time. If not, a fairly high-resolution TIN is usually part of the orthorectification process and vendors will usually provide this TIN along with the photographs. Most vendors will also be willing to provide a complete high-resolution digital terrain model, but this can cost a considerable sum. City or county terrain models will usually be held in the local GIS/information systems department. If a city or county has a GIS coordinator, this is the person to contact first.

Land-cover, soil type, and floodplain maps

Typically these will be distributed by state geological survey bureaus or the Soil Conservation Service. All three types of maps are important data elements in local planning processes, as the case of the sensitive natural areas ordinance described above shows. Land-cover maps describe the type of vegetation and are most often distributed in GRID format. Soil type is a categorization of surface soils (bedrock, clay, loam, and so on). These are distributed in GRID format, and sometimes as coverages, shapefiles, or as files in ESRI's old interchange (.e00) format. ArcToolbox will perform the necessary conversions. Floodplain maps are usually distributed as shapefiles.

Other useful sources of digital map data

Almost every federal agency or bureau that has a substantive connection to local government produces maps that may be useful to urban land professionals. For instance, the Department of Housing and Urban Development (HUD) (*www.huduser.org/Datasets/gis.html*) produces a series called Research Maps or R-Maps; this is a set of CD–ROMs containing boundary maps for MSAs, central cities, and suburbs, and data from the American Housing Survey, Government Sponsored Enterprises, Home Mortgage Disclosure Act, Low Income Housing Tax Credit program, and the Picture of Subsidized Households. The Bureau of Transportation Statistics (BTS) (*www.bts.gov*) produces a considerable amount of transportation data including maps of all major U.S. transportation facilities. The National Oceanic and Atmospheric Administration (NOAA) (*www.noaa.gov*) produces a number of maps (including nautical charts useful in coastal, lake, and river areas), weather charts, and so on. The Environmental Protection Agency (EPA) (*www. epa.gov*) produces a broad range of environmental data. Their Envirofact Data Warehouse at *www.epa.gov/enviro/index_java.html* includes various Web-mapping engines on a variety of environmental topics. If you are searching for data and do not know the likely department, agency, or bureau that produces it, go to the Federal Geospatial Data Clearinghouse (FGDC) (*www.fgdc.gov*). It is important to remember that state government departments are also collectors, processors, and distributors of map data. State geological survey bureaus and state departments of transportation and natural resources all provide data useful to urban land professionals. Unfortunately, in almost all states, detailed land-use data is held locally (at the city or county levels), and you will have easy access to that data only if local government is GIS friendly, is prepared to invest in making public its data, and has an Internet site that makes data retrieval practicably possible.

U.S. urban analysts are fortunate in having easy and cheap access to huge amounts of useful data and complementary mapping systems. With recent strides in GIS software, both in ease of use and the power of available analysis routines, it is surprising that more urban land professionals don't make greater use of these opportunities in their everyday work.

In this chapter we have focused on simple access issues: how to acquire maps and data, and then connect them. The following four chapters focus on substantive topic areas—social and demographic, economic, transportation, and housing analyses—and give specific guidance (and many more examples) on using the census and GIS for a wide range of urban analyses.

Chapter 3

Using the census
to analyze demographic and social conditions

Counting people to establish congressional representation is the primary justification for a national census. Describing those people has become an equally important part of the census, because it is the basis for many federal, state, and local government programs. In 2000, approximately $283 billion was distributed from the federal government to state and local governments in the form of grants (U.S. General Accounting Office 2003a). Funds were distributed based in large part on census estimates of the population and its characteristics (such as the age distribution, the extent of poverty, and so on). This is why debates over the census are so sharply politicized at times.

Why is detailed social and demographic data useful? Local human services agencies need to define service areas based on the clients they serve. For instance, an agency planning to develop a sheltered employment program for disabled young adults might need to identify the following:

- How many young adults have an employment disability?
- What kinds of disabilities limit their employment?
- Which neighborhoods do they live in?
- What are their economic circumstances?
- How many live in neighborhoods currently served by an existing public transit service?

City planners need to project the size of the population five, ten, or twenty years into the future to decide how the housing supply, parks and recreation facilities, and water and sewer capacity will need to change to accommodate population growth. Projecting population relies on several pieces of information about the current population:

- What is the age, sex, race, and ethnic makeup of the current population?
- How will current birth and death rates affect rates of natural increase?

- How much population change in the past decade was the result of migration?
- What is the current household size for different population cohorts?
- How are household formation rates likely to change in the future?

School district planners need to estimate not just likely future school enrollment, but also how many children may need a variety of supportive services such as bilingual teachers. Questions school district planners may have would include:

- How many non-English speaking immigrant families have moved to the region?
- How many of those families are linguistically isolated (that is, no one over 14 speaks English well)?
- What languages do linguistically isolated families speak at home?
- Which school districts contain the highest number of non-English speaking families?

Planners, human service providers, school districts, and several other special-purpose public and private agencies rely on the descriptive detail provided by the census, along with the count of population. Planning future service provision, writing grant proposals, and designing programs all require data to justify the choice of priorities. Understanding the spatial distribution of target groups is key to delivering services effectively.

The Census of Population and Housing is the single most comprehensive source of population data available at a fine spatial scale. Together with other official data such as the Current Employment Survey (CES) and the Current Population Survey (CPS), it is the basis for intercensal estimates of social and economic change. The American Community Survey (ACS) will in many ways revolutionize our ability to describe local populations from year to year. Estimates of annual changes will be more accurate. However, understanding the decennial census is still essential—the ACS is closely based on the methods and concepts described in this chapter.

As chapter 1 explains, the decennial census does not provide a perfect count of either the population as a whole or its subgroups. Some groups of people, especially recent migrants and minorities, are clearly undercounted, although a variety of statistical techniques are used to correct for this. Because the census is address-based, it is quite inadequate as a count of people who have no fixed address, and no statistical adjustments have been developed to address this deficiency. Understanding these limitations is necessary if we are to use the data appropriately.

The following section of this chapter discusses the major social and demographic variables (economic variables are dealt with in chapter 4). This discussion draws heavily on the Census Bureau's definition of the variables (U.S. Census Bureau 2003a, chapter 7). The third section discusses other widely used data sources, including the other form in which census data is available, the Public Use Microdata Sample (PUMS). The final section provides practical examples of how census data can be used for spatial analyses of demographic and social characteristics. The examples present solutions to two common spatial challenges—identifying trends over time when census geography has changed, and identifying characteristics of neighborhoods that may not coincide with census tract boundaries.

Major population variables

It is often difficult for a newcomer to grasp the intensity of the debate that accompanies the redefinition of census variables. On the one hand, there is a strong inertia because changing definitions complicate the ability to compare trends over time. On the other hand, redefinition allows us to capture new information that enables us to define new kinds of needs and target groups. The constituencies of existing programs may feel threatened by new ways of defining eligibility. A good example is the heated debate over whether "race" should be redefined to include options for people who identify with more than one group.

Understanding the precise definition of the variables is indispensable to using them appropriately. Often, census definitions do not fit within our common-sense understanding of a concept. For example, "families" are defined and counted based on their relationship to the person completing the survey—a household may be counted as a "nonfamily" household if one person answers and a "family" household if another does.

The population section of the decennial census covers three main sets of concepts:
- people, families, and households;
- ethnicity and culture; and
- human capital.

In addition, the decennial census is a rich source of income and employment data. These topics are covered separately in the following chapter.

The count of individuals, families and households, their age, sex, race, and ethnic affiliation are collected in the "short form" questionnaire that every household answers. The other variables are based on the "long form," a questionnaire completed by about 17 percent of households (although sampling rates differ depending on the size and type of place). Chapter 1 dealt with sampling approaches and the issues of accuracy. Chapter 6 will deal with standard errors and confidence intervals in some detail. If absolute precision is important, analyses should be based on these confidence intervals. For most analyses, the "estimates" based on the sample should be adequate. If an issue is highly politicized (such as which neighborhood has more children under 5 living in linguistically isolated households) confidence intervals would obviously provide more defensible results.

Underreporting, misreporting, and other nonsampling sources of error affect all data, not just the sample data. Data based on the sample questions is reported down to the block group level only, because estimates become less accurate at finer levels of detail. Some cross-tabulations of sample data by detailed demographic characteristics are only reported to the census tract level.

People, families, and households

Age

Age is collected for every person. Age is used as a filter for several sample questions, such as educational attainment, which is only asked of people 25 or older. Some analyses (for instance, some population projection models) use age in single-year categories, cross-tabulated by sex, race, and Hispanic origin. This is reported in Summary File 1 (SF 1). For most analyses, the five-year intervals in Summary File 3 (SF 3) will be sufficient. The concept of age-sex cohorts is explained in box 3.1. Median age, a convenient summary of the overall age distribution of a place or tract, is also reported.

Charting median age for the United States shows the significant demographic and social transformations of the past century. In 1900, the median age of the population was 23, similar to that of many developing countries today. By 2000, median age was 35, and more than ten times as many people were 65 or older in 2000 compared to 1900 (Hobbs and Stoops 2002, 57–8). The United States still has a relatively young population compared to other developed countries because of immigration (immigrants tend to be younger). However, some states with high rates of immigration have also attracted many elderly movers from elsewhere in the United States. Florida, for instance, has the highest proportion of people 65 and older and ranks forty-ninth in the proportion of its population 15 or younger.

Although age seems the most straightforward of information to collect, it is not. Analysis of the 1990 Census suggested that many people round their age up to their next birthday or the next birthday ending in a zero or five; so age may be overstated. For Census 2000, age is calculated by date of birth, and respondents are also asked for their age as of April 1, not when they complete the survey. Date of birth will become the main basis for calculating age when the American Community Survey (ACS), which collects data throughout the year, is fully phased in.

Sex

According to the census at least, everyone is classified as male or female. Like age, information on sex has been collected in every census, as it was originally the basis of voting eligibility. A sex ratio is reported, dividing the total number of males by females. Ratios over 100 indicate more males than females. Sex is another dimension along which many other variables, such as employment and income, are reported (see sidebar, page 90).

Households, families, and individuals

In a rather circuitous way, households are defined as all the people occupying a housing unit, while housing units (see chapter 5) are defined as the separate living quarters of a household. "Households" are not the same as "families." Families are a group of individuals related to the householder by blood, marriage, or adoption. Nonfamily households include single people living alone and groups of unrelated people living together as roommates or as unmarried partners.

Box 3.1   Age-sex cohorts

Many of the events that define our lives are in some ways predictable based on our demographic affiliations. The likelihood of school or college enrollment, of employment or unemployment, or of moving away or dying varies depending on who we are—how old we are, our gender, our race and ethnicity. These broad demographic categories certainly do not determine our fate, but they make it easier for a stranger to predict the likelihood of any one of these outcomes.

Consequently, one of the building blocks or starting points of any social or economic analysis is a study of demographic structure—how are residents broken down into particular "cohorts?" Consider the following pair of maps (3.1a and 3.1b) showing age-sex cohorts for each county in Arizona.

Mohave, Yavapai, La Paz, and Gila counties have a much higher proportion of men and women older than 75 compared to Coconino, Navajo, Apache, and Greenlee counties. These last four are more likely to have a disproportionately large number of 5- to 14-year-olds. They also have a very small share of 20- to 24-year-olds, which suggests there is quite high out-migration by young adults. Comparing the actual growth of cohorts since 1990 with the growth we would expect to see from natural processes would explain migration rates more clearly. At this point, we may also want to consider the role of race and ethnicity in these differences. How do cohorts differ when we compare Native Americans with non-Hispanic whites? Maps 3.1c and 3.1d (next page) extend the comparison to include race.

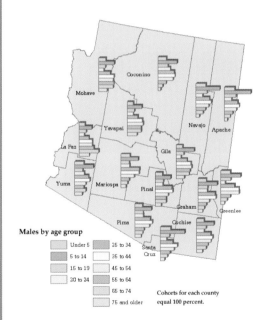

Map 3.1a   Age cohorts for males by county, Arizona.

Source: 2000 Census of Population and Housing

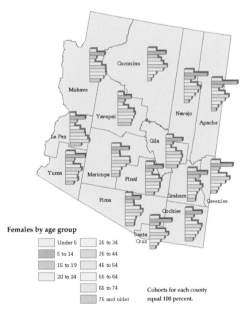

Map 3.1b   Age cohorts for females by county, Arizona.

Source: 2000 Census of Population and Housing

89

Using the census to analyze demographic and social conditions

Box 3.1   Age-sex cohorts (continued)

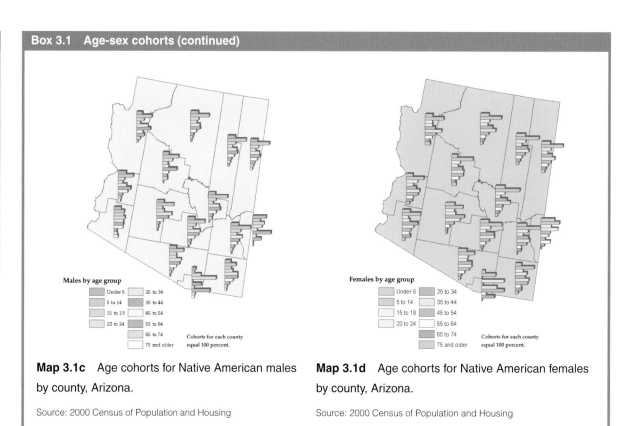

Map 3.1c legend:

Males by age group
- Under 5
- 5 to 14
- 15 to 19
- 20 to 24
- 25 to 34
- 35 to 44
- 45 to 54
- 55 to 64
- 65 to 74
- 75 and older

Cohorts for each county equal 100 percent.

Females by age group
- Under 5
- 5 to 14
- 15 to 19
- 20 to 24
- 25 to 34
- 35 to 44
- 45 to 54
- 55 to 64
- 65 to 74
- 75 and older

Cohorts for each county equal 100 percent.

Map 3.1c Age cohorts for Native American males by county, Arizona.

Source: 2000 Census of Population and Housing

Map 3.1d Age cohorts for Native American females by county, Arizona.

Source: 2000 Census of Population and Housing

Until 1950, men outnumbered women in the United States. Since then, the ratio of men to women reached a low point in 1980, at 94.5 men for every 100 women (Hobbs and Stoops 2002, 62). By 2000, the gap had narrowed to 96.3 men for every 100 women, reflecting higher male immigration and improvements in men's life expectancy. Overall, central cities have more women than men, and sex ratios are narrowest in nonmetropolitan areas. In 2000, only seven states (all in the West) had more men than women with Alaska leading the pack with 107 men for every 100 women. Women outnumber men by the greatest margin in Washington, D.C. (with a ratio of 89 to 100), a typical pattern throughout the Northeast. Nationwide, there were 86 unmarried men over 15 for every 100 unmarried women. Paradise, Nevada, (a suburb of Las Vegas) was one exception, with 118 unmarried men for every 100 unmarried women (Kreider and Simmons 2003).

The householder is the person who answers the survey. This is usually one of the people in whose name the home is owned or rented. But this definition is quite arbitrary, and its arbitrariness means that the same combinations of individuals could be defined in different ways, depending on who is designated as the householder. Consider the case of a man and woman with her own child living together, renting a home jointly. If the man responds as the householder, this would be a household of unrelated individuals (neither the woman nor her child are related to the householder). If the woman responds as the householder, this same group would be described as a family household (the woman and her child) with one nonrelative (the man) in the household. Box 3.2 summarizes the variety of relatives and nonrelatives that could make up a family or a household.

91

Box 3.2 Understanding households and families

Family households are defined by the presence of people related to the householder by birth, marriage, or adoption. Family households are further divided into married couple households and those with no spouse present. Nonfamily households may be a single person or may include an array of other people not related to the householder. Figure 3.1 explains these concepts graphically.

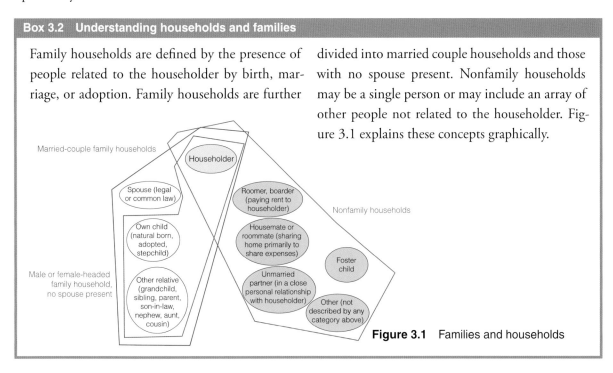

Figure 3.1 Families and households

"Own children" are the householder's children by birth, marriage, or adoption who are unmarried and under the age of 18. "Related children" are under 18 and may be related to the householder in many ways—as nephews, cousins, grandchildren, or daughters-in-law. They may be married or unmarried but would never be the spouse of the householder. One census table shows the number of people in family households who are the child of the householder, regardless of their age.

Because families are defined based on their relationship to the householder, each household contains only one family by definition. Subfamilies, such as an adult child of the householder with her own child, or the householder's brother and his wife and children, are not counted as separate families. However, subfamilies and the numbers of households with subfamilies are reported at the census tract level. Box 3.3 discusses the concept of subfamilies in more detail. Census 2000 introduced detailed tables showing relationships and responsibilities for households that include grandchildren.

Box 3.3   Subfamilies in households

Household formation rates slow when housing prices rise. One indicator of this is the proportion of households that include subfamilies. Although subfamilies are not shown separately in tables presenting the characteristics of families, they are an important component of unmet housing demand. The maps on this page compare the proportion of households with subfamilies in two very different housing markets in New York state—Kings County (Brooklyn) and Onondago County (Syracuse). Subfamilies are far more likely in Brooklyn.

Higher housing prices may explain this, but it is also possible that households in Brooklyn, a higher proportion of which are immigrants, may prefer to live in extended families. Table 3.1 compares housing prices and immigrant populations in the two counties. There may be several reasons why households are more likely to have subfamilies in Brooklyn than in Syracuse.

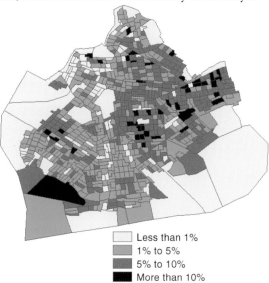

Less than 1%
1% to 5%
5% to 10%
More than 10%

Map 3.2a   Percent of households with subfamilies by census tract, Kings County, New York.

Source: 2000 Census of Population and Housing

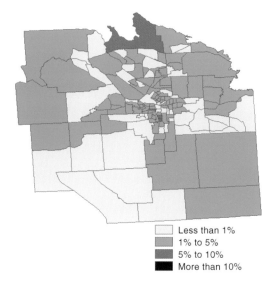

Less than 1%
1% to 5%
5% to 10%
More than 10%

Map 3.2b   Percent of households with subfamilies by census tract, Onondago County, New York.

Source: 2000 Census of Population and Housing

Table 3.1 Foreign-born residents, housing prices, and subfamilies		
	Brooklyn (Kings County)	**Syracuse (Onondago County)**
Foreign born	37.8%	5.7%
Noncitizens	19.9%	2.7%
Entered United States 1990 or later	44.1%	43.3%
Median rent	$672	$550
Median home value	$224,100	$85,400

Source: 2000 Census of Population and Housing, Summary File 3

Marital status is defined by respondents not by their legal status. Unmarried partners are different from roommates—they are in a "close personal relationship" with the householder. In contrast to people who consider themselves to be in common-law marriages, unmarried partners are nonfamily households. Unmarried partners (unlike a couple in a common-law marriage) need not be of opposite sexes. Box 3.4 explores the implications of this new definition.

How many grandparents are responsible for raising their grandchildren? In the Personal Responsibility and Work Opportunity Reconciliation Act of 1996 (PRWORA, otherwise known as the "welfare reform" bill), Congress required the Census Bureau to begin asking this question. Of the 158.9 million people aged 30 or older, 3.6 percent lived in the same household as their grandchildren under 18. Of these, 42 percent (2.4 million people) were the primary caregivers for their grandchildren, and 39 percent of these caregivers had been primarily responsible for their grandchildren for five or more years (Simmons and Dye 2003). Pacific Islanders were most likely to live with their grandchildren (10 percent, compared to 2 percent among non-Hispanic whites, and 8 percent among African-Americans, Hispanics, and Native Americans). However, African-American and Native American grandparents were more likely to be the primary caregivers if they lived in the same household (at 52 percent and 56 percent respectively), compared to 38 percent of Pacific Islander and 35 percent of Hispanic grandparents, suggesting some important cultural differences in family structure.

Marital status is a sample question asked for all members of the household over 15, not just the householder. Because subfamilies are not counted as families, there are more married couples than there are married couple family households. People who are now married include a subcategory of those who are separated. Legally separated couples, those living apart and intending to divorce, and couples living apart because of, in the Census Bureau's quaint term, "marital discord," are in this subcategory. People with an absent spouse are not necessarily separated. A spouse may live away from home because of employment, service in the military, or because they are institutionalized. Thus, the number of married men and women in a place are not always equal—reporting differences, absent spouses, and sample weighting procedures account for these differences.

Each census reflects changes in social mores. Although information on unmarried partners and same-sex couples was planned for inclusion in the 1990 Census, it was only in the 2000 Census that this became politically acceptable. Map 3.3a shows the neighborhood-level distribution of unmarried partner households as a proportion of all households in three counties in the Minneapolis–St. Paul metro area. Unmarried partners appear to be concentrated in relatively few downtown neighborhoods.

However, map 3.3b suggests a different story. As a proportion of nonfamily households, unmarried partner households are more concentrated in outlying rather than central neighborhoods.

Can we use census data to identify gay neighborhoods? Map 3.3c shows the share of all unmarried partner households made up of same-sex couples. The distribution suggests that indeed some neighborhoods (mostly downtown) attract a high proportion of same-sex couples.

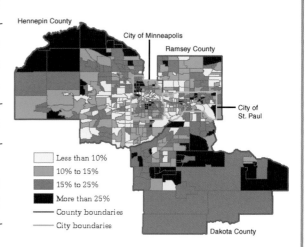

Map 3.3b   Unmarried partner households as a percent of all nonfamily households by census tract in Hennepin, Ramsey, and Dakota counties, Minnesota.

Source: 2000 Census of Population and Housing

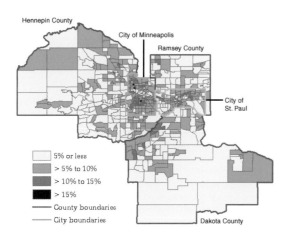

Map 3.3a   Unmarried partner households by census tract in Hennepin, Ramsey, and Dakota counties, Minnesota.

Source: 2000 Census of Population and Housing

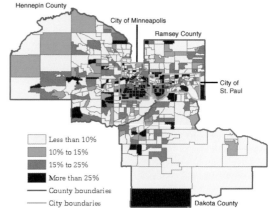

Map 3.3c   Same-sex partners as a percent of all unmarried partner households by census tract in Hennepin, Ramsey, and Dakota counties, Minnesota.

Source: 2000 Census of Population and Housing

While married-couple households are still the slight majority, at 51.7 percent of all households in 2000 (down from 55.2 percent in 1990), their numbers are on the decline. Single-person households increased from 24.6 percent in 1990 to 25.8 percent of all households in 2000. There were striking regional differences in household composition with counties in Utah and Idaho leading the nation in proportion of married couple households and those along the Gulf Coast and Atlantic seaboard (from the lower Mississippi Valley to New England) lagging. In a diverse range of cities, from Seattle, Washington, to Fort Lauderdale, Florida, and St. Louis, Missouri, single-person households made up more than 40 percent of all households. Multigenerational households (see the discussion of grandparents above) were most common in Hawaii, California, and Mississippi, reflecting in part differences by race and ethnicity (Simmons and O'Neill 2001).

Ethnicity and related cultural concepts

Race and Hispanic origin

Defining "race" is not an easy task. Biological or anthropological definitions carry unpleasant connotations. Some countries avoid the question altogether and ask merely about national origin and the cultural group with which the respondent identifies. However, if census questions reflect important social concerns and concepts, race will not disappear from the United States' census questionnaire soon. The Census Bureau asks respondents which race or races, cultural group(s), or national origin(s) they identify with most closely. Thus, "race" is an amalgam of national or ethnic origin concepts that are socially, rather than anthropologically or biologically, defined.

Until the 1990s, the Canadian census did not collect information about race, although a question about ethnic origin (similar to the "ancestry" question in the U.S. census) was used to estimate race. In 1991, a question about aboriginal origin was added, followed by a new question on "visible minority group" in 1996 (Census Canada Web site *www.statcan.ca/english/census2001*).

This ambiguous situation in the United States often results in confusion over "Hispanic origin." It is inaccurate to report Hispanic origin as just another racial category. People of Hispanic origin may be of any race. However, many people of Hispanic origin describe themselves as some "other" race, such as Mexican or Cuban. People may describe themselves as Hispanic because they speak Spanish, because their parents spoke Spanish, or because they have a Spanish surname. Technically, then, Hispanic origin is a purely cultural variable, defined by language

It is only since 1980 that a question has been included on Hispanic origin. Since then, the Hispanic population has more than doubled in size (from 14.6 million to 35.3 million), and in 2000 people of Hispanic origin accounted for a slightly larger proportion of the population (12.5 percent) than people who described themselves as African-Americans (12.3 percent) (Hobbs and Stoops 2002, 78).

or heritage. People from Portuguese- or French-speaking countries in Latin America and the Caribbean are not Hispanic. Europeans from Spain, Asians from the Philippines, and Native Americans from Mexico may all describe themselves as Hispanic.

Race was redefined in an important way in 2000. In previous censuses, people were asked to choose among six categories:

- white,
- black or African-American,
- American Indian or Alaska Native,
- Asian,
- Hawaiian or Pacific Islander, and
- "other."

In 2000, people could choose two or more race categories to reflect mixed parentage, although they still had the choice of "some other race alone." Write-in responses are also accepted—an automated coding system classifies them into one of the five categories. For people reporting more than one race, fifty-seven different combinations of races are possible. These are reported in Summary Files 1 (SF 1) and 4 (SF 4). Box 3.5 explores how this redefinition may affect our understanding of racial identity.

Fifty-seven racial categories are obviously too cumbersome for cross-tabulations of other variables by race. This is dealt with in two ways. In some cases, cross-tabulations summarize responses from all people who reported each race category (for example, "Asian alone or in combination with one or more other races" would include everyone who reported being Asian or part Asian). This solves one of the practical problems resulting from multiracial identities, but people may be counted twice or more. When summarizing characteristics by race, it would be helpful to explain why results do not sum to 100 percent. In other cases however, cross-tabulations are based on people who reported belonging to one racial group only, in which case the 2.6 percent of people reporting more than one race are excluded. In Summary File 4 (SF 4), cross-tabulations are provided for people who reported various combinations of racial affiliations.

Place of birth, national origin, and ancestry

Place of birth and national origin are fairly straightforward questions, but "ancestry" is an even muddier concept than race. Respondents report the state, territory, or foreign country of birth

Box 3.5　Changing definitions of race

The Office of Management and Budget (OMB) had resisted using multiracial classifications for the 1990 Census because many federal reporting requirements were based on the five main racial categories. However the agency agreed to a compromise in 2000. What effect has the inclusion of multiracial reporting options had on the racial profile reflected in the 2000 Census? Map 3.4 shows the proportion of residents in each county in California who were identified as multiracial.

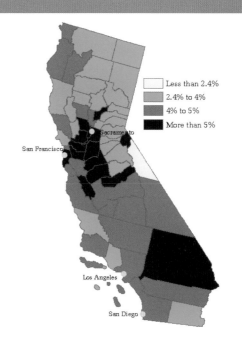

Less than 2.4%
2.4% to 4%
4% to 5%
More than 5%

Sacramento
San Francisco
Los Angeles
San Diego

Map 3.4　Californians reporting two or more races by county.

Source: 2000 Census of Population and Housing, SF1

Surprisingly, residents of Los Angeles (a major gateway city for new migrants) are somewhat less likely to see themselves as multiracial compared to residents of the Bay Area outer suburbs and the agricultural north-central belt. Nevertheless, Los Angeles has one of the highest counts of multiracial residents in the nation, at nearly 200,000.

Table 3.2 shows the distribution of Californians reporting they belonged to a particular racial category, both alone or in combination with one or more other races.

Table 3.2　Multiracial Californians				
	Alone	**Alone or in combination**	**In combination**	**Percent in combination**
White	20,170,059	21,490,973	1,320,914	6.2
African-American	2,263,882	2,513,041	249,159	9.9
Native American	333,346	627,562	294,216	46.9
Asian	3,697,513	4,155,685	458,172	11.0
Pacific Islander	116,961	221,458	104,497	47.2
Other race	5,682,241	6,575,625	893,384	13.6

Source: 2000 Census of Population and Housing, Summary File 1

Box 3.5 Changing definitions of race (continued)

Two groups who make up a tiny overall proportion of the state's population, Native Americans and Pacific Islanders, nearly double in size when we allow people to use more than one racial category to describe themselves. One thing this table illustrates is the care that should be taken in determining whether to use single or multiple racial identities as the basis for analyses. Another conclusion may be that our current conventional notions of "race," though sanitized over the decades to eliminate the biological connotations that dominated earlier census definitions, may be seen as quite misguided by future generations.

Who were the 6.8 million people who reported identifying with more than one racial group? They were more likely to be younger than 18, more likely to report they were Hispanic, and more likely to live in the West. In California alone, 1.6 million people (4.7 percent) reported identifying with two or more races (Jones and Smith 2001). Nearly two thirds of all people who reported they were multiracial lived in just ten states: California, New York, Texas, Florida, Hawaii, Illinois, New Jersey, Washington, Michigan, and Ohio. Overall, 32.6 percent of people describing themselves as multiracial were also of Hispanic origin.

using current political divisions. In contrast, the question about ancestry could be interpreted to refer to the person's parents' place of birth, or the cultural or ethnic group(s)with which the person identifies. Would a person born in Australia of Italian parents describe themselves as Australian or Italian? Would a person born in the United States with three American grandparents and one Turkish grandparent and a Turkish surname describe themselves as of American or Turkish ancestry? Individuals with the identical ancestry may describe themselves in quite different ways or may describe their ancestry differently over time.

A further complication is that the ancestry question is designed to supplement the questions on race and Hispanic origin. People of Spanish, Mexican, Indian, or Japanese ancestry would be lumped in together under "other ancestry groups." Not all ancestry categories are associated with a country—some refer to a cross-national region (Basque) or subregion (Acadian/Cajun). But although regions may be the basis for ancestry, religion is usually not. "Sephardic," "Jewish," or "Sunni Muslim" responses would be classified as "not reported." However, "Hindu" would be coded as East Indian.

Why is ancestry still collected if it is such an ambiguous concept? Migration and suburbanization patterns have attenuated the links between ancestry and place for much of the native-born population. However, distinct ethnic neighborhoods do survive in some places. Ancestry may be a useful way to describe cultural heritage because of (rather than despite) the fact that it

In 2000, about one of every nine U.S. residents was born in a foreign country—31.1 million people, compared to 19.8 million in 1990. More than half of the foreign-born lived in just three states—California, New York, and Texas. Overall, Mexico was the birthplace of 29.5 percent of the foreign-born population, just ahead of Asia (26.4 percent), and the remainder of Latin America, including Central America and the Caribbean (22.2 percent). Europe ranked fourth, at 15.8 percent (Malone, Baluja, Costanza, and David 2003).

is based on self-identification. National origin and place of birth, however, are the appropriate measures of immigrant populations.

Language

Householders are asked whether household members 5 years and older sometimes or always speak a language other than English at home. The language spoken most often or learned first is recorded. Write-in answers are coded into 380 detailed language categories, which are classified into thirty-nine language groups and then summarized into four main groups:

- Spanish,
- other Indo-European,
- Asian and Pacific Island, and
- all other languages.

Clearly, these groups do not reflect actual linguistic relationships. They are based on the number of speakers of each language group that might be found in a sample of the U.S. population. In households where at least one person speaks a language other than English at home, all household members are assigned to that language group, even if they speak only English.

"Language density" shows how many household members speak another language at home (none, some, or all). People who speak a language other than English at home are asked how well they and household members spoke English—"very well," "well," "not well," or "not at all." There are no guidelines for how to interpret this very subjective question. A household where no one older than 14 speaks English only, and no one over 14 speaks English "very well," is classified as linguistically isolated. The concept of "linguistic isolation" is explored further in box 3.6.

Language concepts are important in neighborhoods with significant immigrant populations. Public meetings and information campaigns, such as emergency preparedness, will be more effective if all audiences are included. Where many households are "linguistically isolated," it is essential. Data on language has been collected in every census since 1890, with the exception of 1950. Since 1980, the wording of the questions has not changed.

Foreign migration has fundamentally changed local culture in many cities, but in few so dramatically as Los Angeles and its surrounding area. Map 3.5a shows the proportion of households speaking English at home. Anglo households are clearly in the minority through much of the inner city.

How many households that speak a language other than English at home are "linguistically isolated?" A household where no one over 14 speaks English only, and no one over 14 speaks English "very well," is classified as linguistically isolated. Map 3.5b shows the proportion of non-English-speaking households classified as linguistically isolated.

Linguistically isolated households are more common in the same central city neighborhoods, but there are pockets of linguistic isolation in some suburbs, including suburbs where a high proportion of households speak English at home. How does linguistic isolation vary by the language spoken at home? Map 3.5c and Map 3.5d show the proportion of Spanish-speaking and Asian-language-speaking households who are linguistically isolated.

Overall, a higher proportion of households speaking an Asian language at home are linguistically isolated, but those households are less concentrated in contiguous census tracts.

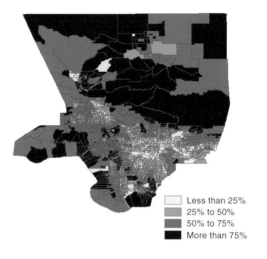

Less than 25%
25% to 50%
50% to 75%
More than 75%

Map 3.5a   English speakers by census tract, Los Angeles County, California.

Source: 2000 Census of Population and Housing

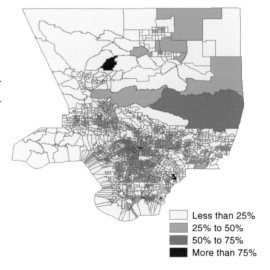

Less than 25%
25% to 50%
50% to 75%
More than 75%

Map 3.5b   Linguistically isolated non-English speakers by census tract, Los Angeles County, California.

Source: 2000 Census of Population and Housing

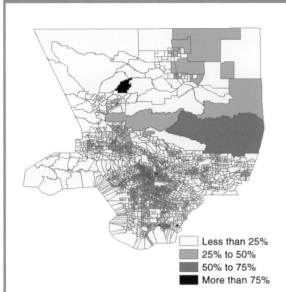

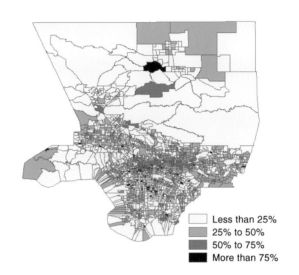

Less than 25%
25% to 50%
50% to 75%
More than 75%

Less than 25%
25% to 50%
50% to 75%
More than 75%

Map 3.5c   Linguistically isolated Spanish speakers by census tract, Los Angeles County, California.

Source: 2000 Census of Population and Housing

Map 3.5d   Linguistically isolated Asian-language speakers by census tract, Los Angeles County, California.

Source: 2000 Census of Population and Housing

Given the rise in the number of foreign-born U.S. residents, it should be no surprise that the number of people speaking a language other than English at home has increased, from 14 percent (31.8 million people) in 1990 to 18 percent (47 million people) in 2000. The majority of these people (55 percent) reported they spoke English "very well." However, a growing minority of the population (8.1 percent of the total in 2000, up from 6.1 percent in 1990) do not (Shin and Bruno 2003, 3). Accommodating people with less than perfect English skills will be increasingly important for local governments. The top ten languages spoken in 2000, along with their rank in 1990, are shown here:

1. Spanish (1)
2. Chinese (5)
3. French (2)
4. German (3)
5. Tagolog (6)

6. Vietnamese (9)
7. Italian (4)
8. Korean (8)
9. Russian (15)
10. Polish (7)

Using the census to analyze demographic and social conditions

Citizenship and year of entry

Citizens are

- people born in the United States or its territories,
- people born abroad of United States citizens, and
- foreign-born people who have naturalized.

All other residents of the United States are noncitizens, but the census does not distinguish among permanent residents, legal temporary residents (such as students or refugees), and undocumented ("illegal") immigrants. Nevertheless, we know that undocumented noncitizens are undercounted. Year of entry to the United States is reported for all noncitizens and naturalized citizens. Many other characteristics, such as linguistic isolation or the likelihood of homeownership, are related to the "cohort" of immigration. These questions were asked in the identical way in 1990, allowing comparability.

Of foreign-born residents who moved to the United States since 1990, only 13 percent have become citizens; 40.3 percent of the total foreign-born population were citizens in 2000, almost identical to the proportion in 1990 (Malone, Baluja, Costanza, and Davis 2003, 2).

Migration

In addition to foreign immigration, the census also reports on population shifts within the United States. Respondents are asked where they lived five years ago. Tables distinguish among

- people living in the same county,
- a different county in the same state, or
- a different state broken down by the four main census regions.

Those living outside the United States are divided by whether they lived

- in Puerto Rico (including movers within Puerto Rico),
- in other U.S. territories and possessions, or
- in a foreign country or at sea.

Tables also show movement among metropolitan areas (MAs), nonmetropolitan areas, and within MAs by central city or suburban locations.

Although there have been minor changes in how missing responses are allocated, this data is comparable with that collected in the 1980 and 1990 Censuses.

State-to-state migration patterns reflect both short-term economic factors, as people follow jobs or move to the suburbs, and longer-term demographic factors, such as the migration of retirees from northeastern and midwestern states to the south and west. Nevada, Arizona, and Georgia were the states with the highest net domestic inmigration from 1995 to 2000; Hawaii, Alaska, and New York had the highest net domestic outmigration (Perry 2003).

However, migration patterns differ when we look at different demographic groups. Young, single, college-educated adults (who were the most likely of any group to have moved during the previous five years) moved to the states with high domestic inmigration, but they also moved disproportionately to states that had net outmigration over the period—California, Alaska, and Maryland. Young educated singles made up a much higher proportion of people who moved to central cities, compared to suburbs or nonmetropolitan areas. They were also much more likely to move to larger metropolitan areas such as New York, Los Angeles, Chicago, and the Washington–Baltimore area, which experienced net outmigration overall (Franklin 2003, 9).

Human capital concepts

Disability

Identifying people with disabilities is an important prerequisite for planning supportive services. Different types of services are needed for people with a self-care disability compared to an employment disability. Census 2000 made significant changes to the way "disability" is defined, to improve the data's usefulness for service providers. More precise information is collected on the nature of the person's disability, and it is collected for all people aged 5 or older, not just those over 15 (box 3.9, later in the chapter, explains these changes in detail).

Householders are asked whether household members 5 years or older have long-term sensory disabilities (blindness, deafness, or severe vision or hearing impairments), or movement disabilities (substantial limits on walking, reaching, lifting, or carrying). A second question asks whether the person has a physical, mental, or emotional condition lasting six months or more that substantially limits any of four categories of activity:

- mental activity
- self-care (such as bathing, eating, or dressing)
- going outside the home alone or
- employment

People are disabled if they are

- five or older and have a sensory, physical, mental, or self-care disability;
- sixteen or older and have a "going outside the home" disability; or
- between 16 and 64 and have an employment disability.

Educational attainment

Educational attainment is an important indicator of the employment prospects of people in a neighborhood. Adults who have not graduated from high school and those who have not completed a college degree have much weaker employment and earnings prospects than those with at least a bachelor's degree.

> Educational attainment has widened the earnings gap considerably from 1975 to 1999. In 1975, full-time, year-round workers with a bachelor's degree earned 1.5 times the wages that someone with a high school diploma only would earn. By 1999, they earned 1.8 times as much. For those with an advanced degree, the ratio increased from 1.8 in 1975 to 2.6 times as much in 1999. The gap widened on the other end, too. People who had not graduated from high school earned 90 percent of high school graduates' wages in 1975, but only 70 percent as much in 1999 (Day and Newburger 2002, 3).

Respondents are asked for the highest level of education completed by each household member 25 or older. High school graduates are those who received a diploma, not all those who completed the twelfth grade. Those who have completed some college but not graduated are shown in two categories:

- "some college credit, less than one year"
- "one or more years of college, no degree"

Professional graduate degrees (in medicine, law, and theology) are classified above master's degrees (such as MSW or MBA). Courses at trade schools or company training are not included in the definition of "educational level," unless they are accepted for credit toward a degree at a regular school or college.

School enrollment

School enrollment is asked for all people 3 years old or older. "Enrolled" people attended a public or private school or college (including nursery school or preschool) between February 1, 2000, and the time of enumeration. Enrollment in a trade or business school, company training, or tutoring, would not count unless the education would be accepted for credit at a regular school or college. Public schools and colleges (supported and controlled by federal, state, or local government, including tribal governments) are distinguished from private ones. For people aged 16 to 19, school enrollment (and high school graduation) is cross-tabulated with employment or service in the armed forces. Box 3.7 explores this data in more detail.

Box 3.7   School enrollment and employment in St. Louis, Missouri

Employment status is closely associated with educational attainment. People who do not graduate from high school are more likely to be unemployed. One census table shows the links among school enrollment, educational attainment, and employment for young adults (those aged 16 to 19). Comparing these factors across places, however, suggests that educational attainment has different consequences for employment depending on where the person lives. Figure 3.2a compares young adults in three counties in the St. Louis metropolitan area: St. Louis City (the inner city of the metro area), the inner-ring suburbs of St. Louis County, and the outer suburbs of St. Charles County.

Young adults living in the inner city are less likely to be enrolled in school, and those not enrolled in school are less likely to be high school graduates. But among those who did graduate from high school, inner city residents are more likely to be unemployed. And, fewer inner city residents that did not graduate from high school are likely to be employed than suburban residents that did not graduate from high school. Although educational attainment affects employment prospects, employment also interacts with residence (and, most likely, race).

Figures 3.2b and 3.2c (next page) compare the experiences of young whites and young African-Americans in the three counties.

The experience of young white adults is fairly similar to that of all people aged 16 to 19—residence really seems to matter in determining employment prospects. One difference is that unemployment rates are lower everywhere for young white high school graduates who are not enrolled in school.

Young African-Americans, however, differ somewhat from the overall picture. The disparities between people growing up in the inner city and in the suburbs are much sharper—St. Charles residents are far more likely to have graduated from high school. However, for the small proportion of African-American St. Charles residents who did not graduate from high school, the job market available appears much worse than the job market available to inner city residents (and worse than the job market available to white non-high-school graduates in the county). Race matters, but it interacts with residence in complex ways.

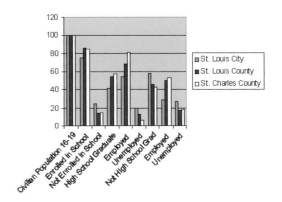

Figure 3.2a   Employment, school enrollment, and residence of young adults 16 to 19, greater St. Louis area, Missouri.

Source: 2000 Census of Population and Housing, Summary File 3

Using the census to analyze demographic and social conditions

Box 3.7 School enrollment and employment in St. Louis, Missouri (continued)

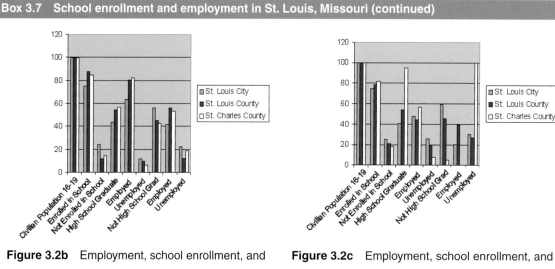

Figure 3.2b Employment, school enrollment, and residence for young whites 16 to 19, greater St. Louis area, Missouri.

Source: 2000 Census of Population and Housing, Summary File 3

Figure 3.2c Employment, school enrollment, and residence for young African-Americans 16 to 19, greater St. Louis area, Missouri.

Source: 2000 Census of Population and Housing, Summary File 3

The individual variables discussed in this section become much more interesting and useful when we consider how characteristics differ among different demographic or economic groups. Table 3.3 shows the available cross-tabulations of data by demographic and economic characteristics.

Other major data sources

Social and demographic data is collected by a wide variety of federal, state, and local agencies. Unfortunately, many databases do not include geographic identifiers, and samples are not always large enough to draw conclusions about the characteristics of people in particular places. This section discusses the major sources of supplementary data and explains how they could be used to supplement census data. Four main types of data are covered:

- demographic data from other Census Bureau surveys and population estimates
- health and vital statistics data from the National Center for Health Statistics and other sources
- rural community data from the Economic Research Service of the U.S. Department of Agriculture
- other social indicators from the U.S. Department of Health and Human Services, Department of Education, and the Federal Bureau of Investigation

In addition to these data sources, census microdata from the Public Use Microdata Sample (PUMS) files allow more detailed manipulation of census data (explained in box 3.8). PUMS are also widely used for transportation and housing analyses. Although microdata is only

	Sex	Age	Race	Hispanic origin	Family type	House-hold type	Disability status
Table 3.3			**Available cross-tabulations of demographic and cultural data**				
Sex by age	P8	P8	P145A-G	P145H-I			
Family or subfamily type		PCT3			PCT4, PCT5, PCT8, PCT9	PCT6, PCT9	
Household type		P11, P12, P13, P146	P146A-G	P146H-I			
Marital status	P18, PCT7	PCT7					
Household size						P14	
Unmarried partners	PCT1						
Nonfamily households	PCT2	PCT2					
Children		P12			P15, P16, P17	P10, P12	
Language and ability		P19, PCT10, PCT13, PCT14	PCT62A-G	PCT11, PCT62H-I			
Place of birth by citizenship			PCT63A-G	PCT63H-I			
Residence in 1995			PCT64A-G	PCT64H-I			
Disability status	P42, PCT26-33	P41, P42, PCT26-32, PCT34	PCT67A-G, PCT68A-G	PCT67H-I, PCT68H-I			
School enrollment	P36, PCT23, PCT24, PCT33	P38, PCT23, PCT24	P147A-G, P149A-G	P147H-I, P149H-I			PCT33
Educational attainment	P37, PCT25	P38, P148, PCT25	P148A-G, P149A-G	P148H-I, P149H-I			PCT33

Note: Relevant Summary File 3 tables are listed for each pair of variables with cross-tabulated data. Variables that are not cross-tabulated have blank cells.

available at very broad spatial scales, the detailed analyses of relationships among variables allow users to estimate answers to questions that could only otherwise be addressed by commissioning special tabulations. A variety of other data available at less detailed spatial scales is summarized in table 3.4.

Box 3.8   Public Use Microdata Sample (PUMS)

Census data is also released as microdata files, enabling researchers to investigate relationships among characteristics without the constraints imposed by the published cross-tabulations. Microdata is made up of individual records for housing units and people. However, to protect confidentiality, only samples of the data are released, at quite broad spatial scales. PUMS data is available as a 5-percent sample for Public Use Microdata Areas (PUMAs), which generally have a population of at least 100,000, and as a 1-percent sample for Super-Public Use Microdata Areas (Super-PUMAs), which are much larger in size (about 400,000 population). Super-PUMAs are composed of contiguous PUMAs and do not cross state lines. For place of residence in 1995 and place of work, data is also reported at the PUMA and Super-PUMA level (U.S. Census Bureau 2003f).

Occupied and vacant housing units, and the group quarters population, are included in the sample. The 5-percent sample includes less detail for each record than the 1-percent sample. Several other methods of disclosure limitation are used to protect confidentiality, including data swapping, top-coding of variables, age perturbation, and collapsing of categories (U.S. Census Bureau 2003f). The samples are stratified and drawn from households and individuals receiving the long form. The two samples are drawn independently and include weights for each record that allow users to estimate the frequency of a particular characteristic or set of characteristics for the population. A

more detailed explanation and example of the use of weights, confidence intervals, and other analytic issues related to PUMS is provided in chapter 6.

PUMS will also be released for the data collected in the American Community Survey and the Supplementary Surveys that precede the full implementation of the ACS. For the Supplementary Surveys, PUMS are only released for entire states; this protects confidentiality while protecting minimum standards of data quality (U.S. Census Bureau 2003e).

Why are microdata useful to someone interested primarily in spatial analysis? For some kinds of questions, census tabulations do not provide enough detail. For instance, if we were interested in the school enrollment, adolescent dropout, and employment rates in families who migrated to the area from another state or country (or families who are linguistically isolated), available cross-tabulations are of little use. However, PUMS could be used to estimate the proportion of children of recent immigrants (or children in linguistically isolated families) who have not completed high school and are not enrolled in school. We could apply those proportions to the neighborhood-level data on immigrant or linguistically isolated families to estimate the number of children in the neighborhood who meet these criteria. The estimates would be approximate, but they would be a reasonable basis on which to plan for supplementary education or employment and training programs.

	Table 3.4 Nonspatial demographic and social data sources		
Data source	**Type of information**	**Spatial descriptors**	**Where can I find this?**
Survey of Program Dynamics	Longitudinal survey (1996–2001) of welfare recipients to analyze the effect of welfare reform (PWORA of 1996). Includes data on education and training, child well-being, family structure, migration, work schedules, childcare and child support, and income and expenditures.	National	www.sipp.census.gov/spd
Emergency Temporary Assistance for Needy Families (TANF) Data Report System	Race of each family member enrolled in TANF system.	States	www.acf.dhhs.gov
Community Service Assurance Reporting System	Service to minorities and people with limited English proficiency by 2,852 hospitals receiving federal grants.	Service area of hospitals covered in system	smelov@os.dhhs.gov
National Study of Assisted Living for the Frail Elderly	Role of assisted living facilities in meeting the needs of elderly people with disabilities.	National	aspe.hhs.gov/daltcp/home.shtml
National Aging Programs Information System	Services delivered under the Older Americans Act, and client profiles by disability status and race/ethnicity.	State and some substate areas	www.aoa.gov/prof/agingnet/NAPIS/napis.asp
National Survey of Homeless Assistance Providers and Clients	Types of programs and services available to homeless persons, and profile of client population.	Sample of seventy-six metropolitan and nonmetropolitan areas	www.census.gov/prod/www/schapc/NSHAPC4.html
Adoption and Foster Care Analysis and Reporting System	Characteristics of children placed in foster care or those adopted with the involvement of the state child welfare agency.	States	www.acf.dhhs.gov/programs/cb
National Child Abuse and Neglect Data System	Information on reports of child abuse and neglect, services provided, perpetrators and agency workforce. Forty states provide more detailed information on the characteristics of victims and their families.	States	www.acf.dhhs.gov/programs/cb
Runaway and Homeless Youth Management Information System	Characteristics and demographics of youth (under 27) served, and services provided by the RHY program.	States and individual grantee agencies	By request to the Family and Youth Services Bureau of the DHHS
Center for Mental Health Services (CMHS) Client/Patient Sample Survey	Demographic, clinical, and service use of clients in a sample of CMHS programs.	National	By request to the Center for Mental Health Services of the DHHS
Survey of Mental Health Organizations, General Hospital Mental Health Services, and Managed Care Organizations	Sample survey of patients served, capacity, funding, and so on.	States	By request to the Center for Mental Health Services of the DHHS

Using the census to analyze demographic and social conditions

Table 3.4 Nonspatial demographic and social data sources (continued)			
Data source	**Type of information**	**Spatial descriptors**	**Where can I find this?**
Drug Abuse Warning Network	Data on drug-related visits to a national sample of hospital emergency departments, and drug-related deaths.	National and forty-eight metropolitan areas	By request to the Substance Abuse and Mental Health Services Administration of the DHHS
Drug and Alcohol Services Information System	Substance abuse treatment programs, services and use, and client-level data on admissions, discharge, and demographics.	States	www.samhsa.gov
National Household Survey on Drug Abuse	Sample of noninstitutionalized population (25,089 in 1998) collecting information on health status, use of services, demographic and socio-economic characteristics, and substance use.	National	www.samhsa.gov

Census population estimates and projections

In each year between decennial censuses, the Census Bureau constructs estimates of the population by age, sex, race, and Hispanic origin. The estimates are based on a cohort-component population estimation model. Cohorts are categories defined by age, sex, race, and Hispanic origin. Cohort-component models estimate the change to each cohort resulting from three different sources (components) of change: birth, death, and migration. Fertility rates are calculated for each cohort of women to estimate the number of births. Cohort-component models are widely agreed to be the soundest method of population estimation and projection. A more detailed description of the precise version of the model the Census Bureau uses is available at *eire.census. gov/popest/topics/methodology/coasro.php.*

Several data sources are used to estimate the size of each component of change. Birth and death certificates cover the obvious. Migration is estimated based on

- Internal Revenue Service data on tax returns,
- Social Security records,
- Medicare enrollment records,
- armed forces data,
- group quarters data, and
- other Census Bureau sources.

It is quite possible to construct your own cohort-component models to project population estimates five or ten years into the future. It probably does not make sense to construct separate estimates of current population. The data the Census Bureau uses to estimate migration is likely far superior to the sources an individual analyst would have access to. Because estimates and projections are based on models, they become progressively less reliable at smaller scales. Constructing estimates at less than the county level (unless the county is very large) is usually a bad idea. Instead, if it is important to adjust tract population, a cruder measure of the tract share of total county change may be less problematic. An example is provided in chapter 5.

Vital statistics and health

Population projections and estimates are based on current vital statistics—data on births and deaths broken down by age, sex, race, or Hispanic origin. The National Center for Health Statistics (NCHS) is the central repository for information on births and deaths. However, state departments of public health may provide more recent data in usable formats, down to the county level. Links to state public health sites may be found at *www.cdc.gov/nchs/about/major/natality/sites.htm.*

County level information on cause of death by age, sex, race, and Hispanic origin helps identify vulnerable populations. Crime, HIV/AIDS, substance abuse, and preventable childhood diseases are examples of public health issues that may affect neighborhoods differently. Analyzing health threats affecting neighborhoods may be the starting point for estimating preventive service needs. A useful source of mortality data by county, the Compressed Mortality File, is available from the Centers for Disease Control at *wonder.cdc.gov/wonder/help/mort.html.*

Two other data sources provide health-related information at the state and county level. The State and Local Area Integrated Telephone Survey (SLAITS), developed by the National Center for Health Statistics, is a random-digit dialing survey based on the sampling frame of the National Immunization Survey, which surveys nearly one million households annually. In addition to standardized questions that provide comparative data across states, agencies can commission specific topics or subgroups of questions. Special topics have included health insurance coverage, child well-being, and access to healthcare. Not all topics are collected for every state. Microdata is available from the SLAITS Web site at *www.cdc.gov/nchs/slaits.htm.*

The Community Health Status Indicators Project provides health and health-related data at the county level, and compares health status among places. The database is available on CD–ROM from the Public Health Foundation at *www.phf.org/data-infra.htm.* It includes information on

- demographic and health characteristics,
- behavioral risks,
- preventive service use,
- access to health resources, and
- estimates of at-risk target populations.

Rural and nonmetropolitan communities

How can analysts generalize or draw meaningful comparisons among different nonmetropolitan areas without subsuming them all into one category? Employment, poverty, or demographic trends may differ significantly among different categories of nonmetropolitan counties. The Economic Research Service (ERS) of the U.S. Department of Agriculture offers several approaches. Two approaches classify counties by population size and by whether they are part of, adjacent to, or remote from a metropolitan area. The Rural-Urban Continuum divides counties into nine categories:

Table 3.5 The Rural–Urban Continuum		
Metropolitan counties	**Nonmetropolitan counties**	
	Adjacent to a metro area	**Not adjacent to a metro area**
1. More than 1,000,000	4. Urban population more than 20,000	7. Urban population more than 20,000
2. 250,000 to 1,000,000	5. Urban population 2,500 to 19,999	8. Urban population 2,500 to 19,999
3. Less than 250,000	6. Urban population less than 2,500	9. Urban population less than 2,500

Source: Economic Research Service. Measuring Rurality: Rural-Urban Continuum Codes. *www.ers.usda.gov/Briefing/Rurality/RuralUrbCon.*

The revised Rural-Urban Continuum Codes reflect the changes made to the definition of metropolitan, urbanized, and rural areas in 2000. An alternative classification is based on the concept of urban influence. The Urban Influence Codes also divide counties into nine categories, but they are defined a little differently:

Table 3.6 Urban Influence Codes			
Metropolitan counties	**Nonmetropolitan counties**		
	Adjacent to a large metro area	**Adjacent to a small metro area**	**Not adjacent to a metro area**
1. Large—in a metro area with more than 1,000,000 people	3. Contains a city of at least 10,000 people	5. Contains a city of at least 10,000 people	7. Contains a city of at least 10,000 people
2. Small—in a metro area with fewer than 1,000,000 people	4. Does not have a city of at least 10,000 people	6. Does not have a city of at least 10,000 people	8. Contains a town of 2,500 to 9,999 people
			9. Does not contain a town of at least 2,500 people

Source: Economic Research Service, USDA. Measuring Rurality: Urban Influence Codes. *www.ers.usda.gov/Briefing/Rurality/UrbanInf.*

Urban Influence Codes may be more useful in states with both large and small metropolitan areas. As of late 2003, they have not yet been updated to reflect changes based on the 2000 Census.

A different approach classifies counties on measures of primary economic activity and other social policy indicators. County Typology Codes distinguish between eleven types of nonmetropolitan counties—six nonoverlapping economic types and five overlapping policy types, shown in table 3.7.

As of early 2004, the typologies have not yet been updated to incorporate 2000 Census data. The typologies provide a convenient way for analysts of statewide or regional trends to summarize local area characteristics.

Table 3.7 County Typology Codes	
Economic types	**Policy types**
Farming-dependent: Counties with 20 percent or more of labor and proprietor's income from farming	Retirement-destination: Counties with 15 percent or more inmigration from people over 60
Mining-dependent: Counties with 15 percent or more of labor and proprietor's income from mining	Federal lands: Counties with 30 percent or more of their land area federally owned
Manufacturing-dependent: Counties with 30 percent or more of labor and proprietor's income from manufacturing	Commuting-dependent: Counties with 40 percent or more of workers working outside their county of residence
Government-dependent: Counties with 25 percent or more of labor and proprietor's income from government	Persistent poverty: Counties with 20 percent or more of all residents in poverty in 1960, 1970, 1980, and 1990
Services-dependent: Counties with 50 percent or more of labor and proprietor's income from services	Transfers-dependent: Counties with 25 percent or more of total personal income derived from transfer payments
Nonspecialized: Remaining counties not classified under any of the above	

Source: Economic Research Service, USDA. Measuring Rurality: County Typology Codes. *www.ers.usda.gov/Briefing/Rurality/ Typology.*

A final resource the Economic Research Service offers is a summary indicator of rural natural amenities (McGranahan 1999). The Natural Amenities Scale is based on six measures—four of them climate-related (warm winter, winter sun, temperate summer, low summer humidity), plus topographic variation, and water area.

Children and families

The Personal Work Opportunity and Responsibility Act of 1996 (the "welfare reform" bill) replaced Aid to Families with Dependent Children (AFDC) with Temporary Assistance to Needy Families (TANF). Since then, agencies have faced the challenge of tracking the outcomes of reform (Weinberg, Huggins, Kominski, and Nelson 1997). The Office of the Assistant Secretary for Planning and Evaluation (ASPE) of the Department of Health and Human Services has sponsored Welfare Outcomes Grants for research on enrollment in the TANF program, including new applicants and those leaving the program, in some states and large counties. To protect the confidentiality of files, researchers must submit a research proposal and sign a confidentiality agreement. Data is available for thirteen states, plus the District of Columbia, and four large counties. More information, including reports on the research completed thus far, is available at *aspe.hhs.gov/hsp/leavers99/datafiles/index.htm.*

The Federal Child Care Information System (FCCIS) reports demographic data on families receiving child care funded by federal sources. The data is available at the county level. Researchers must request access to the data and confidentiality provisions must be agreed to. The Child Care Bureau of the Administration on Children, Youth, and Families of the DHHS is the responsible agency. The Head Start Program Information Report is another potentially useful data source that can be analyzed at the city and state level. The database collects information about the characteristics of children enrolled in the program (including their health and special services received), and their families (including income, employment, and special services received). The Web site is at *www.acf.dhhs.gov.*

Education

The National Center for Education Statistics provides a variety of data, mostly summarized by Area Education Agency but some available at the school district level. Annual school enrollment, school financing, dropout rates, and other indicators of education quality are available at *www.nces.ed.gov/ccd/ccddata.asp.* However, in most cases the best source of detailed data at the school district level will be the relevant state department of education or association of school boards. Data on children with special education or other support needs, children from families with incomes low enough to qualify for school lunch subsidy programs, and educational facilities such as Internet and computer access may all be useful indicators of the relative quality of education and the need for services in particular school districts.

Crime

Uniform Crime Reports are assembled annually by the FBI from more than seventeen thousand law enforcement agencies, including universities and colleges, as well as cities and counties. The easiest way to find reports at the city and county level is through HUD's State of the Cities database (discussed in chapter 5). This database summarizes annual reports of property and violent crimes for each city within a metropolitan area and the surrounding suburbs. The database can be accessed at *socds.huduser.org/FBI/FBI_Home.htm.* For more detailed information on crime, local law enforcement agencies should be able to provide address data that could be geocoded.

Using the census

How can we combine census and other data sources to answer questions about the spatial distribution of particular sorts of people? This section explores two examples of typical analyses in more detail, chosen to demonstrate how spatial analysts can deal with two kinds of spatial definition problems that decennial census data poses:

- Geographic definitions (of tracts, block groups, Traffic Analysis Zones, places, and MSAs) are based on characteristics such as population size and incorporated areas, which change regularly. When geographic boundaries change to reflect this, it is difficult to use the data to determine trends over the decade. Creative strategies are needed to enable comparisons over time when geographic boundaries change.
- Neighborhoods are an important unit for planning analyses, because they are the local scale at which services are provided. Census tracts (with an ideal size of about 4,000 people) are

roughly the size of neighborhood service areas, but census tract boundaries do not necessarily coincide with neighborhood boundaries. Tracts may contain very different populations with different service needs. How can we aggregate census data at a scale that coincides with "real" neighborhood boundaries? Analytic techniques can be used to group areas with similar populations.

Example one: Analyzing trends despite changing census geography

Nevada was one of the fastest-growing states in the nation during the 1990s. But mapping and understanding the dimensions of population change is complicated by the fact that census geographic definitions changed to reflect population growth. As the reader may recall from chapter 1, census tracts are intended to be "small, relatively permanent geographic subdivisions" (U.S. Census Bureau 1997, 1). However, the optimal size for census tracts is 4,000 people, and the maximum size is 8,000. Many census tracts in Nevada (and elsewhere) grew much larger than this maximum during the 1990s. In 2000, Nevada's census geography was split up to form many new census tracts. How can we make sense of trends using geographic indicators that change over time?

Consider the following hypothetical example. A human services agency in Douglas County, Nevada, is writing a grant application to expand services to elderly people with self-care disabilities in the county. Without in-home services, elderly people with self-care disabilities are forced to move to expensive assisted living or nursing home facilities. The agency provides in-home services to clients in a limited area but plans to use grant funds to add more service providers in those places where the potential client population has grown fastest since 1990.

The population aged 65 and older in the county has grown from 3,352 in 1990 to 6,257 in 2000, and it is fair to assume that the service needs of elderly disabled individuals have grown proportionately. However, it is unlikely that growth has been evenly spread throughout the county. The agency faces two challenges in comparing 1990 and 2000 data. First, the definition of disabilities changed significantly in the 2000 Census. Second, the geographic definitions in the county have also changed significantly. How can the agency analyze trends over the decade while accounting for these changes?

The first step will be to understand how census definitions of disabilities have changed and to determine if the information reported in 1990 can be compared with the information for 2000. The wording of the questions in each year is a good starting point. Box 3.9 explains the difference in concepts in more detail.

Once we have determined that the concepts measured in 1990 are similar enough to the concepts measured in 2000 to allow useful comparison, the second step is to deal with the changing geography. The Census Bureau provides Census Tract Relationship files identifying changes in each state. Box 3.10 explains the changes in census tract boundaries in Douglas County between 1990 and 2000.

Using the census to analyze demographic and social conditions

In 1990, the census questionnaire asked the following questions about disabilities:

18. Does this person have a physical, mental, or other health condition that has lasted for 6 or more months and which -

    a.   Limits the kind or amount of work this person can do at a job?

        Yes   No

    b.   Prevents this person from working at a job?

        Yes   No

19. Because of a health condition that has lasted for 6 or more months, does this person have any difficulty -

    a.   Going outside the home alone, for example, to shop or visit a doctor's office?

        Yes   No

    b.   Taking care or his or her own personal needs, such as bathing, dressing, or getting around inside the home?

        Yes   No

The questions were asked for all people aged 15 or older.

In 2000, the questions read as follows:

16. Does this person have any of the following long-lasting conditions:

    a.   Blindness, deafness, or a severe vision or hearing impairment?

        Yes   No

    b.   A condition that substantially limits one or more basic physical activities such as walking, climbing stairs, reaching, lifting, or carrying?

        Yes   No

17. Because of a physical, mental, or emotional condition lasting 6 months or more, does this person have any difficulty in doing any of the following activities:

    a.   Learning, remembering, or concentrating?

    b.   Dressing, bathing, or getting around inside the home?

    c.   (Answer if this person is 16 YEARS OLD OR OVER.) Going outside the home alone to shop or visit a doctor's office?

    d.   (Answer if this person is 16 YEARS OLD OR OVER.) Working at a job or business?

The questions were asked for all people aged 5 or older (except as indicated). An important difference in 2000 was that a more specific question was asked about the nature of the person's disability. In 2000, the definition of "a health condition" was also made more specific to include "a physical, mental, or emotional condition." However, the substance of the question about self-care limitations has remained almost identical; the one difference is that some kinds of "health conditions" (such as an emotional condition) may have been excluded by a respondent in 1990, but not in 2000. We could conclude that 1990-reported numbers of people 65 or older with a self-care limitation could be compared with the number reported in 2000 with the caveat that the identification of a health condi-tion has been made clearer and thus may include more people in 2000 than it did in 1990. This is a minor limitation, however.

Box 3.10   Tracking changes in census tracts from 1990 to 2000

Census Tract Relationship Files are the starting point for understanding tract changes. They can be found at: *www.census.gov/geo/www/relate/rel_tract.html.*

Unfortunately, the files and instructions are not necessarily intuitive. For each state, two files are available showing the relationship between each 1990 tract or part of a tract and each 2000 tract or part of a tract. One of these files uses population to define the relationship, and the other uses street-side mileage. Two additional files are available, listing the 1990 and 2000 tracts that changed significantly (by more than 2.5 percent of its population). These two files are useful to consult to see if the tract(s) you are concerned with have changed, but the relationship files are the ones that help explain the nature of the change.

We will use the population-based relationship file. Download the relevant state files from the above Web site and import the text relationship files into a spreadsheet or database. The files are in fixed-width format, so you will need to consult the record layouts to do this. Record layouts are found in the Web site referenced above. Give the fields names. You will see something that looks like this (we limited the file to just one county in Nevada, Douglas):

	C	D	E	F	G	H	I	J	K	L	M	N	O	P
1	TRACT90	TRSUF90	PTFLAG90	T00POP90TR	PCTPOP90T	STFIPS00	COUNTY00	TRACT00	TRSUF00	PTFLAG00	T00POP00TR	PCTPOP00T	AREAPOP	LANDAI
2	0001	00	P	12880	356	32	005	0001	01		4586	1000	4586	8
3	0001	00	P	12880	299	32	005	0001	02	P	3856	1000	3856	685
4	0005	00	P	12881	0	32	005	0001	02	P	3856	0	0	
5	0001	00	P	12880	343	32	005	0001	03		4423	1000	4423	108
6	0002	98		6631	1000	32	005	0002	00	P	6679	993	6631	172
7	0003	00	P	4081	1	32	005	0002	00	P	6679	0	3	24
8	0004	00	P	2658	17	32	005	0002	00	P	6679	7	45	48
9	0003	00	P	4081	468	32	005	0003	01		1909	1000	1909	57
10	0003	00	P	4081	531	32	005	0003	02		2169	1000	2169	18
11	0004	00	P	2658	983	32	005	0004	00		2613	1000	2613	28
12	0001	00	P	12880	1	32	005	0005	01	P	6938	2	15	
13	0005	00	P	12881	537	32	005	0005	01	P	6938	998	6923	218
14	0001	00	P	12880	0	32	005	0005	02	P	5958	0	0	
15	0005	00	P	12881	463	32	005	0005	02	P	5958	1000	5958	8
16	0006	00		2128	1000	32	005	0006	00		2128	1000	2128	462
17														
18														

Figure 3.3

The left-hand list of tracts are the 1990 tracts. Those marked P in the PTFLAG90 field were split in 2000. Those marked P in the PTFLAG00 field were merged from different parts of tracts in 2000. TOT00POP shows the 2000 population of the tract areas as they were defined in 1990. PCTPOP90 shows the percent of the 1990 tract that was split off to become part of the 2000 tract shown in the right-hand list (the decimal place is missing, so divide by 10 to get the actual percentage). Each record then shows one piece into which tracts would be divided if we overlaid a map of 2000 tracts on one of 1990 tracts and identified each polygon separately.

The relationships shown in the file could be represented schematically as follows:

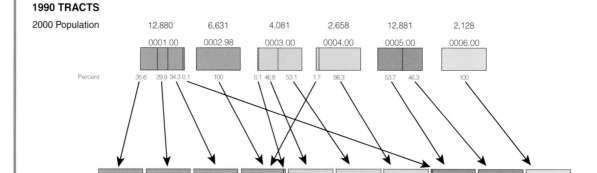

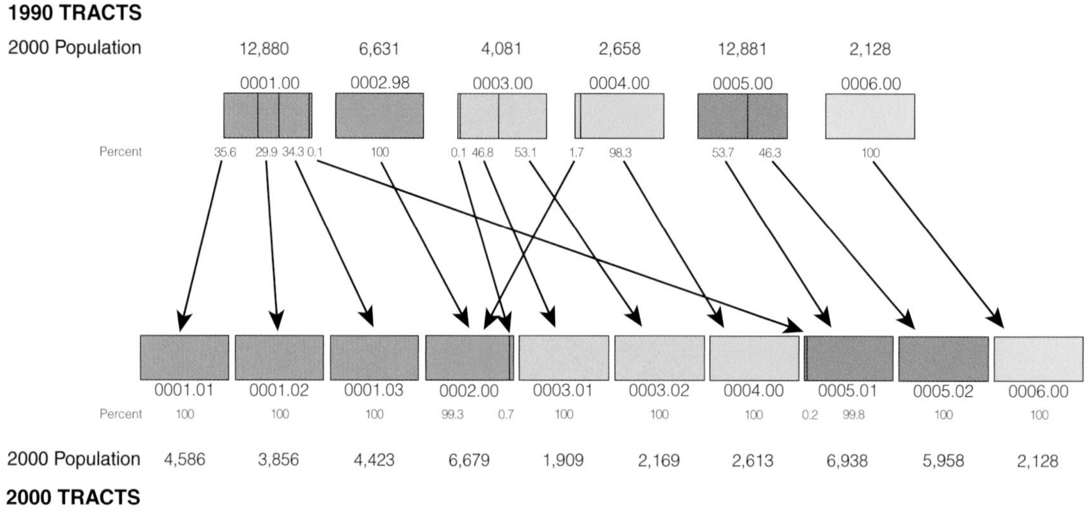

1990 TRACTS

Figure 3.4   Changing census tract definitions, Douglas County, Nevada.

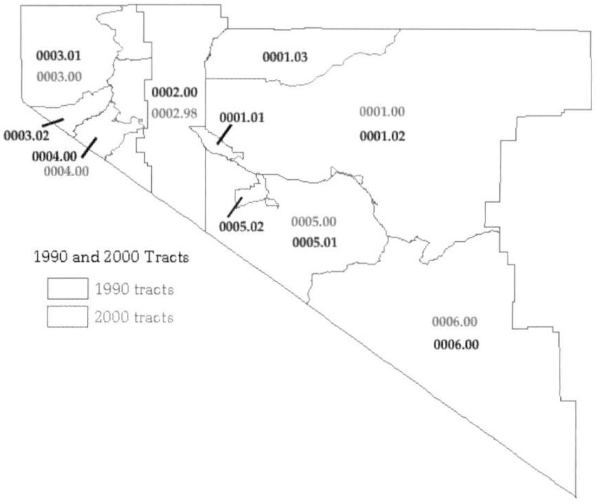

2000 TRACTS

This can be rather confusing, as some splits involved zero percent of the population. There were very minor redrawings of boundaries in these cases. Map 3.6 shows the 1990 tracts overlaid with the 2000 tracts.

Map 3.6   Census tract changes 1990–2000, Douglas County, Nevada.

Source: 1990 and 2000 Census of Population and Housing

As we are concerned with a population rather than a transportation question, the appropriate file is the one that compares changes based on population. We will need the 1990 and 2000 census tract data on self-care disabilities for people 65 and older. For 1990, we can calculate the number of elderly people with a self-care disability for each portion of tracts that were split or merged. Then, from the 2000 data, we can use the 2000 estimate to calculate the proportionate change in potential clients in each tract. Box 3.11 shows the calculations in detail for each tract.

Box 3.11   Estimating population changes from 1990 to 2000

The population-based Census Tract Relationship file enables us to calculate the share of 1990 population characteristics for each of the census tracts defined for 2000. For each 2000 tract, we know the proportion of the 1990 tract that was split or merged to form the new tract. We can use these proportions to estimate the number of people with a particular characteristic—in this case, the number of people 65 and over with a self-care disability. Table 3.8 details these calculations.

Table 3.8   Estimating changes in the population with disabilities

2000 tract	1990 tract	% 1990 tract population in 2000 tract	Elderly with self-care disability 1990	Elderly with self-care disability 2000	Change 1990–2000
0001.01	0001.00	35.6%	18.16 (51 x .356)	79	+60.1
0001.02	0001.00	29.9%	15.25 [(51 x .299)+(39 x 0)]	37	+21.75
	0005.00	0%			
0001.03	0001.00	34.3%	17.49 (51 x .343)	45	+27.5
0002.00	0002.98	100%	12.07 [(12 x 1)+(67 x .001)+ (0 x .017)]	67	+54.9
	0003.00	0.1%			
	0004.00	1.7%			
0003.01	0003.00	46.8%	31.36 (67 x .468)	15	-16.36
0003.02	0003.00	53.1%	35.58 (67 x .531)	0	-35.6
0004.00	0004.00	98.3%	0 (0 x .983)	8	+8
0005.01	0001.00	0.1%	20.99 [(51 x .001)+ (39 x .537)]	97	+76.0
	0005.00	53.7%			
0005.02	0001.00	0%	18.06 [(51 x 0)+(39 x .463)]	49	+30.1
	0005.00	46.3%			
0006.00	0006.00	100%	17 (17 x 1)	34	+17

We can now estimate the tracts where the demand for services has grown fastest (and the tracts where it is likely that demand has declined).

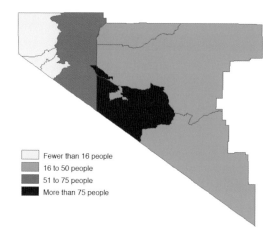

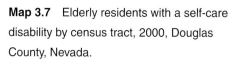

Map 3.7 Elderly residents with a self-care disability by census tract, 2000, Douglas County, Nevada.

Source: 2000 Census of Population and Housing

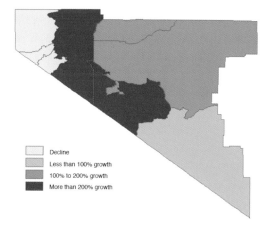

Map 3.8 Change in elderly residents with a self-care disability by census tract, 1990–2000, Douglas County, Nevada.

Source: 1990 and 2000 Censuses of Population and Housing

Map 3.7 shows the number of potential clients in each tract, and map 3.8 shows the proportionate change in their numbers since 1990.

Growth has been most rapid in those tracts that also had the highest number of elderly people with a self-care disability in 2000. The agency has a strong rationale to add service providers in these parts of the county. Identifying these clear trends and demonstrating how they will inform service expansion plans will likely strengthen the agency's application for human services grant funds.

Example two: Identifying the need for "neighborhood-based" services

What is a neighborhood? Sociologists, planners, and community residents are likely to provide quite different definitions. Residents may define their "neighborhood" as narrowly as their street block, while planners are more likely to use "neighborhood" as a synonym for "subarea" or "planning district" (Peterman 2000 provides a useful overview of the concept of "the neighborhood"). In practice, "neighborhoods" are often defined based on census tract boundaries, a convenient if not always accurate basis for defining service needs and targets. However, tracts are not necessarily defined based on social homogeneity. In some cases, a more fine-grained analysis of residential patterns is needed than the simple assumption that census tracts define real neighborhoods.

Consider the following hypothetical problem in Polk County, Iowa, of which Des Moines, the state capital, is the largest city. Immigration and population loss have altered the city's demographic profile—younger racial and ethnic minority families have moved into older neighborhoods abandoned by a previous generation of primarily white suburbanites. Inner city neighborhoods appear to have attracted most of these new families, many of whom are headed by a single parent and are renters.

A social service agency is planning to develop an after-school enrichment program aimed at children in lower-income minority families. How should they design and deliver both their outreach program and the services they provide? Would services be most accessible if they were neighborhood-based? If so, how should neighborhoods be defined? How should priority neighborhoods be chosen? The agency needs to answer the following questions:

- Where do lower-income minority families live? Are they concentrated in particular neighborhoods?
- Are there contiguous or clustered neighborhoods in which services should be located to reach the greatest number of children?

Our first task is to identify places where relatively high proportions of target children live. As we have seen, the census provides a rich array of information on school enrollment, income, family type, and the relationship among these characteristics and basic demographic characteristics such as age, race, and Hispanic origin. However, much of this information is obtained from the sample questionnaire asked of about one in six residents, and thus it is only available at the tract and the block group level. Using sample-based information is likely to trap us in a set of assumptions about how target families are distributed across the city. A better strategy for this problem may be to use the information collected from every household, which is available down to the block level.

Three characteristics provide the basis for an analysis that could be performed at a fine-grained spatial scale. The median age of residents will identify those places with high proportions of children and young families. Race is available for everyone. Identifying lower-income households is impossible using nonsample data, but renter households can be identified. Renters are more likely to be lower-income, and the proportion of renters could be used as a substitute for income or poverty. Cluster analysis is used to identify how these three characteristics are associated at three different spatial scales—the census tract, the block group, and the block. Cluster analysis is a useful technique that enables us to group areas based on their similarity on several dimensions. Box 3.12 explains the cluster analysis used to group tracts in more detail. Map 3.9 shows the location of the "clusters" of tracts the analysis identifies.

The three dimensions used to cluster tracts—median age, percent of residents identifying themselves as a racial minority, and percent of renters (as an indicator of economic stability)—appear to do a reasonably good job of identifying different types of "neighborhoods" at the tract level. One test of the adequacy of a cluster analysis is to examine variables that were not used to develop the clusters. If there are statistically significant differences among the clusters for these other variables, then the analysis is probably meaningful. The table in box 3.12 shows that tract-based clusters do not distinguish all other resident characteristics equally well. There is still significant diversity within tracts. Are neighborhoods indeed as "integrated" and diverse as the

Box 3.12   Cluster analysis of census tracts

Cluster analysis is a multivariate technique that groups cases based on their similarity to one another on the chosen variables. It may be easiest to think of it as a multidimensional cross-tabulation. To be grouped together, cases must be similar on all of the variables used to define the cluster. This makes it especially useful for analyses of complex "objects" such as neighborhoods or living environments.

Cluster analysis was performed using three variables: the percent of people describing themselves as minority, the proportion of renters, and the median age of the population. Several clustering options were explored, but a four-group cluster produced the most consistent results across all geographic levels. Two clusters had a predominately white population; one of these had a somewhat older population, and a lower than average proportion of renters. The other predominately white cluster had a higher than average proportion of renters (although there are still many homeowners in this neighborhood).

The other two clusters had much higher than average proportions of minority residents. Of these, one had more than two-thirds of its households renting. In the other cluster, about three out of five households owned their own home.

The usefulness of the clusters was explored by cross-tabulating other variables across the groups; in many cases, the variables were significantly related to the clusters. Table 3.9 shows the results of the cluster analysis performed for census tracts. Variables in bold were used to define the clusters. The remainder of the table shows the differences among the clusters on several other dimensions. Statistical significance (the probability that differences among categories are due to chance) is reported in the table note.

Table 3.9 Cluster analysis of tracts				
Resident characteristics	**White owners**	**White renters**	**Minority owners**	**Minority renters**
% minorities	**6.4**	**12.8**	**71.4**	**41.4**
% renters	**20.0**	**44.0**	**40.7**	**68.9**
median age	**37.0**	**32.4**	**29.6**	**30.5**
% Hispanic**	2.7	6.6	14.0	12.6
% under 18*	25.3	23.9	34.1	25.3
% 65 and older	12.8	10.8	9.4	10.9
% family households**	69.2	58.0	69.0	42.7
% single-mother families**	7.8	13.4	24.5	23.4
% married couple with children families*	36.4	32.7	27.1	28.4
average household size*	2.5	2.3	3.0	2.4
average family size**	3.0	3.0	3.6	3.3
Notes: (1) ** = probability < .001 * = probability < .01. (2) Variables in bold-face were used to cluster tracts.				

Unlocking the census with GIS

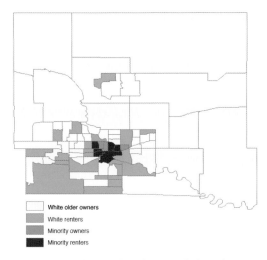

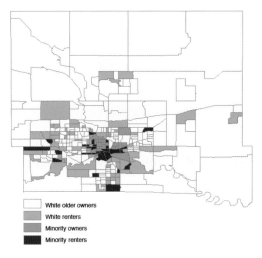

Map 3.9 Analyzing the characteristics of census tracts, Polk County, Iowa.

Source: Calculated from 2000 Census of Population and Housing, SF1

Map 3.10 Analyzing the characteristics of block groups, Polk County, Iowa.

Source: Calculated from 2000 Census of Population and Housing, SF1

tract profile suggests, or are the tracts defined so broadly that they incorporate many different communities?

Map 3.10 explores this question. The same variables were used to cluster block groups (see box 3.13). This is a somewhat different picture than is presented in map 3.9. "Neighborhoods" with predominately minority renters are dispersed over a wider area when we consider characteristics at the block group level rather than the tract level.

But are block groups providing a sufficiently fine level of detail? Map 3.11 shows clusters of blocks with the different characteristics. The clusters of blocks are far more sharply defined statistically than either block groups or tracts. They have far less diversity than clusters at cruder spatial scales, and there are significant differences among the clusters of blocks, as the table in box 3.14 shows.

Blocks may provide a better basis for defining outreach and service provision areas. The characteristics of the population in the "minority younger renters" cluster—more children, more single-mother headed families, and fewer homeowners—are similar to those of the children the agency plans to serve. While a tract-level analysis suggested there is a compact, quite clearly defined "neighborhood" with these characteristics, the block-level analysis suggests a much more dispersed pattern of need. In fact, the block level analysis suggests that an exclusively "neighborhood-based" approach may be misguided. Given the staff costs involved in outreach and services, trying to serve children where they live may require too dispersed a strategy. Instead, a centralized program that provides transportation to one location may reach the largest share of the targeted group. By avoiding assumptions about the correct spatial level at which to estimate need, the agency has avoided an expensive mistake.

These examples demonstrate the role that spatial analysis can play in refining and improving our interpretation of the rich array of social and demographic information the census offers. GIS analysis promises to cast new light on traditional public policy and planning decisions that have often been based on unclear assumptions about the role that space plays.

Box 3.13   Cluster analysis of block groups

The same variables (the percent of people describing themselves as minority, the proportion of renters, and the median age of the population) were used to explore clusters of block groups. Table 3.10 shows the results of the cluster analysis performed for census tracts. Variables in bold were used to define the clusters. The remainder of the table shows the differences among the clusters on several other dimensions. Statistical significance (the probability that differences among categories are due to chance) is reported in the table note.

The clusters defined for block groups were fairly similar in profile to those defined for tracts. Only one of the additional variables tested was not significantly different among clusters: the proportion of residents 65 or older.

Table 3.10 Cluster analysis of block groups				
Resident characteristics	**White owners**	**White renters**	**Minority owners**	**Minority renters**
% minorities	**6.2**	**11.4**	**60.7**	**24.9**
% renters	**14.0**	**38.0**	**41.0**	**73.0**
median age	**37.4**	**34.2**	**29.2**	**33.8**
% Hispanic**	2.6	5.4	17.0	9.6
% under 18**	25.2	23.9	33.5	19.5
% 65 and older	13.0	11.4	8.9	13.4
% family households**	71.2	59.6	67.7	39.8
% single-mother families**	7.6	11.9	24.7	19.0
% married couple with children families**	25.5	20.3	19.1	11.3
average household size**	2.5	2.4	2.9	2.0
average family size**	3.0	3.0	3.5	2.9
Notes: (1) ** = probability <.001. (2) Variables in bold-face were used to cluster tracts.				

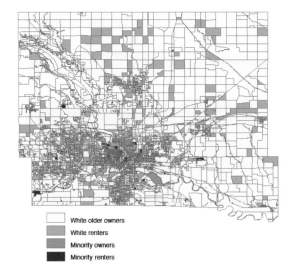

White older owners
White renters
Minority owners
Minority renters

Map 3.11 Analyzing the characteristics of blocks, Polk County, Iowa.

Source: Calculated from 2000 Census of Population and Housing, SF1

Box 3.14 Cluster analysis of blocks

Once more, the same variables were used to analyze clusters among census blocks. Table 3.11 shows the block-level clusters are the sharpest; the differences among the four groups of tracts are very clear. At both the block group and the tract level, two categories—white renters and minority owners—are ambiguous. Although a group of tracts with a high proportion of minorities also has a home-ownership rate higher than average for minority households, there are still a significant share of renters in the group. At the block level analysis, this is not the case.

Table 3.11 Cluster analysis of blocks				
Resident characteristics	**White owners**	**White renters**	**Minority owners**	**Minority renters**
% minorities	**5.0**	**9.1**	**61.3**	**62.2**
% renters	**8.8**	**68.9**	**24.1**	**83.6**
median age	**39.1**	**35.0**	**32.7**	**28.7**
% Hispanic**	2.2	3.7	17.7	18.9
% under 18**	24.8	20.4	30.6	29.3
% 65 and older**	13.1	11.6	11.1	6.6
% family households**	75.7	51.0	71.7	64.2
% single-mother families**	6.5	15.8	16.1	27.7
% married couple with children families**	37.2	29.0	33.0	29.1
average household size**	2.6	2.2	3.1	2.8
average family size**	3.0	2.7	3.6	3.3
Notes: (1) ** = probability <.001. (2) Variables in bold-face were used to cluster tracts.				

Box 3.14   Cluster analysis of blocks (continued)

The additional variables tested are all significantly related to the groups of blocks. Blocks with high proportions of minorities and a majority of renters are different from predominately white majority renter blocks—they are more likely to contain family households, have a higher share of people under 18, and have a lower share of people 65 or older. They are also the areas where mother-headed families are most likely to live.

Chapter 4

Using the **census**
to **analyze economic conditions**

Economic indicators are at the heart of many of our policy decisions. From the dramatic effects that quarterly unemployment estimates have on politician approval ratings, to the use of poverty rates to identify target neighborhoods for a plethora of antipoverty programs, economic data is key. Income, employment, and poverty rates define much of our understanding of particular places. But where does this data come from? How is it constructed? How should we use it?

Economic development planners need to target redevelopment incentives to those locations where unemployment and poverty are the greatest problems. They would need to identify target neighborhoods based on questions such as the following:

- Where are unemployment rates highest?
- Where do people in poverty live?
- What are average earnings in neighborhoods that have seen high rates of job loss?

Human services agencies developing welfare-to-work initiatives such as job-training programs need to understand the link between human resource development and employment prospects. Questions they would need to ask include

- Which occupations have seen the fastest growth in the region over the past decade?
- What are the skill requirements of entry-level jobs in those occupations?
- Where do current welfare recipients live, and how does this compare to where the fastest growth in accessible jobs has occurred?

Developers exploring the market potential for a retail development would assess the feasibility of a prospective project by investigating the following questions:

- What is the income distribution and family structure of households within the market area of the proposed development?
- How many local area residents would be in the labor market pool on which the development would draw?
- How many competing stores are there in the local market area, and what proportion of regional sales do they capture?

Decennial census data, along with other sources of economic data, provides a starting point for all these questions. Unlike social and demographic data, which is only systematically collected at the federal level every decade, economic data is collected in a wider variety of formats and time periods. The decennial Census of Population and Housing is one (but not the only) source. The decennial census collects economic information about people based on where they live. The Economic Census, in contrast, collects information about businesses based on where the firms do business. It is conducted every five years, in years ending in two or seven. A series of monthly surveys conducted by the Census Bureau and the Bureau of Labor Statistics provide yet another source of "official" data on economic trends. Some of these are based on where people live, and some are based on where they work.

Major economic variables in the Census of Population and Housing

The economic variables in the decennial census are based on the "long form," a questionnaire completed by about 17 percent of households (although sampling rates differ depending on the size and type of place). Chapter 1 dealt with sampling approaches and accuracy, and standard errors and confidence intervals are dealt with in some detail in chapter 6. If absolute precision is important, analyses should be based on these confidence intervals. For most analyses, the "estimates" based on the sample should be adequate. If an issue is highly politicized (such as which neighborhood has more children under 5 living in poverty) confidence intervals would obviously provide more defensible results.

Underreporting, misreporting, and other nonsampling sources of error affect all data, not just the sample data. Data based on the sample questions are reported down to the block group level only, because estimates become less accurate at finer levels of detail. Some cross-tabulations of sample data by detailed demographic characteristics are reported only to the census tract level. The discussion that follows draws heavily on the Census Bureau's definition of variables (U.S. Census Bureau 2003a, chapter 7).

Income in 1999

Income questions are asked of the sample population 15 and older. Total census income:

Includes:	But excludes:
gross earnings (wages or salary, self-employment income)	capital gains
interest and dividends	money from the sale of property, unless selling property was the person's business
rents and royalties	"in kind" income from food stamps, housing assistance, medical care, and so on
trusts and estates	loans
Social Security or retirement, survivor or disability pensions	tax refunds
Supplemental Security Income (SSI)	support from family members living in the household
public assistance or welfare payments	gifts and lump-sum inheritances
other sources not excluded	other lump-sum amounts

Income is reported for the previous full year for households, families, and individuals. Household (or family) income includes that of all members of the household (or family) aged 15 or older. However, earnings are only reported for people aged 16 or older. Box 4.1 explains the various combinations of people for which income is reported. Households and families are defined by their living arrangements in April 2000, while income data is for 1999. In households (or families) where an earner had moved out by April 2000, reported income would be less than actual income in 1999, and vice versa. However, this affects only a small number of households and families.

Underreporting is more likely for "unearned" income-interest, dividends, and net rental income, or for public assistance. The Census Bureau uses procedures to correct for these deficiencies based on responses to other questions about employment and other characteristics. Income-related questions have varied slightly in their wording since 1970. Two changes occurred for the 2000 Census: (1) self-employment income no longer distinguishes between farm and nonfarm sources, and (2) income from Supplemental Security Income is now distinguished from public assistance income.

Extreme caution should be used in comparing census-reported income with other sources. It differs in important ways:

- IRS-reported income for tax purposes includes several sources (capital gains, for instance) that the census excludes, and people with very low incomes are exempted from filing tax returns, but not from completing the census.
- Social Security Administration earnings data is based on employer's reports and tax returns of self-employed people. It excludes some classes of workers and thus is not comparable to census income data.

Box 4.1   Measuring income

Income is reported for several different arrangements of people. The following chart compares commonly used measures of income for the Jackson, Mississippi, metropolitan area:

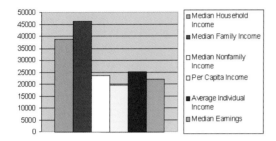

Figure 4.1   Measures of income in Jackson, Mississippi

Households include single people as well as large families, so median household income is usually lower than median family income. "Nonfamily" households include a greater share of single-person households, so we would expect their median incomes to be lower still than median household incomes. The calculation of median income for households and families includes those with no income in the previous year.

However, average individual income is based only on people aged 15 or older who had some income (an aggregate is provided; the average is calculated here). In contrast, per capita income is the mean income calculated for every person (including children). It may provide a better measure of the relative wealth or poverty of a community, because it eliminates differences that can stem from household structure.

• The Bureau of Economic Analysis of the Department of Commerce publishes income data based on business and government sources, and as with tax data the concept is defined differently than it is in the census.

Thus, census income data is merely one of several sources that could be used to estimate local area incomes. Which is preferable depends on the purposes for which it is to be used. The only comparable source is the Current Population Survey (CPS). This is the appropriate source for updating decennial data until the ACS is fully phased in (see the section of this chapter on "other sources").

Poverty status in 1999

Poverty status is calculated from questions about income. Poverty measures are important tools for determining eligibility or priority needs for a wide variety of federal programs, from Head Start and the National School Lunch Program (NSLP) to the Low Income Home Energy Assistance Program (LIHEAP). The poverty threshold (poverty "level" is a widely used but less precise term) is defined nationwide by the federal government.

Poverty thresholds differ for different types of households. A three-person family with no children would have a lower poverty threshold ($13,032) than a family of one adult and two children ($13,423). A person aged 65 or older would have a lower poverty threshold than a younger person. For people living in families, total family income is used to decide whether they

Poverty thresholds were originally based on assumptions about food expenditures. Now, current poverty thresholds are revised annually to reflect changes in the Consumer Price Index (CPI) (Fisher 1997). Because the threshold is not adjusted for regional, state, or local variations in the cost of living, many federal programs base program eligibility on the area median income instead. The U.S. Department of Health and Human Services uses a different version of the measure; "poverty guidelines" simplify poverty thresholds and use different standards for Alaska and Hawaii, two high-cost states. More information on poverty guidelines is available at the Department of Health and Human Services Web site, *aspe.hhs.gov/poverty/contacts.htm.*

Box 4.2 Comparing poverty rates in Houston, Texas

Poverty rates differ for different categories of people. Figure 4.2 shows 1999 poverty rates for different categories of individuals, families, and households in Houston. Proportionately more individuals are poor than families or households. Children are more likely to be poor than elderly people. Married couples with children are the least likely of any group to be poor, but nearly one third of families headed by a single woman with children are poor.

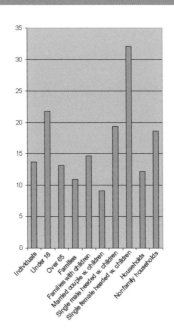

Figure 4.2 Percentage in poverty in Houston, Texas

are in poverty or not. For those living in nonfamily households, the decision is based on the individual's, not the household's, income.

However, poverty status is reported for different types of households, based on the poverty status of the householder. Thus, a household composed of an elderly woman with an income below poverty level and two lodgers who have above-poverty level incomes would be classified as a household in poverty, although not all of its members are. Similarly, a subfamily with an income below poverty level would not be identified as a household in poverty if the householder had an income above the poverty threshold. However, individual poverty counts would include the elderly woman only in the first household, and the subfamily members in the second household. Counts of individuals in poverty are thus more reliable than counts of households in poverty. Box 4.2 compares poverty rates for different combinations of individuals, families, and households in Houston, Texas.

Poverty status is not determined for people in

- institutions;
- military group quarters;
- college dormitories; or
- for unrelated individuals in a household aged 15 or younger, who are most often foster children.

Other people living in noninstitutional group quarters (such as boarding houses and homeless shelters) would be included in the count. Because the poverty threshold is so low, the Census Bureau also reports people in increments above and below the threshold.

Employment and labor force status

Employment questions only include people 16 years or older. Unlike the income questions, employment questions ask people about their experience during a "reference week," the calendar week prior to the week the survey was completed. Employed people include those

- who worked at any time for pay during the reference week,
- who did more than fifteen hours of unpaid work for a family business or farm, and
- who were temporarily absent from work (for vacation or illness for example) but not laid off.

Unemployed people include

- the temporarily laid off who expected to return to their job within six months (or at a specific date) and who were available for work during the reference week, and
- those who did not have a job but were actively looking for work during the reference week or the previous three weeks and were available for work.

The "labor force" includes both employed and unemployed people. A subcategory, the civilian labor force, would not include people on active duty in the U.S. armed forces. The labor force does not include

- people involved in unpaid work around the home, such as childcare or home repairs, or unpaid volunteer work, unless they were actively seeking work and available for employment;
- full-time students without a job and not seeking a job;
- seasonal workers interviewed in the off-season who were not looking for work;
- people in institutions, even though they may have worked during the reference week, perhaps in a sheltered employment program;
- people who did incidental unpaid work for a family business or farm (fewer than fifteen hours).

The distinction between unemployed people and those not in the labor force rests on the definition of "job-seeking" activities. These include

- registering at an employment office,
- meeting with prospective employers,
- investigating possibilities for opening a business or professional practice,
- placing or answering advertisements,
- writing letters of application, or
- being on a union or professional register.

"Discouraged workers" are a more difficult group to identify. People who have given up searching after long periods of unemployment would no longer be in the labor force. Analyses comparing local and regional labor force participation rates for different demographic groups should supplement comparisons of unemployment rates to ensure that these "hidden" unemployed are considered.

Employment may be understated by people who have irregular or unstructured jobs. The number of people reporting they were "at work" during the reference week is probably overstated, and the number "with a job, not working" is likely understated. Reference weeks differ, so we may not have a consistent picture of employment, unlike the Current Population Survey, which always refers to the same week. Questions about employment have been asked in similar ways since the 1970 Census.

Census employment data differs from other employment data. The Current Employment Statistics (CES) survey counts people employed at each establishment. A person with two jobs could be counted twice. Some types of workers—private household workers and the self-employed—are excluded. People under 16 may be included in CES employment counts. The most important difference is that the census counts people where they live, while establishment-based data counts them where they work.

Estimates of unemployment based on compensation claims are also different from census estimates. They exclude

- people who have exhausted their benefits but are still looking for work;
- new workers who are not yet eligible for benefits; and
- those who lose jobs not covered by unemployment insurance, such as domestic servants, farm laborers, or the self-employed.

However, these estimates may include people who worked only a few hours during the week, if they are eligible for benefits. The census would count these people as "employed." Claims may also be filed in a different place than the worker's residence.

Box 4.3 Employment status and work status in Albuquerque, New Mexico

It is easy to confuse "employment status" (whether someone worked in the reference week) with "work status" (whether the person worked at any time during the previous year). Figure 4.3 compares the two concepts.

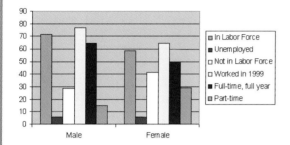

Figure 4.3 Employment status and work status in Albuquerque, New Mexico

In each case, the same number of people is used to calculate proportions. The number of people in the labor force in April 2000 is determined by the number of people employed or looking for work (this chart includes people in the armed forces as well as the civilian labor force, so the definition is consistent with the definition of work in the previous year). A higher proportion of people worked in 1999 than were in the labor force in 2000. This may be accounted for by people who retired in the interim, discouraged workers who are not defined as "unemployed" because they were not actively seeking work, or those who work seasonally and were neither working in April 2000 nor looking for work.

A higher proportion of men than women are in the labor force, and men are more likely than women to work full-time, full year (fifty to fifty-two weeks, including paid vacation). In part, this probably reflects the fact that women are more likely to leave the labor force while raising young children. However, the population sampled includes all those aged 16 and older. There are more elderly women than elderly men, so at least some of the difference also reflects the larger proportion of women who are retired.

Work status in 1999

In contrast to employment questions, work status questions ask about work history during the previous full year. Box 4.3 explains the difference between "employment status" and "work status" in more detail. People 16 or older who worked at least one week during the year are classified as "worked in 1999." "Work" is defined as it is in the employment questions, so it does not include unpaid work in the home (a source of continuing bitterness, perhaps, to many an overworked at-home parent). Service in the armed forces counts as work.

Full-time, year-round workers are those usually working thirty-five hours a week or more, at least fifty weeks of the year. There may be some underreporting by people who worked for very short periods, and because some people exclude paid vacation time from their weeks worked. The data is comparable back to the 1960 Census. "Workers" are defined differently in some related tables, such as journey to work and class of worker, which refer to employment during the reference week, not work status during the previous year. Care should be taken that the precise definition is understood.

Place of work

People who worked at some time during the reference week are asked for the exact address (or nearest street or intersection), place, whether the place was inside city limits, and the county, state (or country), and ZIP Code of the job. For people with more than one job, it would be the location of the job where they worked the most hours. People who worked in several locations are asked for the place where they began their workday. People with jobs but not at work in the reference week are not included, so "place of work" does not necessarily reflect total local employment.

Box 4.4 Workplace and regional economies

Many residents of rural and nonmetropolitan places commute long distances to work in metropolitan areas. The example of northeastern Nebraska illustrates what county of work and place of work data might suggest about regional economies. Map 4.1a shows the proportion of employed county residents who work within and outside their county of residence and the share that work outside the state.

Among workers in Dakota County (adjacent to the Sioux City, Iowa, MSA), nearly half work in Iowa rather than Nebraska. Counties along the northern border with South Dakota, and further south along the Iowa border, have some workers commuting out of state. Burt County, which borders the Omaha MSA, has a fair amount of commuting out of the county. However, the counties with the highest out-of-county commuting rates, Stanton and Pierce, are fairly remote from the Omaha MSA. People here appear to be commuting instead to neighboring nonmetropolitan counties with stronger labor markets.

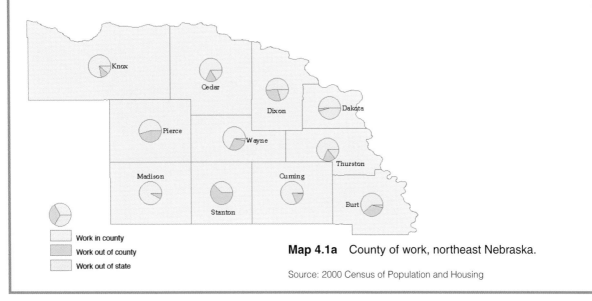

Map 4.1a County of work, northeast Nebraska.

Source: 2000 Census of Population and Housing

Work in county
Work out of county
Work out of state

Box 4.4   Workplace and regional economies (continued)

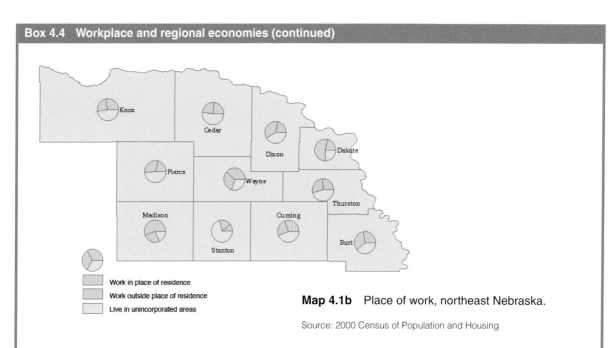

Map 4.1b   Place of work, northeast Nebraska.

Source: 2000 Census of Population and Housing

Map 4.1b examines the share of workers employed in the place where they live. In Stanton County, a majority of employees live in unincorporated areas. Of those that live in a city, only a tiny share work there too. An exception to this pattern is Madison County, which has a larger town (Norfolk). This is the single county where a majority of people work in the place they live. The majority of working people in Nebraska must travel outside their place of residence to find employment, reflecting a regional economy centered on a few larger cities and towns, which depend in part on a large rural labor force.

Place of work is summarized by whether people worked within or outside the county, place, state, or metropolitan area where they lived. Box 4.4 illustrates the concept in rural Nebraska. Within metropolitan areas, places inside or outside the central city are distinguished. For residents of twelve selected states, place of work is also shown by the Minor Civil Division (MCD) (usually cities, towns, and townships) of their home.

Place of work questions were asked in similar ways since the 1980s, but only since 1990 have they been asked of the full sample. Place of work is the basis for other questions about the journey to work, which are explained in chapter 6.

In many situations we need to know not where workers live but where they work. The Census Bureau also re-organizes place of work information in this way and summarizes it in relation to the place of work. This is published as a separate data set, the Census Transportation Planning Package (CTPP). The CTPP shows the spatial distribution of jobs. We use this data set in the first example in this chapter.

Industry and occupation

Industry and occupation data have many uses. Analysts can use it to

- track labor force trends in local, state, and national economies;
- assess equal employment opportunity in different industries and occupations, enabling employers to develop affirmative action plans;
- identify local industrial clusters;
- identify hazardous industries in the local economy.

"Industry" describes the type of activity at a person's place of work, while "occupation" describes the type of work that a person does. For instance, a single factory may forge metals. All employees, no matter what they actually do, will be classified as working in the metal forging industry. Some may be metal furnace tenders, others lathe setters, others secretaries or foremen, and so on. However, each person also will be classified by his or her occupation, which reflects the work actually done in the plant. To complicate matters further, the single factory (or "establishment") may also be part of a larger enterprise engaged in other types of industries. This is discussed further in the section on the economic censuses. For the purposes of the decennial Census of Population and Housing, a person's "industry" is determined by the type of activity in the place of work (usually, this is the establishment level).

Industry, occupation, and class of worker are reported for the job held during the reference week, or the most recent job of an unemployed person. Like "place of work," industry and occupation are also limited by the fact that they refer to the "primary" job, not all jobs held.

The classification system for both industry and occupation changed dramatically in 2000. Industries, previously classified by the fourteen-category SIC (Standard Industrial Classification) code, are now classified by the twenty-category NAICS (North American Industrial Classification System) code. Both systems are hierarchical, meaning that sectors of the economy are broken down into increasingly narrow subsectors. Box 4.5 explains the SIC system.

The SIC divisions are based on an economy structured around producing and transporting goods. However, we no longer live in that sort of economy. Apart from the fact that the production of many goods has moved to lower-cost labor regions (manufacturing accounts for fewer than 20 percent of jobs), the real drivers of the modern world economy are more abstract. The production and distribution of information—through software development, the creation of hedge and derivative financial products, or nightly news and talk shows—adds far more "value" to the economy than the production of the TV sets or computers that deliver the information. This is the change that NAICS seeks to capture.

NAICS was jointly developed by Canada, Mexico, and the United States to replace each of those countries' old systems. A standardized classification system across the three countries was needed to simplify some of the provisions of the North American Free Trade Agreement (NAFTA) treaty. Moreover, for higher-level groupings, NAICS statistics conform to the latest revision of the United Nations International Standard Industrial Classification (ISIC, Revision 3).

Box 4.5 The Standard Industrial Classification system

The Standard Industrial Classification (SIC) system breaks an economy down into eleven divisions:

Table 4.1 SIC code divisions and included major groups	
Division	**Included major groups**
A—Agriculture, forestry, and fishing	Major groups 01–02, 07–09
B—Mining	Major groups 10, 12–14
C—Construction	Major groups 15–17
D—Manufacturing	Major groups 20–39
E—Transportation, communications, electric, gas, and sanitary services	Major groups 40–49
F—Wholesale trade	Major groups 50–51
G—Retail trade	Major groups 52–59
H—Finance, insurance, and real estate	Major groups 60–65, 67
I—Services	Major groups 70, 72–73, 75–76, 78–84, 86–89
J—Public administration	Major groups 91–98
K—Nonclassifiable establishments	Major group 99
Note: Standard Industrial Classification 1987, see U.S. Office of Management and Budget (1987).	

Major groups are sometimes called two-digit sectors, and they are further broken down into constituent industry groups (three-digit) and industries (four-digit). The following example shows the hierarchical logic of this arrangement:

Table 4.2 Example of SIC hierarchy			
Division	**Major group**	**Industry group**	**Industry**
D—Manufacturing	20. Food and kindred products	201. Meat products	2011. Meat packing plants 2013. Sausages and other prepared meat products 2015. Poultry slaughtering and processing

The SIC manual describes the precise activities of each industry (U.S. Office of Management and Budget 1987).

Box 4.6   NAICS

There are twenty sectors in the NAICS and 1,170 detailed industries for the United States

The main "divisions" in NAICS are called "sectors" and are defined by two-digit codes. "Subsectors" perform the same functions as "major groups" in the SIC system.

Table 4.3 NAICS sectors and included subsectors	
Sector	**Included subsectors**
11—Agriculture, forestry, fishing, and hunting	Subsectors 111–115
21—Mining	Subsectors 211–213
22—Utilities	Subsector 221
31, 32, 33—Manufacturing	Subsectors 311–316, 32–327, 331–337, 339
42—Wholesale trade	Subsectors 421–422
44, 45—Retail trade	Subsectors 441–448, 451–454
48, 49—Transportation and warehousing	Subsectors 481–488, 491–493
51—Information	Subsectors 511–514
52—Finance and insurance	Subsectors 521–525
53—Real estate and rental and leasing	Subsectors 531–533
54—Professional, scientific, and technical services	Subsector 541
55—Management of companies and enterprises	Subsector 551
56—Administrative and support and waste management and remediation services	Subsectors 561–562
61—Education services	Subsector 611
62—Health care and social assistance	Subsectors 621–624
71—Arts, entertainment, and recreation	Subsectors 711–713
72—Accommodation and food services	Subsectors 721–722
81—Other services (except public administration)	Subsectors 811–813
92—Public administration	Subsectors 921–928

The most important change NAICS introduced was to split the single "services industries" SIC sector into eight separate sectors (51, 54, 56, 61, 62, 71, 72, 81) (U.S. Office of Management and Budget 1998). An interesting illustration is to consider how the new NAICS sector, 71 (arts, entertainment, and recreation) was dealt with in the SIC system. In SIC Division I, services, subsector 79 (amusement and recreation services) we find the following industry groups:

Box 4.6   NAICS (continued)

- 791—Dance studios, schools and halls
- 792—Theatrical producers (except motion picture), bands, orchestras, and entertainers
    - 7922—Theatrical producers (except motion picture)
    - 7929—Bands, orchestras, and entertainers
- 793—Bowling centers
- 794—Commercial sports
    - 7941—Professional sports clubs and promoters
    - 7948—Racing, including track operation
- 799—Miscellaneous amusement and recreation services
    - 7991—Physical fitness facilities
    - 7992—Public golf courses
    - 7993—Coin-operated amusement devices
    - 7996—Amusement parks
    - 7997—Membership sports and recreation clubs
    - 7999—Amusement and recreation services not elsewhere classified

This last industry group ranges from fortune-tellers, phrenologists, and astrologers to sports professionals, gambling establishments, and hunting guides.

The NAICS classification reflects the way our leisure time has been transformed:

- 711—Performing arts, spectator sports, and related industries:
    - 7111—Performing arts companies (including theater, dance, music, and "other")
    - 7112—Spectator sports (sports teams, racetracks, and other)
    - 7113—Promoters of performing arts, sports, and similar events
    - 7114—Agents and managers for artists, athletes, entertainers, and other public figures
    - 7115—Independent artists, writers, and performers
- 713—Amusement, gambling, and recreation industries:
    - 7131—Amusement parks and arcades
    - 7132—Gambling industries
    - 7139—Other

There are also methodological reasons for preferring NAICS over SIC, but their discussion is beyond the scope of this book. Box 4.6 explains the NAICS system.

The Standard Occupational Classification system (SOC) also has undergone a restructuring at least as important as those for industrial codes. SOC 2000 is a large methodological shift in the classification of occupations. SOC, like SIC and NAICS, is hierarchical. Box 4.7 compares the SOC system used in 1990 with the SOC system used in 2000.

The redefinition of these important categories raises problems for those comparing trends in employment structure. Most current economic data is published according to the NAICS

Box 4.6   NAICS (continued)

Map 4.2a shows the proportion of Manhattan's population employed in the "arts, entertainment, and recreation" industrial sector.

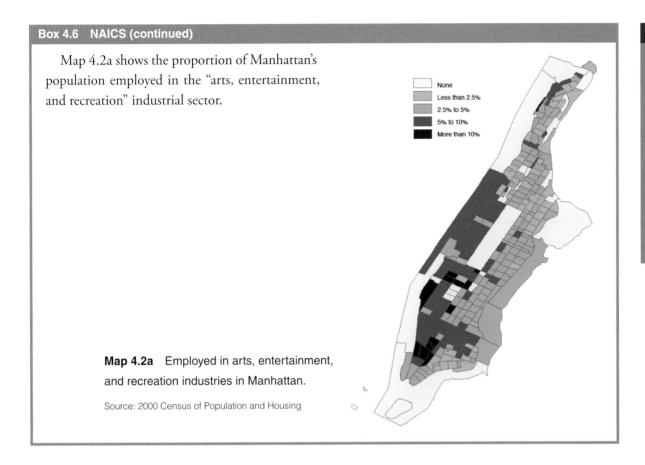

	None
	Less than 2.5%
	2.5% to 5%
	5% to 10%
	More than 10%

Map 4.2a   Employed in arts, entertainment, and recreation industries in Manhattan.

Source: 2000 Census of Population and Housing

code, but almost all historical data, and a considerable volume of current derived data, is still published using the old SIC system. There is a translation matrix available aiding the movement across these two systems; see appendix B of North American Industrial Classification System, United States, 1997 (U.S. Office of Management and Budget 1998). To make matters even more complex, the population census has its own industry and occupation coding systems. Fortunately, the Census 2000 industry system is explicitly based on NAICS, and the occupation system is explicitly based on SOC 2000. The Census Bureau publishes "crosswalks," which are tables that allow translation between the various coding schemes. The crosswalks can be found at *www.census.gov/hhes/www/ioindex/index.html*. Crosswalks are also available in appendix G of the technical documentation to Summary File 3 (U.S. Census Bureau 2003a). The industry and occupation breakdowns provided in the Summary File 3 tables are not very detailed, so the crosswalks are fairly straightforward to use. However, they are more complex with more detailed data sets such as the Public Use Microdata Sample (PUMS).

One particularly useful crosswalk translates Census 1990 codes, NAICS codes, and Census 2000 codes. Thus "crop production" is listed under "017" in Census 2000, "111" under NAICS, and "010" in the 1990 Census, while "beverage manufacturing" is listed as "137" in Census 2000, "3121" in NAICS, and "120" in Census 1990. The crosswalks can be downloaded, saved,

Box 4.7   SOC and occupational coding

Occupations are categorized in a manner similar to industries. The federal interagency SOC Revision Policy Committee (SOCRPC) decided to fundamentally restructure the SOC system for the 2000 Census. In some important regards the differences between the 2000 SOC system and the earlier occupational classification system are greater than those between the SIC system and NAICS. The revised system has twenty-three major groups divided into 96 minor groups, 449 broad occupations, and 821 detailed occupations. The major groups are described in the table below:

Table 4.4 SOC major groups and names	
Major group code	**Name**
11-0000	Management occupations
13-0000	Business and financial operations occupations
15-0000	Computer and mathematical occupations
17-0000	Architecture and engineering occupations
19-0000	Life, physical, and social science occupations
21-0000	Community and social service occupations
23-0000	Legal occupations
25-0000	Education, training, and library occupations
27-0000	Arts, design, entertainment, sports, and media occupations
29-0000	Healthcare practitioners and technical occupations
31-0000	Healthcare support occupations
33-0000	Protective service occupations
35-0000	Food preparation and serving related occupations
37-0000	Building and grounds cleaning and maintenance occupations
39-0000	Personal care and service occupations
41-0000	Sales and related occupations
43-0000	Office and administrative support occupations
45-0000	Farming, fishing, and forestry occupations
47-0000	Construction and extraction occupations
49-0000	Installation, maintenance, and repair occupations
51-0000	Production occupations
53-0000	Transportation and material moving occupations
55-0000	Military specific occupations

Note: SOC 2000, see U.S. Office of Management and Budget (2000).

Box 4.7 SOC and occupational coding (continued)

"Life, physical, and social science occupations" (19-0000) is divided into four minor groups, one of which is "life scientists" (19-1000). "Life scientists" contains various broad occupations including "biological scientist" (19-1020) and the latter contains detailed occupations such as "microbiologist" (19-1022). Each occupation has six digits. Major groups end with "0000," minor groups with "000," and broad occupations "0." The SOC manual is available for purchase from the National Technical Information Service (U.S. Office of Management and Budget 2000).

Map 4.2b shows the proportion of Manhattan residents in the arts, entertainment, and recreation occupations. Comparing this map with map 4.2a (in box 4.6) shows the importance of differentiating industry of employment from job occupation. People working in the arts, entertainment, and recreation *industries,* for instance, may be in a variety of occupations; they include personal service providers (hairdressers and makeup artists), along with professionals such as lawyers and accountants. However, these people would not be reflected in counts of people in arts, entertainment, and recreation *occupations.* People in arts, entertainment, and recreation

Map 4.2b Employed in arts, entertainment, and recreation occupations in Manhattan.

Source: 2000 Census of Population and Housing

occupations may be working in a variety of different industries, such as graphic designers employed by large corporations, and piano players employed by department stores.

143

Using the census to analyze economic conditions

and converted into databases allowing fairly straightforward conversions among the various industrial coding systems and somewhat more difficult conversions among the occupational systems. Spreadsheet versions of some of the crosswalks are also available. The first example in the final section of this chapter illustrates this process. Box 4.8 provides detailed instructions on how to deal with the changes.

The decennial census provides a powerful way to understand the economic status and employment patterns of individuals and households. Cross-tabulations of income, employment, and poverty with demographic characteristics offer a rich source of data for analyzing local economies. Table 4.5 summarizes the available cross-tabulations in the published tables.

Box 4.8 Detailed instructions for using crosswalks

Most of the industry and occupational breakdowns in Summary File 3 of Census 2000 are not very detailed, making crosswalks fairly straightforward. For instance, the table "P49 sex by industry for the employed population 16 years and over" breaks down employees into the equivalent of two-digit (and some three-digit) NAICS codes. Likewise, "P50 sex by occupation for the employed civilian population 16 years and over" mostly breaks down employees only so far as "minor groups"; only in a few cases does it go as far as "broad occupations."

When downloading industry and occupation tables from Summary File 3 using FactFinder you will be prompted to download a .pdf file with Census 2000 and NAICS or SOC codes for each listed (click on the Detailed Industry Code List or Detailed Occupation Code List links below the table). It is always useful to download and print these lists as they allow you to understand better the SF3 data and also allow you to connect to other industry and occupation data sources. Also click on the link that reads **Table P49 With Codes,** or whatever table number you have chosen, and download and print that .pdf file.

If you want to use census data on individuals (for instance PUMS), you will need to become more familiar with detailed industrial and occupational classifications and adept at using detailed crosswalks.

If you download data from FactFinder as suggested in chapter 2, industries and occupations are identified not by names or codes but by variable numbers. For table P50, variable P050011 (picked at random) has the descriptive data element name: "The employed civilian population 16 years and over: male; computer and mathematical occupations." To find out the appropriate codes associated with this variable and name, look at the contents of the .pdf document "Table P50 with codes." The document indicates that "Computer and mathematical occupations" consists of Census 2000 occupation codes 100 through 129 or SOC 2000 code 15-0000. So, variable P050011 in table P50 consists of males in SOC code 15-0000.

Variable P050013 has the descriptive data element name "Employed civilian population 16 years and over: male; architects; surveyors; cartographers; and engineers." Using the same lookup system, this variable covers males in SOC 17-1000 through 17-2000, or, using Census 2000 codes, 130 through 153.

The Economic Census

The decennial Census of Population and Housing collects important information about the economic circumstances of people and households tied to their home location, but it does not collect information about the economy of those places. In 1810, a few questions about manufacturing were included in the census of that year, but by the 1950s a completely separate integrated census had emerged to measure economic activity at the business level. Until 1992, separate censuses were conducted for different industrial sectors (the Census of Manufacturing, Census of Retail Trade, and so on). In 1997, the sector-specific surveys were collapsed into one Economic Census with only two separately defined surveys remaining: the Census of Mineral

	Sex	Age	Race	Hispanic origin	Family type	Household type	Disability status
				Table 4.5 Available cross-tabulations of income and employment data			
Employment status	P43, P150, PCT35, PCT69	P38, PCT35	P150A-G, PCT68A-G, PCT69A-G	P150H-I, PCT68H-I, PCT69H-I	P44-46, PCT70		P42, PCT26-PCT32, PCT68
Work status	P47, PCT71, PCT73		PCT71A-G, PCT73A-G	PCT71H-I, PCT73H-I			
Workers in family					P48		
Industry	P49, P51						
Occupation	P50						
Household income		P55, P56, P57, PCT72	P151A-G, P152A-G, P153A-G, PCT72A-G	P151H-I, P152H-I, P153H-I, PCT72H-I			
Family income		PCT37	P154A-G, P155A-G, P156A-G	P154H-I, P155H-I, P156H-I	PCT37, PCT38, PCT40-41		
Nonfamily income	PCT42, PCT43	PCT43					
Per capita income			P157A-G	P157H-I			
Individual income	PCT44, PCT45		P158A-G	P158H-I			
Earnings 1999	P84, P85, P86, PCT46-8, PCT73		PCT73A-G, PCT74A-G	PCT73H-I, PCT74H-I			
Poverty status	PCT49, PCT53, PCT55, PCT75	P87, P89, P92, P159, PCT49, PCT50, PCT53, PCT55	P159A-G, P160A-G, PCT75A-G, PCT76A-G	P159H-I, P160H-I, PCT75H-I, PCT76H-I	P90, P160, PCT52, PCT59-61, PCT76	P89, P92, P93, PCT55, PCT56	
Armed forces status	P39	P39	P149A-G	P149H-I			

Note: Relevant Summary File 3 tables are listed for each pair of variables with cross-tabulated data. Variables that are not cross-tabulated have blank cells.

Industries and the Census of Transportation, Vehicle Inventory, and Use Survey (Hovland, Gaulthier, and Micarelli 2000).

The Economic Census is conducted every five years (in years ending in two or seven). Instead of surveying households, it surveys business *establishments*—a single plant (or part of a plant devoted to one type of output and keeping a separate set of books), in contrast to an *enterprise,* which is the entire company. An enterprise may consist of many establishments, though usually it will not. Logically, a multi-establishment enterprise may consist of establishments in many different industrial sectors.

Like the decennial census, answering the Economic Census is mandatory, and similar confidentiality protections govern the publication of the data. Consequently, detailed data is rarely available at a disaggregated spatial scale. Data is reported at the national, state, county, and place level (for places over 2,500), and at the ZIP Code level. Some establishments could not be assigned to a particular state; these are treated in one of three ways:

- Nationwide, with a state FIPS equivalent code of 97.
- Foreign, including ships at sea, with a state FIPS equivalent code of 98.
- Offshore; for instance, mining or construction operations. If an offshore enterprise could be assigned to a state, it was, and it also was given a pseudo-county code. If an offshore enterprise could not be assigned to a state, it would be assigned an abbreviation corresponding to one of three coastal regions—AT (Atlantic), NG (Northern Gulf of Mexico), and PC (Pacific).

Within consolidated cities and counties, data is reported separately for incorporated places with more than 2,500 residents, and for the balance of the consolidated city (or county) for all smaller places. Although data is geocoded to the census tract and block level, data is not tabulated at this level.

The 1997 Census was mailed to approximately 3.7 million companies (enterprises), to collect data on about five million business locations (establishments). For very small businesses, the Census Bureau uses data from the Internal Revenue Service (IRS) and Social Security Administration (SSA) instead of a survey. This data collection effort covered about 1.5 million small employer firms and fourteen million businesses with no employees (Hovland, Gauthier, and Micarelli 2000, 5).

The Economic Census uses different questionnaires for different industry sectors. Some information is collected from all establishments:

- physical location of activity
- number of employees
- payroll
- value of sales, receipts, or equivalent

However, a wide variety of questionnaires is designed for different industries. Within the construction sector, for instance, eleven different questionnaires were used, while the manufacturing sector was surveyed using 35 different "short-form" and 218 different "long-form" questionnaires (Hovland, Gauthier, and Micarelli 2000). The data collected focuses on several broad categories of issues:

- cost of labor (including fringe benefits, subcontractors, hours worked)
- cost of supplies (materials, purchased services)
- operating expenses (rent, fuel, and so on)
- depreciable assets, capital expenditures, and debt payments
- inventories and value of assets
- sources of revenue

- employment by occupation
- legal form of organization, ownership, and control

In 1997, the NAICS system was introduced, restructuring the definitions of sectors used in the Economic Census. For instance, "accommodations and food services" was moved from the services industry sector to the retail trade sector, and "communications industries" was moved from the SIC sector "Transportation, Communications, Electric, Gas and Sanitary Services" to the new NAICS classification "Telecommunications." In each census, product lines are revised to reflect changing consumption patterns. New product lines with an expected value over $50 million are added, and lines with an expected value below $25 million are deleted or merged (Hovland, Gauthier, and Micarelli 2000).

Downloading Economic Census data

There are three main data series:
- industry series
- subject series
- geography (or area) series

The first provides detailed information on the various NAICS sectors with very limited geographical breakdowns. The second provides data on more specialized topics such as merchandise line sales for the retail sector. The third provides geographic data down to the place (greater than 2,500 population) and ZIP Code levels. Economic Census data is published on CD–ROM available in depository libraries and for purchase. The CD–ROMs come with their own special data access software, which will need to be installed on your computer. However, the data on the CD–ROMs are held in .mdb databases, the same format used by Microsoft Access, personal geodatabases in ArcMap, and any database manager using the Microsoft JET engine. More advanced users will probably want to use one of these programs to access Economic Census data.

Data can be downloaded as a series of reports from *www.census.gov/econ/www/index.html,* but it is probably more useful to use American FactFinder at *www.census.gov,* which includes download choices for the Economic Census that mirror those for the Census of Population and Housing. The download options described in chapter 2 will work with very little modification. As with the Census of Population and Housing, choose the **Data Sets** button on the left hand side of FactFinder, and then select the **Economic Censuses and Surveys** tab. Most often you will need to choose from the **Geographic Quick Reports** series. In the following screen capture from FactFinder, we have generated data for Iowa City, Iowa, to the two-, three-, and four-digit levels. The geographic data includes six variables: the NAICS industry code, the industry description, the number of establishments, the number of employees, annual payroll, and shipments or sales and receipts (figure 4.4, next page).

Notice the "D" in the annual payroll and shipments/sales/receipts columns. The "D" indicates the application of nondisclosure rules. The small letters "a" through "m" in the employment column indicate nondisclosure but nevertheless provide size ranges for employment: "a" is

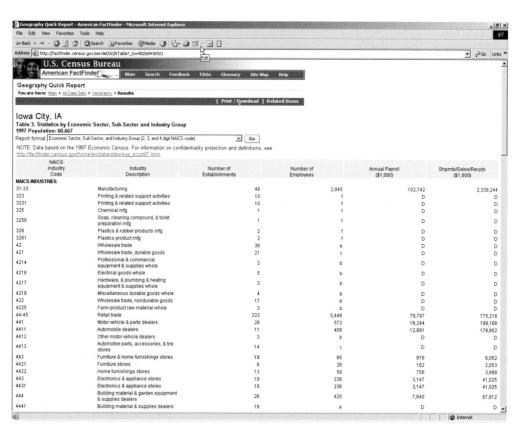

Figure 4.4

the range 0–19 employees, "b" the range 20–99 employees, and so on (the size range categories are dealt with in detail in the second example at the end of this chapter).

Quick reports on industries can be generated in a similar way, as the following figure on NAICS 315111 (sheer hosiery mills) demonstrates. Notice in this figure that the meaning of the various alphabetical letters is visible (figure 4.5).

Further download options are available from the Economic Census main page at *www.census. gov/epcd/www/econ97.html*. This page also has links to metadata and other background information and contains the bridge between the SIC system and NAICS. However, at the time of writing, download choices on this page varied widely in their ease of use. Note that more detailed and specialized data tend not to be available for download in standard database formats. In these instances, users should either buy the Economic Census CD–ROM or use the CD–ROMS at their local depository libraries.

Note that the 1992 Economic Census CD–ROMs are organized in broadly similar ways to the 1997 Economic Census. The most important difference is the use of the SIC system instead of NAICS. The 1992 discs use a DOS-based data access software called GO™. The data files are in .dbf format, and any database manager capable of reading dBase files can be used to extract data.

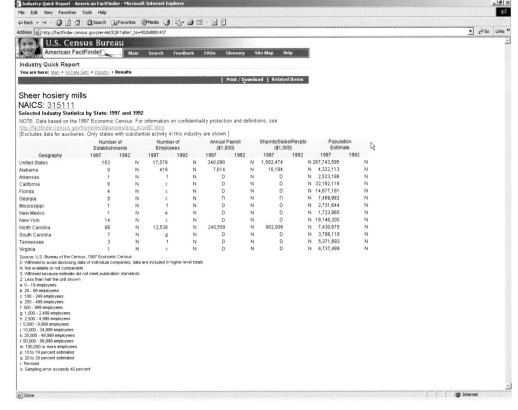

Figure 4.5

The CD–ROM series is divided into various volumes:

- Volume 1 NAICS Report Series consists of disc set 1f, which now supersedes 1a through 1e. It includes complete geographic, line size, and other subject series data for all sectors. The set consists of three CD–ROMs: 1f-1, 1f-2, and 1f-3.
- Volume 2 Special Series consists of disc set 2d, which supersedes 2a through 2c. This includes the 1997 Economic Census for Outlying Areas, Business Expenses, Nonemployer Statistics (including those for 1998), Puerto Rico Geographic Area Series and Subject Series, Minority-Owned Businesses, Women-Owned Businesses.
- Volume 3 ZIP Code Statistics consist of disc set 3. The information in Volume 3 is not available through FactFinder.

Other major economic data series

A vast array of economic data is collected by a variety of federal, state, and local agencies. Unfortunately, many databases do not include geographic identifiers, and samples are not always large enough to draw conclusions about the characteristics of people in particular places. Nevertheless, current national data sources can be used to supplement and update decennial census data. The remainder of this section discusses the major sources of supplementary economic data and explains how they could be used to supplement census data.

Other employment, income, establishment, and enterprise statistics produced by the Census Bureau

Current Population Survey

The Current Population Survey (CPS) is the primary source of data on the labor force. The CPS March supplement is the standard source of annual data on unemployment trends and the official source of estimates of poverty rates. The Census Bureau and the Bureau of Labor Statistics (BLS) share responsibility for the CPS. It is conducted monthly (during the week that includes the nineteenth of the month) for a sample of approximately 50,000 households. Households are in the sample for four months, out for eight months, and back in for four months before being replaced by a different household. This sample design is intended to balance continuity with continual replenishment of households (U.S. Department of Labor, Bureau of Labor Statistics, and U.S. Census Bureau 2002).

The labor force status of the working-age population and the demographic characteristics of those who are employed, unemployed, and not in the labor force are explored in greater detail in the CPS than in any other survey. Related topics such as school enrollment, job tenure, displacement, and veteran status are often covered in supplementary questions. Other sponsors may also pay to include questions unrelated to labor force activity. Family size, computer use, and voting patterns are examples of topics that have been included in monthly surveys.

Although the Current Employment Statistics survey (CES, discussed below) also collects employment data, it is quite different from the CPS. It is employer-based and does not cover the self-employed, unpaid workers in family businesses, farm workers, or those who are unemployed or not in the labor force.

Although the CPS provides a wealth of labor force information, its usefulness for spatial analysis is limited. States are the lowest level of geography for which the CPS provides statistically reliable estimates. Nevertheless, the CPS can be a useful source for analyses of trends at the state level.

Small Area Income and Poverty Estimates (SAIPE)

This Census Bureau program provides current estimates of income and poverty for states, counties, and school districts. Estimates are based not on surveys but on models of the relationship between

- census measures of income and poverty,
- earnings and employment data from tax returns,
- food stamp use,
- employment data from the Bureau of Economic Analysis, and
- the CPS.

Standard errors are estimated. Estimates are somewhat more reliable for states than for counties. For counties, estimates are in fact three-year averages centering on a particular year rather than annual averages.

County-level estimates cover

- number of people in poverty,
- number of related children aged 5 to 17 in families in poverty,
- number of children under 18 in poverty, and
- median household incomes.

For each school district, estimates cover

- total population,
- population aged between 5 and 17, and
- number of children between 5 and 17 in families in poverty.

The number of poor children under 5 is estimated for states only. Estimates are usually produced every two years (for odd-numbered years).

The SAIPE would be useful to update estimates of families and children in poverty from the 2000 Census. However, because estimates are based on a series of regression models, and because the data on which they are based is drawn from different sources than the decennial census, the SAIPE are not directly comparable to census estimates. It would be important to explain apparent inconsistencies. Table 4.6 describes important nonspatial sources of related data.

Table 4.6 Selected nonspatial economic data			
Data source	Type of information	Spatial descriptors	Where can I find this?
Survey of Income and Program Participation (SIPP)	Longitudinal study of income, assets, and expenditures, and participation in income-support programs (such as food stamps, Medicare, or Temporary Assistance to Needy Families (TANF) for a sample of about 8,000 households a month	National	www.bls.census.gov/sipp
Panel Study of Income Dynamics (PSID)	Longitudinal study begun in 1968 with approximately 7,000 families in the sample in 2001. Provides a variety of economic and demographic data including family composition changes and residential location. Supplements have addressed education, health, and wealth.	National	psidonline.isr.umich.edu/Guide/Overview.html

Annual Survey of Manufactures (ASM) and other sector-specific surveys

The ASM, conducted in non-Economic Census years (all years except those ending in two and seven), provides annual data on manufacturing firms with one or more employees. Data includes employment, payroll, value-added, value of shipments, capital and energy expenditures, inventories, and so on. There are three main reports. Statistics of Industry Groups and Industries (AS)-1 presents detailed information down to the six-digit NAICS level. Value of Product Shipments (AS)-2 provides shipment information on 473 six-digit and around 1,500 seven-digit NAICS codes. The Geographic Area Series (AS)-3 has data at the state level for a more limited set of NAICS codes. For information, go to *www.census.gov/mcd*.

There are various other special monthly, quarterly, and annual surveys that perform much the same function as the ASM but for other sectors of the economy. Like the ASM, most of these have little or no geographic disaggregation. Surveys cover construction, retail, wholesale, transportation, services, and industrial production.

Construction: See *www.census.gov/const/www.*
- New Residential Construction
- New Residential Sales Characteristics of New Housing
- Manufactured Housing
- Construction Spending (Value Put in Place)
- Residential Improvements

Retail: See *www.census.gov/econ/www/tasmenu.html.*
- Advance Monthly Sales for Retail and Food Services
- Monthly Retail Sales and Inventories
- Annual Retail Trade Survey

Wholesale: See *www.census.gov/econ/www/retmenu.html#WHOL.*
- Monthly Wholesale Trade Survey
- Annual Wholesale Trade Survey

Transportation: See *www.census.gov/econ/www/tasmenu.html.*
- Service Annual Survey

Service Sectors: See *www.census.gov/econ/www/servmenu.html.*
- Service Annual Survey

Current Industrial Reports (CIR): This program, which was started in 1904, provides monthly, quarterly, and annual data on industrial activity. The program reports on economic activity in important commodity areas. There is no geographical breakdown. Go to *www.census.gov/cir/www/index.html.*

County Business Patterns (CBP)

This is an annual series on employment (full- and part-time workers who are on the payroll on March 12), payroll, and number of establishments by industry for states, counties, metropolitan areas, ZIP Codes, and the United States. It is widely used for economic analysis down to the county level. The main alternative to this series is ES202 (Covered Employment and Wages), discussed below. ES202 covers slightly more of the U.S. workforce than does CBP, and data is probably slightly more reliable. CBP excludes self-employed persons, employees of private households, railroad employees, agricultural production workers, and most government employees.

However, CBP data is sometimes easier to work with, and, for many urban analyses, there is little reason to prefer one series over the other. The CBP series goes back to 1946 allowing for long-term historical analyses (earlier ES202 suffers from considerable interstate variation in data quality). From 1998 onward, CBP has been published only electronically (Web pages, CD–ROM, and .pdf files).

CBP data is extracted from the Census Bureau's Business Register, a file of all known companies. The Annual Company Organization Survey and Economic Census provide individual establishment data for multilocation firms. Data for single-location firms is obtained from various programs including the Economic Census, the Annual Survey of Manufactures, and the Current Business Surveys, together with records of the Internal Revenue Service (IRS), the Social Security Administration (SSA), and the Bureau of Labor Statistics (BLS). For CBP data and information on the program, go to *www.census.gov/epcd/cbp/view/cbpview.html*. CBP data is used in the multiplier example later in this chapter.

Enterprise Statistics (ES)

CBP presents data on establishments. As we explained earlier, a manufacturing establishment is best thought of as a single plant. But it is often necessary to find information on entire companies (enterprises). An enterprise may consist of multiple establishments and various auxiliary establishments such as headquarters offices, research and development facilities, and data processing centers. The most important source of enterprise (as opposed to establishment) data is the Enterprise Statistics (*www.census.gov/csd/ent*) program. Unfortunately, this program was not funded for 1997, so for data more recent than 1992 it is necessary to use the Statistics of U.S. Business listed below. Data includes sales, employment, payroll, form of organization, and enterprise industry classification. Supplementary data for large companies includes inventories, assets, fringe benefits, capital and research and development (R&D) expenditures, and depreciation. Data for auxiliaries include sales, employment and payroll, billings, inventories, capital, R&D expenditures, and selected purchased services. Data is disaggregated by enterprise employment size, receipts, three-digit industry code, and state. For data and information, go to *www.census.gov/csd/ent*.

Statistics of U.S. Businesses (SUSB)

Statistics of U.S. Businesses is developed from the same database that is used to produce County Business Patterns, but CBP classifies establishments by the employment size of the establishment rather than the employment size of the entire enterprise. Statistics of U.S. Businesses data is extracted from the Standard Statistical Establishment List (SSEL), a file of all known single- and multi-establishment employer companies. The Economic Census is the primary source for industry and geography classifications. The annual Company Organization Survey provides individual establishment data for multiestablishment companies. Data for single-establishment companies is obtained from the Annual Survey of Manufactures and the Current Business Surveys, as well as from records of the IRS, SSA, and BLS. This series replaces the Enterprise Statistics series of the 1992 Economic Census. For information and data see *www.census.gov/csd/susb/susb.htm*.

Survey of Business Owners (SBO)

This series provides statistics that describe the composition of U.S. businesses by gender, race, and ethnicity. Additional statistics include owner's age, education level, veteran status, and primary function in the business; family- and home-based businesses; types of customers and workers; and sources of financing for expansion, capital improvements, or start-up. See *www.census.gov/csd/sbo* for details.

Survey of Minority-Owned Business Establishments and Survey of Women-Owned Business Establishments (SMOBE and SWOBE)

This series provides data on business owners' race, ethnicity, and gender based on the Economic Census (SMOBE/SWOBE data is available for years ending in two and seven) and various other data sources. The data covers firms, sales and receipts, employees, and payroll, and is tabulated for states, counties, places, and metropolitan areas. For data and information on this series, go to *www.census.gov/csd/mwb*.

Nonemployer Statistics

This series provides data (sales, receipts, and so on) for establishments with unpaid employees, usually the self-employed and unincorporated partnerships. Data is obtained from the business income tax returns filed with the IRS. Nonemployers do not get census questionnaires (payroll tax records are the way that the Census Bureau keeps tabs on businesses in noncensus years), and therefore they are not included in any of the other core business statistics put out by the bureau. Exceptions are the minority- and women-owned business reports, where nonemployers are included in the "all firms" category. For a detailed description of what is covered by the Nonemployer Statistics, go to *www.census.gov/epcd/nonemployer/view/cov&meth.htm*.

Note that for the Nonemployer Statistics the Census Bureau equates a business mailing address with a business establishment. A business that sells from a mobile vehicle or temporary stand is an establishment for the purposes of Nonemployer Statistics and it will be assigned to the owner's mailing address. Nonemployer businesses may use leased or contract employees, in which case the payroll for the business is still zero, keeping the business in the nonemployer universe. However, if the firm has large business receipts, then it will be dropped from the nonemployer universe. For data, go to *www.census.gov/epcd/nonemployer*.

Census of Governments

This is actually part of the Economic Census; we include it here as a separate entry since the data looks very different from the rest of the Economic Census. This data set includes information on government organization, employment, and finances (including revenue, expenditure, debt, assets, employees, payroll, and benefits).

Census Transportation Planning Package (CTPP)

This data set is discussed in the first example in this chapter and fully in chapter 6. It is a re-ordering of Census of Population and Housing data so that places of residence can be connected geographically with places of work.

Building Permits

This series provides data on new construction summarized to the place and county levels, including numbers of buildings, units, and construction costs. It is updated monthly. See chapter 5 for a more complete description of this data.

Other Census Bureau Economic Data

Go to *www.census.gov/econ/www* for a gateway to all other nonspatial census economic data including exports, detailed information in the performance of industrial sectors, and so on.

Major employment and related data series produced by the Bureau of Labor Statistics (BLS)

Covered Employment and Wages (ES202)

This program, usually called ES202, provides the best source for employment and wage data by industry in the United States. It covers all workers covered by state unemployment insurance (UI) laws and federal workers covered by the Unemployment Compensation for Federal Employees (UCFE). UI coverage, and thus ES202 data, is comparable across states (for variation see BLS Handbook of Methods chapter 5, available at *www.bls.gov/opub/hom/homch5_a.htm*). ES202 covers about 98 percent of all nonfarm waged civilian jobs. The data is establishment (place of work)-based. It parallels the data in the Census Bureau's County Business Patterns (CBP). ES202 provides the basis for the Quarterly Census of Employment and Wages discussed below. The main annual publication is called *Employment and Wages;* data is also available for download in flat-file formats or interactively on Web pages (some download options are discussed in the second example at the end of this chapter). States also publish their own ES202 data and often provide useful county-by-county information.

ES202 is often the preferred data set for those analyzing employment at the local level. Outside of years ending in two or seven, the main alternative to ES202 is CBP. CBP is not quite as comprehensive as ES202. It excludes agricultural workers and household workers; ES202 includes some of these workers. Moreover, some of the data in CBP comes from sample surveys, whereas ES202 comes directly from covered establishments each year. CBP and ES202 treat administrative employment differently. Note that ES202 has an advantage over the Current Employment Statistics (CES) program, which is based on a sample of 390,000 establishments. In fact, ES202 is used to benchmark CES employment numbers. For further details on the ES202 program, see *www.bls.gov/opub/hom/homch5_c.htm*.

Quarterly Census of Employment and Wages (QCEW)

This program publishes quarterly counts of employment and wages. The census is based on ES202 data and thus is establishment-based (employment and wages are reported by place of work). The quarterly county report is *County Employment and Wages;* there are also more detailed annual reports covering states, industries, metropolitan areas, and large counties. The census covers around 98 percent of all U.S. jobs. For data and background information on QCEW, go to *www.bls.gov/cew/home.htm*.

The Current Employment Statistics (CES) survey

The Current Employment Statistics (CES) survey is conducted monthly, surveying approximately 39,000 employers each month, for a total sample size of about 400,000 establishments. The QCEW program is used as the benchmark for employment in the CES. The CES collects data on

- total jobs,
- hours worked, and
- hourly and weekly earnings by industry.

Data is broken down for about 850 industries by

- women workers,
- production and supervisory workers.

Several indexes are constructed based on the CES. These include

- the health of the economy (measured by employment),
- earning trends and wage inflation,
- industrial production,
- productivity measures, and
- the employment cost index.

Monthly employment data is published by industrial sector by state and metropolitan area. Annual average earnings, weekly hours worked, and other data is available by sector for states.

The CES would be a useful benchmark to estimate current employment and earnings data by industry. The comparative indexes it provides on several employment- and wage-related topics are also useful. However, care should be taken in using it to update decennial census data, because it defines "employees" differently (as explained above in the discussion of the CPS). For data and background information go to *www.bls.gov/sae/home.htm*.

Local Area Unemployment Statistics (LAUS)

The LAUS program produces annual and monthly employment, unemployment, and labor force data for census regions, divisions, states, counties, metropolitan areas, and many places. It is organized by place of residence of the worker, not by the location of employment opportunities (that is, it is not place of work or establishment data). The CPS is the source of the monthly statistics on unemployment for the nation and the annual average estimate for all states. It is also the main source for the models estimating monthly labor force for the states, the District of Columbia, New York City, and Los Angeles. The CPS is also used in modeling the estimates for the 7,000 substate areas. For data and background information, go to *www.bls.gov/lau/home.htm*.

Mass Layoff Statistics (MLS)

This series reports on mass layoffs (meaning that fifty or more claims for unemployment insurance were filed against an employer in a five-week period). For data and background information, go to *www.bls.gov/mls/home.htm*.

National Compensation Survey (NCS)

This provides earnings data by worker characteristics and establishment characteristics. There is also comprehensive information on employee benefits. The main publication is *Compensation and Working Conditions;* see also the Occupational Employment Statistics below. For data and background information, go to *www.bls.gov/ncs/ocs/home.htm*.

Wages by Area and Occupation

This data set provides wage information for particular occupations. The data is published at the national, division, state, and metropolitan levels. They are derived from the National Compensation Survey, the Occupational Employment Statistics Survey, and the Current Population Survey. For data and background information, go to *www.bls.gov/bls/blswage.htm*.

Occupational Employment Statistics (OES)

The OES Survey is used to produce annual employment and wage estimates for over 700 occupations and 400 nonfarm industries. The estimates are for the nation, state, and metropolitan areas. The main publication series is called *Occupational Employment and Wages.* Urban land professionals will find another publication, *Occupational Outlook Handbook,* particularly useful. This provides information on training qualifications, earnings, working conditions, and outlook for 250 occupations. For data and background information on OES, go to *www.bls.gov/oes/home.htm*.

Injuries, Illness, and Fatalities (IIF)

This program covers illnesses, injuries, and deaths on the job. Incidence rates by industry are recorded. Data is derived from the Census of Fatal Occupational Injuries, the Survey of Occupational Injuries and Illnesses, and the Survey of Respirator Use. It is possible to download the entire database from the IIF site. For data and background information, go to *www.bls.gov/iif/home.htm*.

Economic data and analysis produced by the Bureau of Economic Analysis (BEA)

State and local personal income

This provides data on various measures of income at the state and local level. The BEA uses Quarterly Census of Employment and Wages (QCEW) data as the base for developing the wage and salary component of personal income. For data and further information, go to *www.bea.doc.gov/bea/regional/spi*.

Gross state product

This series reports state product figures, including breakdowns by industry. For data and further information, go to *www.bea.doc.gov/bea/regional/gsp.htm*.

Regional Input-Output Multipliers (RIMS II)

RIMS II multipliers are used to measure the regional economic impact of public- and private-sector projects such as airport construction, military base closings, and so on. RIMS II multipliers are based on the BEA's national input-output model, which covers just under five hundred industries. Input-output (I-O) models are widely used in economic impact analysis; essentially I-O models try to capture the interindustry relationships (for instance, the existence of one firm will create economic opportunities for other firms) that exist in all economies and then use these relationships to predict what is known as the "indirect" and sometimes "induced" economic impact of a project. A handbook (U.S. Bureau of Economic Analysis 1997) provides a full description of the RIMS II system. The handbook is available on the BEA Web site at *www.bea.doc.gov/bea/regional/rims*. There are two main private sector alternatives to RIMS II: IMPLAN® and Regional Economic Models, Inc. (REMI®) models.

Special programs and state employment data

The various federal agencies responsible for producing data also produce specialized data products. For instance, we have requested (at cost) special data runs from the SSEL (Standard Statistical Establishment List) database. There are many other official data sources that provide data on local economies that urban analysts often use. States and some larger cities also publish a considerable amount of economic data. One final note: much of the economic data covered here is summarized in the Statistical Abstract of the United States, the County and City Data Book, and State and Metropolitan Area Data Book, discussed in chapter 1.

Using the census for local economic analyses

Census data (from both the Census of Population and Housing and the Economic Census) is widely used to answer a variety of questions about local economic conditions. This section of the chapter explores two examples of analyses in more detail. The examples were chosen to illustrate practical solutions to some of the analytic challenges that census data poses:

- Definitions of variables change over time, and variables are defined differently in different data sources. Analyzing trends in the industry and occupation of jobs over time faces both problems. Creative strategies are needed to compare data based on household surveys with that based on establishment surveys and to compare data from the early part of the 1990s with the current data available from the 1997 Economic Census and the 2000 Census of Population and Housing.

- Linking employment (or earnings) data collected at places of residence to employment or earnings data at places of work is key to many analyses, but that process entails using a variety of sources and reconciling differences in variable definition and spatial scale between sources.

- Finally, the issue of nondisclosure presents much larger problems for users of the Economic Census than the Census of Population and Housing. Developing a consistent method of dealing with nondisclosure is a crucial part of using the Economic Census (and related data) at the local level.

Example one: Designing a residential relocation component for a family self-sufficiency program

Since the welfare reform act (the Personal Responsibility and Work Opportunity Reconciliation Act, PWROA, of 1996), moving welfare recipients off assistance rolls and into the workforce has been a priority for state and local agencies. A wide range of approaches to these so-called "welfare to work" programs has emerged. Job training and education have obviously been important, but research has also identified residential location and access to transportation as a key component of labor force participation.

Consider the following hypothetical scenario. Assume that the local department of human services and the public housing authority in Flint, Michigan, want to coordinate a program aimed at expanding job opportunities for single mother-headed households in poverty. One component of the program will address job-readiness skills and childcare, but another component builds on the findings of the link between residential location and labor force participation. The housing authority plans to provide program participants with housing assistance to enable them to move to neighborhoods where employment prospects are better. In order to design the program, officials need to answer several questions:

- Are mother-headed households in poverty concentrated in some neighborhoods in the metropolitan area?
- Are there differences in the concentration of households in poverty by race?
- Is there a relationship between single-mother labor force participation, or work experience in the previous year, and residential location?
- Where are entry-level jobs located in the metropolitan area?

An innovative program in Chicago, the Gautreaux program (named for the court case that mandated it), provides lessons for welfare-to-work programs (Rosenbaum 1996). The Chicago Housing Authority was found guilty of furthering racial segregation in public housing; the judge ordered the agency to redress the problem by offering housing assistance (in the form of Section 8 certificates) to minority public housing residents of segregated projects. The tenants could use the certificates to move anywhere in the Chicago metro area, as long as the neighborhood did not have a concentration of poor or minority residents. Later, the program was amended to allow people to move to any neighborhood of their choice, regardless of its characteristics.

Kaufman and Rosenbaum's (1992) evaluation of the Gautreaux program revealed several important policy implications. The children in households who moved to low-poverty suburban communities were far more likely than the children in households who moved to other poor neighborhoods to complete high school and attend college. Furthermore, the mothers (households were almost exclusively mother-headed) were far more likely to work if they lived in low-poverty suburbs than if they lived in typical inner city neighborhoods. This effect held even for women who had never previously been in the labor force.

These findings supported an important body of existing research on the "spatial mismatch" hypothesis (Kain 1992). Kain argued that unemployment was high among racial minorities living in inner city neighborhoods because people were isolated from where labor markets were growing. Thus, poverty was at least in part a reflection of unequal access to transportation or unequal access to residential options in economically prosperous suburbs.

Based on this analysis, the agencies hope to identify neighborhoods that should be targeted for outreach efforts to encourage participation in the program, and neighborhoods that program participants should be encouraged to move to in order to enhance their employment prospects.

The first step will be to investigate whether Flint has neighborhoods of concentrated poverty, and whether single-mother families of different races are more or less likely to live in areas of concentrated poverty. Using 2000 Census of Population and Housing tables identifying the types of households in poverty, and the race of household heads, we can construct the following set of maps that show Flint MSA, an area that comprises Gennessee County.

Map 4.3 provides a simple description of the percent of people in poverty in each census tract in the metropolitan area. The highest proportion of people is concentrated in the central city, and some neighborhoods have more than 50 percent of people in poverty. Does the distribution of families in poverty differ in similar ways?

Map 4.4 shows there are fewer neighborhoods with very high proportions of families in poverty, as we would expect given that single adults and elderly people have higher poverty rates than families overall. How does this distribution change when we consider only the types of families the program will target—single-female-headed households with children under 18? Map 4.5 examines this group.

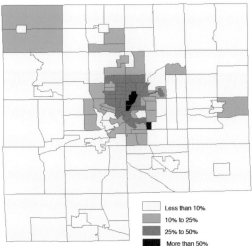

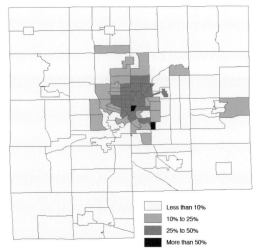

Map 4.3   Percent of people in poverty by census tract, Flint MSA (Gennessee County), Michigan.

Source: 2000 Census of Population and Housing

Map 4.4   Families in poverty by census tract, Flint MSA (Gennessee County), Michigan.

Source: 2000 Census of Population and Housing

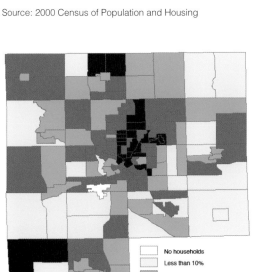

Map 4.5   Mother-headed families in poverty by census tract, Flint MSA (Gennessee County), Michigan.

Source: 2000 Census of Population and Housing

Poverty rates are clearly much higher for mother-headed families in the metro area. Map 4.5 suggests that areas where mother-headed families are more likely to be in poverty are fairly widely distributed through the metropolitan area. Not all of these families live in neighborhoods where overall poverty rates are high. However, we suspect that some of these neighborhoods may have quite small numbers of mother-headed households. We know that there are racial differences in the proportion of families that are mother-headed, and that Flint has some racially segregated neighborhoods. Map 4.6 and Map 4.7 compare the location of poverty-level mother-headed families by race.

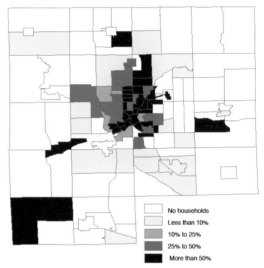

Map 4.6 White mother-headed families in poverty by census tract, Flint MSA (Gennessee County), Michigan.

Source: 2000 Census of Population and Housing

Map 4.7 African-American mother-headed families in poverty by census tract, Flint MSA (Gennessee County), Michigan.

Source: 2000 Census of Population and Housing

Quite different racial patterns emerge. While white mother-headed families in poverty are distributed throughout most of the metro area, no white mother-headed families live in several of the inner city census tracts that exhibited the greatest overall concentrations of poverty ("no households" indicate tracts where no mother-headed families lived, whether in poverty or not). African-American mother-headed families, in contrast, do not live in the majority of the suburban portions of the metro area. They are concentrated primarily in central city tracts, and are more likely to be poor if they live in the inner city. There are a few scattered suburban tracts where poverty rates are fairly high for these families, but this group is less likely to be poor if they live in a suburban neighborhood.

Another way to look at the distribution is to consider how the total number of white and African-American mother-headed families in poverty is distributed—in other words, what

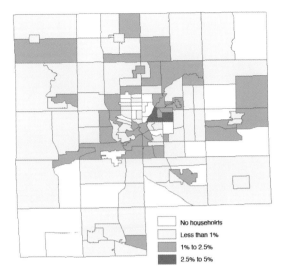

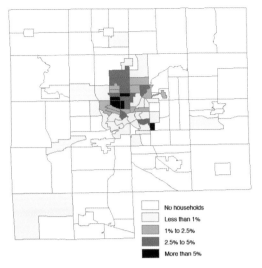

Map 4.8 Distribution of white mother-headed families in poverty by census tract, Flint MSA (Gennessee County), Michigan.

Source: 2000 Census of Population and Housing

Map 4.9 Distribution of African-American mother-headed families in poverty by census tract, Flint MSA (Gennessee County), Michigan.

Source: 2000 Census of Population and Housing

proportion live in each census tract? While white families are somewhat concentrated in a small central city area, they tend to be widely spread throughout the metropolitan area (as map 4.8 shows). The same is not true of African-American families, many of whom live in inner city neighborhoods and very few (or none) of whom live in most suburban neighborhoods (see map 4.9).

So, in answer to our first two questions, we can conclude that although mother-headed families are as likely to live in poverty in the suburbs as they are in the central city portions of the metro area, African-American mother-headed families are both more likely to live in neighborhoods with high overall poverty rates and are more likely to be poor if they live in those neighborhoods than if they live in suburban low-poverty neighborhoods. White mother-headed families in poverty are much less likely to live in inner city neighborhoods and are widely distributed throughout the metro area.

Next, we turn to the question of whether there is a relationship between residential location and labor force participation or employment for mother-headed families. Maps 4.10, 4.11, and 4.12 explore the relationship between work status in the past year and residential location. In very few neighborhoods did more than half of mother-headed families in poverty work full-time, full-year.

However, single mothers in poverty were quite likely to have worked part-time or part-year in many suburban neighborhoods. In most inner city neighborhoods, relatively small proportions worked either part- or full-time. Are we seeing the effects of racial differences here, of residential differences, or some other factor—such as the comparative age of children? Is this a full picture of the effects of either on employment given that it excludes mother-headed

Using the census to analyze economic conditions

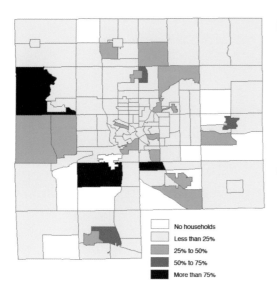

Map 4.10 Mother-headed families in poverty, worked full-time and year-round, by census tract, Flint MSA (Gennessee County), Michigan.

Source: 2000 Census of Population and Housing

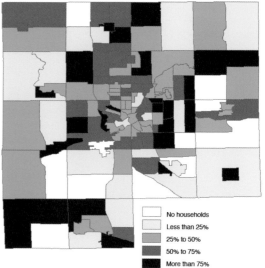

Map 4.11 Mother-headed families in poverty, worked part-time or part year, by census tract, Flint MSA (Gennessee County), Michigan.

Source: 2000 Census of Population and Housing

Map 4.12 Mother-headed families in poverty, did not work in 1999, by census tract, Flint MSA (Gennessee County), Michigan.

Source: 2000 Census of Population and Housing

households who are not in poverty? A better approach may be to consider employment status for all single-mother-headed households, comparing those with very young children who would need daycare and those with children of school age. Unfortunately, only labor force status is broken down this way, so we use it as a substitute for work experience in the past year. Overall, women with school-age children were more likely to be in the labor force than women with young children, and white mothers were more likely to be in the labor force than African-American mothers.

Maps 4.13a, 4.13b, 4.14a, and 4.14b examine labor force participation differences by race and age of children. Among single white mothers metrowide, 78 percent of those with children under 6, and 83 percent of those with school-age children, were in the labor force. Few or no white single-mother-headed families live in inner city neighborhoods. Of those that do, labor force participation rates (especially for those with school-age children) are lower in many inner city neighborhoods compared to suburban areas.

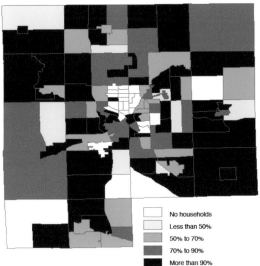

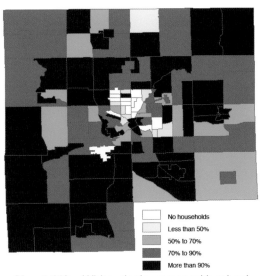

Map 4.13a White, single women with children under 6, in labor force, by census tract, Flint MSA (Gennessee County), Michigan.

Source: 2000 Census of Population and Housing

Map 4.13b White, single women with school-age children, in labor force, by census tract, Flint MSA (Gennessee County), Michigan.

Source: 2000 Census of Population and Housing

Maps 4.14a and 4.14b perform the same comparison for African-American mother-headed families. Overall, their labor force participation rates are lower, at 70 percent for those with children under 6, and 72 percent for those with school-aged children. For those living in inner city neighborhoods, labor force participation rates appear to be lower than in the surrounding suburban neighborhoods. The relationship between place and labor force participation is less clear for mothers with school-age children.

165

Using the census to analyze economic conditions

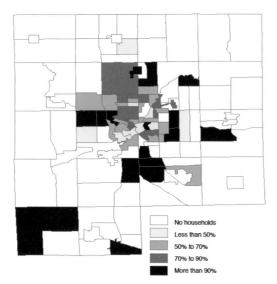

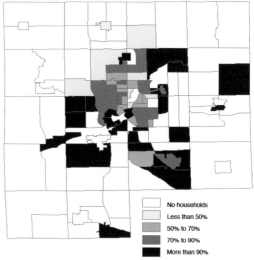

Map 4.14a African-American single women with children under 6, in labor force, by census tract, Flint MSA (Gennessee County), Michigan.

Source: 2000 Census of Population and Housing

Map 4.14b African-American single women with school-age children, in labor force, by census tract, Flint MSA (Gennessee County), Michigan.

Source: 2000 Census of Population and Housing

What can we conclude about the relationships among residence, race, and labor force participation? While African-American mothers' participation is lower than white mothers', residential location appears to affect white mothers in similar ways—those living in high-poverty, inner city neighborhoods are somewhat less likely to be in the labor force than those living in low-poverty suburbs.

To determine whether there was in fact a relationship, we performed a bivariate correlation analysis of the percent of families in poverty and the percent of women with children of different ages in the labor force[1]. As table 4.7 shows, for both white and African-American women, neighborhood poverty level and labor force participation rates were not significantly correlated for those with children under 6 (in other words, living in a high- or low-poverty neighborhood appears to have little impact on whether the woman was in the labor force or not). For those with school-age children, however, there was a significant, negative correlation between neighborhood poverty levels and labor force participation for both white and African-American women (although the relationship was somewhat more significant for white mothers, which may be a function of the wider range of tracts in which white mothers lived). Mothers living in high-poverty neighborhoods were less likely to be in the labor force than those in low-poverty neighborhoods. Given that African-American families are far more likely to live in high-poverty

[1]Bivariate correlation analysis helped us determined whether each pair of variables were linearly related (or correlated) and whether each relationship was statistically significant. The correlation statistics shown in table 4.7 indicate the direction of the relationship between each variable. A negative value shows that the variables vary inversely; in other words, as the percent of families in poverty in a tract increases, the percent of women in the labor force decreases. The statistics also show the linearity of each relationship. The closer the statistic is to 1 (or-1), the more linear the relationship between the variables (that is, pairs of values for individual cases will vary less). Table 4.7 also shows the probability that the observed relationships are due to chance (that is, whether they are statistically significant).

Table 4.7 Relationship among race, residence, and labor force participation	
Percent of women in the labor force who are:	**Correlation with percent of families in poverty in the tract**
White	
With children under 6	-.113
With children 6 to 17	-.491**
African-American	
With children under 6	-.089
With children 6 to 17	-.286*
Note: *= probability < .05; **=probability < .001.	

neighborhoods, this is likely to account in part for their lower overall labor force participation rates. Residential relocation may be a justifiable welfare-to-work strategy.

The final question we must address is where the entry-level jobs available to women with little job experience and limited skills are located. For this, we need to look for workplace-based data on job occupations. This is not available in the Census of Population and Housing tables, but the data is published in the Census Transportation Planning Package (CTPP). CTPP data is available at the Traffic Analysis Zone (TAZ) level, which is not quite as detailed as the tract data we have used to this point, but it is adequate as an indicator of which neighborhoods offer the best entry-level job prospects. Chapter 6 explains Traffic Analysis Zones in more detail.

The 2000 CTPP had not yet been released as of mid 2004, so for the purposes of this hypothetical example we will use 1990 CTPP data for Flint. If this were a real-world analysis, this would obviously be hopelessly out of date! However, it will be sufficient to illustrate the process. Our first question is: how should we define entry-level jobs? Box 4.9 explores this in more detail.

We have identified the following occupational groups where entry-level jobs are likely to grow most rapidly over the next decade:

- healthcare support occupations
- food preparation and serving-related occupations
- building and grounds cleaning and maintenance occupations
- personal care and service occupations
- office and administrative support occupations
- sales and related occupations

All of these occupations are grouped into four categories used in 1990:

- sales
- administrative support
- service occupations, except protective and households services
- handlers, equipment cleaners, helpers, and laborers

Box 4.9   Defining entry-level jobs

What counts as an "entry-level" job? The obvious answer is a job that doesn't require any experience. But, inexperienced people have different entering qualifications, and an entry-level job for a college graduate would be different from an entry-level job for a high school graduate. For this example, we are dealing with single mothers moving off welfare; although some may have some college or have completed a degree, the median education level of those who have completed the "job readiness" component of the program will be a high school diploma.

The Bureau of Labor Statistics provides detailed statistics ranking occupations by their potential for growth over the next decade, for different levels of education. This query function (along with several other search options for occupational statistics) is available at *www.bls.gov/emp/home.htm#data*.

We used the query function specifying no college education and "short-term on the job training" to identify occupations for which this would be a typical level of qualification. We sorted occupations by their projected growth: "average annual job openings due to growth and net replacement needs, 2000–2010." The top twenty occupations listed are shown in table 4.8.

These occupations fall into the following occupational groups:

- healthcare support occupations
- food preparation and serving related occupations
- building and grounds cleaning and maintenance occupations
- personal care and service occupations
- office and administrative support occupations
- sales and related occupations

Table 4.8 Occupations and earnings			
Occupation	**Percent change in employment, 2000–2010**	**Average annual job openings, 2000–2010**	**Median annual earnings**
Retail salespersons	12.4	207,000	$16,670
Food preparation and serving workers	30.5	202,000	$13,550
Cashiers, except gaming	14.2	198,000	$14,460
Waiters and waitresses	18.3	148,000	$13,350
Laborers and freight, stock, and material movers	13.9	99,000	$18,810
Office clerks, general	15.9	95,000	$21,130
Janitors and cleaners, except maids and house-keeping cleaners	13.5	74,000	$17,180
Stock clerks and order filers	8.5	74,000	$18,210
Security guards	35.4	69,000	$17,570
Teacher assistants	23.9	57,000	$17,350

Box 4.9   Defining entry-level jobs (continued)

Child care workers	10.6	53,000	$15,460
Nursing aides, orderlies, and attendants	23.5	50,000	$18,500
Packers and packagers	19.3	49,000	$15,660
Receptionists and information clerks	23.7	49,000	$20,040
Landscaping and grounds-keeping workers	29.0	48,000	$18,300
Food preparation workers	16.9	47,000	$15,360
Maids and housekeeping cleaners	5.1	44,000	$15,410
Counter attendants, cafeteria, food concession, and coffee shop workers	14.4	39,000	$13,970
Home health aides	47.3	37,000	$17,120
Truck drivers, light or delivery services workers	19.2	37,000	$22,350

Source: Bureau of Labor Statistics, Occupational Employment, Training, and Earnings data. *www.bls.gov/emp/home.htm#data*.

We can now use place-of-work-based data for the Flint metropolitan area to identify where jobs in these occupational groups were concentrated. Map 4.15 shows the locations of jobs by Traffic Analysis Zone. Overlaid on the TAZ map is a map of 2000 census tracts, the unit of analysis we have used until now. A comparison with map 4.3 shows that jobs are most numerous in many tracts with low poverty levels, particularly in the western and southeastern suburbs. And jobs are most numerous in neighborhoods where few or no African-American mother-headed families live.

A residential relocation strategy aimed at expanding choices in and around these census tracts, rather than just in any low-poverty census tracts, would provide the best chance of success. Map 4.16 shows the tracts that meet two criteria:

- a poverty rate less than 10 percent
- five hundred or more entry-level jobs

This analysis suggests that residential relocation may improve labor force participation rates among mothers heading families in poverty (especially African-American mothers, who are most likely to live in neighborhoods of concentrated poverty). It also provides a basis for deciding the neighborhoods that relocation efforts should target.

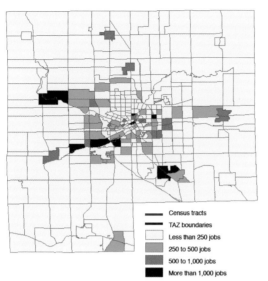

Census tracts
TAZ boundaries
Less than 250 jobs
250 to 500 jobs
500 to 1,000 jobs
More than 1,000 jobs

Map 4.15 Estimated entry-level jobs by Traffic Analysis Zone (TAZ), Flint MSA (Gennessee County), Michigan.

Source: 1990 Census Transportation Planning Package

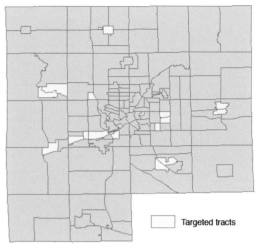

Targeted tracts

Map 4.16 Target tracts for housing assistance, Flint MSA (Gennessee County), Michigan.

Source: Calculated from 2000 Census of Population and Housing and the 1990 Census Transportation Planning Package

---

Box 4.10   Downloading CTPP data

The CTPP data is available as two CD–ROM series (a state series and an urban series—you will need the urban series for the example in this chapter); the data can also be downloaded from the Web using the TranStats site (*www.transtats.bts.gov/DataIndex.asp.* Click on **C** in the alphabetical listing and then choose **CTPP**).

The maps and the attribute tables on the CD–ROMs can be read by TransCAD, a GIS that focuses on transportation issues. All map layers on the CD–ROMs are stored in native TransCAD format, and they would need to be translated in order to use them in another GIS system. (Trans-CAD has extensive translation capabilities). For those without this software, each CD–ROM comes with a copy of TransVU™-CTPP Edition that will allow the download of data and the viewing of

map layers. This software works only on Windows 95® and Windows 98. If you are using a later version of Windows, you will need to download the NT version of this software. Go to *www.bts.gov* and select "Help," then "Census Transportation Planning Package (CTPP) 1990," and then select the updated software. This version will work on Windows NT machines, and, although it will give error messages, will, in many instances, generate the necessary data files on Windows 2000 and Windows XP machines.

Install the software, and in the Open Dataset window, select "Urban" under **Element** and then select a transportation region under **Region** (you will be prompted to install a transportation region—transportation region codes are listed on the back of the CD–ROM

Box 4.10   Downloading CTPP data (continued)

case). Under **Summary Level** choose "TAZ" (or whatever is appropriate), and under **CTPP Part** choose "2. Place of Work" (this and other CTPP terminology are discussed in detail in chapter 6). This will create data summaries at the TAZ level organized by the place-of-work (as opposed to place-of-residence) of workers. On Windows 2000 and XP machines you may need to open the Open Dataset window a few times to select all the necessary information. On these machines you will get various error messages (all of which you can ignore). Then go to **File,** then **Choose Tables,** and then select the variable(s) you may need, for instance, "U202 sex by occupation." A data table will be generated with the information. You will then need to export the table: go to **File,** then **Export** and choose **.dbf** as the file type and give the file a name. The data (now in dBase format) can be read in ArcMap or your database manager.

Documentation on the downloaded variables is available in the DOCs folder on the CD–ROM in files called CTPP_1 (covering the place-of-residence variables), CTPP_2 (covering the place-of-work variables), and CTPP_3 (covering the matrix journey-to-work variables). For further detailed download instructions for CTPP 1990 see Srinivasan and Christopher (2001).

Since the maps on the CD–ROM are all in TransCAD format, if you do not have a license to that program, you will need to generate your map layers using some other method. There are two options:

1. You can generate TAZ maps using one of the methods described in chapter 2. Note that for 1990 TAZ layers you will need to use a pre-2000 edition of TIGER/Line, otherwise the zones in your maps may not correspond to the zones on the CTPP CD–ROMs. Your local metropolitan planning organization (MPO) will likely have this data if you cannot find it on the Web.

2. The CTPP section of the TranStats Web site has downloadable copies of all map layers already translated into shapefile format.

As we indicated above, the CTPP section of the TranStats Web site also allows the download of all attribute data. As with the CD–ROMs, users must choose the element and part of the CTPP, summary level, region and year, and then the variables to download. The data is delivered in zipped .csv format—this is a text format readable in ArcMap, Access, Excel, and many other programs.

The 2000 CTPP should be available to the public sometime in the second half of 2004. The data will come with new access software not compatible with TransVU-CTPP. Later, it will also be available on the TranStats Web site.

Example two: Local economic impact analysis and creating a multiplier for a local economy

An important part of local economic impact analysis is developing reliable multipliers for a local economy. Multipliers allow analysts to predict the total economic impact of some change to a local economy. For instance, if a small county were the site of a new tractor plant that would employ two hundred people, we would want to know what the total impact would be on local employment. If we had calculated the local employment multiplier of 1.2, then 200 x 1.2 =

240; in other words, we would forecast a total of 240 new jobs locally. If the multiplier were 1.5, then we would forecast a total of 300 new jobs, and so on.

There are a number of different methods for calculating multipliers. In most instances a full input-output model may be necessary. Such models are expensive and should be used only by economic impact specialists. As a result, analysts who need an immediate estimate of the likely size of a local multiplier may have to turn to other methods. One option is to use the RIMS II multipliers, available from the Bureau of Economic Analysis and discussed earlier in this chapter. It is quite possible to calculate a multiplier very quickly using what is known as the economic base technique. However, economic base multipliers are crude, and multipliers based on other methods—such as input-output or income-expenditure—should almost always be preferred if they are available. The various economic impact analysis techniques are discussed in Davis (1990).

In an economic base analysis, the multiplier is based on the ratio of local employment involved in export activities (so-called Basic Employment or E_{Bk}, the subscript B indicating basic, the subscript k indicating the local region, and E signifying employment) and local employment not involved in export activities (so-called Nonbasic Employment or E_{Nk}). In other words, for a certain level of export activity, a certain level of nonexport activity is required. Thus, any increase in export activity will increase the level of nonexport activity. In essence, the economic base model assumes that export activity (or more correctly export demand) drives all local employment activity. Calculating basic and nonbasic employment usually relies on some form of location quotient. A location quotient is an equation that, for each sector of a local economy, divides up employment into that which directly satisfies export demand (E_{Bik} with the subscript i indicating a particular industrial sector) and that which does not (E_{Nik}). Application of the economic base technique is discussed in some detail in Klosterman (1990).

In the following example we will calculate an economic base multiplier for Buchanan County, Iowa. Buchanan is a small, rural county. Our aim is to estimate the total employment impact of a new exporting tractor plant that is going to employ two hundred people.

The basic data, downloads, translation, and queries

For this analysis we will use county-level employment data from County Business Patterns rather than from the two major alternative sources, ES202, or the Economic Census. CBP, like ES202 and unlike the Economic Census, is published annually. In the case at hand, if we used data from an Economic Census year, we would be restricting our analysis to relatively aged data. We prefer CBP to ES202 here because the former is slightly easier to use than the latter, and the omissions in CBP will be unimportant in the analysis we plan to undertake. However, we will discuss downloading and using ES202 data since, in many instances, there is good reason to prefer this data source.

We will need a complete employment data set for the county we are analyzing and a complete set for the United States, since the United States will be our comparison region. Instead of using the standard economic download tools on the census Web site (these will not generate easy-to-use data), go to the CBP home page (*www.census.gov/epcd/cbp/view/cbpview.html*) and then click on the link "Download County, State, U.S., or Puerto Rico to use with your favorite spreadsheet or database software (1988–2001)." This will enable you to download a complete set of data for an area. You will then choose the year (we have chosen 2001, the last data year available at the time of writing) and then select a state or the entire United States. In this case we will download for Iowa, and then for the entire United States. The files will appear on the Web browser and will need to be saved in text (.txt) format. At this point we have two text files, which we have called "us2001.txt" and "ia2001.txt."

> Downloading ES202 data is nearly as simple as CBP. Go to the Bureau of Labor Statistics main download data page (*www.bls.gov/data/home.htm*) and for the database labeled "State and County Employment and Wages from Covered Employment and Wages (2001 forward)" click on the flat-file icon. This will take you to the BLS's FTP site, where you will be able to select a data file to download. Select the data year (in this case, 2001), the region size (in this case, county), and then select a state. In this case we select the zipped file "CN19IA01.ZIP" (in other words, Iowa data), then download the file and extract it. The resulting text file can then be imported into a database. Note that the file is not comma or tab delimited. It is in fixed file text format. What this means is that individual fields are only distinguishable by knowing the character position of the field. In order to use the file you will need a description of the file format. This is available in the DOCUMENT folder of the FTP site (in this case *ftp://ftp.bls.gov/pub/special.requests/cew/DOCUMENT*). The file describing the layout of the data file is called "layout.txt." This will allow you to define fields manually. However, the BLS has created a convenient import specification file using Microsoft Access. The file and information on how to use it is available in the DOCUMENT folder. This will automate the process of converting the text file into an Access database table.

These files will need to be imported into a database manager. For new users the temptation will be to bring them into a spreadsheet instead, but *don't*. You will need the Structured Query Language (SQL) capabilities of a database manager to organize the data. The files we have downloaded are in comma delimited format, meaning that each field is separated by a comma. Microsoft Access will read comma delimited text files as will ArcMap and most other standard database programs. The first line in the text file will become the field headers in an Access data table.

Once the file "ia2001.txt" has been imported, we will need to run a query so that we only have data for Buchanan County, not for all of Iowa. The county field is called "fipscty," thus the query will read something like "fipscty = 019" depending on the database manager used (see chapter 2 for more on SQL queries). We will save the result of this query and call it "buchanan2001." Another query will be necessary to join "buchanan2001" to "us2001" (which we imported into an Access data table from "us2001.txt").

The main issue here is that for the United States every NAICS code has been provided (there are no disclosure problems), but at the county level only some NAICS codes will be available. You will need to perform what is known as a one-to-one query join on the NAICS codes (the join could be performed in Access, ArcMap, or any other relational database manager). These joins are discussed in chapter 2. What this means is that only the NAICS codes that exist in both tables will be in the resulting joined table. Thus, U.S. level data for many NAICS codes will be lost. In all but counties with tiny economies this will not be a problem for our analysis; remember that our purpose is to define what sectors export from our chosen county. The resulting joined table will only include the level of sectoral detail found in the county file. In this case we are left with only two- and three-digit codes and an employment number in the top row for the entire country and entire county. We could refine this join by including only those fields that we will finally need (the NAICS code, employment flag, and employment) and deleting all other fields. Advanced users may want to combine the first and second queries into a single query. Once the query(ies) has been accomplished we will need to export the resulting table into spreadsheet format and then open it. Figure 4.6 shows the first forty-eight records as they appear in Microsoft Excel.

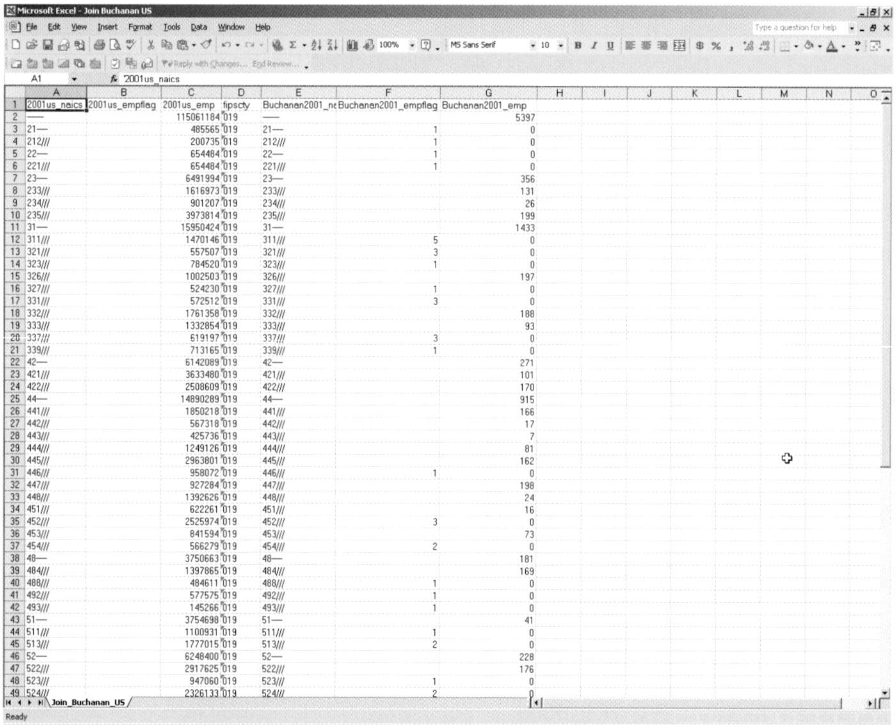

	2001us_naics	2001us_empflag	2001us_emp	fipscty	Buchanan2001_na	Buchanan2001_empflag	Buchanan2001_emp
2	——		115061184	019	——		5397
3	21—		485565	019	21—	1	0
4	212///		200735	019	212///	1	0
5	22—		654484	019	22—	1	0
6	221///		654484	019	221///	1	0
7	23—		6491994	019	23—		356
8	233///		1616973	019	233///		131
9	234///		901207	019	234///		26
10	235///		3973814	019	235///		199
11	31—		15950424	019	31—		1433
12	311///		1470146	019	311///	5	0
13	321///		557507	019	321///	3	0
14	323///		784520	019	323///	1	0
15	326///		1002503	019	326///		197
16	327///		524230	019	327///	1	0
17	331///		572512	019	331///	3	0
18	332///		1761358	019	332///		188
19	333///		1332854	019	333///		93
20	337///		619197	019	337///	3	0
21	339///		713165	019	339///	1	0
22	42—		6142089	019	42—		271
23	421///		3633480	019	421///		101
24	422///		2508609	019	422///		170
25	44—		14890289	019	44—		915
26	441///		1850218	019	441///		166
27	442///		567318	019	442///		17
28	443///		425736	019	443///		7
29	444///		1249126	019	444///		81
30	445///		2963801	019	445///		162
31	446///		958072	019	446///	1	0
32	447///		927284	019	447///		198
33	448///		1392626	019	448///		24
34	451///		622261	019	451///		16
35	452///		2525974	019	452///	3	0
36	453///		841594	019	453///		73
37	454///		566279	019	454///	2	0
38	48—		3750663	019	48—		181
39	484///		1397865	019	484///		169
40	488///		484611	019	488///	1	0
41	492///		577575	019	492///	1	0
42	493///		145266	019	493///	1	0
43	51—		3754698	019	51—		41
44	511///		1100931	019	511///	1	0
45	513///		1777015	019	513///	2	0
46	52—		6248400	019	52—		228
47	522///		2917625	019	522///		176
48	523///		947060	019	523///	1	0
49	524///		2326133	019	524///	2	0

Figure 4.6

Spreadsheet columns A, B, and C are for the national data; columns D, E, F, and G are the Buchanan County data. Before calculating the location quotient, the flagged records will need dealing with, as will remainders. Notice in cell G3, employment in Buchanan County for NAICS 21 is listed as "0" but there is a flag in the "Buchanan2001_empflag" field indicating that the data is not listed due to nondisclosure rules. The flag has the value "1." Depending on the database manager used the flag may also be an "A." The flags have standard meanings:

A (or 1) 0–19 employees
B (or 2) 20–99 employees
C (or 3) 100–249 employees
E (or 5) 250–499 employees
F (or 6) 500–999 employees
G (or 7) 1,000–2,499 employees
H (or 8) 2,500–4,999 employees
I (or 9) 5,000–9,999 employees
J (or 10) 10,000–24,999 employees
K (or 11) 25,000–49,999 employees
L (or 12) 50,000–99,999 employees
M (or 13) 100,000 or more employees

So, the zero employment number will have to be replaced by the midpoint of the appropriate range. In the current example, flags 1, 2, 3, 5, and 6 are included in our processed data file, and should be replaced as follows:

1 with midpoint 10
2 with midpoint 60
3 with midpoint 175
5 with midpoint 375
6 with midpoint 750

The general process is straightforward, but care must be taken to start at higher-level NAICS codes and work *down* to lower-level codes. In this case we start with the two-digit sectors, replacing flags with the midpoints shown above. Once this is done, all two-digit sectors should be summed and any difference between this summation and the employment figure for the entire county should be used to adjust the midpoints inserted (use a standard prorated adjustment[2]). After adjustment, sum all two-digit codes again and make sure they equal the employment number for the entire county. If they do not, then a mistake has been made.

At this point we are ready to adjust the three-digit codes. Again, replace flags with midpoints, and then *within a two-digit sector,* sum all three-digit sectors. Take the difference between the summation and the two-digit employment number to adjust the original three-digit midpoints (again, always use a prorated adjustment). Sum the three-digit numbers *within a two-digit sector,* again making sure they equal the two-digit number. If they do not, then a mistake has been

[2]Add up all two-digit employment including estimated midpoints from flagged data. Subtract from this total employment for the county, in this case 5,397. The difference (indicated by δ) must then be distributed across the estimated midpoints. Sum all the two-digit midpoints estimates used (indicated by σ). Then, for each midpoint (M) adjust up or down using the equation: adjustment factor = $\delta \times (M_n / \sigma)$. This same method can be used with three-digit midpoints. In this case, each set of three-digit midpoints within a particular two-digit sector is adjusted individually.

	A	B	C	D	E	F	G	N
	2001us_naics	2001us_empflag	2001us_emp	fipscty	Buchanan2001_n	Buchanan2001_empflag	Buchanan2001_emp	Final Employment Estimate
1								
2	—		115061184	019	—		5397	
3	21—		485565	019	21—	1	0	9
4	212///		200735	019	212///	1	0	9
5	22—		654484	019	22—	1	0	9
6	221///		654484	019	221///	1	0	9
7	23—		6491994	019	23—		356	356
8	233///		1616973	019	233///		131	131
9	234///		901207	019	234///		26	26
10	235///		3973814	019	235///		199	199
11	31—		15950424	019	31—		1433	1433
12	311///		1470146	019	311///	5	0	549
13	321///		557507	019	321///	3	0	128
14	323///		784520	019	323///	1	0	7
15	326///		1002503	019	326///		197	197
16	327///		524230	019	327///	1	0	7
17	331///		572512	019	331///	3	0	128
18	332///		1761358	019	332///		188	188
19	333///		1332854	019	333///		93	93
20	337///		619197	019	337///	3	0	128
21	339///		713165	019	339///	1	0	7
22	42—		6142089	019	42—		271	271
23	421///		3633480	019	421///		101	101
24	422///		2508609	019	422///		170	170
25	44—		14890289	019	44—		915	915
26	441///		1850218	019	441///		166	166
27	442///		567318	019	442///		17	17
28	443///		425736	019	443///		7	7
29	444///		1249126	019	444///		81	81
30	445///		2963801	019	445///		162	162
31	446///		958072	019	446///	1	0	7
32	447///		927284	019	447///		198	198
33	448///		1392626	019	448///		24	24
34	451///		622261	019	451///		16	16
35	452///		2525974	019	452///	3	0	122
36	453///		841594	019	453///		73	73
37	454///		566279	019	454///	2	0	

Figure 4.7

made. Repeat for the next two-digit sector. The result will be a new set of county employment numbers. The results—to NAICS 454—are shown in figure 4.7.

Calculating the multiplier

We are now ready to undertake the basic location quotient analysis and then calculate the multiplier. The location quotient is calculated:

$$LQ_{ik} = \frac{\dfrac{E_{ik}}{E_k}}{\dfrac{E_i}{E}}$$

The lack of a *k* subscript indicates national data; thus E_i is national employment in industry *i,* and *E* is total national employment across all industries. The location quotient compares the relative size of a particular sector in the local economy to the relative size of the national sector. If a particular sector is relatively larger locally than nationally, then it is exporting. A location quotient greater than one indicates an exporting sector. Note that the location quotient analysis should be done at the greatest level of industrial disaggregation[3]: in this case, the three-digit level except for NAICS 99 where only two-digit data is available. Analysts must be careful not to double count; in other words, beware of counting employment in a three-digit sector and then counting that same employment again by including employment in the two-digit sector that encompasses the three-digit one. Where the location quotient is greater than one, nonbasic employment in industrial sector *i* in region *k* is calculated:

[3]This helps resolve what is known as the cross-hauling problem in economic base analysis.

$$E_{Nik} = \frac{1}{LQ_{ik}} \times E_{ik}$$

For each sector, basic employment is the difference between total employment in that sector and nonbasic employment in it. All basic and all nonbasic employment across all three-digit sectors (and, in this case, one two-digit sector, NAICS 99) must then be summed to give E_{Bk} and E_{Nk}, respectively. The multiplier is then calculated:

$$\text{Economic Base Multiplier} = 1 + \frac{E_{Nk}}{E_{Bk}}$$

The results of the analysis are presented in table 4.9. The multiplier is 2.5, meaning that, on average, for every ten export jobs in the county, an additional fifteen service jobs will exist. This multiplier is high for a local economy of this sort. In other words, 2.5 should be treated as a very high estimate of the true multiplier. In the case of the new two-hundred-employee tractor plant in Buchanan County, we estimate a likely top end impact of five hundred jobs.

As Klosterman (1990) notes, the sort of economic base analysis we have undertaken to this point is crude. One result of this is that our multiplier is too high. The analysis should be adjusted to take into account productivity and per capita income differentials between the nation and the county, and we should also pay closer attention to imports and exports at the national level. Klosterman (1990) provides the equations to undertake such an analysis. We will not do that here, but we will make a few comments on the data needed for his suggested adjustments.

The productivity differential adjustment requires the calculation of v_i, the ratio of regional (in this case, county) value-added per employee in industrial sector i to national value-added per employee in that sector. This data is not available in CBP or ES202. The Annual Survey of Manufactures provides value-added and employee data down to four-digit NAICS sectors. Moreover, data for 2001 exists (go to *www.census.gov/mcd/asmdata/2001/us00.htm*). The problem here is that the data is only for manufacturing and is only for the entire state of Iowa, not Buchanan County. The Economic Census has 1997 data on value-added and employees at the county level, but for Buchanan County, there is only one set of numbers for all of manufacturing, NAICS 31-33 (go to *www.census.gov/epcd/www/ec97stat.htm* to find the data).

The issue is, should an adjustment be made on the basis of more detailed industry productivity numbers that are only available for the entire state, or should an adjustment be made on the basis of the industrially aggregated (and older) data for Buchanan County? Both courses of action involve compromise and error. The appropriate strategy will depend to a large extent on local knowledge. Does Buchanan County's economy work in much the same way as the state's, or is there reason to believe that the county is very different from the state? The point to remember is that with economic data, analysts often must choose between geographic disaggregation and industrial disaggregation.

The other two sets of data required for adjustment are easier to locate. County income is available from the State and County Data Book, and appropriate export data (though in a form different from that used by Klosterman (1990)) can be derived from Foreign Trade Statistics (go to *www.census.gov/foreign-trade/statistics*).

These two examples demonstrate different strategies for using census and related data sources to answer typical economic and employment questions. In the first, the spatial analysis capabilities of GIS are emphasized; in the second, the database management capabilities of GIS are more important. Both, we hope, make the point that there are a rich variety of sources available to analysts with basic computational and GIS skills, but that this rich variety itself poses pitfalls to the unwary. Asking the right questions about data before jumping into an analysis is key to avoiding these pitfalls.

Table 4.9	Adjusted, basic, and nonbasic employment, location quotient, and economic base multiplier, Buchanan County, Iowa, 2001				
NAICS	Adjusted employment	Location quotient	Nonbasic	Basic	Multiplier
21----	9.0	0.4			
212	9.0	1.0	9.0	0.0	
22----	9.0	0.3			
221	9.0	0.3	9.0	0.0	
23----	356.0	1.2			
233	131.0	1.7	75.8	55.2	
234	26.0	0.6	26.0	0.0	
235	199.0	1.1	186.4	12.6	
31----	1,433.0	1.9			
311	385.1	5.6	69.0	316.1	
321	179.7	6.9	26.2	153.6	
323	10.3	0.3	10.3	0.0	
326	197.0	4.2	47.0	150.0	
327	10.3	0.4	10.3	0.0	
331	179.7	6.7	26.9	152.9	
332	188.0	2.3	82.6	105.4	
333	93.0	1.5	62.5	30.5	
337	179.7	6.2	29.0	150.7	
339	10.3	0.3	10.3	0.0	
42----	271.0	0.9			
421	101.0	0.6	101.0	0.0	
422	170.0	1.4	117.7	52.3	
44----	915.0	1.3			
441	166.0	1.9	86.8	79.2	
442	17.0	0.6	17.0	0.0	
443	7.0	0.4	7.0	0.0	
444	81.0	1.4	58.6	22.4	
445	162.0	1.2	139.0	23.0	
446	7.0	0.2	7.0	0.0	
447	198.0	4.6	43.5	154.5	
448	24.0	0.4	24.0	0.0	

451	16.0	0.5	16.0	0.0	
452	122.1	1.0	118.5	3.7	
453	73.0	1.8	39.5	33.5	
454	41.9	1.6	26.6	15.3	
48----	181.0	1.0			
484	169.0	2.6	65.6	103.4	
488	4.0	0.2	4.0	0.0	
492	4.0	0.1	4.0	0.0	
493	4.0	0.6	4.0	0.0	
51----	41.0	0.2			
511	5.9	0.1	5.9	0.0	
513	35.1	0.4	35.1	0.0	
52----	228.0	0.8			
522	176.0	1.3	136.9	39.1	
523	7.4	0.2	7.4	0.0	
524	44.6	0.4	44.6	0.0	
53----	54.0	0.6			
531	46.3	0.7	46.3	0.0	
532	7.7	0.3	7.7	0.0	
54----	87.0	0.3			
541	87.0	0.3	87.0	0.0	
55----	54.0	0.4			
551	54.0	0.4	54.0	0.0	
56----	54.0	0.1			
561	46.3	0.1	46.3	0.0	
562	7.7	0.5	7.7	0.0	
61----	9.0	0.1			
611	9.0	0.1	9.0	0.0	
62----	1,025.0	1.5			
621	100.0	0.5	100.0	0.0	
622	618.5	2.6	238.5	380.0	
623	257.0	2.1	125.3	131.7	
624	49.5	0.5	49.5	0.0	
71----	28.0	0.3			
711	4.0	0.2	4.0	0.0	
713	24.0	0.4	24.0	0.0	
72----	393.0	0.8			
721	10.2	0.1	10.2	0.0	
722	382.8	1.0	382.8	0.0	
81----	236.0	0.9			
811	63.0	1.0	63.0	0.0	
812	44.2	0.7	44.2	0.0	
813	128.8	1.0	127.4	1.4	
99----	8.0	1.6	4.9	3.1	
Total			3,221.5	2,169.5	2.5

Chapter 5

Using the **census** *to **analyze housing issues***

Like many clichés, the truism that "all housing is local" is more complex than it appears at first. Housing markets vary significantly within metropolitan areas; adjacent neighborhoods may face quite different challenges, and even tiny rural towns have a "wrong" side of the tracks. Developers, community planners, human service providers, historic preservationists, and banks all rely on a detailed spatial understanding of how housing markets work.

Developers may want to know whether a new rental development for young singles would succeed in a neighborhood. They would ask questions such as these:

- How many competing properties are available?
- Is homeownership so affordable that few will rent for more than a few months?
- Is the neighborhood attractive enough for young singles? (Density of restaurants, bars, and health clubs, and access to major employment centers matter, as does the age and occupational profile of the current population.)

Community planners may want to target housing rehabilitation funds to blocks where concentrations of poorly maintained homes blight surrounding properties. They would need to answer questions like the following:

- What is the relationship between housing age and property values?
- What kinds of households are more likely to occupy older homes, and would they meet income eligibility guidelines for rehabilitation assistance from federal block grant funds?
- How much home improvement has occurred on the block and in surrounding areas, and how much private (bank) financing has supported it?

Human services providers may need to establish guidelines for energy efficiency improvements for low-income elderly households in small rural communities. Questions of interest include the following:

- How are low-income elderly households distributed?
- What kinds of homes do they occupy, and what kinds of fuels are used?
- What are their energy, property tax, and total housing costs?
- How do these expenditures compare with those of other households in their community?

Banks need to demonstrate the extent to which they meet community reinvestment needs. One part of this is evaluating the share of the market they hold for loans to different types of households. Evaluating market share entails answering questions such as these:

- What is the share of owner-occupied homes in the neighborhoods in the service area?
- Does the bank's distribution of home mortgage loans match the distribution of homeowners within the community?
- What proportions of residents in each neighborhood are low- or moderate-income, and what proportions of each group are homeowners?
- How does the bank currently serve each of these groups?
- How many renters have incomes sufficient to purchase a home?
- Which neighborhoods have sufficient potentially qualified renters to justify targeting marketing efforts there?

For each of these questions, the Census of Population and Housing is the starting point. Despite its limitations, the decennial census is the single most comprehensive source of consistent data on local housing markets. The twenty-seven housing items collected—combined with the demographic data—allow planners, urban analysts, neighborhood groups, and others to answer a wide variety of questions at progressively finer levels of spatial detail. The detailed spatial scale enables us to compare conditions across places, often a crucial justification for some kind of action somewhere. Most data is also consistently available across time, so we can identify trends important for future-oriented decisions.

In the late 1980s, Congress proposed cutting costs by dropping most housing items from the census. City and state governments were outraged, and private-sector industry organizations such as the National Association of Realtors℠ offered to volunteer their members to collect this information if the Census Bureau could not afford to (Lavin 1996). Each decade, the battle over information versus costs versus "paperwork reduction" and intrusion on individual privacy continues.

However, the majority of housing items (like many demographic items) are protected by the fact that some piece of legislation, somewhere, requires the federal government to allocate funds or set priorities based on some attribute of communities as measured by the Census of Population and Housing. For instance, cities prepare consolidated plans to justify Community Development Block Grants (CDBG) or HOME block grants from the federal government. Consolidated plans rely on information from the census on housing affordability and inadequacy, and the groups of consumers who are most vulnerable. Allocations of Low Income Housing Tax Credits (LIHTC) are higher in census tracts identified as "difficult development areas" or "qualified census tracts," which are determined based on income and housing cost information from the census and other sources. Census data is integral to public policy decisions of many sorts.

The Census of Population and Housing does have some significant gaps. Until this decade, data was collected only every ten years, so analysts faced the continuing problem of updating information. Once the American Community Survey is fully operational (see chapter 1), timeliness will be a less significant issue. Other data sources such as building codes, mortgage lending reports, and local agencies are an important supplement to decennial data.

The chapter is organized as follows: the next section discusses the major groups of variables and explains the available links between demographic and housing data. The third section discusses other widely available data sources that supplement or update decennial census data. The final section provides two practical examples of spatial analyses using census and other sources to answer typical questions about local housing conditions.

Major census housing variables

Census variables are defined very precisely, but not necessarily intuitively. In the topsy-turvy world of the census, families are not always families, and homes may have occupants but be counted as vacant. As with all census information, understanding the precise meaning of the variables is the key to using the data effectively. In some cases, the prepared tables may not address the data in exactly the way we need. Special tabulations can be ordered from the Census Bureau, but in many cases the expense and time involved makes this unattractive. Microdata (the Public Use Microdata Sample, or PUMS) avoids this problem, but at the cost of spatial detail. There are ways around this constraint; some examples are shown in the final section of this chapter.

Housing variables can be divided into three main topics:

- status and type of units
- conditions and attributes of units
- cost and financing of units

Numbers of units, whether they are occupied or vacant, and owner-occupied or rented, are based on the "short form" (the 100 percent questionnaire). These items are reported down to the block level, so they can be compared at very fine spatial scales.

For the remaining items, the data is based on a sample of approximately 17 percent of the universe (although sampling rates differ by the size of place and other factors). Chapter 1 dealt with sampling approaches and the issues of accuracy, standard errors, and confidence intervals in some detail. If absolute precision is important, analyses should be calculated with these standard errors in mind. For most analyses, the "estimates" based on the sample should be adequate. If an issue is highly politicized (such as precisely which neighborhood has more low-income elderly homeowners), confidence intervals would obviously provide more defensible results.

Although the 100 percent questions aim to reflect the "universe," underreporting, misreporting, and other errors (including changes happening between the collection date and the reporting date) undermine this aim. Data from sample questions are provided down to only the block group level, because estimates are not accurate enough beyond this point. Sample data cross-tabulated by detailed demographic characteristics such as age or race are often reported only to the census tract level. The following discussion draws heavily on the Census Bureau's definition of variables (U.S. Census Bureau 2003a, chapter 7).

Status and type of units

Number of units

What is a housing unit? This may seem the most obvious of issues, but it isn't. The concept of a housing unit is different than the more inclusive concept of living quarters. Living quarters include all kinds of group living arrangements (from sheltered care facilities and college dormitories to prisons), and all kinds of structures—from those intended for human habitation to a variety of nonresidential structures or places such as abandoned warehouses, tents, vans, and the streets. A housing unit, in contrast to a place where people live, is defined as follows:

- a residential structure (such as an apartment, single-family home, or mobile home);
- a portion of a structure wherein a household lives separately from other households that may occupy the structure;
- a structure with direct access from the outside or through a common hall that is not part of anyone else's living space.

For vacant units, it may be difficult for the enumerator to decide whether these criteria apply. If so, the judgment is based on the previous occupants. "Residential structures" include boats, recreational vehicles, tents, or vans, if they are occupied by someone as his or her usual place of residence. If they are occupied only temporarily or are vacant, they are not housing units.

Since the first housing census in 1940 until 1990, housing units were defined fairly consistently. For the 2000 Census, two changes were made. The concept of "eating separately" is no longer part of the definition of "living separately." This eliminates the dilemma faced since questions about eating arrangements were dropped after 1970. It makes the definition of a housing unit consistent with the United Nations' definition. The definition of nonfamily households also changed in 2000. The size of households of unrelated individuals was no longer used to distinguish "housing units" from "group quarters." Until 1990, households of more than nine unrelated individuals were reported as occupying group quarters rather than a housing unit. Very few households fit this category, so this is a minor change. Vacant rooms in hotels and motels were classified as housing units until 1980, if at least 75 percent of occupants were permanent residents. Beginning in 1990, they are only "housing units" if they are occupied as a permanent residence.

This may seem like a rather lengthy discussion of a basic concept, but it is surprising how much dissension this particular concept can generate!

Group quarters

"Group quarters" is in the population file, not the housing file, because it counts people rather than "housing units" or households. However, we discuss the variable here to clarify the comparison with housing units. People living in group quarters (not occupying a housing unit) are divided into two categories:

- the institutionalized population living in supervised care or custody, such as prisoners and residents of nursing homes or juvenile care facilities
- the noninstitutionalized population who are not in supervised care or custody, such as college dormitories, military bases, and group homes

The division is based on whether people are free to come and go as they please. Live-in nursing home or prison staff would be counted as noninstitutionalized even though they live in an institution.

In 1990, the count of the "noninstitutionalized" population included homeless people—in shelters, abandoned buildings, or on the street (that is, not occupying a housing unit). The count of people in public places was done by enumerators on a designated night (S-night). This count was notoriously inaccurate, and advocates conducting independent enumerations claimed that many sites were not visited by enumerators (U.S. General Accounting Office 1991, 10). For Census 2000, the Census Bureau conducted a Service-Based Enumeration in partnership with local governments, advocacy organizations, and other agencies. The enumeration was not intended to be a count of homeless people. By counting people at emergency and transitional housing shelters, soup kitchens, and certain outdoor locations, it was intended to provide a reliable estimate of people without conventional housing who needed services. However, the data on emergency and transitional shelter residents proved unreliable, and it was combined with other data on people in noninstitutional group quarters, such as facilities for victims of natural disasters (U.S. General Accounting Office 2003b). We still do not have a good solution to the methodological challenges of counting a population that is not attached to actual places, although there are several defensible approaches. It is ironic that the people with the most acute "housing problems" do not show up in our data about housing problems.

Occupied and vacant units

An "occupied housing unit" is the usual place of residence of a household. But what if the household has more than one home? Each household can only occupy one home at the time of the census. Their "usual place of residence" would be the place they spend most time. Vacant units are those not occupied by anyone at census time, unless their residents are temporarily away, perhaps on vacation or business. And, temporarily occupied units such as time-share condominiums or weekend cabins are always vacant, even if they are occupied at census time.

Homes sold or rented but not yet occupied are vacant. So are homes under construction, if they have all exterior windows and doors installed and usable floors. If even one window or door is missing, they are not yet housing units. Condemned homes or those that have deteriorated so they are open to the elements are not counted as housing units, and thus not counted as vacant. But boarded up homes are still counted as units, and thus would count as vacant.

Six types of vacant units are reported:

- for rent
- for sale
- sold or rented but not yet occupied
- for seasonal or recreational use
- homes for migrant workers
- "other"—the boarded up and abandoned

It is obviously a mistake to include seasonal holiday cabins in the count of vacant available units in a county, or to mix homes sold and awaiting occupants in with the abandoned and boarded up. Box 5.1 shows that including seasonally vacant units would lead to a large over-calculation of real vacancies in many cases.

Box 5.1   Understanding vacancy rates in Bay County, Florida

Estimates of vacancy rates may vary widely depending on the proportion of seasonally vacant units in a community. Map 5.1a shows overall vacancy rates by census tract in the Panama City–Lynn Haven MSA, which comprises Bay County, Florida.

When we adjust for seasonally vacant units, however, we see a different pattern and scale of vacancies (see map 5.1b). Although there are still many vacant for-rent and for-sale units in the community, they are concentrated in just a few census tracts.

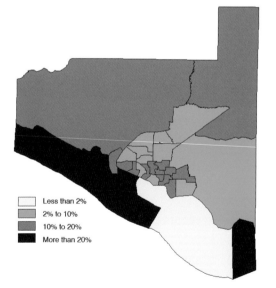

Less than 2%
2% to 10%
10% to 20%
More than 20%

Map 5.1a   Overall vacancy rates by census tract, Panama City–Lynn Haven MSA (Bay County), Florida.

Source: 2000 Census of Population and Housing

Box 5.1   Understanding vacancy rates in Bay County, Florida (continued)

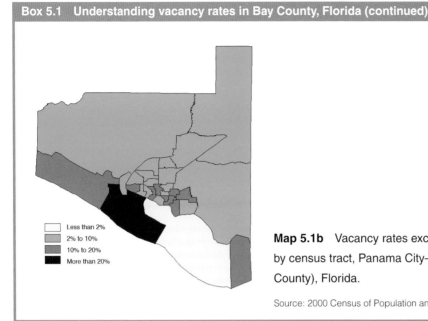

Less than 2%
2% to 10%
10% to 20%
More than 20%

Map 5.1b   Vacancy rates excluding seasonal units, by census tract, Panama City–Lynn Haven MSA (Bay County), Florida.

Source: 2000 Census of Population and Housing

The American Community Survey (ACS) will make a couple of important changes to measures of vacancy rates. Vacant units will be identified only when a sample of one of every three nonrespondents is followed up with a personal visit. So, estimated vacancy rates may not be directly comparable to rates reported in the 2000 and earlier censuses. The "usual place of residence" of a household will be wherever the household is living when they are enumerated, as long as they are living there for at least two months (Griffen and Obenski 2002; U.S. Department of Housing and Urban Development 2002a). The ACS will be conducted throughout the year, so we may see changes in reported occupancies in popular "snowbird" winter destinations like Arizona, Texas, and Florida, and similar changes in the places snowbirds leave behind for the winter. This will have important effects on several issues such as local government eligibility for federal assistance. Some communities will lose out, but the change will more accurately reflect actual populations and service needs.

Tenure

All occupied units are defined as either owned or rented. If the owner or co-owner lives in the house, even if that person has only a contract to purchase, installment loan, or purchase agreement rather than a mortgage, it is owner-occupied. Owner-occupied homes may be on leased or rented land such as a mobile home lot. The questionnaire now clarifies that debt is no disqualification for ownership. Apparently, some respondents believed the bank owned their home if they

Homeownership rates reached their highest point (66.2 percent) in 2000, reversing a small decline from 64.4 percent in 1980 to 64.2 percent in 1990. Low interest rates and income growth played an important role in this improvement. Over the past century, homeownership rates declined most sharply (from 47.8 percent in 1930 to 43.6 percent in 1940) during the Depression. However, the next decades saw the most rapid increases, as postwar federal supports for homeownership and rapid suburbanization increased the proportion of owners to 55 percent in 1950 and 61.9 percent in 1960 (Woodward and Damon 2001). Ownership rates continue to differ sharply by race, with 71.3 percent of white households owning homes, compared to 46.3 percent of African-American households.

had a mortgage. They may still believe this, but they are now directed to describe themselves as homeowners. All other occupied housing units are counted as rented, even if the occupant pays no rent. Military housing, caretaker apartments, and borrowed vans would all be rented for no cash rent.

Homeownership rates are often used to measure prosperity and neighborhood stability, but "ownership" includes many variants:

- occupants of mobile homes paying installment loans to dealers for a unit on rented land
- tenants with a contract to purchase the home they are leasing, often at an exorbitant interest rate with few legal protections
- new owners with negative equity in declining markets

Number of rooms and bedrooms

"Rooms" are enclosed areas suitable for year-round use. They include kitchens but not bathrooms, finished recreation rooms or enclosed porches but not pullman or strip kitchens. Unfinished attics and basements, halls, foyers, or utility rooms are not habitable rooms. Rooms are enclosed by a floor-to-ceiling partition (not just shelves or cabinets) but need not have a door. Before 1990, only rooms in units designed for year-round occupancy were counted.

"Bedrooms" would be rooms listed as such when advertising a home for sale or rent, even if the room is used for some other purpose now, such as a study. An efficiency apartment has no bedroom. Before 1990, bedrooms had to be used for sleeping; a room used as a study, for instance, was not a bedroom. This small change in definition matters if you are using census data to identify trends in home size over time.

Units in structure

This is one of the key variables you would use to describe the local housing stock. "Structures" are buildings separated from neighboring buildings by space or by walls that extend from ground to roof. Stores, office spaces, and other nonresidential uses are not counted as housing units, but mixed-use structures are not identified separately.

Single units: Detached single units are surrounded by space, while attached single units are separated from others by a ground-to-roof wall. Mobile homes with a permanent room addition, or with a permanent foundation, are single-family detached units, not mobile homes.

Multiple units: Units are not separated from one another by space or by ground-to-roof walls. They include row houses, apartments, and stacked duplexes. Two- to four-unit structures are technically "single-family" homes, while structures with five or more units are "multifamily" housing.

Type of ownership is different to type of structure. Row houses, town homes, and even single-family attached homes may be owned as *condominiums.* Condos are not a type of structure but a form of ownership where what is owned is a "box of air," with all land, common spaces, and exterior structures owned by the condominium association to which the homeowner pays dues. Apartments or other multiple unit structures (or even single-family homes) could be owned as *cooperatives,* where what is owned is a share in a corporation that gives the owner the right to occupy a particular unit owned by the corporation. Row houses or attached units separated by ground-to-roof walls could be owned through fee-simple ownership as zero-lot line units. In this case, the householder owns the land on which the unit is placed, and there is no common property unless a separate homeowners association exists to own it. It is also possible to own the home but lease the land on which it sits.

Mobile homes: Mobile homes include those without permanent attached structures or permanent foundations. Trailers used only for business or as extra sleeping space are not counted as separate housing units. In contrast to conventional homes, completed mobile homes for sale on a dealer's lot are not yet counted as housing units. The Department of Housing and Urban Development (HUD) defines mobile homes as "manufactured housing"; manufactured housing includes a range of prefabricated, modular, and factory-built homes that would be classified as single detached units once installed on a permanent foundation. There is a fine dividing line between these units and some of the larger "mobile homes" manufactured today. The practical distinction rests on whether the unit could be moved, even if this would require the addition of wheels. In most states, tax assessors treat mobile homes as personal property, while identical units on permanent foundations are classified (and taxed) as real estate. Cross-tabulations of unit type by tenure refer to the structure only; owner-occupied mobile homes include those on a rented lot in a park and those placed on the owner's land.

Numbers of mobile homes have grown rapidly during the postwar decades, from just 315,000 units in 1950 to nearly 8.8 million in 2000. They are concentrated in the South, making up 11.6 percent of the region's total inventory, compared to 7.6 percent of the nation's total. In South Carolina, 20.3 percent of homes are mobile homes; but they make up a tiny share of the stock in most Northeastern states, accounting for just 3 percent of units in the region as a whole (Bennefield and Bonnette 2003, 10).

Boat, RV, van, etc.: In 2000, the "other" category was revised to this more specific definition—any kind of living quarters occupied as a housing unit not included in the above definitions. Only structures occupied as permanent living quarters are counted as units in this definition; consequently, vacancy rates for this category of units are always zero.

In 1970 and 1980, seasonally vacant homes were not reflected in "units in structure." As of 2000, the question was asked on a sample basis, so trends may not be entirely comparable with figures for 1990 because of sampling error. In 1980, an additional question was asked about "units at this address"; this data is not comparable because multifamily structures may have more than one street address.

"Units in structure" are cross-tabulated separately for vacant units and by tenure, age, and race of householder. Box 5.2 demonstrates the calculation of vacancy rates for different types of units in Guilford County, North Carolina, of which Greensboro is the center and the largest city.

Box 5.2   Understanding different housing markets, Guilford County, North Carolina

Single-family, two- to four-unit structures, multi-family, and mobile homes exist in quite different kinds of markets. "Units in Structure" allows us to understand these market differences. Overall vacancy rates (shown in map 5.2a) do not necessarily reflect conditions for single-family, multi-family, or mobile homes.

While overall vacancy rates are low in only a handful of tracts, vacancy rates among single-family detached homes (shown in map 5.2b) are low in many parts of Guilford County.

Multifamily vacancy rates (see map 5.2c) are much higher—often in the same tracts where the supply of single-family homes is tight.

Vacancy rates for mobile homes (shown in map 5.2d), in contrast, are very low in many neighborhoods. The county's residents clearly face very different housing choices depending on the type of home they search for. The picture would become more complex still if we were to differentiate owner-occupied from rental housing of different types.

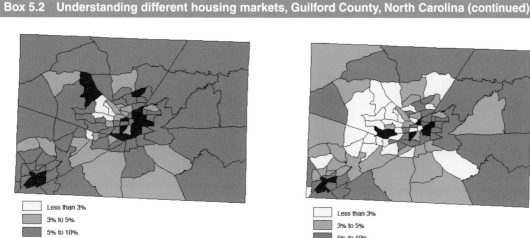

Less than 3%
3% to 5%
5% to 10%
More than 10%

Map 5.2a Overall vacancy rates by census tract, Guilford County, North Carolina.

Source: 2000 Census of Population and Housing

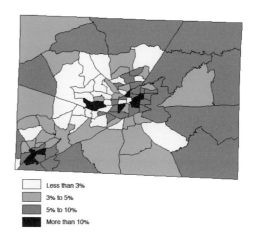

Less than 3%
3% to 5%
5% to 10%
More than 10%

Map 5.2b Vacancy rates by census tract for single detached homes, Guilford County, North Carolina.

Source: 2000 Census of Population and Housing

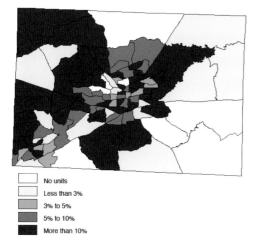

No units
Less than 3%
3% to 5%
5% to 10%
More than 10%

Map 5.2c Vacancy rates by census tract for multi-family homes, Guilford County, North Carolina.

Source: 2000 Census of Population and Housing

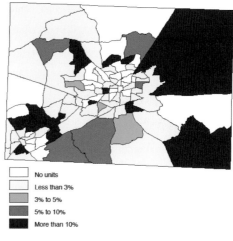

No units
Less than 3%
3% to 5%
5% to 10%
More than 10%

Map 5.2d Vacancy rates by census tract for mobile homes, Guilford County, North Carolina.

Source: 2000 Census of Population and Housing

Conditions and attributes of units

Plumbing facilities

Complete plumbing facilities include hot and cold piped water, a flush toilet, and a bathtub or shower, located inside the unit but not necessarily in the same room. Before 1990, facilities had to be for the exclusive use of the residents of the unit. Dropping this requirement in 1990

Mortgage lenders distinguish among types of structures. Structures with four or fewer units are treated as "single-family units," eligible for low-priced conventional mortgages if they are owner-occupied. Structures with five or more units are classified as multifamily, and loans are usually made on different (less lenient) terms than single-family loans. Loans for rental housing are made on commercial rates. Mobile homes classified as real estate are in principle eligible for more attractively priced single-family loans. Those classified as personal property are usually financed through dealer installment loans, or high-priced personal loans. The type of financing available to mobile home owners may have an important effect on long-term value appreciation (or depreciation).

increased the number of units with complete plumbing; in 1980, about a quarter of units classified as lacking complete plumbing had the facilities listed, but other households could use them.

This is one of the few measures of housing condition and quality included in the decennial census. As a measure of housing quality, it is limited. Very few homes had incomplete plumbing facilities in 2000, although we know a much larger number of units were inadequate in some other way. The American Housing Survey (AHS) provides much more detailed information on housing condition. An example in the final section of this chapter shows how the AHS can be used to estimate local housing quality.

Kitchen facilities

Complete kitchen facilities include a sink with piped water, a range (or cook-top and oven), and a refrigerator. Homes with a microwave or portable cooking equipment but no range, or an icebox but no refrigerator, have incomplete kitchens. This provides another measure of housing adequacy but does not directly address the condition of the unit. It is cross-tabulated with data on whether meals are included in rent, so units that do not require complete kitchens can be identified. Before 1990, data was collected only for year-round units, but the data is otherwise comparable to earlier censuses.

Year structure built

The year the structure was built is not necessarily the year it was converted to a housing unit. For mobile homes, houseboats, RVs, and so on, "year built" is the manufacturer's model year. Because this variable relies on the memory (or guess) of the occupant or, for vacant units, neighbors, it may be an unreliable measure. Box 5.3 compares the reported cohorts of housing age in Lawrence, Kansas, in the 1990 and 2000 Censuses. In 2000, the optional response "don't know" was eliminated, although it was unclear whether this improved the accuracy of responses for older homes.

One difficulty with the variable "year built" is that it often relies on the respondent's (or sometimes neighbor's) guess about the home's age. Figure 5.1 shows reported age cohorts for homes in Lawrence, Kansas, from the 1990 and 2000 Censuses.

Even after accounting for the fact that as many as half of the homes reported as built between 1989 and March 1990 may have been built in 1990, there is quite a large discrepancy in the number of homes reported as "built in the 1980s." Under- and overestimates vary by decade with no discernible pattern; although some variation may be attributable to demolitions, more is likely a result of inconsistent data.

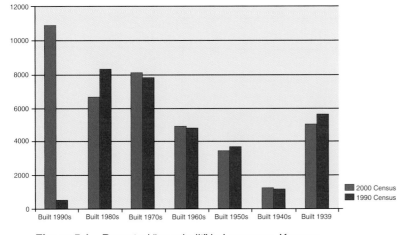

Figure 5.1   Reported "year built" in Lawrence, Kansas.

Age is obviously not necessarily a good proxy for condition; neighborhoods with older homes and stable property values are likely to have homes in good condition. However, age can be used as a basis, along with other data, to estimate the likelihood of lead paint contamination or other significant physical problems.

> Overall, 15 percent of homes were built before 1940, but age differs sharply by region— just less than 30 percent of homes in the Northeast were old, compared to only 7.2 percent of homes in the South. Five states (Iowa, Massachusetts, New York, Pennsylvania, and Vermont) and the District of Columbia have more than 30 percent of homes built before 1940 (Bennefield and Bonnette 2003).

Occupants per room

Dividing the number of people in the household by the number of rooms provides a measure of overcrowding. HUD defines units with more than one person per room as overcrowded; those with more than 1.5 people per room are severely overcrowded. Like the definition of affordability (discussed below), this is in part a cultural standard based on assumptions about housing adequacy. Overcrowding is an important measure of housing quality. While it is a minor problem in most places, it is growing in significance in very high-priced markets and in places with high concentrations of very poor households.

Overall, 5.7 percent of homes were overcrowded, and 2.7 percent were severely overcrowded in 2000 in the United States. Renters were much more likely to be overcrowded, at 11 percent compared to 3.1 percent of owners. Overcrowding also differed by race, with just less than 2 percent of non-Hispanic whites overcrowded, compared to 8.5 percent of African-Americans, 14.8 percent of Native Americans, 20.5 percent of Asians, and 25.7 percent of Native Hawaiian or Pacific Islanders. Among Hispanic households, a surprising 29.3 percent were overcrowded. Residents in the West were most likely to be overcrowded, with 10.9 percent of homes with more than one person per room, and 6.1 percent severely overcrowded. Foreign-born householders accounted for 63.5 percent of all severely overcrowded households (Bennefield and Bonnette 2003, 15).

Overcrowding may indicate that families are doubling up, that household formation is slowing, or that few adequately sized homes are available. It may also reflect different housing expectations or preferences of recent immigrants. The incidence of overcrowding in California is explored further in box 5.4.

Year householder moved into unit

Migration patterns and neighborhood stability can be estimated from this indicator of mobility. It always refers to the most recent move to the current home (not, for instance, to another apartment at the same address). Renters and owners may be expected to have different rates of mobility. Rapid turnover may indicate a neighborhood with significant problems, a

Box 5.4   Overcrowding in California

California, along with Hawaii, led the nation in the proportion of overcrowded households in 2000. Map 5.3a shows the proportion of households who were crowded in each county; map 5.3b shows the proportion who were severely overcrowded, with more than 1.5 people per room. California alone accounted for about 36 percent of all severely overcrowded units (Bennefield and Bonnette 2003, 12).

The likelihood of overcrowding differs significantly by tenure. Map 5.3c and Map 5.3d compare the proportion of severely overcrowded owner and renter households.

Box 5.4 Overcrowding in California (continued)

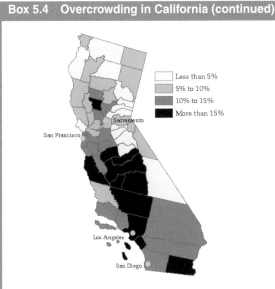

Map 5.3a Overcrowded households by county, California.

Source: 2000 Census of Population and Housing

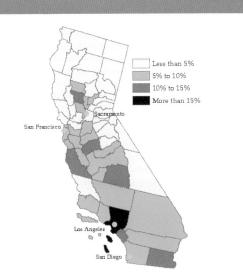

Map 5.3b Severely overcrowded households by county, California.

Source: 2000 Census of Population and Housing

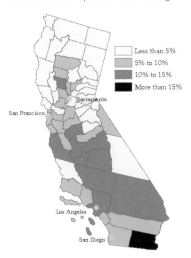

Map 5.3c Overcrowded owner households by county, California.

Source: 2000 Census of Population and Housing

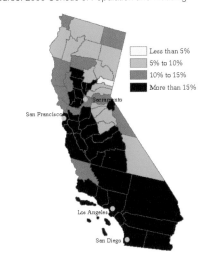

Map 5.3d Overcrowded renter households by county, California.

Source: 2000 Census of Population and Housing

Using the census to analyze housing issues

neighborhood dominated by mobile young adult renters, or a neighborhood that is gentrifying fast. The demographics of the population, trends in housing prices, and the balance between rental and owner-occupied households are important factors to bear in mind (alongside new construction) in explaining higher (or lower) mobility rates.

Nearly one in five of all households had moved in the fifteen months prior to the 2000 Census, while less than one in ten had lived in the same house for more than thirty years. Renters were far more mobile—38.8 percent had moved recently, compared to 13.5 percent of homeowners. Mobility differed sharply by age, with two-thirds of those under 25 moving recently, compared to 5.8 percent of those aged 75 to 84 (Bennefield and Bonnette 2003, 4).

House heating fuel

Each home is classified by the one type of fuel used most often to heat the home. Solar energy was included as a possible response beginning in 1990. In locations where heating is a necessity, units that report no fuel used may provide another indicator of poor housing quality. Similarly, in high-cost heating environments, reliance on electricity or wood may also indicate a quality problem. Data about fuel can be correlated with other more detailed data on costs and usage from the Residential Energy Consumption Survey (see table 5.2). Although the census questionnaire collects information about energy costs, this is not shown in the summary tables. It is only reflected in the calculation of monthly housing costs or gross rent.

Telephone service available

Telephone service has been seen as a basic necessity in the United States for some decades, ensuring access to emergency services and many other forms of assistance. Households that lack telephone service may be less prepared for health emergencies or other disasters. Estimating homes without a telephone available may also be useful for determining whether a telephone survey would reach an adequate sample of different types of households. In 2000 (in contrast to 1980 and 1990) respondents were asked whether the telephone was in service. Households where the telephone had been disconnected (for example, for nonpayment) would not be counted as having phone service available.

Vehicles available

These are the working vehicles available for all uses by household members, not the vehicles owned. Employer-owned cars kept at home would be counted if they could also be used for nonwork trips, but vehicles used only for business purposes would not be counted. Cars, vans, and trucks of one-ton capacity or less are included but not motorcycles, semis, or dismantled or immobile vehicles. Estimating housing units without a vehicle available may be useful for identifying particularly vulnerable households (such as elderly households) who may need easily accessible or home-based services. However, the question does not ask whether household members have driver licenses.

Numbers of vehicles may be used to estimate trip generation rates; households with four cars usually generate more trips (for instance, by teenagers) than those with only one car. The variable may also be used to identify relationships between population density and vehicles. For instance, do homes in dense traditional neighborhoods have fewer cars available than homes in suburban neighborhoods with similar socio-economic profiles? There have been no significant changes to this variable since 1980.

Housing costs and financing

Contract rent, gross rent, and rent asked

"Rental" units are all those not occupied by an owner, not only those for which rent is paid. Homes occupied as a condition of employment such as a minister's house or caretaker's apartment, or those owned by a friend or family member who allows the occupant to live there rent-free, are rentals with no cash rent.

Box 5.5   Comparing contract and gross rent in Knoxville, Tennessee

Contract rent may or may not include utilities and other services; gross rent includes comparable services and is a more consistent variable. Information is also collected on the rent for vacant units (asking rent). Figure 5.2 compares contract rent with gross rent and asking rent in Knoxville.

If we used contract rent to describe the housing market, we would overestimate the number of low-priced units (which probably do not include utilities) and underestimate the number of high-priced units. Because "asking rent" shows the contract rent for vacant units, it may or may not include similar services. Consequently, the gross rents of vacant units would be higher on average than the distribution shown here.

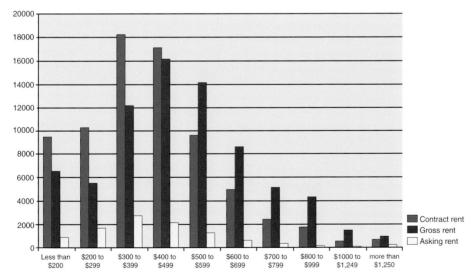

Figure 5.2   Comparing contract and gross rent in Knoxville, Tennessee.

There is an important difference between *contract* rent (the monthly rent contracted for regardless of the kinds of services included, such as utilities or meals) and *gross* rent. Gross rent is derived from several questions—it includes the contract rent and the average estimated monthly cost of utilities (electricity, gas, water, and sewer) and fuels, if these are paid by the renter. Of the two, gross rent provides a better measure for comparison. Contract rent distributions may be skewed by including units with and without paid utilities. Box 5.5 shows the different distributions of contract rent, gross rent, and asking rent for homes in Knoxville, Tennessee.

Contract rent is the total paid from all sources. So, a tenant with a government housing subsidy or with a roommate who pays half the rent would report the total paid, not just his or her share. For units that include business premises, contract rent is the amount paid for the residential portion of the unit only. However, "live-work" units would likely not be defined as separate residential and business premises. Condominium fees or cooperative carrying charges paid separately by the renter are included in the contract rent.

Aggregate gross rent is tabulated separately for units with and without meals included. Where there are many congregate housing units (not group living quarters, which are not counted as housing units), it would be helpful to separate out the number of units with meals included. Average rents could be calculated for those units to adjust the overall gross rent distribution. Gross rent is also shown for units of different sizes.

"Rent asked" is a useful indicator of the supply of units. For instance, vacancy rates may be around normal (5 percent), but there may be a very tight supply of available units with affordable rents. In 1990 and previous censuses, "rent asked" may be less reliable, because 35 percent of cases (in 1990) had missing data and were thus allocated to a rent category. However, contract rent was collected for all units in 1990 and earlier censuses but collected from only a sample in 2000. "Gross rent" was redefined in 2000 to ask about water and sewer costs, not just water costs.

Gross rent as a percentage of income

This ratio measures the affordability of the housing stock. Federal, state, and local housing programs assume that households paying more than 30 percent of their gross income in rent are "cost-burdened." Those paying more than 50 percent for rent are defined as "severely cost-burdened." Housing assistance is usually targeted to cost-burdened households. Cross-tabulations by race and ethnicity, income, age, and type of unit make it easy to identify the households most likely to have affordability problems.

Units with no cash rent and households that reported no income or a net loss in 1999 are not included in this ratio. The ratio is based on gross rent as a percentage of gross income, not tenant payments. So, households with housing assistance may be shown as "cost-burdened," but may pay no more than 30 percent of their income in rent. Accurately reflecting affordability

An interesting and useful application of rent and income data can be found in an annual report from the National Low Income Housing Coalition. The most recent report, *Out of reach 2003: America's housing wage climbs,* can be found at *www.nlihc.org/oor2003.* It includes a searchable function that will provide estimates of rental affordability for any county or metropolitan area in the nation. Using HUD estimates of median family income, fair market rents (FMR), and census data, the *Out of reach* reports calculate the percent of renters unable to afford a two-bedroom home at FMR and estimate a "housing wage" (the hourly wage a renter would have to earn to afford a home of a particular size). Changes in the "housing wage" provide a useful index of changes in affordability.

problems in a local housing market requires additional data on the numbers of households receiving assistance (local public housing authorities would be the best source of this).

Value

This variable refers to owner-occupied homes and vacant homes for sale. Estimates of the value of vacant units may be more reliable than estimates for occupied units, because "value" is based on a sales or asking price (although it does not differentiate between new and existing homes for sale). For occupied units, it is based on the owner's estimate of the home's value. It is easy to see how "value" could be randomly under- or overestimated, unless the owner has a relatively current appraisal. Values may be systematically underestimated by owners who bought their homes decades ago and have little knowledge of the local real estate market. Other owners may overestimate the value of their homes. Property tax-based estimates of market prices may be a helpful check. Many local assessor's offices have assessed values online.

Value includes the value of the land as well as the home. It is important to note the universe for which data is tabulated. Care should be taken to ensure that the appropriate tabulation is used, as box 5.6 demonstrates (next page).

Mortgage status and selected monthly owner costs

"Mortgage status" distinguishes between homes owned free and clear and those with a loan secured by the property. Loans include deeds of trust, land contracts, home equity loans, and conventional mortgage loans from a bank or broker. Data is collected separately on each loan, and monthly owner costs are tabulated separately for owners with and without a mortgage.

Like "gross rent," monthly owner cost is estimated from several questions. It is the sum of payments for

- all loans secured by the property,
- real estate taxes,

A variable may have very different values depending on the universe for which it is tabulated. "Specified owner-occupied (or vacant for-sale) units" include only single-family homes (not mobile homes) on less than ten acres without a business or medical office on the premises. Thus, "specified units" would include single-family condominium units but not those in multi-unit structures. Approximately 80 percent of all owner-occupied homes are included in this definition (Bonnette 2003, 3). Value is tabulated separately for mobile homes (which also include estimates of the value of the land, even if the home is on a rented lot) and for all owner-occupied units (including those excluded from the above description). "All owner-occupied units" includes homes in multi-unit structures and single-family homes on more than ten acres, as well as mobile homes. Map 5.4a shows the difference between the median value of all owner-occupied units and the median value of specified owner-occupied units, by census tract, in the El Paso MSA, Texas.

Map 5.4b and map 5.4c explain this difference; they show the median value of specified owner-occupied homes and owner-occupied mobile homes respectively. Mobile homes have much lower values on average, so when they are included in the calculation of value they lower the median substantially in many tracts.

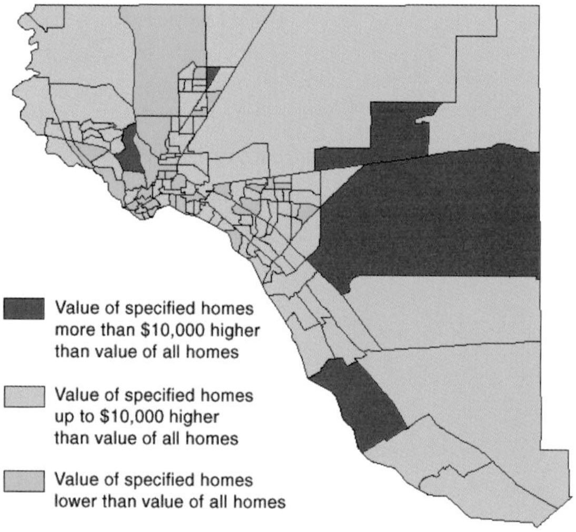

Value of specified homes more than $10,000 higher than value of all homes

Value of specified homes up to $10,000 higher than value of all homes

Value of specified homes lower than value of all homes

Map 5.4a Comparing median value of all owner-occupied homes and specified owner-occupied homes by census tract, El Paso MSA, Texas.

Source: 2000 Census of Population and Housing

- property insurance, and
- utilities and fuels.

It may also include

- monthly condominium fees,
- installment loan payments (not secured by the property), and
- lot rent and other charges associated with mobile homes.

Monthly costs are tabulated separately for all owner-occupied units, selected owner-occupied units (see definition in box 5.6 above), and owner-occupied mobile homes. Mortgage status and owner costs were collected from all sampled units beginning in 2000, not just single-family owner-occupied units, mobile homes, and condominium units.

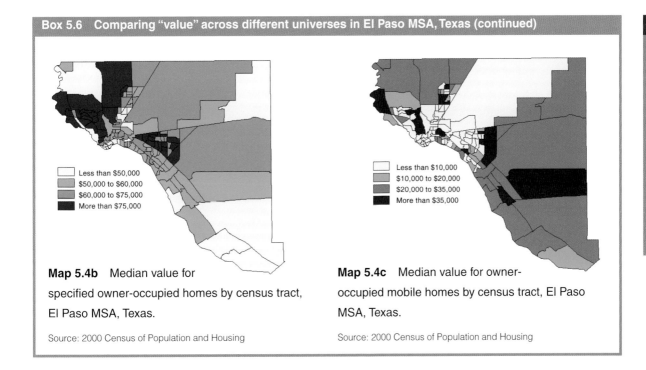

Less than $50,000
$50,000 to $60,000
$60,000 to $75,000
More than $75,000

Less than $10,000
$10,000 to $20,000
$20,000 to $35,000
More than $35,000

Map 5.4b   Median value for specified owner-occupied homes by census tract, El Paso MSA, Texas.

Source: 2000 Census of Population and Housing

Map 5.4c   Median value for owner-occupied mobile homes by census tract, El Paso MSA, Texas.

Source: 2000 Census of Population and Housing

Only 30 percent of homeowners had no mortgage in 2000, down from 35 percent in previous decades. This may reflect the increasing popularity of home equity loans. The national median monthly cost for owners with a mortgage was $1,088, but ownership was more expensive in the West ($1,289) and Northeast ($1,274). Hawaii had the highest monthly costs at $1,636, followed by New Jersey ($1,560). West Virginia ($713), Arkansas ($737), and Mississippi ($752) had the lowest monthly owner costs for those with mortgages (Bonnette 2003, 7).

Monthly owner costs as a percentage of income

This ratio measures the affordability of homeownership, but it should be used with more caution than the rental affordability ratio. Rents tend to increase regularly to reflect market prices, but homeownership costs do not. Protection from inflation in housing costs is one of the most widely recognized benefits of ownership. Thus, the ratio of monthly housing costs to income reflects a wide range of experience and choices, from long-established owners who spend a minor share of their income on housing, to new homeowners struggling to afford "as much house as they can buy." The year the household moved in may significantly affect both owner costs and affordability. Another complicating factor is that the estimate includes all mortgage payments. Home equity loans and other mortgage-type debt may be used for consumer expenditures, but this would skew estimates of ownership costs upward.

Ratios of selected owner costs to income provide a measure of potentially cost-burdened households, but a more relevant measure of affordability may be how many current renters could afford to become homeowners given the available stock of for-sale housing. This entails more complex calculations relying on assumptions about down payments, typical interest rates, and other associated ownership costs (utilities, insurance, and property taxes). Fannie Mae's *True Cost Calculator*^{SM} (*www.fmcalcs.com/tools-tcc/fanniemae/ calculator*) is a convenient way to estimate the price a home buyer of any given income level could afford. It offers a "what-if" calculation with varied down payment and total household debt options.

Lenders typically use a ratio of housing costs to gross income to calculate how much debt a household can afford. These ratios are flexible; a typical standard is 28 percent of income for housing, but recent attempts to expand home lending have pushed the "acceptable" ratio up as high as 36 percent or beyond.

Selected physical and financial conditions

This cross-tabulation summarizes the incidence of housing problems for owners and renters. The "selected" conditions are as follows:

- units lacking complete plumbing
- units lacking complete kitchen facilities
- units with more than one occupant per room
- selected monthly owner costs, or gross rent, more than 30 percent of income (that is, cost-burdened households)

Tables showing how housing characteristics vary for households of different races, ages, and incomes bring meaning to the bald facts. Table 5.1 summarizes the links between housing variables and socio-economic ones. Remember, though, that "households" are classified by the characteristics of the householder, not the characteristics of its members. Household-level data certainly loses some detail. For instance, an elderly women living with her son and his large family in a two-bedroom apartment would not show up in tables reporting housing overcrowding by age of householder. A household made up of an elderly white man and an African-American lodger and her two children would not show up in tables reporting rental housing cost-burdens by race. However, simplification makes it easier to investigate which broad types of households experience a particular problem.

The cross-tabulation shows the extent to which physical and financial problems are clustered in particular units.

Table 5.1 Available cross-tabulations of housing and demographic characteristics

	Age	Race	Hispanic origin	Income	Poverty status	Household size	Household type	Occupants/ Room
Tenure	H14, H19, H21, H43, HCT24	H11	H12, H13	HCT11	HCT22, HCT24	H17, HCT2, HCT3	H19, HCT1	H20, H21
Unit type	HCT4, HCT14	HCT30A-G	HCT30H-I	HCT14		HCT3		
Year built	HCT5, HCT15			HCT15	HCT23			H49
Year moved in	HCT7, HCT16	HCT31A-G	HCT31H-I	HCT16				
Plumbing		HCT34A-G	HCT34H-I		HCT22			H22, H49
Telephone	H43	HCT32A-G	HCT32H-I		HCT27			
Vehicles	H45	HCT33A-G	HCT33H-I					
Kitchen		HCT35A-G	HCT35H-I					
Occupants/ Room	H21	HCT29A-G	HCT29H-I		HCT22			
Gross rent		HCT36A-G	HCT36H-I	HCT18				
Rent as % income	H71	HCT39A-G	HCT39H-I	H73				
Value	H78	HCT40A-G	HCT40H-I	HCT17				
Monthly owners costs		HCT44A-G	HCT44H-I					
Owner costs as % income	H96	HCT47A-G	HCT47H-I	H97				

Note: Relevant Summary File 3 tables are listed for each pair of variables with cross-tabulated data. Variables that are not cross-tabulated have blank cells.

Other sources of housing data

While decennial census data provides the most comprehensive and consistent source of data for local housing analyses, it is limited in scope and currency. Many housing questions require additional data. Three main sources of data are discussed in this section:

- data collected through the Construction Division of the Census Bureau (housing starts and building permits);
- data collected or estimated by the U.S. Department of Housing and Urban Development (HUD) and other federal agencies;
- data collected by state agencies.

Additional sources (such as the American Housing Survey, or AHS) provide valuable data on housing trends but lack the spatial detail of the census. Box 5.7 describes the AHS in more

Box 5.7 The American Housing Survey (AHS)

Conducted biannually on a sample of approximately fifty-five thousand housing units nationwide, the AHS provides a statistically reliable summary of housing characteristics and trends in the central city, suburban, and nonmetropolitan parts of the four census regions. In addition to the national survey, forty-four metropolitan areas are surveyed every four years, and the sample provides a reliable picture of conditions and trends in the central city and suburban portions of that metro area. Although the AHS cannot be used for detailed spatial analyses, the greater level of detail it provides on housing and neighborhood characteristics can make it an extremely useful source for many background analyses.

In addition to breakdowns by metropolitan, central city, suburban, and nonmetro areas, published AHS tables compare characteristics by several categories. Standard cross-tabulations contrast owners and renters, homes built in the past four years, mobile homes, and those with moderate or severe physical problems. Elderly, African-American, and Hispanic households, those who moved in the past year, and those with incomes below the poverty level are shown separately. Many researchers use AHS microdata rather than published tables, so they are not limited by published cross-tabulations.

One of the most valuable aspects of the AHS is the level of detail it provides on specific housing conditions, such as visible problems with roofs, siding, windows, foundations, and equipment failures. This provides a much better basis for evaluating the adequacy of existing housing. Square footage, number of bathrooms, and other amenities (such as air-conditioning) provide a more precise picture of how the housing stock has changed over time. Perceptions and objective indicators of neighborhood quality, and the reasons the household moved to a particular house and neighborhood, provide other ways to measure resident satisfaction with housing choices. More detailed financial data (including source of down payment, type of mortgage including term and interest rate, and the year the mortgage was originated) also supplement census data.

An example of how the AHS may be used to supplement census data is presented at the end of this chapter. AHS microdata was used to estimate the proportion of homes of different ages that had moderate or severe physical inadequacies. Microdata can be downloaded from the HUD Web site (*www.huduser.org/datasets/ahs.html*) in SAS or ASCII format, or from the census Web site using the DataFerret data extraction system (*www.census.gov/hhes/www/ahs.html*). DataFerret is easier to use when only a small subset of variables is of interest. Microdata provides much greater flexibility in estimating typical trends for a region, even though the sample size is too small to draw conclusions about a particular state.

detail. A variety of other national surveys provides useful information on topics such as vacancy rates, rental housing ownership and management, and residential financing. Although they are not available at a detailed spatial scale, the broader trends identified may be useful benchmarks for developing local estimates of housing characteristics. Table 5.2 summarizes several sources of information on national trends.

Table 5.2 Selected nonspatial data for estimating national or regional trends			
Data source	**Type of information**	**Spatial descriptors**	**Where can I find this?**
American Housing Survey	See box 5.7	Four census regions, metropolitan/non-metropolitan and urban/rural, forty-four selected metro areas. Microdata available.	*www.huduser.org/ datasets/ahs.html or www.census.gov/hhes/ www/ahs.html*
Housing Affordability	Based on the Survey of Income and Program Participation (1995); estimates the availability of homes affordable to households of different income levels.	Nine census divisions, metropolitan/non-metropolitan and central cities/suburbs.	*www.census.gov/hhes/ www/housing/hsgaffrd/ afford95/aff95src.html*
Property Owners' and Managers' Survey	Census Bureau survey of managers or owners of about 16,300 occupied and vacant rental homes; data includes maintenance, management, tenant policy, financial characteristics, property and owner characteristics.	Four census regions, metropolitan/non-metropolitan and urban/rural. Microdata available.	*www.census.gov/hhes/ www/poms.html*
Housing Vacancies and Homeownership	Based on Current Population Survey and AHS. Data includes rental and homeowner vacancy rates, the characteristics of vacant units, and the characteristics of homeowners.	States and forty-four metropolitan areas annually; estimates of total housing inventory for four census regions.	*www.census.gov/hhes/ www/hvs.html*
Survey of Market Absorption	Census Bureau survey of newly constructed buildings with five units or more (drawn from the Survey of Construction). Data includes how soon units are rented or sold after construction completion by type of unit (privately financed, subsidized or not, rental, condominium, cooperative or time-share).	National	*www.census.gov/hhes/ www/soma.html*
Residential Finance Survey	Decennial Census Bureau survey of about 68,000 property owners and lenders; data on property, mortgage and financial characteristics for owner-occupied and rental housing, including multifamily homes.	Nine Census divisions, metropolitan/non-metropolitan, central cities/suburbs. Microdata available.	*www.census.gov/hhes/ www/rfs.html*
Residential Energy Consumption Survey	Surveys of 5,000 households; demographics, physical characteristics of homes, appliances used, types of fuel, energy usage and spending (from Energy Suppliers Survey).	Nine Census divisions, metropolitan/non-metropolitan, plus four states (CA, FL, NY, TX). Microdata available.	*www.eia.doe.gov/emeu/ recs/contents.html*
Federal Reserve Board Conventional Mortgage Interest Rates	Weekly survey of interest rates for conventional mortgages.	National	*www.federalreserve.gov/ releases/h15/data.htm*

Table 5.2	Selected nonspatial data for estimating national or regional trends (continued)		
Data source	**Type of information**	**Spatial descriptors**	**Where can I find this?**
U.S. Housing Market Conditions	Variety of quarterly housing-related data assembled by HUD from several sources.	National, with some regional data	*www.huduser.org/ periodicals/ushmc.html*
Freddie Mac Primary Mortgage Market Survey	Weekly survey of lenders to determine mortgage rates for various fixed and adjustable rate mortgages; other quarterly surveys are conducted on refinancing activity and home prices.	National (based on 125 representative lenders)	*www.freddiemac.com/ news/finance/index.html*
Fannie Mae National Housing Survey	Annual survey of approximately eighteen hundred individuals; includes data on perceptions of homeownership, use of home equity loans, understanding of home-buying process, and experience of discrimination.	National	*www.fanniemae.com*
Manufactured Homes Survey	Census Bureau survey with monthly regional estimates of manufactured home placement, sales prices, inventories, and annual estimates including characteristics of homes.	Four census regions	*www.census.gov/const/ mhs*

Spatial data from the Census Bureau

The Construction Division collects and reports monthly information on building permits for places issuing permits (about nineteen thousand cities and counties). Data reported includes the following:

- number of permits issued for residential structures of different types (single unit, two to four units, and five or more units)
- number of units within each type of structure
- value per unit

Single unit structures include both detached and attached units, as long as a ground-to-roof wall separates units and they do not share facilities (such as heating and cooling systems). Building permits are a useful way to analyze trends in residential construction and to update estimates of the housing stock. Unfortunately, information on demolition is no longer collected and must be obtained from local sources. Permits are reported at the place but not the census tract level. Permits issued in the unincorporated portions of counties are reported separately in a single category for each county.

There are several things to bear in mind when using building permit data:

- First, it is just that—data on building permits, not data on housing starts or housing completions. According to Census Bureau surveys, construction is undertaken within three months for all but a very small percentage of units authorized by permit (New Residential Construction Documentation, *www.census.gov/const/www/newresconstdoc.html*).

- Second, although the Census Bureau takes several steps to verify reported data and to develop estimates where reports are not available, there may be local anomalies that bias the results. Permit requirements may be unevenly enforced, especially in unincorporated locations.
- Third, the value reported for building permits may not be the same as the actual cost of construction, and the Census Bureau warns that the value data may not be reliable enough to compare across areas (New Residential Construction Documentation, *www.census.gov/const/www/newresconstdoc.html*).
- Fourth, monthly building permit reports are obtained from only a sample of smaller jurisdictions, while all nineteen thousand permit-issuing jurisdictions are surveyed for annual permit activity, so annual data is more reliable for smaller places than monthly data.
- Finally, the boundaries of permit-issuing areas change over time as a result of annexations, new incorporations, and so on, and this should be borne in mind when developing longitudinal comparisons.

Spatial data from other federal agencies

The U.S. Department of Housing and Urban Development (HUD) is an important source of data on several topics; a useful guide to the data sets HUD maintains is the *Guide to PD&R Datasets* (U.S. Department of Housing and Urban Development 2002b).

HUD also publishes CD–ROMS with geographically coded data. The most recent (volume three) contains seven data sets:
- American Housing Survey data aggregated at the metropolitan statistical area (MSA) zone (about 100,000 households)
- Government Sponsored Enterprises and Home Mortgage Disclosure Act data aggregated at the census tract
- Low Income Housing Tax Credit data at the project address level
- The Picture of Subsidized Households in 1998 aggregated by census tract or by project address
- State of the Cities data aggregated by MSA, central city, suburbs, and census place
- Enterprise Zone/Empowerment Community data
- New Market Initiatives data

HUD has commissioned special census tabulations at the census tract level. These tables enable localities to complete the housing market analyses required for the consolidated plans they are required to submit every five years to identify and prioritize needs and develop strategies to meet needs. These tables provide much greater detail on housing needs for different categories of low-income households. For instance, they show housing quality and housing affordability problems broken down by family type, race, and ethnicity, and the standard income categories used in federal programs. A description of the special tabulations commissioned is available at *www.huduser.org/datasets/cp.html.*

Eligibility for most federal programs is based on a series of statutory income categories:

- Extremely low-income households earn less than 30 percent of the area median income.
- Very low-income households earn between 30 percent and 50 percent of median income.
- Low-income households earn between 50 percent and 80 percent of median income.

Income cut-offs are calculated separately for households of different sizes. To complicate the issue, other cut-offs are used for other programs. Eligibility for Low Income Housing Tax Credit (LIHTC) projects, for instance, is 60 percent of median income, and some targeted homeownership programs use 115 percent of the median. Eligibility varies depending on local circumstances, rather than a nationwide standard (such as the poverty threshold, discussed in chapter 4). Standard census tables do not use these income categories, which is why the special tabulations will be helpful.

HUD updates annual estimates of median family incomes to set eligibility levels for several of its programs. It also develops annual estimates of fair market rents (FMRs) to set maximum rents covered by housing assistance vouchers. Estimates are available at the county and metropolitan levels; they can be useful benchmarks for estimating current income levels and rental housing costs at a more detailed spatial scale. However, the reliability of estimates can vary among places, and it is important to understand where they come from.

Median family income estimates

These are published annually, and can be downloaded at *www.huduser.org/datasets/il.html.* They update 2000 Census data (which collected information on 1999 incomes) using annual data on state-level changes in median family income. Estimates were updated from 1999 to 2000 using the Current Population Survey P-60 series data (chapter 4 describes the CPS). Beginning in 2001, estimates are based on data from the American Community Survey (ACS) data, which has a larger sample than the CPS and provides more precise local estimates. Next, Bureau of Labor Statistics (BLS) data on average local wage changes is used to determine whether income estimates should be adjusted because wages increased faster (or slower) than expected given ACS-based estimates of income change. Income data may also be adjusted by findings from the American Housing Survey in the years it is conducted.

If estimated incomes are lower than the previous year's, estimates are not reduced. Some income estimates were lower in 2000/2001 than in 1999/2000 because the adjustment factor came from a different source (the ACS, not the CPS). However, reported family median incomes were not adjusted downward.

HUD estimates for 1999 (based on updated 1990 Census data) were compared with 2000 Census data. The comparison suggested that median family incomes were underestimated using HUD's update methodology. The problem was more severe in nonmetropolitan areas.[1] Because the ACS is based on a larger sample, we can expect more accurate estimates of median family income by the end of this decade.

HUD calculates "statutory" income limits for very low-income families from these estimates. In principle, the statutory limit for very low-income families is 50 percent of the area median family income. But limits may be adjusted to take into account local housing costs and will never be lower than limits based on the state nonmetropolitan median family income. The "very low-income" limit is 50 percent of estimated median family incomes in only 669 nonmetro counties and 196 metro areas. So, changes in median income should not be based on changes in the "very low-income" limit.

Fair market rents (FMRs)

Fair market rents are another statutorily required set of annual estimates and can be downloaded from *www.huduser.org/datasets/fmr.html.* They are used to establish a fair payment standard for federal rental assistance. FMRs are estimates of gross rent (shelter plus all utilities) for a "moderately priced" unit of standard quality.

"Moderately priced" used to be defined as the forty-fifth percentile of rents (45 percent of units would rent for less than the FMR). In a cost-cutting measure in 1996, Congress redefined "moderately priced" to the fortieth percentile of rents, effectively lowering the federal payment standard. FMR is used primarily for the Section 8 Housing Assistance program. Households with assistance pay 30 percent of their income in rent, and the federal government makes up the balance between their payment and the fair market rent. If they can only find (or prefer) a more expensive apartment, the household would end up paying more than 30 percent for rent.

FMRs are estimated for each metro area and nonmetro county for two-bedroom "standard quality" units. They do not include subsidized units, because they are intended to reflect market prices. These are adjusted, based on ratios from the decennial census, to derive FMRs for smaller and larger units. The ratios for larger units are higher, because it is generally more difficult for larger families to find appropriately sized rentals.

FMRs are based on three sources of survey data:
- the most recent decennial census
- the American Housing Survey (for regions and the forty-four metro areas surveyed)
- random digit dialing (RDD) telephone surveys

[1]HUD estimates of 1999 median family income were within 10 percent of census reports of 1999 median family income in 88.6 percent of metropolitan areas but only 64.5 percent of nonmetropolitan counties. HUD estimates were more than 10 percent below census estimates in 10.7 percent of metro areas and 32.7 percent of nonmetro areas (FY 2003 HUD Income Limits Briefing Material. *www.huduser.org/datasets/il/fmr03/index.html*).

"Regional rent change" factors are calculated based on the AHS and survey data and are used to update annual FMR estimates for metro and nonmetro areas. For the 102 metro areas that have their own annual Consumer Price Index (CPI) survey, the rent and utility components of that CPI are used instead of regional rent change factors.

FMRs may be less precise measures of rental costs in smaller, lower-cost areas. They are based on the higher of the estimated local FMR or the statewide average FMR of nonmetropolitan counties. An earlier comparison of FMR estimates and 1990 Census data showed that FMRs were overestimated in 60 percent of nonmetropolitan counties, compared with 21 percent of metropolitan areas (U.S. Department of Housing and Urban Development 1999). Several methodological changes were made as a result. Nonmetro FMRs are now based on individual counties rather than county groups. RDD surveys provide finer detail on rent inflation by region, instead of using the regional CPI.

RDD surveys are not perfect measures of increases in rental costs. They may overestimate the supply of "standard-quality" units because they don't collect information on quality. On the other hand, they may underestimate "standard quality" units because they survey only units with a telephone. Surveys exclude public housing units, units built in the past two years, seasonal units, and those owned by relatives or that charge no cash rent. Overall, HUD claims that RDD surveys have a high degree of statistical accuracy—there is a 95 percent likelihood that the rent estimates are within 3 or 4 percent of the actual fortieth percentile rent (fair market rents for the Section 8 Housing Assistance Payments Program. *www.huduser.org/datasets/fmr.html*). Once the ACS is phased in, RDD surveys won't be necessary. Annual estimates of fortieth percentile FMRs based on the ACS will be far more reliable.

Financial data

Most mortgage lenders are required by the Home Mortgage Disclosure Act (HMDA) to report information on each loan application they receive. The data can be downloaded at *www.ffiec. gov/hmda*. HMDA's main purpose is to show the volume of mortgage credit flowing into particular neighborhoods, but it can also be used as a good indicator of where different types of people are buying or refinancing homes. Banks, savings and loans, credit unions, and mortgage brokers with assets over $30 million are covered by HMDA if they have headquarters in a metropolitan area. The data is incomplete in nonmetropolitan areas, but in recent years as the mortgage lending industry has consolidated, HMDA's coverage in nonmetro areas has improved in most states. HMDA data provides information at the census tract level. It includes demographic information on the race and gender of borrowers and co-borrowers, household income, and the loan amount. Comparisons can be drawn between loans approved and rejected, conventional and government-insured loans, and loans sold to different entities. Four categories of loans are reported:

- home purchase loans (for rental or owner-occupancy)
- home improvement loans
- refinancing loans
- multifamily loans

Unfortunately, HMDA doesn't include information on the terms of loans, so it is a less useful source for examining "subprime" lending, a major home financing issue in many neighborhoods. HUD publishes a list of specialized subprime lenders that can be used to estimate (very roughly) the extent of subprime lending.

A second source of home financing information is the Public Use Database on the Government Sponsored Enterprises (GSEs). Data can be downloaded at *www.huduser.org/datasets/gse. html.* Fannie Mae (the Federal National Mortgage Association) and Freddie Mac (the Federal Home Loan Mortgage Corporation) are government-backed secondary mortgage markets (known collectively as the GSEs) that purchase loans from mortgage lenders with funds raised through securities and bond issues. Together, they buy about 55 percent of single-family home loans. The GSE data is provided in different formats: for single-family (one to four units) and multifamily (five or more units) loans. For each type of mortgage, one file has a census tract identifier along with demographic information about the borrower (age, race, gender, income, and whether the borrower was a first-time buyer). The loan amount is shown, but not the original sales price of the home. Although the GSEs report the loan-to-value ratio and other characteristics of loans purchased, this information isn't linked to the geographic identifiers. Because GSE data covers only some home financing activity, it is less useful as a general indicator of neighborhood trends, but may be of interest for specific questions about patterns of investment.

Assisted housing data

Unfortunately, data not required by statute is collected and reported only intermittently. However, the data set A Picture of Subsidized Households in 1998 *(www.huduser.org/datasets/assthsg. html)* provides census tract and project address data on the characteristics of tenants of HUD-subsidized housing. It includes public housing, privately owned subsidized housing, and Section 8 certificate and voucher holders. Although it has not been updated since 1998, it is useful for identifying locations of subsidized housing. The data should be adjusted to reflect housing that has been demolished or is no longer subsidized. HUD regional offices can provide this information. The tenant and rent information and the census tract summaries of Section 8 recipients are obviously outdated. Local public housing authorities should be able to provide the locations of Section 8 recipients at the ZIP Code level if not the census tract level.

A database on rental housing developed through the Low Income Housing Tax Credit (LIHTC) Program is updated annually. It is available at *www.huduser.org/datasets/lihtc.html.* This program accounts for a large share of new subsidized units. The database is coded by the project address and includes numbers and sizes of units but few details on tenants or rents. State agencies may be more reliable sources for this because their databases are updated more frequently.

Data from state and other agencies

In each state, several agencies are involved in housing markets in one form or another. Housing finance authorities, community and economic development agencies, departments of revenue or taxes, health and human services, energy, and even transportation, may be valuable sources of housing-related data.

Housing value

State departments of revenue or taxes play an important role in estimating, projecting, and equalizing property taxes. In most states, an annual sales ratio study is conducted based on the assessed value of different types of property. Data is collected on aggregate market sales, and single-family properties are separated out from other types of residential property. Sales that were likely not at market prices—such as sales between relatives, seller-financed sales, or sales resulting from the settlement of an estate or as part of divorce proceedings—are excluded.

Data is typically reported at the county level and usually distinguishes between the urbanized and rural portions of the county or between incorporated and unincorporated places. However, these definitions may not match Census Bureau definitions. If the data is to be used at a finer level of detail than the county, care should be taken in determining the precise spatial definition used.

Sales ratio studies can be a useful way to estimate increases in home value in countywide markets. They may be more reliable than owner estimates of value in the census, because they are based on actual recorded sales. However, they do not distinguish between sales of new and existing homes. In places with lots of new construction, they may overestimate increases in value. Thus, they should be looked at alongside building permit data. Because sales ratios are reported for entire taxing jurisdictions, they do not capture neighborhood-level differences in appreciation.

An additional source of data on housing value is the National Association of Realtors. It assembles data on existing home sales prices by metropolitan area, which can be found at *www. realtor.org/research.nsf/pages/EHSPage?OpenDocument.* Data on housing affordability, housing starts, new home prices, and other topics are also available from the National Association of Home Builders at *www.nahb.org.*

Mobile home data

Neither building permit data nor sales ratio studies (in most states) cover mobile homes. In most states, mobile homes are legally classified as real estate if they are fixed to a permanent foundation on a site the homeowners own or on which they hold a long-term lease. They would be shown in building permit data only if the locality requires a permit for construction of a permanent foundation, so they usually do not show up in the count of new units.

If mobile homes are not fixed to a foundation or are located on land that the owner only has a short-term rental contract to occupy, they are treated as personal property (or "chattel"). They are then taxed as personal property, not real estate, and are usually licensed by the state department of transportation. Departments of transportation usually report license and registration information only at the county level, but the annual data can be useful for estimating trends.

Manufactured home placement data is only available for states. Because homes are shipped to dealers that may serve a multicounty area, more detailed local information is not routinely available. Motor vehicle registration offices should be able to provide information on the number of new manufactured homes registered each year. They may be able to report registered homes by owner address, which could be geocoded. For rented manufactured homes (accounting for about 16 percent of manufactured homes nationally) this information may be less reliable, unless units are owned by a park owner.

Subsidized housing data

State agencies concerned with housing finance and community development should be able to provide address data on several types of subsidized housing:

- HOME and the Community Development Block Grant-funded projects
- Low Income Housing Tax Credit (LIHTC) projects
- Mortgage Revenue Bond (MRB) financed projects and homeowner financing
- other locally subsidized programs such as down payment or first-time home buyer assistance, housing trust fund, and other special-purpose programs

Data on the income level of households served and some household characteristics (such as race and household type) should be available for the federal block grant programs at a minimum. Many states maintain similar databases to evaluate their own programs. Projects may not be geocoded, but project addresses should be available. States are also required to prepare statewide consolidated plans and may have collected other data for the analysis of housing markets or housing needs.

"Special needs" data

Health and human services agencies are often responsible for licensing assisted-living facilities, group homes, and nursing homes that provide specialized housing along with services. They may be able to provide detailed information on costs and the population served. To estimate service needs, they should also have data on individuals with mental or physical disabilities. In many states, health and human services departments are responsible for emergency assistance, homeless shelters, and specialized assistance programs for people with disabilities. Health and human service agencies should be a valuable source of information on housing circumstances for people with special needs, although client confidentiality is always an issue.

The federal Low Income Energy Assistance Program (LEAP) may be coordinated through a department of health and human services or human rights. The program collects information on energy usage and assistance needs, and weatherization or energy-efficiency programs. The responsible agency would be a good source of data on these housing quality issues.

Departments of public health collect and analyze a variety of epidemiological data, some of which (such as lead poisoning) may be housing related. State attorney's offices may have data on housing discrimination cases or landlord-tenant disputes. Education departments must collect information on homeless school children, and many collaborate with other agencies in sponsoring statewide studies of homelessness.

Using the census

This chapter began with several examples of questions that local governments, developers, or service agencies may have about local housing circumstances. We will deal with two examples chosen to demonstrate how spatial researchers can deal with three important limitations of the census:

- Geographic census data is only available in cross-tabulations to protect confidentiality. Public Use Microdata Sample (PUMS) data (discussed in chapter 3) is in record format, but confidentiality prohibits PUMS from being made available at any level of spatial detail below the metropolitan. Special tabulations can be ordered, but this is costly and usually not possible until all standard census products have been released. Creative strategies are needed to estimate distributions of characteristics not shown in the standard tables.

- Decennial census data is soon outdated, and estimates must be updated if it is to be used several years after the census was conducted. This problem is approaching resolution with the progress of the American Community Survey, and recent place level data available for ACS pilot areas makes this a minor problem in some places. Nevertheless, the rest of us will need an updating strategy for the next several years.

- The census does not collect information on every topic of interest to researchers and must often be linked with other data to answer specific questions. Some important supplementary sources were described in the previous section of this chapter. A creative researcher will be able to track down other helpful sources and, if time and financing permit, design surveys to provide what secondary sources cannot.

Example one: Estimating the need for new affordable senior housing

Housing needs analysis is a widely used technique to determine where, or to whom, new housing investments should be targeted. Analyses are often done area wide to determine the priority that should be placed on meeting different segments of need. This is the primary purpose of the consolidated plan required by HUD for localities that receive block grant funds. Needs analyses for the consolidated plan are based on the special census tabulations HUD commissioned. However, housing needs analyses are also done for specific types of development—for instance, new starter homes for first-time buyers or apartments aimed at young professionals. Property developers, public agencies investing in specific types of housing, or banks considering whether to provide a mortgage base their decisions in part on analyses that demonstrate the need for the proposed development in a specific place. Here, we explore an example analyzing a specific type of need, because consolidated plan methodologies are pretty clearly laid out and the special tabulations ensure that the more general analyses will be straightforward.

In this hypothetical example, we'll assume a developer is considering constructing a new twenty-four-unit efficiency apartment complex aimed at elderly households with limited incomes in some neighborhood of Rockford, Illinois. The project would be funded with housing tax credits, and tenant incomes will be limited to 50 percent of the area median income (using HUD's "very low-income" limit). Before setting to work identifying a suitable site, the developer wants to ensure the complex will be located in a neighborhood with a demonstrable need for new, affordable senior housing. If the need for the new development can be persuasively demonstrated, the project application will score higher and will more likely be funded.

Estimating the need for this development entails several assumptions. Restricting the analysis to renters only would be a mistake; there may be current elderly owners who find the costs or work involved in maintaining their own home a burden. Some owners may be willing to sell and move into rental housing. This is why homeownership rates tend to decline with age. So, one assumption is that all elderly households within the appropriate income range would be potential tenants. Another assumption is that elderly households are currently located in neighborhoods with a reasonable mix of services. Although the development might attract some tenants to a low-density suburban site, elderly households may be more reliant than others on convenient retail and services. Thus, the development would be most attractive in a location where elderly households currently live. A third assumption is that new housing would be most valuable in locations where the supply of affordably priced units is tightest, and where elderly renters are most likely to be cost-burdened. A housing needs analysis sets out to answer the following questions:

1. How many households are in need of more affordable housing, and how many are prospective tenants for the new development? To answer this question for the hypothetical example here, we need to know

- How many households are elderly (65 and older)?
- How many of these households have incomes within the qualifying range?
- How many of these households are currently cost-burdened (paying more than 30 percent of their income for rent)?

Other specific examples may examine different segments of need; for instance, the need for starter homes affordable to low-income first-time homebuyers would involve identifying renter households with incomes sufficient to qualify for a mortgage of a particular size.

2. How many units are currently available to serve the needs of these prospective tenants? To answer this question, we need to know

- the number of rental units of a suitable size for smaller elderly households
- the number of units (both occupied and for rent) renting for a similar price to the proposed development.

For a different example, we might look at the existing supply of homes affordable to low-income first-time homebuyers.

Once we can answer these two sets of questions, we will be able to identify neighborhoods with a deficit of apartments suitable for and affordable to elderly households of limited means. After narrowing down possible locations through this analysis, the developer would have a clearer idea of where to search for suitable sites. More detailed financial appraisals would identify the characteristics of competing properties in those locations, estimate operating costs and absorption rates, and thus project income, and draw conclusions about the financial feasibility of the development. However, these later stages of analysis would primarily rely on locally generated data rather than census data.

Our first step is to identify where elderly households live. Map 5.5 shows the spatial distribution of elderly households (headed by someone 65 years or older) by census tract for Winnebago County, of which Rockford, in the southeast sector, is the largest city.

Next, we need to know how many elderly households have incomes within the target range for the project. Box 5.8 explains how we could approach this.

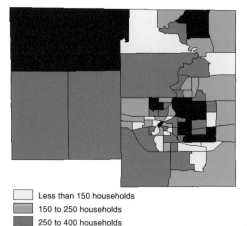

☐	Less than 150 households
▨	150 to 250 households
▤	250 to 400 households
■	More than 400 households

Map 5.5 Number of elderly households by census tract, Winnebago County, Illinois.

Source: 2000 Census of Population and Housing

One complication is that these income figures show the distribution for 1999, and assume it is now 2005. How do we update these estimates? Box 5.9 explains how we could do this.

Next, we need to identify the neighborhoods where elderly renters are most likely to have affordability problems. Map 5.7 (page 219) shows the proportion of elderly households paying more than 30 percent of their income for rent.

Box 5.8   Estimating income-eligible elderly households

What income would a household need to live in the prospective development, and what income would qualify the household to live there (given tax credit rules)? Assuming the prospective rent is $350 (for an efficiency unit), households would have to earn at least $14,000 a year to afford the rent (assuming rent is no more than 30 percent of gross income). The eligible income for a very low-income single person household in Winnebago County is $20,950 (this is the fiscal year 2003 limit, but we will use it for illustrative purposes). Using the single person income limit is more restrictive, but efficiency apartments would be more suitable for a single person than a couple.

The income distribution for elderly households is our starting point, but the intervals for which income is reported do not match our income range. Nevertheless, using simple ratios we can calculate the likely number of households within our range in each tract. Assuming that households are evenly distributed within each income category, we can calculate the proportion of households in the $10,000 to $14,999 category that are likely to have incomes between $14,000 and $14,999 (and similarly for those in the $20,000 to $24,999 category with incomes between $20,000 and $20,950).

Table 5.3 Estimating eligible elderly households			
Income category	Elderly households	Proportion eligible	Estimated number
$10,000–$14,999	28	0.2 ($14,999–$14,000) / ($14,999–$10,000)	5.59
$15,000–$19,999	39	1	39
$20,000–$24,999	20	0.19 ($20,950–$20,000) / ($24,999–$20,000)	3.8
Total:			48.39

Box 5.9   Updating estimates of income-eligible households

One approach to updating estimates is to assume that area wide increases in median family income have changed the income distribution of all area residents in similar ways. We could calculate income growth rates from changes in the HUD-estimated median family income and apply them to the income categories reported for 1999. However, elderly households are more likely to be on fixed incomes, and thus area wide income growth rates may be a poor choice. In reality, their incomes are likely to have stagnated. One compromise is to calculate the growth rate in the national median incomes of households aged 65 or older (from the Current Population Survey), compare that rate to the overall increase in national median incomes, and assume that income increases for elderly households in Winnebago County have occurred at the same fraction of the rate of overall income increases in the city. Thus, while family incomes in Winnebago County have grown by an average

Box 5.9 Updating estimates of income-eligible households (continued)

of 2.5 percent a year between 1999 and 2003, we estimate that the incomes of elderly households in the city have grown by 0.97 percent a year.

In addition, we would want to update estimates of the elderly population. Small area population estimates are notoriously unreliable; a better (and simpler) alternative is to use census-reported estimates of population by demographic groups (discussed in chapter 3) to calculate area wide rates of change for the elderly population and apply these rates to the elderly population in each census tract. Growth rates for the county's elderly population were used to estimate how the elderly population

of individual census tracts has grown. Table 5.4 shows how these two adjustments would change our calculations.

Thus, the number of elderly households within our eligible income range may have decreased very slightly, from 48.39 to 48.37, as a result of increases in income. We would obviously round these estimates off, but decimal places are shown in the tables. Although the difference is small, across several census tracts it has the potential to add up to a significant error. Map 5.6 shows the estimated distribution of eligible elderly households.

Table 5.4 Updating income estimates				
1999 income category	**Estimated 2005 income category**	**Elderly households 2005**	**Proportion eligible**	**Estimated number**
$10,000–$14,999	$10,488–$15,731	28.18	0.33 ($15,731–$14,000)/ ($15,731–$10,488)	9.3
$15,000–$19,999	$15,732–$20,976	39.26	0.99 ($20,950–$15,732)/ ($20,976–$15,732)	39.07
$20,000–$24,999	$20,977–$26,220	20.13	0	0
Total:		87.57		48.37

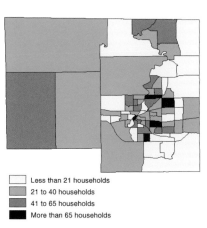

Less than 21 households
21 to 40 households
41 to 65 households
More than 65 households

Map 5.6 Income-eligible elderly households by census tract, Winnebago County, Illinois.

Source: Calculated from 2000 Census of Population and Housing

Now we turn to the next question: how many comparably sized and priced units are available to serve these households? Once again, we face the problem of interpreting within the categories summarized in the census tables; box 5.10 explains how we deal with this issue.

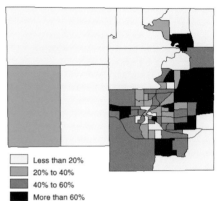

Less than 20%
20% to 40%
40% to 60%
More than 60%

Map 5.7 Cost-burdened elderly renter households by census tract, Winnebago County, Illinois.

Source: Calculated from 2000 Census of Population and Housing

---

Box 5.10 Estimating units of comparable size and price

Although we know the distribution of occupied rental units of different sizes by broad categories of gross rent, we do not know how many units there are of similar size with rents within $50 of the proposed project rents nor how many vacant for-rent efficiency units there are. This time, before performing the calculations using 2000 data, it would be more efficient to calculate an updated rent distribution before proceeding.

As our study area is a metropolitan area for which increases in fair market rents are probably reasonably reliably estimated, we could calculate an adjustment factor based on increases in FMRs since 2000 and use that as we did to adjust income categories in box 5.9. Local information on rent increases from appraisers or real estate agents (or from rent surveys) would be another way to esti-

mate rent inflation over the five-year period. For this example, we use increases in FMRs to estimate that rents have increased by 2.2 percent annually. It would also be useful to check whether new units of a similar size have been built locally, so we could update estimates of numbers of units (this information would be needed for a more detailed analysis of financial feasibility). For this example, we will assume no new efficiency apartments have been added to the stock of potentially affordable units. Table 5.5 shows the distribution of units of different sizes within updated gross rent categories and calculates the number that are likely to rent for within $50 of our proposed rent (between $300 and $400). This estimate is more likely to identify units of adequate quality; many apartments renting for less than $300 may have serious deficiencies.

Box 5.10   Estimating units of comparable size and price (continued)

Rent category 2000	Rent estimates 2005	Number of efficiencies	Proportion of comparable rent	Estimated units
Less than $200	less than $221	48	0	0
$200–$299	$222–$332	14	0.29 ($332–$300) / ($332–$222)	4.02
$300–$499	$333–$553	64	0.305 ($400–$333) / ($553–$333)	19.52
Total:		126		23.54

Table 5.5   Estimating comparably priced units

These estimates cover occupied rental units, but it may be useful to perform a similar calculation for vacant for-rent units for which we do not have any information about unit size. One approach would be to calculate what proportion of units within each rent category are efficiencies (which we could base on the gross rent by number of bedrooms table).

Rent category	Proportion of efficiencies	Number of vacant for-rent units	Estimated efficiencies for rent
Less than $200	.55	0	0
$200–$299	.37	7	2.59
$300–$499	.25	14	3.5
Total:		21	6.09

Table 5.6   Estimated efficiency apartments for rent

At this point, we are able to calculate a ratio of affordable efficiency apartments to income-eligible households, shown in map 5.8.

Although we would expect this to mirror the distribution of cost-burdened elderly renters, it may not; other households (such as students or low-income single adults) also compete for affordable efficiency apartments. Nevertheless, the two measures together give us a useful perspective on the need for new affordable efficiency apartments. Neighborhoods with high proportions of cost-burdened elderly renters and a high ratio of affordable efficiency apartments to elderly households may be locations where rental assistance would be effective, and new construction may not be needed. Neighborhoods with higher than average proportions of cost-burdened elderly renters and lower than average ratios of affordable efficiencies to elderly households, however, are likely to be those where new construction of such units would be justified.

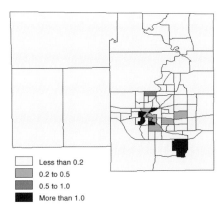

Map 5.8 Ratio of affordable efficiencies to income-eligible elderly households, Winnebago County, Illinois.

Source: Calculated from 2000 Census of Population and Housing

Legend:
- Less than 0.2
- 0.2 to 0.5
- 0.5 to 1.0
- More than 1.0

Map 5.9 identifies census tracts (identified by cross-hatching) that meet all three of our criteria:

- a higher than median number of income-eligible elderly households
- a higher than median proportion of elderly renters are cost-burdened
- a lower than median ratio of affordable efficiency apartments to income-eligible elderly households

Tract shading shows the total number of eligible elderly households. We can assume that tracts with more elderly residents have an adequate mix of services and amenities for elderly residents. A more refined analysis could supplement this by geocoding grocery stores, drug stores, healthcare, and other service agencies. Tracts were identified using a select function in ArcMap. A logical statement was constructed (using Query Builder, as shown in figure 5.3, next page) using median cut-points for these three fields.

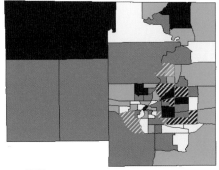

Legend:
- Less than 150 elderly households
- 150 to 250 elderly households
- 250 to 400 elderly households
- More than 400 elderly households
- Tracts meeting need criteria

Map 5.9 Census tracts meeting need criteria, Winnebago County, Illinois.

Source: Calculated from 2000 Census of Population and Housing

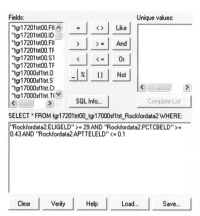

Figure 5.3

Two clusters of tracts meet the three criteria for need and appear to be attractive locations for elderly households. These clusters should be the targets of efforts to locate a site for the proposed project.

This example shows how census data can be used at a microscale to analyze the need for a specific project. Census data is also a useful way to provide a more general picture of housing conditions in order to identify particular problems that policy-makers should address. The next example demonstrates how the census can be used in combination with other data to determine the incidence of homes in poor condition and those with lead-based paint and to estimate the households potentially affected by the problem. Here, a GIS-based approach enables several layers of data to be considered simultaneously to identify priority locations for a targeted rehabilitation program.

Example two: Estimating housing rehabilitation needs

Southwest Iowa has a relatively affordable housing stock, but it is much older than the national average and thus more likely to be affected by lead-based paint and somewhat more likely to have other quality problems. This hypothetical example shows how we might construct an estimate of the need for housing rehabilitation programs in the region.

To develop an effective program, we need to know the scale of housing quality problems and the number of households likely to need public assistance to resolve them. We also need to establish criteria to weigh the relative need for and impact of any program. Short of conducting a detailed survey throughout the region to determine the incidence and severity of the housing quality problem for different households in different communities, census data combined with other sources can provide reasonable estimates of the problem sufficient to guide program design.

The census is not a very rich source of data on housing condition, but because it provides information on the age of housing it can be used as a basis for estimating some aspects of housing condition. Box 5.11 explains how other sources can be combined with census data to estimate housing quality problems.

Box 5.11   Estimating housing quality problems

How can census data be used as the basis for estimating how many homes are of inadequate quality or have lead paint contamination? Combining census data on housing age with other sources that address housing quality is a reasonable substitute for an expensive detailed survey of the actual housing stock. The American Housing Survey collects much more detailed data on housing condition and can be used as a basis for estimates of the proportion of homes in different age cohorts with moderate or severe quality problems. In addition, HUD conducted an extensive national survey in 1995 of lead paint contamination in homes of different ages (U.S. Department of Housing and Urban Development 1995). This report provides a statistically reliable set of estimates of the proportion of homes with lead-based paint in different age cohorts and in different regions.

We use the AHS to calculate how many homes in the sample with similar location (nonmetropolitan Midwest) and age characteristics have moderate or severe physical inadequacies. Table 5.7 shows the percentage of homes in each age cohort with moderate or severe inadequacies, and the percentage likely to have lead-based paint.

Most housing rehabilitation programs have a cutoff date and do not rehabilitate homes built after a particular date (for many, this is the mid-1970s). After 1976, lead-based paint was prohibited and homes built since then are unlikely to be contaminated. We could apply these percentages to the number of homes built in each age cohort to estimate how many are likely to have one of these characteristics.

Table 5.7 Estimating inadequate units			
	Moderate inadequacies	**Severe inadequacies**	**Lead-based paint**
Built before 1940	6.44%	2.53%	88%
Built 1940–1949	3.19%	1.06%	92%
Built 1950–1959	1.03%	1.37%	92%
Built 1960–1969	0.65%	0.97%	76%
Built 1970–1979	1.59%	1.77%	76%

Using the age distribution of homes from the census, we can estimate the percentage of homes that are moderately or severely inadequate or that may have lead-based paint. Because the estimates of this percentage are based on a sample, we could also calculate upper and lower bounds to the estimates using the confidence intervals reported. Map 5.10 shows the number of physically inadequate units by census tract in the region; map 5.11 shows the number of homes likely to have lead-based paint.

Relatively few homes have moderate or severe physical inadequacies, but the scale of the lead-based paint problem is vast. If rehabilitation funds were targeted to homes with both physical inadequacies and lead-based paint, the program would have the greatest impact. Remediating lead paint in a majority of homes in most communities would be a dauntingly expensive program. We

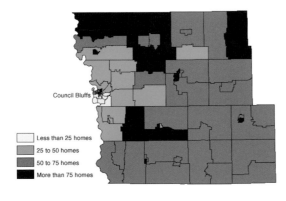

Map 5.10 Estimated moderately or severely inadequate homes by census tract, southwest Iowa.

Source: Calculated from 2000 Census of Population and Housing and 2001 American Housing Survey

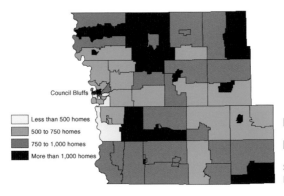

Map 5.11 Estimated homes with lead-based paint by census tract, southwest Iowa.

Source: Calculated from 2000 Census of Population and Housing and HUD (1995)

also know that Iowa's population is aging, and that in many communities (especially nonmetropolitan ones) elderly households make up a significant share of residents. Elderly households are more likely to occupy older homes. Lead-based paint is primarily a problem for households in the child-bearing and rearing years, so households with heads aged up to 45 years are likely to be most affected by lead-based paint.

Map 5.12 shows another source of information from the Iowa Department of Public Health. Children under 6 are tested every year in each county; the map shows the proportion of children tested who had elevated blood lead levels. A set of priority locations for lead-based paint abatement is emerging. Targeting remediation funds to those locations with larger proportions of affected children would be justified, but impact on the quality of the housing stock will also be an important goal.

Who should be responsible for removing this hazard? Because the data is broken down by tenure, we can estimate the number of owner and renter households affected. Renter households could be assisted in two ways: by requiring property owners to resolve the problem or by enabling affected households to move to other units. Resolving problems for renters will require different funding sources: housing assistance or direct subsidies to property owners. A separate analysis could identify the availability of better quality units that renters could afford with assistance, and determine which strategy would be appropriate in each place.

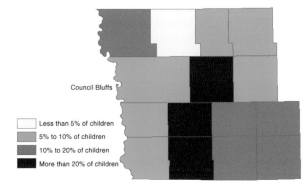

Map 5.12   Estimated affected children by county, southwest Iowa.

Source: Calculated from 2000 Census of Population and Housing, HUD (1995), and Department of Public Health (2000)

Legend:
- Less than 5% of children
- 5% to 10% of children
- 10% to 20% of children
- More than 20% of children

Owner households are more likely to need direct assistance in place. Of the affected owner households (those headed by someone younger than 45), it is likely that at least some have sufficient income to resolve the problem themselves. We could assume that the households in greatest need of assistance are those with incomes below poverty. Summary File 3 provides information on the poverty status of potentially affected households by age category. More assistance will be needed in locations with more owners in poverty. Map 5.13 shows estimates of the proportion of potentially affected owner households with incomes below poverty level.

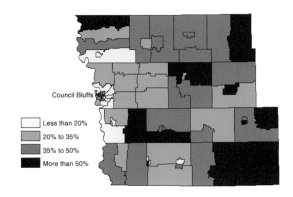

Map 5.13   Proportion of estimated affected owner households in poverty by census tract, southwest Iowa.

Source: Calculated from 2000 Census of Population and Housing and HUD (1995)

Legend:
- Less than 20%
- 20% to 35%
- 35% to 50%
- More than 50%

Where should assistance be targeted? Map 5.14 highlights those tracts that meet three criteria:
- More than 20 percent of children tested in the county had high blood-lead levels.
- More than 20 percent of potentially affected owner households are in poverty.
- More than 5 percent of homes are estimated to have moderate or severe physical problems.

A similar select query function to that shown in the first example was used to identify the tracts that meet these three criteria. They are shaded blue in map 5.14.

An effective housing rehabilitation program would target those locations with the greatest proportion of affected children and those locations where housing quality and owners' ability to resolve problems are poorest. While there is a need for rehabilitation funds throughout this region of the state, the highlighted locations are justifiably priorities for funding.

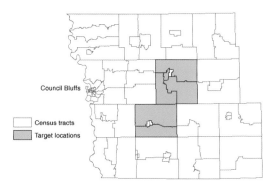

Council Bluffs

☐ Census tracts
■ Target locations

Map 5.14 Target census tracts for housing rehabilitation, southwest Iowa.

Source: Calculated from 2000 Census of Population and Housing and HUD (1995)

Identifying targeted locations for rehabilitation programs is just one example of how census data can be used to guide program design. Similar analyses could have identified locations where first-time home buyers face the greatest constraints because of the mismatch between incomes and housing prices or face the greatest difficulty obtaining home loans, locations where tenant-based assistance may be more appropriate than subsidizing new construction because of the ample available supply of rental units, or places where mobile home rehabilitation and replacement programs are most needed.

Although the census is widely used for several mandatory purposes, it has the potential to contribute to many other policy decisions. It is easy to forget that desktop census analysis has only been possible since the 1990 data was released. Only with the increased accessibility of geographic census products and GIS analysis packages during the past decade has it become possible to use the census to its full potential. Geographic analysis promises new ways of asking questions and understanding their answers, but it will only do so if it is easily accessible to decision makers, their advisors, and the public. Chapter 7 explores these issues.

Chapter *6*

Using the *census*
*to **analyze transportation issues***

Understanding people's travel patterns can help evaluate infrastructure investment needs, identify mismatches between homes and jobs, and predict patterns of suburban growth. While the Census of Population and Housing collects only a few pieces of information about travel and transportation resources, this information allows transportation planners to analyze several important questions. The role of GIS in analyzing transportation questions is particularly well developed, as we would expect given the fundamentally spatial nature of the topic.[1]

Public sector agencies need to plan for the growing congestion on our roads. For instance, a state transportation agency deciding whether to increase road capacity in a county would need to answer the following questions:

- How many trips are being made, and how many are being made by each mode (car, bus, and so on)?
- Where do trips begin and end?
- What time of day do trips begin, and how long do they take?
- How are future travel patterns likely to change?

City planners need to forecast travel demand in their comprehensive plans. In addition to understanding the existing transportation networks, they need demographic and social information such as the following:

- How many people are old enough to drive?
- How many people work outside the home?
- What is the income distribution of households?
- What is the education level and occupation of workers?
- Where do people work?

[1] Paul Hanley, an assistant professor in the graduate program in Urban and Regional Planning at the University of Iowa, contributed to this chapter. His research and teaching focus is on transportation and environmental issues.

Regional planning agencies are required to meet federal and state environmental mandates. For example, a region that does not meet the air quality standards of the Clean Air Act Amendments (a "nonattainment" region) must document its efforts to comply. Census data can be used to document changes in

- total vehicle miles traveled,
- number of single-occupancy vehicles,
- use of mass transit, and
- travel time.

Economic development planners may need to estimate the commuting shed from which a business will draw workers. Questions they might have include

- Where do people of working age live?
- How many are in the labor force?
- What are their occupations?
- Is the location drawing in workers from outside its boundaries, or is it exporting workers to other locations?

The focus of transportation planners has widened beyond just building new roads to include finding ways to reduce travel demand and to reduce impacts on the natural and social environment. These new questions have created a demand for more sophisticated, dependable transportation data and analysis methods. The Census of Population and Housing collects consistent, comparable information on one primary transportation topic—the journey to work. This data can be linked to a variety of the demographic and economic characteristics of people and households discussed in previous chapters. While the tables provided in Summary File 3 allow one to summarize work trips for people living in a particular place, census tract, or county, the data is provided in two other formats widely used for analyses.

The special-purpose Census Transportation Planning Package (CTPP) links travel characteristics by place of residence to travel characteristics by place of work. The origin-destination data in the CTPP can be used to update travel demand forecasting models for a particular city, or to investigate commuting patterns along a particular corridor. The Public Use Microdata Sample (PUMS) samples the responses collected in the long form to provide individual-level data that can be analyzed much more flexibly than the cross-tabulations in Summary File 3 allow. For instance, the likelihood that someone with a particular income and occupation would travel to work alone in a car rather than take a bus or train can be estimated using PUMS.

The chapter is organized as follows: the next section discusses the variables collected in the decennial census and explains the available links between demographic, economic, and travel data. The major formats in which this data is made available are explained in this section. The third section of the chapter discusses other widely available data sources that supplement or update decennial census data. The final section provides two examples of analyses using census and other sources to answer typical questions about local transportation issues.

Transportation data collected by the census

The census has asked about people's journey to work since 1960. There have been a few changes since then, and it is important to understand these if you plan to analyze trends over time. The census transportation questions are asked in the sample (long form) questionnaire. Sampling rates differ by size of place, but overall about one in six households (17 percent) are surveyed about their travel behavior. Thus, the data reported is in fact an estimate. Given the high fixed costs entailed in most new transportation investments, it is often important to ensure greater accuracy by calculating the confidence interval for each estimate. Chapter 1 dealt with the basic principles of sampling approaches and the issues of accuracy, standard errors, and confidence intervals. A later example in this chapter shows how confidence intervals would be calculated in an analysis using the PUMS.

In addition to journey to work (collected for each employed person), information is collected about the vehicles available in each household. So, there is transportation data in both the "population" and "housing" segments of the decennial census. While there is some overlap in the variables covered in this and previous chapters, the same information can be used for very different purposes. So, for consistency of treatment, we chose to tailor each discussion to the purpose for which the data is likely to be used. The discussion below draws heavily on the definition of variables provided by the Census Bureau (U.S. Census Bureau 2003a, chapter 7). The variables are published in different formats, each of which is discussed once we have explained the variable definitions.

There are some important limitations in the coverage of the transportation data the census provides. Because only work trips are covered, a significant amount of travel (including travel by children, the elderly, and others who are not in the labor force or unemployed) is not reflected in this data. Other types of transportation issues (transportation infrastructure, freight movement, long distance travel, and so on) are not reflected in decennial census data either, although aspects are covered in the economic censuses. Other data sources (discussed in the following section) supplement some of these gaps.

Place of work

Place of work data is used to estimate commuting from home to work. The question is asked of people who are 16 years and older and who worked during the week before completing the questionnaire. People are asked for the primary place of employment for the job they worked that week, and information is collected for the exact street address, place (or whether the job was outside an incorporated place), county, and metropolitan area (if applicable). The data does not cover a specific week. It also excludes the work trips of employed people who were away from work during the previous week and work trips to a second job. Thus, the total number of jobs in a particular place may be underestimated. If someone (for example, a construction laborer) travels to different job sites, then the person is asked to report the place were the majority of work time was spent. This may produce a temporary spike in the number of jobs within a geographic region. Place of work data is also discussed in box 4.4 in chapter 4. Beginning in 1990, "place of work" was imputed based on answers to the other transportation questions if responses were missing, and the "not reported" category was eliminated.

Usual means of transportation

For each person who was 16 or older and worked outside his or her home in the previous week, information is collected about the primary travel mode ("means of transportation") used for the home-to-work trip. Only one travel mode is reported. If an individual used more than one means, such as driving to a park-and-ride and then riding a train to complete the journey, the person was required to report only one—the means used for the longest distance. The information is limited because it does not capture any multimodal trips (or any trips other than the work trip). Beginning in 1990, automobiles, trucks, and vans are no longer identified separately. When comparing vehicle use from the 1990 and 2000 Censuses with that of earlier years, the combined total of automobiles, trucks, and vans should be calculated from the earlier censuses. Box 6.1 examines what the data can tell us about work trips in Minneapolis–St. Paul, Minnesota.

Box 6.1   Mode of travel to work

Reducing the number of people driving alone to work is an important part of meeting Clean Air Act Amendment mandates in metropolitan areas. In recent decades, the effect of urban form on modes of travel has been an important concern of transportation and land-use planners. Do people choose different modes of transportation if they live in different kinds of neighborhoods? We investigate this question for three counties in the Minneapolis–St. Paul metro area. Map 6.1a shows the proportion of workers driving to work alone in each tract. In many suburban tracts, more than 90 percent of workers commute to work alone in their car, truck, or van. However, less than half of workers drive alone in the centrally located tracts.

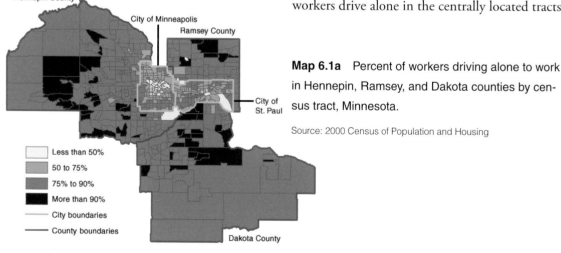

Map 6.1a   Percent of workers driving alone to work in Hennepin, Ramsey, and Dakota counties by census tract, Minnesota.

Source: 2000 Census of Population and Housing

Box 6.1 Mode of travel to work (continued)

Does the proportion of people taking public transit vary in similar ways between neighborhoods? Map 6.1b suggests a strong relationship, with high rates of public transit use concentrated in central city neighborhoods.

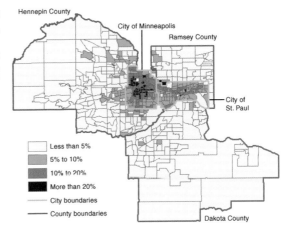

Map 6.1b Percent taking transit to work in Hennepin, Ramsey, and Dakota counties by census tract, Minnesota.

Source: 2000 Census of Population and Housing

The difference is even more marked when we consider people who walk to work. Map 6.1c shows that in just a handful of centrally located tracts, more than 20 percent of people walk to work, but in very few suburban tracts do more than 5 percent of people walk to work.

Better balancing housing and jobs throughout the metro area may allow more people the opportunity to walk to work or to take public transit.

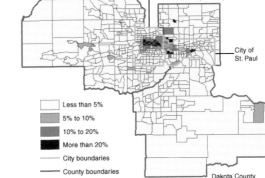

Map 6.1c Percent walking to work in Hennepin, Ramsey, and Dakota counties by census tract, Minnesota.

Source: 2000 Census of Population and Housing

Number of persons in the vehicle

Vehicle occupancy rates are shown for those who traveled to work by car, truck, or van. This data, along with the estimates of total workers, allows us to calculate the number of vehicles being used for the home-to-work trip. Vehicle occupancy rates provide important data for measuring progress toward attaining Clean Air Act travel reduction goals. For the 2000 Census, the 1990 response categories of "five people" and "six people" were collapsed into a single category.

Using the census to analyze transportation issues

Time of departure for work

The time the person leaves home to travel to work is reported separately. This data allows us to calculate peak work travel hours. The data collected may not be precisely accurate, as it relies on the memory of the person responding (who is not necessarily the worker), and there is some evidence that responses are rounded to the nearest quarter hour. This is mostly an issue when using microdata, as Summary File 3 reports even peak hour times in half-hour categories. A different limitation is that respondents are asked to report only one typical time at which they begin the trip for the primary job held. For people who work flexible or variable hours, or more than one job, the data will be inaccurate.

Although the decennial census focuses only on work trips, work and work-related trips in fact make up only a minority of daily trips—17.7 percent, compared to nearly 45 percent of trips for personal and family business, according to the 2001 National Household Transportation Survey. Even social and recreational trips (27.1 percent of daily trips) outrank work trips (U.S. Bureau of Transportation Statistics 2003, figure 7). Consequently, the most trips are not made during the morning peak hour (7 to 8 A.M., when about 6.2 percent of all trips are made). The busiest hour is 3 to 4 P.M., with about 8.3 percent of all trips occurring during that time. In fact, a higher proportion of daily trips are made each hour between 11 A.M. and 7 P.M. than are made from 7 to 8 in the morning (U.S. Bureau of Transportation Statistics 2003, table A-12).

Usual travel time to work

The typical length of the work trip is reported in minutes rather than by distance, so it takes into account congestion and other factors. Again, this data relies on the memory of the person responding (who is not necessarily the worker), and there is some evidence that responses are rounded to the nearest five-minute interval. This may affect the precision of a travel forecasting model calibrated with microdata and may affect the aggregate time traveled reported in Summary File 3. However, the error is likely to be random. Reported travel time can be interpreted as peoples' perception of the length of their trip. Box 6.2 investigates the change in travel time to work in California from 1990 to 2000.

Vehicles available

The above variables have all referred to the work trips of individuals; this variable is collected for households. The number of vehicles available for all uses by household members is reported, not the vehicles owned. Employer-owned cars kept at home would be counted if they could also be used for nonwork trips, but vehicles that may be used only for business purposes would not be counted. Cars, vans, and trucks of one-ton capacity or less are included, but not motorcycles

Box 6.2   Length of the work trip in California

Rising housing prices, population growth, and suburban sprawl have increased commuting times throughout the nation. Map 6.2a shows the proportion of workers who commuted for an hour or more in California in 1990. In only one county (Riverside) did more than 15 percent of workers travel for more than an hour to work.

By 2000, the proportion of workers who had work trips of an hour or longer had risen in most counties. Map 6.2b shows that eight counties had more than 15 percent of workers traveling for an hour or more.

Which counties experienced the largest proportionate increases in work trips of an hour or more? Map 6.2c compares changes in the proportion of long work trips from 1990 to 2000. The proportion of people commuting an hour or more declined in three counties, but it doubled in four counties, all of them surrounding the Bay Area.

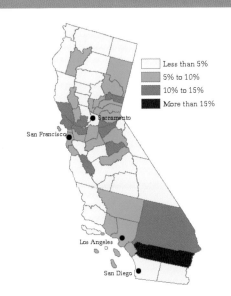

Map 6.2a   Percent of California workers by county commuting an hour or more one way in 1990.

Source: 1990 Census of Population and Housing

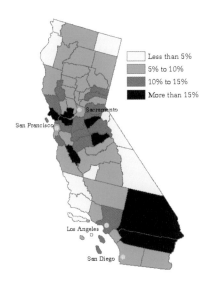

Map 6.2b   Percent of California workers by county commuting an hour or more one way in 2000.

Source: 2000 Census of Population and Housing

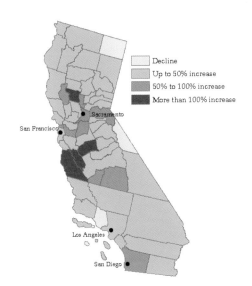

Map 6.2c   Change in number of workers by county commuting at least one hour each way, 1990 to 2000.

Source: Calculated from 1990 and 2000 Censuses of Population and Housing

233

Using the census to analyze transportation issues

and semis, or dismantled or immobile vehicles. Numbers of vehicles may be used to estimate trip generation rates; households with four cars generate more trips (for instance, by teenagers) than those with only one car.

The Census Bureau first asked the journey-to-work questions in the 1960 Census, so analysts have four snapshots of transportation over the decades. There have been some small changes to the questions during this period, which should be borne in mind if you plan to analyze changes over time. Table 6.1 shows the changes the Census Bureau made to the questions between the 2000 and 1990 Censuses. Changes were also made to the way responses were processed. In 1980 only about half of the long-form responses were used in tabulations, but all responses were used in 1990 and 2000. Another constraint the user may face in making direct comparisons is the coarseness of the geographic level used in the 1960 and 1970 Censuses versus the 1980, 1990, and 2000 Censuses. To make comparisons over the four decades, the current census geography should be aggregated to that of the earlier census.

Table 6.1 Changes to the transportation variables from 1990 to 2000 Census	
Variable	**Change between 1990 and 2000 Census**
22. Place of work	No major changes.
23a. Means of transportation to work	No major changes.
23b. Carpooling	The 1990 response categories "5 people" and "6 people" were collapsed to "5 or 6 people" for Census 2000. In 2000, the upper category was "7 or more people" whereas in 1990 it was "10 or more people."
24a. Departure time	No major changes.
24b. Minutes to work	No major changes.
43. Vehicles available	The upper limit category changed to "6 or more" in 2000. For 1990, the upper limit category was "7 or more."

Source: U.S. Census Bureau 2002a.

Only a few cross-tabulations of transportation and demographic variables are provided in Summary File 3. These are shown in table 6.2.

Another tabulation, the "County-to-County Worker Flow" file, shows the number of workers by place of residence and place of work. Home and work locations are identified by county and minor civil division. The data can be downloaded as an Excel or text file for the United States as a whole, or for individual states, at *www.census.gov/population/www/cen2000/commuting.html*. For each state, two files are available. One shows where people work by their county of residence, and the other shows where people live by the county they work in. Files are also available for worker flows by minor civil division (MCD) for the twelve states that have MCDs. Worker flow data identifies statewide commuting patterns that are helpful in determining infrastructure expansion needs. They are also used to identify patterns of suburbanization and labor sheds. Box 6.3 presents an example of how worker flow data can be used to estimate commuting sheds.

Table 6.2   Available cross-tabulations of transportation and demographic characteristics

	Age	Race	Hispanic
Place of work	P26, P27, P28, P29		
Usual means of transportation	P30		
Number of persons in the vehicle	P35		
Time of departure for work	P34		
Usual travel time to work by public and private transit	P32, P33		
Vehicles available	H45	HCT33A - G	HCT33H - I

Source: U.S. Census Bureau, 2003a

Far more detailed relationships between travel patterns and demographic and economic characteristics are published in two other data products, the Public Use Microdata Sample (PUMS), and the Census Transportation Planning Package (CTPP). These are designed to serve different research needs than Summary File 3.

Public Use Microdata Samples

The Public Use Microdata Samples (PUMS) are samples of the long-form responses—in other words, a sample of a sample. The PUMS consists of individual records for people and households, rather than summaries of distributions by place. Unlike the summary tables, PUMS allows you to create your own descriptive summaries and to test for relationships between

---

Box 6.3   County-to-county worker flows in Iowa

Iowa, like many agricultural states, has an extensive road network linking rural residents to urban centers. Farm-to-market roads were built on section lines beginning in the nineteenth century, followed by the construction of the interstate system in the middle decades of the twentieth century. The increasing centralization of economic activity in metropolitan centers has increased county-to-county commuting substantially over recent decades.

Using the County-to-County Worker Flow files, map 6.3a shows the percentage of each county's workers actually employed in that county. The counties containing Iowa's largest cities all manage to retain over 80 percent of their workers in-county. Without exception, these counties also had more nonresident commuters traveling into them for work than resident commuters traveling out of them.

Notice too the draw that counties with large cities had on the workers of surrounding counties (see map 6.3b). This is most apparent in the eastern and central parts of the state, particularly Polk County (the county containing the state capital, Des Moines). Polk County is a major employment destination for residents of most of the counties surrounding it. So are Linn County (Cedar Rapids), Johnson County (Iowa City), and Black Hawk County (Waterloo). Unsurprisingly, as the commuting sheds of Iowa's bigger urban areas have grown, so the average Iowan's commute has lengthened substantially.

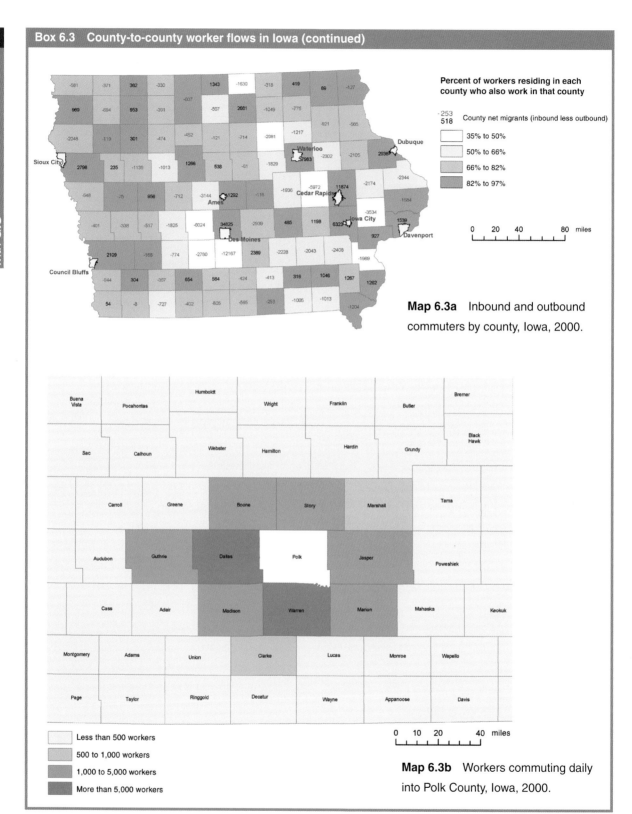

Box 6.3   County-to-county worker flows in Iowa (continued)

Percent of workers residing in each
county who also work in that county

-253
518   County net migrants (inbound less outbound)

35% to 50%

50% to 66%

66% to 82%

82% to 97%

0   20   40   80   miles

Map 6.3a   Inbound and outbound
commuters by county, Iowa, 2000.

Less than 500 workers

500 to 1,000 workers

1,000 to 5,000 workers

More than 5,000 workers

0   10   20   40   miles

Map 6.3b   Workers commuting daily
into Polk County, Iowa, 2000.

variables. Microdata is an improvement over the fixed summary tables for analyses involving statistical or econometric models. For example, the relationships between people's choice of travel mode and personal characteristics, such as income and access to vehicles, can be used to calibrate a discrete choice model. An example in the final section of this chapter illustrates the use of PUMS data in transportation analyses.

PUMS is released in two sample sizes:

- A 1-percent sample—a set of responses sampled at a 1:100 ratio from the census long form, containing the maximum range of socio-economic characteristics but low geographic resolution
- A 5-percent sample—a 1:20 sample of the long form responses at a higher geographic resolution than the 1-percent sample, but with a smaller range of characteristics

The 1-percent PUMS data can be downloaded at *www.census.gov/Press-Release/www /2003/ PUMS.html* and the 5-percent PUMS at *www.census.gov/Press-Release/www/2003/PUMS5.html.* Technical documentation, including file structure and record layouts, is available at these sites (U.S. Census Bureau 2003f).

Two geographic levels, Public Use Microdata Areas, or PUMAs, are used for PUMS. The 1-percent sample is released for Super-PUMAs, an area with a population of at least 400,000. The 5-percent sample is released for a PUMA, which must have a population of at least 100,000. Since the sizes of the PUMAs are defined by population, the spatial area covered by the PUMA varies by PUMS sample size and region within the states. A PUMA in a region with low population density would be larger than in a region with high population density. State census data centers defined the current PUMAs using population totals from the 2000 Census. Maps of PUMAs and Super-PUMAs are provided on the sites listed above.

Because this data is provided for a sample of individuals, the Census Bureau takes several steps to protect the confidentiality of sampled respondents. The broad spatial definition of PUMAs and Super-PUMAs protects confidentiality to some extent, but other data processing strategies are used as well. "Top-coding" collapses reporting categories at the top end of the scale (for instance, if a person's actual income is $250,000, it is reported as being only in the greater than $200,000 category). "Age perturbation" modifies peoples' ages in households with ten or more people. "Record swapping" exchanges a sample of individual records with another sample selected from a neighboring area and is used when reporting frequency tables (U.S. Census Bureau 2003f).

The PUMS records contain the complete responses from the long form. As with other census products, housing and population characteristics are released in two separate data files. The population and housing files are linked through a common data field, SERIALNO, that links individuals to the households to which they belong.

It is important to remember that PUMS is a weighted sample of responses from the census long form, which is itself a weighted sample. The issue of sampling error is thus much more likely to be important when dealing with PUMS, especially if it is used for statistical or econometric

Box 6.4 Accuracy, sampling errors, and sample design for PUMS

Because the information contained in the PUMS is a sample, the results derived from it must be treated as estimates and not exact values. For instance, the reported percentage of workers within a PUMA that use a bus as their main mode of travel to work is only an estimate of the true percentage of bus riders. The sampling process introduces two types of errors: sampling and nonsampling errors. As the reader may remember from the discussion in chapter 1, sampling errors are random (if the sample has been randomly drawn from the population) and can be estimated mathematically, while nonsampling errors may be either random or nonrandom (in which case they cannot be estimated mathematically).

Calculating the standard error of the sample quantifies the variability of the sample data. The more varied the individual responses are from the true mean response, the greater the standard error will be. As the standard error increases, the reliability of the estimate decreases. Sampling error can be calculated based on the variability in the responses and the sampling design used (such as simple random, stratified, cluster, and so on). The Census Bureau provides estimation methods and

equations for the sampling error for each variable, referred to as a standard error, based on the sampling design used for that variable (U.S. Census Bureau 2003f). For example, to estimate the standard error of the total number of workers in a Super-PUMA and the proportion of those using a car, truck, or van you would need to use the design factor method and the equations presented in chapter 5 of the technical documentation (U.S. Census Bureau 2003f).

The standard error calculated can be used to calculate a confidence interval around your estimated value. Box 6.6 later in this chapter illustrates these calculations. A confidence interval is the range within which we can expect the average value of a characteristic (calculated over all possible samples) to fall, with a specific level of probability. For example, the 95 percent confidence interval for the mean income of workers who chose a ferry boat as their primary mode of transportation for their journey to work and resided in Super-PUMA 34070 (Hudson County, New Jersey) is $95,398 and $99,696. We could say with 95-percent confidence that the "true" mean income of ferryboat commuters is within this range.

models. Box 6.4 explains how to approach this issue, and the first example in the final section of this chapter illustrates the calculation of confidence intervals around the PUMS estimates.

Census Transportation Planning Package

The Census Transportation Planning Package (CTPP) is designed specifically by the Census Bureau and the Bureau of Transportation Statistics for transportation analysis. However, as one of the examples in chapter 4 showed, the CTPP is also a very useful data source when we need to find the location of employment opportunities. The data is derived from the census long form. The CTPP differs from other census-based products in that it summarizes information about people at both their home and work locations. The package contains demographic, occupational, industrial, residential, transportation, and travel-to-work data. Unlike the limited number of tables contained in Summary File 3, the CTPP has many cross-tabulations of population and household information with transportation characteristics. The CTPP uses a special geographic unit, the Traffic Analysis Zone (TAZ), for tabulating the results. The TAZ is the lowest level of geography for which data is published in the CTPP.

The state and urban elements: Two data series are published. The state element has data summarized to the place (with populations greater than 2,500), county, and state levels. It is useful for understanding commuting between counties and between places. The urban element is organized by transportation region and provides data on commuting patterns within each region. The data is organized by TAZ, although higher levels of census geography are also available.

Place of residence or work: In 1990 the state and urban elements were organized into three parts:

- Part A: Place of residence—the data is summarized by the area (county, place, and so on) where the worker lives.
- Part B: Place of work—the data is summarized by the area (county, place, and so on) where the worker works.
- Part C: Journey to work (JTW)—these are matrix tables measuring flows between homes and work places summarized to some area level (county, place, and so on).

Traffic Analysis Zones: A TAZ is a spatial aggregation of census blocks. Prior to each census, state departments of transportation (DOTs) and metropolitan planning organizations (MPOs) define the number and geographic boundaries of local TAZs, using the same boundary features used to define census blocks. This process is explained in chapter 1. The size of a TAZ is in part a function of population—TAZs can be as small as a single city block in areas with high population density, or many times larger than a city block in areas with low population density.

TAZs are most useful for travel analyses if they meet the following criteria:

- contiguity
- compactness
- complete coverage of the study area
- homogenous land use and demographics
- boundaries that follow natural and constructed land features that physically restrict access

Using existing census blocks to define TAZs may not meet all of the above criteria. Blocks are not defined based on homogeneous land uses and demographics, and their boundaries are not necessarily defined by natural or constructed features that limit accessibility, such as bridges.

In some cases, existing TAZs must be aggregated. For example, if an analyst is developing a travel forecasting model using only the primary road network, then the existing TAZs might be too small, requiring unreasonably long connectors from each TAZ to the primary road system. A GIS is invaluable for this task, easily merging both the spatial boundaries and the attribute data. Map 6.4 contains the TAZ boundaries defined for Johnson County, Iowa, in the 2000 Census. As you can see, many of the TAZs are not contiguous to or traversed by a primary road, so they will require long centroid connectors. To avoid this problem, a new set of TAZs could be created from the existing zones. Map 6.5 shows the result of dissolving the existing TAZ boundaries into new regions that better (though not fully) match the primary road network.

2000 CTPP: The 2000 CTPP (scheduled for release in 2004) is structured similarly to the 1990 CTPP to allow comparability. Data from part 1 (organized by place of residence) will be

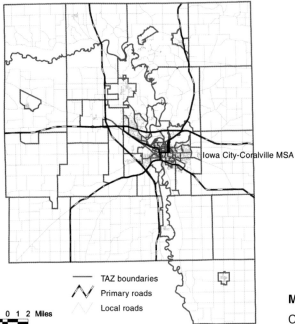

TAZ boundaries
Primary roads
Local roads

1 0 1 2 Miles

Map 6.4 2000 TAZ boundaries, Johnson County, Iowa.

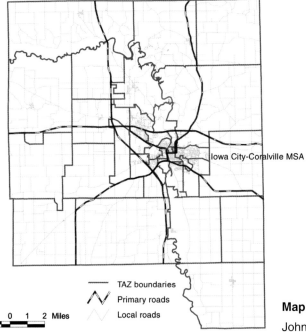

TAZ boundaries
Primary roads
Local roads

1 0 1 2 Miles

Map 6.5 Adjusted 2000 TAZ boundaries, Johnson County, Iowa.

available at twelve geographic levels: state, county, county subdivision, place, census tract, block group, MSA/CMSA, urban area, PUMA, MPO region, combined zone, and TAZ.

Note that the 2000 CTPP will be in a proprietary format so that without the special access software, the data will not be directly accessible from the CD–ROMs. If you need a complete data set in ASCII format, the Journey to Work and Migration Branch of the Census Bureau will provide it.

Accessing the CTPP: The 1990 CTPP is available as two series of CD–ROMS (the state element and the urban element) and is also downloadable from the TranStats Web site *(www. transtats.bts.gov/DataIndex.asp)*. The CD–ROM package contains the TAZ boundary files, but they are all in Caliper's TransCAD GIS format. These must be translated if you use a different GIS program. Fortunately, the TAZ boundary files for 1990 and 2000 can be downloaded like any other census geography from the TIGER/Line system, though for the 1990 boundaries it is crucial that you download from pre-2000 TIGER/Line files (see the instructions in chapter 2 for download options). Map layer files in shapefile format are also available from the CTPP section of the TranStats Web site, obviating the need for any translation if you are working with ESRI software.

For the 1980 and 1990 CTPPs, the Caliper Corporation developed software, TransVU-CTPP, for accessing and displaying CTPP data in both tabular and map formats. The software is available free of charge from the Bureau of Transportation Statistics (BTS) (go to *www.bts.gov/help,* choose **CTPP Compact Discs 1990,** and then select the upgraded software). An earlier version of the software (for Windows 95 and Windows 98 machines) is also available on the CTPP CD–ROMS. See chapter 4, box 4.10 on using TransVU-CTPP and see Srinivasan and Christopher (2001) for alternative procedures to move the data from the proprietary format into a general GIS format. Even the newer TransVU-CTPP will have problems on Windows 2000 and Windows XP machines. Box 4.10 has instructions on overcoming these problems. The software is still necessary for obtaining and viewing the 1980 Census TAZ boundaries, then referred to as traffic zones. The 1990 CTPP data tables are held in dBase format, which most GIS programs are able to read directly. The 2000 CTPP will have entirely new access software, CAT (CTPP Access Tool).

Uses and limitations of the CTPP: The CTPP allows you to examine existing travel characteristics at a variety of geographic summary levels. For example, the origin-destination data can be used in updating travel demand forecasting models or for examining commuting patterns along a given corridor. The place of work data can be used to determine the spatial location of labor demand at the micro scale (this is not available from any other published census data source) and the distance workers are prepared to travel. The place of residence data provide an equivalently micro sense of labor supply characteristics. The advantage of the CTPP over the Summary File 3 data products is the inclusion of demographic and transportation data that is not included in the summary tables. An advantage over the use of PUMS is the ease of using the CTPP tables and the availability of geographic summary levels other than the PUMAs.

The CTPP suffers from the same limitations as other census products. It only provides a snapshot of existing conditions every ten years. The data is subject to error, and changes to census geography limit comparisons across census years. Moreover, it lacks any information on the transportation infrastructure and changes to that infrastructure.

Workers-at-work and employment estimates from other census sources: The main use of the CTPP is to analyze commuting patterns from home to work; a central organizing concept in CTPP is thus employment. But when comparing CTPP results with other employment data sources there are a few issues to keep in mind. There is a slight difference in the census definition of workers-at-work and employed persons with the result that the national numbers for these two differ by a considerable amount (128,279,228 for workers-at-work versus 129,721,512 for the civilian employed, Census 2000). Moreover, the total number of jobs will differ from the number of employed persons. A person may hold a number of jobs, there are seasonal fluctuations in employment that the census adjusts for, and there are also weekly absenteeism adjustments. Thus if we used part two of the CTPP to give some sense of labor demand at a particular location, we would in reality be summing workers working at that location. But data from other sources, especially establishment data sources such as County Business Patterns, ES202, or the Economic Census, would provide a more complete estimate of employment (or jobs) at that location. For a discussion of these issues in a CTPP context, and for recommendations on adjustments to the CTPP, go to the CTPP May 2003 and January 2004 Status Reports at *www.fhwa.dot.gov/ctpp/articles.htm.*

Other transportation data

The census-based data we have discussed until this point covers one primary transportation issue—the journey to work. However, there are other important issues. Nonwork travel and travel by people who are unemployed or not in the labor force is also an important area of policy concern (especially trips by people who are disabled, elderly, or have very low incomes). Nonwork trips account for an increasing share of traffic. The journey-to-work data collected in the decennial census does not reflect this, nor does it reflect long-distance travel.

The transportation infrastructure, congestion, safety, environmental impacts, and freight transportation are important topics covered by other data sources. This section discusses other data sources that supplement the information collected in the decennial census.

The National Household Transportation Survey

The National Household Transportation Survey (NHTS), conducted for the first time in 2001, collects information on daily and long-distance travel for the nation. It combines the coverage of the National Personal Transportation Survey (NPTS) and the American Travel Survey (ATS), previously performed by the Federal Highway Administration and the Bureau of Transportation Statistics. The NPTS collected information about daily trips using a travel diary for each respondent. The ATS surveyed long-distance trips (seventy-five miles or more) taken during the two-week period prior to the survey. The NHTS combines these collection techniques.

NHTS collects information on all trips, not just work trips. Trips for personal and family, and social and recreational purposes are by far the majority of daily trips. Combined, they account for nearly 72 percent of daily trips, compared to work trips, which account for less than 15 percent (U.S. Bureau of Transportation Statistics 2003a, figure 7). Information is also collected on demographic characteristics, trip characteristics (mode, length, time and day of week, and vehicle occupancy), and vehicle characteristics (model year, annual miles driven, and so on). Many aspects of travel behavior can be cross-tabulated with household and individual characteristics. Data on long-distance trips is broken down by purpose, as well as mode and distance.

> In 2001, men and women made the same average number of daily trips—4.1. In previous years, the NPTS had found that women made more trips than men. This is interesting because it may suggest that the distribution of household responsibilities among men and women has become more even. While employed people made an average of 4.5 daily trips, those who were not employed still made a significant 3.7 daily trips on average. Even those with a medical condition that limited their travel made an average of 2.8 trips outside the home each day (U.S. Bureau of Transportation Statistics 2003a, table A-9).

The NHTS is a valuable source of information on a variety of travel issues, but it covers a limited sample of households (26,000 nationwide), and thus it is not useful at a more detailed spatial scale than the nine census divisions. However, localities may cover the costs of sampling their jurisdictions at a higher rate. Nine jurisdictions financed an additional 40,000 household surveys in 2001. In these places the NHTS can be used for a wider range of local analyses.

> These jurisdictions paid for additional data:
> - Baltimore, Maryland
> - Des Moines MPO, Iowa
> - Edmonson, Carter, Pulaski, and Scott counties, Kentucky
> - Lancaster MPO, Pennsylvania
> - Oahu MPO, Hawaii
> - State of Hawaii, except Oahu
> - New York state
> - Texas
> - Wisconsin (Oak Ridge National Laboratory at *nhts.ornl.gov/2001/html_files/faq.shtml*)

The NHTS data set can be downloaded from *nhts.ornl.gov/2001/index.shtml.* Like PUMS, the data is made up of individual records for each member of the households surveyed. Files can be downloaded in SAS, ASCII, or dBase format, or you can construct tables interactively. The 1990 and 1995 NPTS surveys are also available online. A user's guide is available at *nhts.ornl. gov/2001/usersguide/index.shtml.*

Other sources of data about individual and household travel

Data on commuting costs is collected in some of the economic databases described in chapter 4. The Survey of Income and Program Participation (SIPP), for instance, includes valuable national level information on transportation issues faced by people on welfare and those making the transition from welfare to work.

A recent analysis of 1999 SIPP data found that the working poor (defined as those with an income less than $8,000) spent nearly 10 percent of their income on commuting, compared to the 4 percent that workers spend on average. For those who used their own vehicle (66 percent of the working poor), about 21 percent of their income was spent on commuting, compared to 13 percent for those who took public transit. Lower cost alternatives such as carpooling, biking, and walking were much more widely used by the working poor than others (U.S. Bureau of Transportation Statistics 2003b).

Special purpose surveys are also conducted periodically. In 2002, the Bureau of Transportation Statistics surveyed a sample of about 5,000 people with and without disabilities to identify significant transportation needs. Based on the 2002 National Transportation Availability and Use Survey, it is estimated that approximately six million people with disabilities have problems with transportation, and about half a million do not leave their home primarily because of transportation difficulties (U.S. Bureau of Transportation Statistics 2003c).

Neither SIPP nor the National Transportation Availability and Use Survey can provide any spatially specific data, but the topics they cover are important for many local transportation planning issues. They can be a helpful supplement for local analyses.

Environmental data related to transportation

The Aerometric Information Retrieval System (AIRS) data from the National Air Quality Database (sponsored by the Environmental Protection Agency, or EPA) is a valuable source of data about a significant transportation impact. It provides data on ambient concentrations of air pollutants at monitoring sites in cities and towns throughout the United States. It has been collected annually since 1996. The data can be downloaded at *www.epa.gov/air/data.*

The Hazardous Material Incident Reporting System (HMIRS) provides data about another kind of environmental impact—spills of hazardous materials during transportation. The data has been collected annually since 1995 and is available at *hazmat.dot.gov*.

Highway facilities, congestion, and safety data

The Highway Performance Monitoring System (HPMS) provides a wealth of information on arterial and collector roads, and more limited data on all public roads, summarized by urbanized, small urban, and rural areas. The Federal Highway Administration collects the information in partnership with state and local governments and MPOs. Data on highway condition, performance, future investment needs, and air quality is available annually. The data can be downloaded at *www.transtats.bts.gov*.

The Highway Congestion (Urban Mobility) study provides information on trends in mobility and congestion for sixty-eight urban areas. Driver-hours of delay, traffic rate index, and congestion cost per year are some of the analytic indicators provided. It has been available annually since 1982 and can be found at *mobility.tamu.edu/ums*.

The Fatality Analysis Reporting System (FARS) provides information on crashes involving fatalities, including vehicle and personal characteristics. It has been available annually since 1991 and can be found at *www-fars.nhtsa.dot.gov*.

The Federal Highway Administration's Highway Safety Information System (HSIS) provides accident and traffic volume data for a small group of states (California, Illinois, Maine, Michigan, Minnesota, North Carolina, Utah, and Washington). The data is available for 1991 to 1999. It can be found at *www.hsisinfo.org*.

Public transit data

The National Transit Database collects financial and operating information from more than six hundred transit providers serving both urban and rural areas. It provides a valuable resource describing mass transportation programs. The data is collected annually and has been available since 1996. The data may be downloaded at *www.ntdprogram.com/NTD/ntdhome.nsf?OpenDatabase*.

Useful information is also available from a summary database of the Federal Transit Administration Grant Assistance Programs. Funding levels are shown for each FTA program, by state and urban areas. The data is available at *www.fta.dot.gov*. Further transit data is available from the Federal Transit Administration (FTA at *www.fta.dot.gov*) and the American Public Transit Association (*www.apta.com*).

Freight movement data

The Commodity Flow Survey (CFS), sponsored by the Bureau of Transportation Statistics and the Census Bureau, estimates the flow of goods and materials by mode of transportation. The CFS surveys mining, manufacturing, wholesale trade, selected retail industries, and selected auxiliary establishments, such as warehouses, for the value, weight, mode of transportation, and the origins and destinations of the commodities shipped. The survey has been conducted since 1963 roughly every five years with major revisions occurring in 1993 and 1997. In 1993 and 1997, the CFS contained information on all modes of shipment a commodity uses from origin to destination. Prior to 1993, the survey tracked only the primary mode of transport.

The 1997 CFS sampled about 100,000 establishments resulting in approximately five million recorded shipments. The CFS includes a five-digit Standard Classification of Transported Goods code, value, weight, modes of transport, the ZIP Codes of origin and destination, and whether the freight was packed in containers, a hazardous material, or an export. The data is released at several geographic levels including states, which can be broken down into selected metropolitan areas and the remainder of the state.

1997 CFS data is available free of charge on CD–ROM from the Bureau of Transportation Statistics; contact their order desk at (202) 366-3282. The CD–ROM contains software for viewing, modifying, and extracting data tables as well as maps that define the metropolitan areas. Tabulated results from the 1997 CFS compiled by the Bureau of Transportation Statistics can be obtained online at *www.bts.gov/ntda/cfs* or from the TranStat Web site at *www.transtats. bts.gov.*

Economic Census

The Economic Census (*www.census.gov/epcd/www/econ97.html*) (in 1992 and earlier, the Census of Transportation, Communications, and Utilities) and the associated Service Annual Surveys (SAS) (*www.census.gov/svsd/www/sashist.html*) (previously Transportation Annual Surveys) provide data on transportation companies and commodity movement. Use of the Economic Census was described in chapter 4. Data in the SAS include operating revenue, percent of motor carrier freight revenue by commodity type, weight of shipments handled, length of haul, shipment country of origin and destination, and vehicle fleet inventory.

Additional transportation data resources

There is a vast amount of additional official and semi-official transportation data that may be useful to urban land professionals. Most of the data is disaggregated geographically, at least to the state level, though sometimes also to lower levels of geography. However, even data that is only available at the national level can still be useful to urban land professionals since it may provide a national context for local conditions. Probably the best place to start is the BTS's publication *National Transportation Statistics* (U.S. Bureau of Transportation Statistics 2002a). This is a compilation volume covering most of the data collected by the Department of Transportation and its various agencies and bureaus. It covers the road, rail, air, pipeline, and maritime transportation systems. There are also special sections on the movement of goods, the performance of the physical systems, safety in the various systems (this also covers multimodal and transit systems), finance, the economic contribution of the transportation sector, and a section on transportation and air pollution. Not only does the publication provide basic data often broken down to the local level, but each table's footnotes provide an invaluable guide to additional data sources. The publication is available at *www.bts.gov/pdc/index.xml.* Note that this publication is different from the Transportation Statistics Annual Report, which provides a broad-brush analysis of some national transportation trends (the content of the latter publication has also changed somewhat over the years). For digital maps of the transportation system, the National Transportation Atlas Database (NTAD), published on a CD–ROM by the BTS, is a fairly comprehensive source. Further descriptions of the physical system and data on usage are available from the following sources:

- Air system: Data on airports, passengers, freight, safety, and aircraft from the Federal Aviation Administration (*www1.faa.gov*). Also see the Office of Airline Information at the Bureau of Transportation Statistics for airport, delay, cancellation, and diversion information.

- Maritime system: Data on the merchant fleet is available from the Maritime Administration (*www.marad.dot.gov*). For the recreational fleet, see the National Marine Manufacturers Association (*www.nmma.org*). For freight movement see U.S. Army Corps of Engineers (*www.usace.army.mil*, in particular Waterborne Commerce of the United States). Safety data is held by the U.S. Coast Guard (*www.uscg.mil/USCG.shtm*) and the NTSB. Personal watercraft safety is at U.S. Coast Guard Office of Boating Safety (*www.uscgboating.org*).

- Pipeline system: Usage and pipeline data is available from the Association of Oil Pipelines (*www.aopl.org*) and Office of Pipeline Safety of the U.S. Department of Transportation (*ops. dot.gov/stats.htm*).

- Rail system: For data on operations, inventory, and so on, see the Federal Railroad Administration (FRA at *www.fra.dot.gov*). Further data is available from the Association of American Railroads at *www.aar.org.* Rail waybill data is at *www.railroaddata.com/rrlinks/ Detailed/6188.html.*

- Road and highway systems: Use and auto, truck, and motorcycle data is available from the Federal Highway Administration (*www.fhwa.dot.gov*). See also the National Highway Traffic Safety Administration (*www.nhtsa.dot.gov*) and the Federal Motor Carrier Safety Administration (*www.fmcsa.dot.gov/factsfigs/dashome.htm*).

- States and Metropolitan Planning Organizations (MPOs) also collect and disseminate transportation data although the type, quantity, and quality vary widely. Areas experiencing important changes to their transportation systems will have local MPOs that are more actively involved in the collection and analysis of transportation data. Some of the major American freight corridors have also been the subject of study. An example is the Upper Midwest Freight Corridor Study (go to *www.uppermidwestfreight.org*; this site has links to the other major corridor organizations). Corridor organizations usually compile data on movements in their corridor.

Using census data for transportation analyses

This chapter began with several examples of questions that planners and others may have about local transportation patterns. We will deal with two examples in more detail; they demonstrate how spatial researchers can deal with two important limitations of the census:

- Most census data is obtained from a sample, so we need to correct for the inaccuracies this introduces as a result of sampling and nonsampling errors. This is especially important when using microdata, which is based on a sample of a sample.

- The census is provided in a variety of different forms, but different data products do not necessarily use the same spatial scale. GIS offers an efficient way to link data available at different geographies, enabling us to answer a wider range of questions than one data product alone allows.

Example one: Calculating the income of commuters in northern New Jersey

If we knew the relationship between the travel mode people chose for their work trip and their other characteristics, such as income, occupation, age, sex, race, and so on, we could predict future modal choice with a greater degree of accuracy. We could use estimates of economic and demographic change to project the demand for different modes in the future.

Consider the following hypothetical case. Assume that a metropolitan planning organization in Hudson County, New Jersey, wants to determine the income of workers who drive alone to work, compared to those who take alternative modes (including carpooling, public transit, and other means). Summary File 3 provides little help, as travel mode is not cross-tabulated with income, or indeed many other variables of interest. However, PUMS provides the individual-level records we could use to construct estimates of these interrelationships. For a more accurate picture, we would also need to construct confidence intervals around these estimates.

Our first step is to download the appropriate PUMS data for the region we are interested in. Box 6.5 explains this process.

How many people in each PUMA are employed? Selecting ESR=1 for our area will tell us how many people in the sample from that PUMA are employed (for Hudson County, 12,438 records). The sum of PWEIGHT for these selected cases will allow us to estimate how many people in the PUMA are employed (for Hudson County, 266,716 people).[2]

Next, we need to know how many people commute to work by each mode. Consulting the record layout codes (U.S. Census Bureau 2003f, chapter 6), we see that TRVMNS (travel mode) is coded "one" for people who drove to work in a car, truck, or van. So, we would select records where ESR=1 and TRVMNS=1, and sum PWEIGHT values for these selected cases to estimate how many people drove to work. Table 6.3 shows the number of workers using each of the twelve listed travel modes. The proportion of workers using each mode could also be calculated.

Finally, we need to know the average income of workers who take each means of transportation to work. We would begin by calculating the aggregate income for those who commute by

[2]For more complex analyses, most statistical packages offer a "weight cases" option that streamlines this step. This example spells out the weighting process to clarify the explanation for new users.

Box 6.5   Downloading PUMS data

First of all, we need to decide which areas we want data for and which data set we should use. Because we want a variety of demographic and employment characteristics, and these are more important to us than greater spatial detail, we should probably choose the 1-percent sample available at the Super-PUMA level. We are interested in Hudson County, New Jersey, so we would choose Super-PUMA 34070.

After downloading the population and housing PUMS files for these areas, we need to join them using the common SERIALNO data field. We are joining each household to several people (a one-to-many join). The data fields we will download for this analysis are PUMA1 (1-percent PUMA number), PWEIGHT (person weight), ESR (employment status), TRVMNS (mode of travel), and EARNS (per capita income). The Record Layout codes (U.S. Census Bureau 2003f, chapter 6) show the values for each variable.

Table 6.3 Estimate of employed workers' mode choice, Hudson County Super-PUMA		
Means of transportation to work	**Estimated commuters**	**Estimated percent**
Car, truck, or van	146,927	55.1
Bus or trolley bus	50,816	19.1
Streetcar or trolley car	576	0.2
Subway or elevated	31,223	11.7
Railroad	4,376	1.6
Ferryboat	2,290	0.9
Taxicab	1,116	0.4
Motorcycle	20	0.0
Bicycle	321	0.1
Walked	21,995	8.3
Worked at home	4,771	1.8
Other method	2,285	0.9
Total	266,716	

Source: Calculated from 2000 PUMA.

each mode (the sum of every person's income). For each record in each mode (each value of TRVMNS) we would multiply EARNS by PWEIGHT and sum the total for that mode. This would give us an estimate of the total income of people who drove to work, people who rode the bus, and so on. To get the average income for each mode, we would divide by the total estimated number of people taking that mode. Table 6.4 shows our results.

We have addressed the basic questions we set out to examine, but we have provided only estimates of the answers. The next issue we must address is the accuracy of these estimates. Although the basic principles of calculating standard errors and using them to construct confidence intervals

Table 6.4 Estimate of the mean income per worker by commuting mode (dollars)	
Means of transportation to work	**Estimated mean income ($)**
Car, truck, or van	34,193
Bus or trolley bus	29,517
Streetcar or trolley car	31,310
Subway or elevated	48,898
Railroad	40,599
Ferryboat	97,547
Taxicab	22,791
Motorcycle	45,000
Bicycle	21,374
Walked	22,134
Worked at home	34,914
Other method	24,858

Source: Calculated from 2000 PUMS.

around these estimates remain the same, calculation methods will vary for different types of estimates. Our first estimate was a total—the number of employed people in each county. Box 6.6 explains how we would calculate standard errors and construct confidence intervals around this estimate.

Box 6.6   Calculating standard errors and constructing confidence intervals for a total

For the first question addressed in this example, we obtained an estimate of 266,716 workers for Super-PUMA 34070, Hudson County, out of a total population of 612,562. We need to know the unadjusted standard error and the design factor for this variable. From table E of chapter 4 of the PUMS technical documentation (U.S. Census Bureau 2003f) we see that the design factor for employment status is 1.2. We would calculate the unadjusted standard error of this estimate as follows:

$$SE(\hat{Y}) = \sqrt{99(\hat{Y})\left(1 - \frac{\hat{Y}}{N}\right)}$$

N = Size (population, households) of geographic area

$\hat{Y}$ = Estimate of characteristic total

Equation 6.1a   Standard error of a total

$$SE(266{,}716) = \sqrt{99(266{,}716)\left(1 - \frac{266{,}716}{612{,}562}\right)}$$

Equation 6.1b   Calculating the standard error

We would multiply this error by the design factor to get the confidence interval for the total

number of workers in Hudson County. We can say with a 95 percent level of confidence that there are between 257,449 and 275,983 workers in Hudson County. We would use this same method to construct confidence intervals around the estimates of numbers of people using each mode.

We may also estimate standard errors and construct confidence intervals around the proportions of workers that we estimated used each mode. The equation is a little different, as box 6.7 shows.

The percentage of workers in Hudson County that commuted by car, truck, or van was 55.1 (see table 6.3). The base of the percentage was 266,716, the total number of workers in the area. We would calculate the standard error of this estimate as follows:

$$SE(\hat{p}) = \sqrt{\frac{99}{B}\, \hat{p}\left(100 - \hat{p}\right)}$$

B = Base of estimated percentage

$\hat{p}$ = Estimated percentage

Equation 6.2a   Standard error of a percentage

$$SE(55.09) = \sqrt{\frac{99}{266{,}716} \times 55.09(100 - 55.09)}$$

Equation 6.2b   Calculating the standard error

The largest design factor of all the characteristics used to make the estimate should be chosen. In this calculation we used two characteristics, employment status and means of transportation, to calculate the proportion using each mode. The design factor for the means of transportation is larger, so you would select 1.3 obtained from table E of chapter 4 of the PUMS technical documentation (U.S. Census Bureau 2003f). We could say with a 95 percent level of confidence that between 51.73 percent and 58.45 percent of workers in Hudson County commute by car, truck, or van.

Finally, we need to do the same for the estimates of average income we calculated. Box 6.8 explains how we would calculate standard errors and confidence intervals for aggregate and average amounts.

Calculating standard errors for aggregates, differences, and means is more complex than calculating them for totals and percentages, because we have to account for variance in all the elements used to calculate these estimates. The aggregate income that we calculated for workers using each mode was based on many individual estimates of income, so to calculate the standard error of the aggregate, we would need to estimate the standard errors for each of these individual estimates.

$$SE(\hat{X}) = 1.88 \times \sqrt{a + b(\hat{X}) + c(\hat{X}^2)}$$

$\hat{X}$ = Estimate of aggregate

Equation 6.3a   Standard error of an aggregate

$$SE(9{,}213{,}236{,}572) = 1.88 \times \sqrt{7569 + 32812284.06(9{,}213{,}236{,}572) - 0.00001(9{,}213{,}236{,}572)^2}$$

Equation 6.3b   Calculating the standard error

We estimated the aggregate income of all workers in Hudson County was $9,213,236,572. We can look up the values for the three parameters for Aggregate Personal Income or Earnings (a, b, and c); they are 7569, 32,812,284.06, and -0.00001 (U.S. Census Bureau 2000b, table B-2000). We can say with a 95 percent level of confidence that the aggregate income of workers in Hudson County is between $7,148,799,684 and $11,277,673,460.

For each of the average incomes we calculated (shown in table 6.4), we can also calculate a standard error. The resulting standard errors and 95 percent confidence intervals are shown in table 6.5.

Similarly, for the average income we calculated, we would need to estimate the variance in income for workers in each mode. This is a time-consuming task. Fortunately, parameters are provided by the Census Bureau for each aggregated variable, and each mean and median (U.S. Census Bureau 2002b, table B-2000 and C-2000). To calculate the standard error of an aggregate variable, we would use the following equation:

For each of the average incomes we calculated (shown in table 6.4), we can also calculate a standard error. The equation for calculating standard errors of means is different from the one for aggregates:

$$SE(\hat{M}) = 1.88 \times \sqrt{a + b \times LOG\ (N)}$$

$\hat{M}$ = Estimated mean

LOG(N) = Natural log function of universe count for mean

Equation 6.4a   Standard error of a mean

$$SE(34193) = 1.88 \times \sqrt{394565.4155 - 20202.20207 \times LOG(146927)}$$

Equation 6.4b   Calculating the standard error

The parameter values for "Per Capita Income" (a and b) are 394,565.4155 and -20,202.202070 (U.S. Census Bureau 2000b, table C-2000). The resulting standard errors and 95 percent confidence intervals are shown in table 6.5.

Table 6.5 Standard error and confidence intervals for mean income per worker (dollars)			
Means of transportation to work	**Standard error**	**Lower confidence interval**	**Upper confidence interval**
Car, truck, or van	1,012.72	32,168	36,218
Bus or trolley bus	1,028.85	27,459	31,575
Streetcar or trolley car	1,094.28	29,121	33,499
Subway or elevated	1,036.16	46,826	50,970
Railroad	1,065.16	38,469	42,729
Ferryboat	1,074.55	95,398	99,696
Taxicab	1,084.87	20,621	24,961
Motorcycle	1,140.90	42,718	47,282
Bicycle	1,102.53	19,169	23,579
Walked	1,041.39	20,051	24,217
Worked at home	1,063.90	32,786	37,042
Other method	1,074.58	22,709	27,007

Source: Calculated from 2000 PUMS, U.S. Census Bureau.

We have now developed defensible estimates of the average incomes of workers taking each available mode. However, in addition to calculating these confidence intervals, we should interpret this data carefully based on our understanding of the limitations of the variables we analyze. In this case, our data reflects the mode of transportation used for the longest part of the trip. If we were able to distinguish between those who walked to the train station and those who drove there, we may find some significant differences within the category of people who took the train to work, for instance.

Example two: Commuters to enterprise zones

Enterprise zones have been widely used by states in the United States as a way of bringing jobs to older inner city neighborhoods. There is some evidence that residents of inner city neighborhoods, particularly minorities, have difficulty accessing buoyant suburban labor markets. The result is higher levels of unemployment for inner-city residents. Enterprise zones are meant to deal with this problem by creating new job opportunities in inner-city neighborhoods. The problem is that labor markets tend to be metropolitan with the result that the inner-city jobs created in enterprise zones may be taken not by inner-city residents, but by suburban commuters. In this example we focus on the Fort Wayne, Indiana, enterprise zone and use 1990 CTPP data to look at commuting flows into the zone.

For this example TAZ maps were downloaded from the CTPP CD–ROMS, as was the journey-to-work data. The data was on the urban element CD–ROMS, in this case number BTS-15-12 IL, IN, which covers all Indiana transportation regions. Region 2760 covers Fort Wayne. The enterprise zone map layer was digitized from paper maps of the enterprise zone using a TIGER/Line-derived street centerline layer.

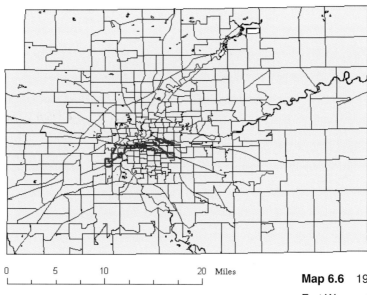

0   5   10   20   Miles

———— Enterprise zone boundaries

———— TAZ boundaries

Map 6.6 1990 TAZs and enterprise zone, Fort Wayne, Indiana, transportation region.

What TAZs cover the enterprise zone? It turns out there is no one-to-one correlation between TAZs and the enterprise zone, as map 6.6 clearly shows. TAZs to be considered part of the enterprise zone could be selected manually (eye-balling each TAZ to identify the ones that should be included) or more rigorously (developing a macro that would measure the extent of each TAZ covered by the enterprise zone and vice versa, and then establishing some overlapping-area criteria for inclusion). In this example we have manually selected TAZs (see map 6.7). The

TAZ-defined enterprise zone is much larger in area than the legally defined zone (colored in red in map 6.7). This will often be the case where a zone is defined by much smaller geographical units than TAZs; in this case the original enterprise zone was defined using city blocks.

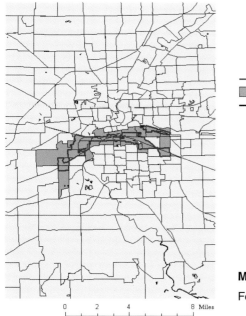

— Enterprise zone boundaries
▨ TAZ defined enterprise zone
— Fort Wayne TAZ boundaries

Map 6.7 TAZs used to define enterprise zone, Fort Wayne, Indiana, transportation region.

The next task is to identify in the attribute table of the map layer which TAZs are included in the enterprise zone definition. In this case we create a new field "EZ" in the TAZ map layer attribute table and give it a value of "1" if it is an enterprise zone TAZ and "0" if not. Note that in the map layer each TAZ is uniquely identified by its FIPS code field "CODE"—for instance, one TAZ has the code "2760 1," another "2760 19," and another "2760 437."

We then download the TAZ journey-to-work data, select the table "U301," which shows "Time leaving home - total and peak by mode" from the universe "Workers 16+ working outside home." The first variable in this table, "U301_0101," is the total daily work trips of workers employed outside the home. These trips are then related to origins (place of residence) and destinations (place of work). So the resulting data indicates how many work trips were made from each origin TAZ to each destination TAZ.

Figure 6.1 (next page) shows the resulting file once opened in ArcMap. The field "FIPS" is the origin TAZ and "FIPS_W" the destination TAZ. Thus twenty-seven people commuted to work from somewhere in TAZ "2760 1" to somewhere in "2760 1," while nine commuted from somewhere in "2760 1" to "2760 4," and so on.

The next task is to join the journey-to-work data to the TAZ map layer; the important thing to remember here is that the map layer could be joined to the data layer in two ways: by residence or by work site. Since we want to find out the residence of people working in TAZs

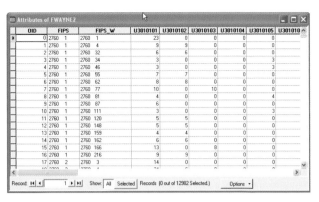

Figure 6.1

we will join by work site. In other words, the field "CODE" in the map layer will be joined to the field "FIPS_W" in the data layer. The result is a new data file with the "EZ" field we defined above. We then run an attribute query where "EZ" is equal to "1" in order to select those records where the destination of workers is the enterprise zone.

The next step is to add, for each TAZ, all workers working in any of the enterprise zone TAZs. The "summarize" function in ArcMap will accomplish this in one step. Figure 6.2 indicates the necessary settings. Note that we are now summing on TAZ of residence. Since one origin TAZ may have workers commuting to a number of different enterprise zone destination TAZs, we need to add all trips to enterprise zone destination TAZs together. Thus we sum on the variable "U3010101" and summarize only on the selected records (in other words, destination TAZs that are in the enterprise zone).

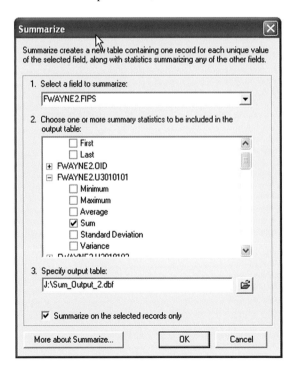

Figure 6.2

At this point all existing joins should be deleted, the new summary file ("sum_output_2.dbf" in this instance) should be opened and should then be joined to the original TAZ map layer. This will allow us to symbolize the results, the origin of those working in the Forth Wayne enterprise zone.

Our results are a little troubling. Although many of those working in the enterprise zone live either in it or close to it, a surprising number commute from far afield, particularly the far northeast and the west (see map 6.8).

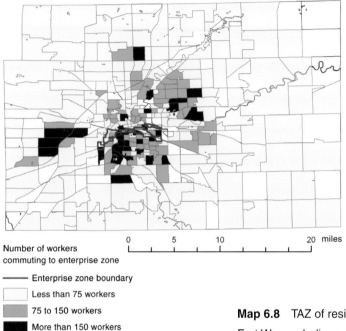

Number of workers
commiting to enterprise zone

——— Enterprise zone boundary

[ ] Less than 75 workers

[ ] 75 to 150 workers

[ ] More than 150 workers

[ ] No data available

Map 6.8 TAZ of residence of those working in the Fort Wayne, Indiana, enterprise zone and living in the Fort Wayne transportation region, 1990.

This same analysis could be undertaken using maps and data downloaded from the TranStats Web site. In this instance, the TAZ map would be downloaded as a zipped shapefile and the journey-to-work data as a zipped .csv text file. Field names will be somewhat different. The origin TAZ field will be "TAZRR" while the destination field will be "TAZRW." The various analysis steps described above will remain the same except that the .csv file will need to be imported into a database.

While many transportation analyses require more detailed information than is available at the geographic summary levels used in Summary File 3, GIS remains an important tool for manipulating and interpreting data. Microdata can be used to identify regional trends and relationships among variables that are useful complements for the limited transportation data available at a fine spatial scale. GIS is also an indispensable tool for joining data available at different geographic levels.

Chapter 7

Strategies *for*
distribution

Finding the right information and analyzing it appropriately to answer your question is a significant accomplishment. But unless the results of this analysis are communicated effectively to their intended audience, the analysis will have little impact on real policy decisions. Urban planners and related urban professionals do not make "expert" decisions in a black box. Instead, they present alternatives, explain their pros and cons, and enable nonexperts (elected decision makers, investors, neighbors, taxpayers, and many others) to decide on the best alternative (or define an entirely new alternative). Clearly communicating the results of complex analyses is at least as important a skill as doing the analyses. Just as GIS can simplify very complex analyses, it is also a powerful way to communicate results to a variety of end users.

There are many excellent guides to producing clear, user-friendly maps. Shading, symbols, annotation, orientation guides, and category decisions all help determine how people will "read" the maps (or other visual aids) presented. While maps are extremely effective tools to communicate results, they may also be misused (intentionally or not) to manipulate and confuse an audience. Designing clear, understandable, and attractive maps is an art. We do not address these important skills in this book. Instead, the reader is referred to one of the many very useful publications on this topic (Dent 1998 and Monmonier 1996 are helpful starting points).

In this concluding chapter, we address two issues related to distributing data that are of particular importance to urban analysts using GIS. The first is the role that GIS can play in organizing databases drawn from many sources and making their contents accessible to a wide variety of nonexpert users. The first section examines the role that GIS-based information banks have played in democratizing access to data. We hope this will stimulate readers to think creatively about local opportunities to use data to empower people and improve the quality of citizen participation in a wide variety of settings.

The second issue is a more practical one—how to distribute maps and map-based data in a cost-effective, user-friendly way. "E-government" initiatives have expanded rapidly in the very recent past, and the learning curve (among software manufacturers as well as analysts) has been steep. Based on a pilot project that we were involved in, we make recommendations for establishing Internet-based information banks that combine ease of use with reliability and widespread accessibility.

Democratizing data

Most of the discussion in this book has focused on the data needs of professional urban analysts—planners in local governments and human services agencies, as well as real estate investors and other business and public-sector users. However, the boundaries between the concerns of professional urban analysts and community-based organizations and neighborhood residents are increasingly fluid. Over the past two decades, community-based organizations have assumed a greater role in defining and implementing solutions to local problems. Community-based initiatives have emerged around issues as diverse as alternative school or healthcare systems, the construction and rehabilitation of affordable housing, environmental cleanup of contaminated land, crime reduction, and alternative transportation. Enabling effective and meaningful citizen participation has become more important for public-sector planners developing innovative solutions in partnership with residents instead of for residents (Sanoff 2000).

Democratizing access to data is a key component of efforts to build community-based capacity and meaningful participation. A major new initiative coordinated by the Urban Institute, the National Neighborhood Indicators Partnership (NNIP) (funded by the Annie E. Casey and Rockefeller foundations), demonstrates a practical approach to "democratizing information." Box 7.1 explains the NNIP in more detail.

Decision making is shaped partly by how one looks at the available evidence. Despite the best intentions of public-sector planners, it is difficult to escape professional conceptual biases about how data should be analyzed and presented. Increasing democratic decision making will entail enabling local residents to frame and answer the questions *they* believe are important.

A good example of how differently local residents may conceptualize and prioritize the same issue is offered by the Urban Institute's Reentry Mapping Network, which helps local communities collect and analyze data about prisoner reentry in their communities (see the National Neighborhood Indicators Partnership Web site at *www.urban.org/nnip/previous_new03.html*). The six initial partners have chosen research topics that focus on quite different issues:

- The Child and Family Center of Des Moines, Iowa, will investigate family reunification and parents' responsibility for recently released prisoners and their families.
- Project COMPASS and the Nonprofit Center of Milwaukee, Wisconsin, will examine ways to strengthen coordination among agencies providing services to released prisoners and their families.
- The Urban Strategies Council of Oakland, California, will educate community stakeholders about the challenges of reintegrating people on parole into the community.
- The Providence Plan of Providence, Rhode Island, will investigate how ex-prisoners' residential mobility affects the likelihood of them accessing services and staying out of prison.
- DC Agenda of Washington, D.C., will investigate the workforce-development opportunities and challenges for serving released prisoners.
- The Center for Community Safety of Winston–Salem, North Carolina, will evaluate the characteristics of neighborhoods that have high concentrations of ex-offenders in order to improve the use and effectiveness of local resources and assets.

Researchers from the Urban Institute's Justice Policy Center and the Metropolitan Housing and Communities Policy Center help communities collect and analyze the data. GIS has provided a powerful way to conceptualize the links between prisoner reentry data and other indicators of community well-being. Users have been able to ask quite different sorts of questions of the data instead of being constrained by one vision of which questions are relevant. For more information about the Reentry Mapping Network, see *www.urban.org/content/PolicyCenters/Justice/Projects/TheReentryMappingNetwork/overview.htm*.

Box 7.1   The National Neighborhood Indicators Project

An interesting example of a practical application of census and other spatial data is the National Neighborhood Indicators Project (NNIP), coordinated by The Urban Institute. By 2003, twenty cities participated in the initiative, building computer-based neighborhood indicators systems that could track changes in several key indicators over time (Tatian 2003). Advances in GIS software and address matching, and the increased availability of electronic data and computers to analyze the data, have enabled this initiative. It has wider application for planning and policy making in many contexts. Indicators are based on several sources of widely available data (Kingsley 1998, 4):

- vital statistics (births and deaths)
- police departments (crimes, police calls, and child abuse and neglect cases)
- public assistance agencies (numbers of needy families, and numbers of people who receive food stamps, general assistance, or free or subsidized medical care or child care)
- school systems (student enrollment, performance, special education programs)
- hospitals and health agencies (hospital admissions, immunizations)
- tax assessors or auditors (parcel characteristics, tax-delinquent parcels, vacant parcels)
- building or planning departments (code violations, building permits, demolitions)
- public housing authorities (public housing units)
- development departments (community development block grant expenditures)
- business directories (employment and economic activity)

Several other indicators could be added to this list. The NNIP focuses on three kinds of activities:

- Cross-site action initiatives. NNIP researchers are able to use locally collected data to compare neighborhood issues and indicators of change across cities. Comparisons of topics such as the impacts of welfare reform, neighborhood health status, prisoner reentry, or arts and culture in community building provide insight into the dynamics of neighborhood change and on the effectiveness of particular programs.
- Tool building and dissemination. This element has focused on developing databases as tools for community action, developing the capacity of neighborhood residents to use data effectively, and developing indicators of neighborhood health and change.
- Direct technical assistance and training. The NNIP provides technical assistance to help groups get started in new cities, including help on topics such as the technicalities of developing a data warehouse, how to design and apply indicators, and how to conduct community surveys (*www.urban.org/nnip/activities.html*).

Democratizing access to data will also help community organizations explain their achievements to philanthropic foundations and other donors. Organizations such as the Rockefeller, Ford, Surdna, and Annie E. Casey foundations play an important role in community-based comprehensive development initiatives (Pitcoff 1997). While traditional community development initiatives tended to emphasize physical development projects (such as housing rehabilitation or business development) that were easy to quantify, comprehensive initiatives go beyond these areas to focus on less easily quantified goals such as building community capacity, improving quality of life, increasing family stability, and reforming local systems. Measuring progress on these more conceptual indicators is a challenge that has required a more creative approach to collecting and analyzing data. While census-based data on employment, school completion, poverty, and other local indicators play an important role, data analysis must also incorporate more qualitative aspects such as residents' perceptions of public safety or the quality of the school system.

> A good example of how data collection and analysis can expand our understanding of community needs and impacts is the Social Assets and Vulnerability Indicators (SAVI) program developed by the Polis Center of Indianapolis (a joint project of Indiana and Purdue universities). SAVI (visit the site at *www.savi.org*) is an electronic GIS database including information on community assets (such as schools, churches, and community centers) and vulnerabilities (crime, public safety, health, and poverty). The site provides interactive mapping capabilities; for instance, the incidence of low-birth weight babies can be compared with the locations of healthcare facilities, outreach programs for mothers, and other indicators. The database can be accessed at public libraries as well as from home computers. A recent initiative introduced it to the school system, and a community-based, service learning project will enable sixth graders to introduce the electronic database to their communities (see "Indianapolis Partner Receives TOP grant" at *www. urban.org/nnip/previous_new03.html*).

Improving access to data (and the tools to analyze it meaningfully) clearly has tremendous potential for supporting and guiding community development initiatives. However, several challenges must be overcome in order to do this:

- Information must be accessible in a variety of formats. In recent years, many have begun to speak of a "digital divide" separating more affluent households with home computers from less-privileged households without home computers, and children in well-funded schools from those in less-advantaged schools. Setting up an interactive Web site alone is not enough; providing public access to computers (in libraries, schools, and community centers) and training on how to use Internet-based data are also important.
- Residents must be motivated to make use of these new resources. "Rational ignorance" is a powerful force; people do not necessarily believe that the effort they are asked to make to participate in important public decisions will pay off. It goes without saying that language should not be a barrier, but other considerations are important too. Information should be not only accessible, but easy and fun to use. Interactive Web sites should be designed with

this in mind. Other formats for presenting information, such as through public access TV shows, small group workshops, and public displays, should be explored.

- Developing consistent, meaningful indicators that are useful for program design and evaluation is also a challenge. It is often difficult to decide what information we might use to decide whether "community capacity" or "quality of life" has improved. It may be even more difficult to collect this information (for instance, through community surveys) consistently over time and ensure it is reliable. A useful guide is provided by the NNIP (Kingsley 1999).

Neighborhood Knowledge Los Angeles (NKLA) tries to address the challenges of providing accessible data that residents are motivated to use. The goals of NKLA are "coordinating public information in ways that assist neighborhoods; increasing government transparency to all residents, especially those who can't afford private access; and narrowing the digital divide by providing reasons that low-income users would want to learn the new technologies" (Richman and Kawano 2000, 1).

NKLA set up an Internet-based information system to track the evidence of disinvestment and decay in some Los Angeles neighborhoods. Using 1995 American Housing Survey data initially, NKLA found that an estimated 154,500 apartments in the city were in need of major repairs, 107,900 were infested with rats, and 131,700 homes did not have working toilets. In response to the public pressure generated by this recognition of an area-wide problem, the city of Los Angeles instituted a comprehensive code enforcement program to inspect all rental units in 1998. Just two years later, more than 400,000 code deficiencies had been fixed as a result (Richman and Kawano 2000, 1).

Once the American Community Survey (ACS) is fully implemented, the availability of timely census data will strengthen indicator projects. Developing neighborhood indicators is an effective way to monitor trends in outcomes for a variety of community development efforts, which may not be reflected in traditional measures of neighborhood vitality. They also provide another way to hold public officials accountable for the results of their decisions (Tatian 2003).

However, perhaps the main value of indicators is their potential in helping community residents take a constructive role in planning for their neighborhood. By democratizing information, indicator projects can make residents meaningful participants in planning and policy making. GIS can be a key component of this democratization. The following section of this chapter explores the issue of distributing spatially based information.

Distributing maps

Distributing maps to your users raises some important questions:

- Do you want to distribute mere images of your map documents or do you want to enable people to use the data and maps interactively?
- Will users have access to compatible GIS software?
- Will you distribute within your organization or to a wider set of users?
- Do you want to use the Internet to distribute information and maps?

The answers you give to these questions will determine, in large part, your distribution strategy. Two general principles apply:

- The wider your intended audience, the more complex the distribution issues.
- The wider the range of GIS skills of your intended audience, the more complex the distribution issues.

For entirely in-house distribution of maps and data, some mapping network system is essential (within the ESRI range of products ArcSDE® does the job), although it is always possible (but massively inefficient) to save data files to a portable medium and walk down the hall and swap files with coworkers. ArcSDE and other similar map networking products are usually implemented by system administrators or GIS consultants for an entire enterprise.

The problem is that even after establishing ArcSDE or a similar system, many in-house users of GIS products—both maps and data—will not be GIS savvy. A program as large and sophisticated as ArcGIS is unlikely to meet the needs of such people. If your target audience includes the general public, the problem is greater, as providing hands-on assistance will rarely be possible. Within an organization it is always possible to develop custom GIS software products that address the needs of novice GIS users. This way GIS administrators know exactly what software products are available within the organization and the capabilities of those products. Consultant programmers can develop such products fairly quickly and cheaply; the software will usually be directly connected to ArcSDE.

However, this strategy is losing ground as Web-based mapping comes to dominate map and data distribution. The advantage of the Web strategy is that the software products need not be entirely customized and may be cheaper and easier to maintain over the long haul. A Web-based distribution strategy also allows you to answer the needs of experienced and inexperienced in-house map users, and the general public, using a single set of tools.

Web-based mapping

A Web-based strategy requires setting up a map server. The map server is a piece of software that runs on a server machine, delivering maps (actually map services) to clients (Web browsers). You will need to decide what sorts of services client browsers should have access to. The nature of the service will determine how (and so some extent what) data is delivered to client machines. The process is both much simpler and, unfortunately, more complex than it sounds. In essence, this is how mapping services work:

- Mapping server software, such as ArcIMS software, must be installed and set up on a server machine.
- Once set up, the GIS administrator assembles the maps to be delivered to clients and also defines how they should be delivered.

This involves deciding whether client machines should see only images of maps, or whether they should have access to the information (the "map feature classes") that underlie the maps. Distributing images poses the fewest technical problems and may meet the needs of very inexperienced users. But static maps are not much use if the audience needs to have access to the data to use maps more interactively. So it may make sense to distribute maps as both image services and feature services for those who need access to the raw data. Different levels of permission can be given for image and feature services, allowing you to control the distribution of your data.

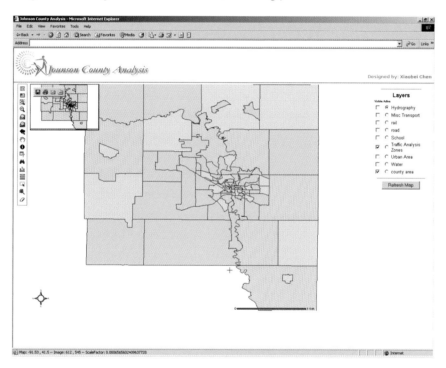

Figure 7.1

Figure 7.1 shows a simple map service delivered to a client browser. The client machine (perhaps a computer in someone's home) requests a map in a Web browser, and the screen, as seen in figure 7.1, is then delivered to the browser. How is it delivered? In this case the user has requested a map of TAZs in Johnson County, Iowa. The request is processed on the server machine, and an image is taken of the resulting map created on the server machine (you could think of the image as a digital photograph of the map created on the server). The image is delivered to the client browser. The user can query the resulting image in various ways such as by zooming or requesting further overlay information. Each request is sent to the server, the server generates the result, creates a digital image of the result, and then sends that image to the client browser for display. For more on Internet mapping, see Harder (1998).

Image services are a good distribution strategy because they use very few resources on client machines. Thus this strategy will work even with old machines using older browser technology. Also, since only images and not the original data are being sent out over the Internet, there is little chance of data being compromised. In some instances this latter issue can be an important consideration. These are the negatives associated with this strategy:

- The server machine must do all the processing (if thousands of clients are logged on at once, this can cause difficulties).
- The strategy will take up more bandwidth as requests and results of requests must be constantly passed between server and client machines slowing down the mapping process on the client machine.
- Users will not have access to the originating feature classes.

The same maps could be delivered to the client as a feature class, and the resulting Web page would look almost identical to the image service in figure 7.1. Delivering maps this way requires installing various additional pieces of ancillary software on client machines. For those using advanced, flexible mapping feature service technology (such as that available in ArcIMS), not all client machines may be capable of upgrading and thus not all client browsers will be able to view the services. Moreover, even on machines capable of upgrading, many users are unwilling to download and install "unknown" software onto their machines. But if users have compliant machines and are willing to install the necessary software, feature services are superior to image services. The feature service delivers the raw maps and data from the server to the client. These are then processed on the client machine itself. The initial download may take some time, but subsequent analysis and manipulation of the data and maps will be much faster. Also, the client machine has the raw data; provided the server gives permission, that data may then be downloaded to the client machine for later use in a variety of ways.

Most casual users would see little difference between the two map services. In both cases a Web browser is used, with a set of icons allowing users to navigate around and query the map's data. For some, a Web browser is not an ideal delivery mechanism, particularly for those whose machines and browser software do not allow feature services to be viewed. ArcExplorer software (available free from ESRI) will perform all map client functions on most personal computer machines. Many will find ArcExplorer considerably more intuitive than a browser. As far as the server machine is concerned, delivering services to ArcExplorer is no different than delivering to a browser. ArcExplorer then functions as a free mini-GIS on the client's desktop. Figure 7.2 (next page) shows the same service as figure 7.1 now delivered to ArcExplorer. The advantage of encouraging clients to use ArcExplorer is that advanced functions can be delivered to client machines, but users have to install only one piece of software from a known provider. Our experience has been that consumer resistance to installing the browser plug-ins necessary for delivering

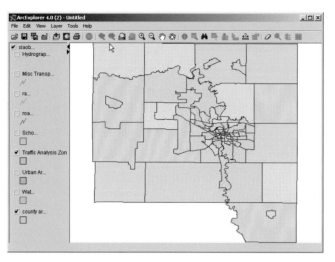

Figure 7.2

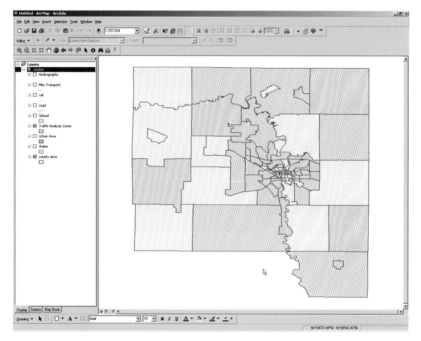

Figure 7.3

a feature service via a browser is likely to be much greater than downloading and installing a single piece of software.

One advantage to setting up image and feature services in this way is that they can also be delivered to clients with advanced GIS knowledge and software. The process here is simple, as illustrated in figure 7.3. In ArcCatalog add a new Internet server, then in ArcMap add data from the Internet server you have set up.

Web-mapping servers such as ArcIMS provide a convenient and powerful way to deliver maps and data to clients. Users are able to access your services using a variety of software—from the near ubiquitous Web browser, to specialized map client software, to a fully-fledged GIS program. The main problem is the difficulty of actually setting up the mapping Web server. With effort, people with some knowledge of GIS and servers can establish a default mapping Web service. But the technology is still very young. Any customization of the services demands a range of more advanced programming (such as JAVA and XML), GIS, and server skills. The software does come with extensive, though difficult to use, documentation on setting up ArcIMS and using JAVA™, XML, and other technologies in your Web sites. If your organization does not have someone with these skills, it may be easier and cheaper in the long run to hire a consultant to set up and maintain your mapping Web services rather than developing in-house ability.

Using map documents

There is an alternative and increasingly popular strategy for distributing maps: delivering "map documents" to clients. This became possible with the release of version 8.2 of ArcGIS. ArcReader™ is a standard document format that is meant to do for maps what the Adobe® Acrobat® reader has done for complex text documents. The process here is straightforward (although there are hidden dangers for the uninitiated). As with Adobe Acrobat, users need to download and install a document reader. ArcReader is available free from the ESRI Web site. The reader is fairly powerful and is, in our experience, much simpler for novice users than the browser-based mapping clients. In our experience, most users are accustomed to dealing with Acrobat .pdf document files and are reasonably comfortable using software they see as a mapping equivalent (the map documents have the .pmf file suffix).

Distributors of .pmf files will have to purchase the ArcPublisher extension to ArcGIS. Once an ArcMap document (.mxd) has been created and saved, an ArcPublisher document version of the same (.pmf) would be created. The ArcPublisher document can then be distributed on the Web, by email or CD–ROM, or any other standard medium.

The benefits of this strategy are all on the client side. Clients get free, easy-to-use software and maps delivered to their machines with the maps looking exactly as they did in ArcMap. ArcReader is powerful enough that typical queries such as zooming, searching for a location, selecting all places with a particular attribute, identifying other attributes of a place, measuring distance, or creating buffers are simple. For maps aimed at a general audience with a variety of interests in the data, this is the strategy we recommend very highly.

In ArcReader 8.3 the difficulties are mainly with setting up and maintaining the server. The .pmf document file does not contain any underlying data, merely the layout structure. Thus, data must also be delivered to client machines. For maps delivered in-house with a shared server or an ArcSDE link this is a minor problem. The document will simply (and transparently) access the raw feature classes from the server. But if the public or other organizations are your primary audience, this is an important problem. A solution which sounds overly complex but which works extremely well in practice (and has the benefit of being entirely transparent to users) is to serve all underlying data using an ArcIMS feature service. This way a user opens a map document in ArcReader and retrieves the underlying data from the mapping server. In this case, Web-mapping services are not set up primarily to serve browser clients (though they may be), but merely to serve map data to distributed map documents. Even though this strategy involves added complexity (not only are you creating map documents but you must serve data on the Web), we have found that it works very well. Users with little prior GIS knowledge seem more at home navigating around a map in ArcReader than they do in either ArcExplorer or in a Web browser. As in ArcMap, users can choose from a "data view" or a "layout view." By developing a layout before you publish the map document, you can then deliver polished map output to users. However, the ArcReader strategy may not be appropriate if users must have direct access to the actual map and data files. Version 9.0 of ArcPublisher/ArcReader allows data to be rolled up with the document files, obviating the need to set up independent map services, though these may still remain useful when the underlying data needs to be updated constantly.

Final comments

Making sense of the rich information in the decennial census and related products requires a clear understanding of the limitations and potential of the data, and a clear idea of how the information will (or could) be used. GIS is an invaluable tool to unlock the potential of this "raw" data. Although it is certainly possible to use census data without a GIS, analyzing information spatially can offer new insights, and the database functions of GIS make it easy to solve many of the problems (such as comparability over time) that some analyses raise.

Using GIS as an effective tool requires some basic understanding of technical issues. To many, this may be intimidating at first. However, the level of technical skills required to access maps and data and link them together are well within reach of those with a basic level of competence with widely used computer software, such as spreadsheets and databases. For more complex tasks, a basic acquaintance with the concepts involved will make it easier to hire and direct a specialized consultant, if the prospect of setting up a map server or incorporating aerial photography threatens to absorb more time than a novice user can justify.

It is important to remember, however, that GIS is just a tool. The most important prerequisites for using it effectively are correctly framing the questions you will use it to answer, understanding the gaps and limitations of the data you use to answer those questions, and understanding the needs and capacities of your audience, whether they be elected officials, civil engineers, or neighborhood residents. The technical skills you will need to develop to use GIS are peripheral to the conceptual, analytic, and communication skills that these prerequisites entail. We hope that readers have as much fun using this guide to developing these varied skills as we had writing it.

Appendix

United States
Census 2000

U.S. Department of Commerce
Bureau of the Census

This is the official form for all the people at this address. It is quick and easy, and your answers are protected by law. Complete the Census and help your community get what it needs — today and in the future!

Start Here
Please use a black or blue pen.

1 How many people were living or staying in this house, apartment, or mobile home on April 1, 2000?

Number of people

INCLUDE in this number:

- foster children, roomers, or housemates
- people staying here on April 1, 2000 who have no other permanent place to stay
- people living here most of the time while working, even if they have another place to live

DO NOT INCLUDE in this number:

- college students living away while attending college
- people in a correctional facility, nursing home, or mental hospital on April 1, 2000
- Armed Forces personnel living somewhere else
- people who live or stay at another place most of the time

➡ Please turn the page and print the names of all the people living or staying here on April 1, 2000.

If you need help completing this form, *call 1-800-471-9424 between 8:00 a.m. and 9:00 p.m., 7 days a week. The telephone call is free.*

TDD – *Telephone display device for the hearing impaired. Call 1-800-582-8330 between 8:00 a.m. and 9:00 p.m., 7 days a week. The telephone call is free.*

¿NECESITA AYUDA? *Si usted necesita ayuda para completar este cuestionario llame al 1-800-471-8642 entre las 8:00 a.m. y las 9:00 p.m., 7 días a la semana. La llamada telefónica es gratis.*

The Census Bureau estimates that, for the average household, this form will take about 38 minutes to complete, including the time for reviewing the instructions and answers. Comments about the estimate should be directed to the Associate Director for Finance and Administration, Attn: Paperwork Reduction Project 0607-0856, Room 3104, Federal Building 3, Bureau of the Census, Washington, DC 20233.

Respondents are not required to respond to any information collection unless it displays a valid approval number from the Office of Management and Budget.

Form D-2

OMB No. 0607-0856; Approval Expires 12/31/2000

List of Persons

➡ Please be sure you answered question 1 on the front page before continuing.

➋ Please print the names of all the people who you indicated in question 1 were living or staying here on April 1, 2000.

Example — Last Name

JOHNSON

First Name   MI

ROBIN   *J*

Start with the person, or one of the people living here who owns, is buying, or rents this house, apartment, or mobile home. If there is no such person, start with any adult living or staying here.

Person 1 — Last Name

First Name   MI

Person 2 — Last Name

First Name   MI

Person 3 — Last Name

First Name   MI

Person 4 — Last Name

First Name   MI

Person 5 — Last Name

First Name   MI

Person 6 — Last Name

First Name   MI

Person 7 — Last Name

First Name   MI

Person 8 — Last Name

First Name   MI

Person 9 — Last Name

First Name   MI

Person 10 — Last Name

First Name   MI

Person 11 — Last Name

First Name   MI

Person 12 — Last Name

First Name   MI

➡ Next, answer questions about Person 1.

FOR OFFICE USE ONLY

A. JIC1   B. JIC2   C. RC1   D. RC4

Form D-2

2

Person 1

Your answers are important! Every person in the Census counts.

➊ **What is this person's name?** *Print the name of Person 1 from page 2.*

Last Name

First Name   MI

➋ **What is this person's telephone number?** *We may contact this person if we don't understand an answer.*

Area Code + Number

➌ **What is this person's sex?** *Mark* ☒ *ONE box.*

☐ Male
☐ Female

➍ **What is this person's age and what is this person's date of birth?**

Age on April 1, 2000

Print numbers in boxes.

Month   Day   Year of birth

➡ NOTE: Please answer BOTH Questions 5 and 6.

➎ **Is this person Spanish/Hispanic/Latino?** *Mark* ☒ *the "No" box if not Spanish/Hispanic/Latino.*

☐ No, not Spanish/Hispanic/Latino
☐ Yes, Mexican, Mexican Am., Chicano
☐ Yes, Puerto Rican
☐ Yes, Cuban
☐ Yes, other Spanish/Hispanic/Latino — *Print group.* ➚

➏ **What is this person's race?** *Mark* ☒ *one or more races to indicate what this person considers himself/herself to be.*

☐ White
☐ Black, African Am., or Negro
☐ American Indian or Alaska Native — *Print name of enrolled or principal tribe.* ➚

☐ Asian Indian   ☐ Native Hawaiian
☐ Chinese   ☐ Guamanian or Chamorro
☐ Filipino   ☐ Samoan
☐ Japanese
☐ Korean   ☐ Other Pacific Islander — *Print race.* ➚
☐ Vietnamese
☐ Other Asian — *Print race.* ➚

☐ Some other race — *Print race.* ➚

➐ **What is this person's marital status?**

☐ Now married
☐ Widowed
☐ Divorced
☐ Separated
☐ Never married

➑ **a. At any time since February 1, 2000, has this person attended regular school or college?** *Include only nursery school or preschool, kindergarten, elementary school, and schooling which leads to a high school diploma or a college degree.*

☐ No, has not attended since February 1 → *Skip to 9*
☐ Yes, public school, public college
☐ Yes, private school, private college

2043

Form D-2

3

8 b. What grade or level was this person attending?
Mark ⊠ ONE box.

☐ Nursery school, preschool
☐ Kindergarten
☐ Grade 1 to grade 4
☐ Grade 5 to grade 8
☐ Grade 9 to grade 12
☐ College undergraduate years (freshman to senior)
☐ Graduate or professional school (for example: medical, dental, or law school)

9 What is the highest degree or level of school this person has COMPLETED? *Mark ⊠ ONE box. If currently enrolled, mark the previous grade or highest degree received.*

☐ No schooling completed
☐ Nursery school to 4th grade
☐ 5th grade or 6th grade
☐ 7th grade or 8th grade
☐ 9th grade
☐ 10th grade
☐ 11th grade
☐ 12th grade, **NO DIPLOMA**
☐ **HIGH SCHOOL GRADUATE** — high school DIPLOMA or the equivalent (for example: GED)
☐ Some college credit, but less than 1 year
☐ 1 or more years of college, no degree
☐ Associate degree (for example: AA, AS)
☐ Bachelor's degree (for example: BA, AB, BS)
☐ Master's degree (for example: MA, MS, MEng, MEd, MSW, MBA)
☐ Professional degree (for example: MD, DDS, DVM, LLB, JD)
☐ Doctorate degree (for example: PhD, EdD)

10 What is this person's ancestry or ethnic origin?

(For example: Italian, Jamaican, African Am., Cambodian, Cape Verdean, Norwegian, Dominican, French Canadian, Haitian, Korean, Lebanese, Polish, Nigerian, Mexican, Taiwanese, Ukrainian, and so on.)

11 a. Does this person speak a language other than English at home?

☐ Yes
☐ No → *Skip to 12*

b. What is this language?

(For example: Korean, Italian, Spanish, Vietnamese)

c. How well does this person speak English?

☐ Very well
☐ Well
☐ Not well
☐ Not at all

12 Where was this person born?

☐ In the United States — *Print name of state.*

☐ Outside the United States — *Print name of foreign country, or Puerto Rico, Guam, etc.*

13 Is this person a CITIZEN of the United States?

☐ Yes, born in the United States → *Skip to 15a*
☐ Yes, born in Puerto Rico, Guam, the U.S. Virgin Islands, or Northern Marianas
☐ Yes, born abroad of American parent or parents
☐ Yes, a U.S. citizen by naturalization
☐ No, not a citizen of the United States

14 When did this person come to live in the United States? *Print numbers in boxes.*

Year

15 a. Did this person live in this house or apartment 5 years ago (on April 1, 1995)?

☐ Person is under 5 years old → *Skip to 33*
☐ Yes, this house → *Skip to 16*
☐ No, outside the United States — *Print name of foreign country, or Puerto Rico, Guam, etc., below; then skip to 16.*

☐ No, different house in the United States

273

15 b. Where did this person live 5 years ago?

Name of city, town, or post office

Did this person live inside the limits of the city or town?

☐ Yes
☐ No, outside the city/town limits

Name of county

Name of state

ZIP Code

16 Does this person have any of the following long-lasting conditions:

	Yes	No
a. Blindness, deafness, or a severe vision or hearing impairment?	☐	☐
b. A condition that substantially limits one or more basic physical activities such as walking, climbing stairs, reaching, lifting, or carrying?	☐	☐

17 Because of a physical, mental, or emotional condition lasting 6 months or more, does this person have any difficulty in doing any of the following activities:

	Yes	No
a. Learning, remembering, or concentrating?	☐	☐
b. Dressing, bathing, or getting around inside the home?	☐	☐
c. (Answer if this person is 16 YEARS OLD OR OVER.) Going outside the home alone to shop or visit a doctor's office?	☐	☐
d. (Answer if this person is 16 YEARS OLD OR OVER.) Working at a job or business?	☐	☐

18 Was this person under 15 years of age on April 1, 2000?

☐ Yes → *Skip to 33*
☐ No

19 a. Does this person have any of his/her own grandchildren under the age of 18 living in this house or apartment?

☐ Yes
☐ No → *Skip to 20a*

b. Is this grandparent currently responsible for most of the basic needs of any grandchild(ren) under the age of 18 who live(s) in this house or apartment?

☐ Yes
☐ No → *Skip to 20a*

c. How long has this grandparent been responsible for the(se) grandchild(ren)? *If the grandparent is financially responsible for more than one grandchild, answer the question for the grandchild for whom the grandparent has been responsible for the longest period of time.*

☐ Less than 6 months
☐ 6 to 11 months
☐ 1 or 2 years
☐ 3 or 4 years
☐ 5 years or more

20 a. Has this person ever served on active duty in the U.S. Armed Forces, military Reserves, or National Guard? *Active duty does not include training for the Reserves or National Guard, but DOES include activation, for example, for the Persian Gulf War.*

☐ Yes, now on active duty
☐ Yes, on active duty in past, but not now
☐ No, training for Reserves or National Guard only → *Skip to 21*
☐ No, never served in the military → *Skip to 21*

b. When did this person serve on active duty in the U.S. Armed Forces? *Mark ⊠ a box for EACH period in which this person served.*

☐ April 1995 or later
☐ August 1990 to March 1995 (including Persian Gulf War)
☐ September 1980 to July 1990
☐ May 1975 to August 1980
☐ Vietnam era (August 1964—April 1975)
☐ February 1955 to July 1964
☐ Korean conflict (June 1950—January 1955)
☐ World War II (September 1940—July 1947)
☐ Some other time

c. In total, how many years of active-duty military service has this person had?

☐ Less than 2 years
☐ 2 years or more

Person 1 (continued)

21 **LAST WEEK, did this person do ANY work for either pay or profit?** *Mark* ☒ *the "Yes" box even if the person worked only 1 hour, or helped without pay in a family business or farm for 15 hours or more, or was on active duty in the Armed Forces.*

☐ Yes
☐ No → *Skip to 25a*

22 **At what location did this person work LAST WEEK?** *If this person worked at more than one location, print where he or she worked most last week.*

a. Address (Number and street name)

(If the exact address is not known, give a description of the location such as the building name or the nearest street or intersection.)

b. Name of city, town, or post office

c. Is the work location inside the limits of that city or town?

☐ Yes
☐ No, outside the city/town limits

d. Name of county

e. Name of U.S. state or foreign country

f. ZIP Code

23 **a. How did this person usually get to work LAST WEEK?** *If this person usually used more than one method of transportation during the trip, mark* ☒ *the box of the one used for most of the distance.*

☐ Car, truck, or van
☐ Bus or trolley bus
☐ Streetcar or trolley car
☐ Subway or elevated
☐ Railroad
☐ Ferryboat
☐ Taxicab
☐ Motorcycle
☐ Bicycle
☐ Walked
☐ Worked at home → *Skip to 27*
☐ Other method

→ If "Car, truck, or van" is marked in 23a, go to 23b. Otherwise, skip to 24a.

23 **b. How many people, including this person, usually rode to work in the car, truck, or van LAST WEEK?**

☐ Drove alone
☐ 2 people
☐ 3 people
☐ 4 people
☐ 5 or 6 people
☐ 7 or more people

24 **a. What time did this person usually leave home to go to work LAST WEEK?**

☐ a.m. ☐ p.m.

b. How many minutes did it usually take this person to get from home to work LAST WEEK?

Minutes

→ Answer questions 25–26 for persons who did not work for pay or profit last week. Others skip to 27.

25 **a. LAST WEEK, was this person on layoff from a job?**

☐ Yes → *Skip to 25c*
☐ No

b. LAST WEEK, was this person TEMPORARILY absent from a job or business?

☐ Yes, on vacation, temporary illness, labor dispute, etc. → *Skip to 26*
☐ No → *Skip to 25d*

c. Has this person been informed that he or she will be recalled to work within the next 6 months OR been given a date to return to work?

☐ Yes → *Skip to 25e*
☐ No

d. Has this person been looking for work during the last 4 weeks?

☐ Yes
☐ No → *Skip to 26*

e. LAST WEEK, could this person have started a job if offered one, or returned to work if recalled?

☐ Yes, could have gone to work
☐ No, because of own temporary illness
☐ No, because of all other reasons *(in school, etc.)*

26 **When did this person last work, even for a few days?**

☐ 1995 to 2000
☐ 1994 or earlier, or never

Form D-2

6

Person 1 (continued)

27 **Industry or Employer** — *Describe clearly this person's chief job activity or business last week. If this person had more than one job, describe the one at which this person worked the most hours. If this person had no job or business last week, give the information for his/her last job or business since 1995.*

a. For whom did this person work? *If now on active duty in the Armed Forces, mark* ☒ *this box →* ☐ *and print the branch of the Armed Forces.*

Name of company, business, or other employer

b. What kind of business or industry was this? *Describe the activity at location where employed. (For example: hospital, newspaper publishing, mail order house, auto repair shop, bank)*

c. Is this mainly — *Mark* ☒ *ONE box.*

☐ Manufacturing?
☐ Wholesale trade?
☐ Retail trade?
☐ Other *(agriculture, construction, service, government, etc.)*?

28 **Occupation**

a. What kind of work was this person doing? *(For example: registered nurse, personnel manager, supervisor of order department, auto mechanic, accountant)*

b. What were this person's most important activities or duties? *(For example: patient care, directing hiring policies, supervising order clerks, repairing automobiles, reconciling financial records)*

29 **Was this person** — *Mark* ☒ *ONE box.*

☐ Employee of a PRIVATE-FOR-PROFIT company or business or of an individual, for wages, salary, or commissions
☐ Employee of a PRIVATE NOT-FOR-PROFIT, tax-exempt, or charitable organization
☐ Local GOVERNMENT employee *(city, county, etc.)*
☐ State GOVERNMENT employee
☐ Federal GOVERNMENT employee
☐ SELF-EMPLOYED in own NOT INCORPORATED business, professional practice, or farm
☐ SELF-EMPLOYED in own INCORPORATED business, professional practice, or farm
☐ Working WITHOUT PAY in family business or farm

30 **a. LAST YEAR, 1999, did this person work at a job or business at any time?**

☐ Yes
☐ No → *Skip to 31*

b. How many weeks did this person work in 1999? *Count paid vacation, paid sick leave, and military service.*

Weeks

c. During the weeks WORKED in 1999, how many hours did this person usually work each WEEK?

Usual hours worked each WEEK

31 **INCOME IN 1999** — *Mark* ☒ *the "Yes" box for each income source received during 1999 and enter the total amount received during 1999 to a maximum of $999,999. Mark* ☒ *the "No" box if the income source was not received. If net income was a loss, enter the amount and mark* ☒ *the "Loss" box next to the dollar amount.*

For income received jointly, report, if possible, the appropriate share for each person; otherwise, report the whole amount for only one person and mark ☒ *the "No" box for the other person. If exact amount is not known, please give best estimate.*

a. Wages, salary, commissions, bonuses, or tips from all jobs — *Report amount before deductions for taxes, bonds, dues, or other items.*

☐ Yes   Annual amount — Dollars

☐ No

b. Self-employment income from own nonfarm businesses or farm businesses, including proprietorships and partnerships — *Report NET income after business expenses.*

☐ Yes   Annual amount — Dollars

☐ Loss

☐ No

2047

Form D-2

7

c. Interest, dividends, net rental income, royalty income, or income from estates and trusts — *Report even small amounts credited to an account.*
☐ Yes   Annual amount — *Dollars*
☐ Loss
☐ No

d. Social Security or Railroad Retirement
☐ Yes   Annual amount — *Dollars*
☐ No

e. Supplemental Security Income (SSI)
☐ Yes   Annual amount — *Dollars*
☐ No

f. Any public assistance or welfare payments from the state or local welfare office
☐ Yes   Annual amount — *Dollars*
☐ No

g. Retirement, survivor, or disability pensions — *Do NOT include Social Security.*
☐ Yes   Annual amount — *Dollars*
☐ No

h. Any other sources of income received regularly such as Veterans' (VA) payments, unemployment compensation, child support, or alimony — *Do NOT include lump-sum payments such as money from an inheritance or sale of a home.*
☐ Yes   Annual amount — *Dollars*
☐ No

32 What was this person's total income in 1999? *Add entries in questions 31a—37h; subtract any losses. If net income was a loss, enter the amount and mark ☒ the "Loss" box next to the dollar amount.*
Annual amount — *Dollars*
☐ None   OR
☐ Loss

➡ Now, please answer questions 33—53 about your household.

33 Is this house, apartment, or mobile home —
☐ Owned by you or someone in this household with a mortgage or loan?
☐ Owned by you or someone in this household free and clear (without a mortgage or loan)?
☐ Rented for cash rent?
☐ Occupied without payment of cash rent?

34 Which best describes this building? *Include all apartments, flats, etc., even if vacant.*
☐ A mobile home
☐ A one-family house detached from any other house
☐ A one-family house attached to one or more houses
☐ A building with 2 apartments
☐ A building with 3 or 4 apartments
☐ A building with 5 to 9 apartments
☐ A building with 10 to 19 apartments
☐ A building with 20 to 49 apartments
☐ A building with 50 or more apartments
☐ Boat, RV, van, etc.

35 About when was this building first built?
☐ 1999 or 2000
☐ 1995 to 1998
☐ 1990 to 1994
☐ 1980 to 1989
☐ 1970 to 1979
☐ 1960 to 1969
☐ 1950 to 1959
☐ 1940 to 1949
☐ 1939 or earlier

36 When did this person move into this house, apartment, or mobile home?
☐ 1999 or 2000
☐ 1995 to 1998
☐ 1990 to 1994
☐ 1980 to 1989
☐ 1970 to 1979
☐ 1969 or earlier

37 How many rooms do you have in this house, apartment, or mobile home? *Do NOT count bathrooms, porches, balconies, foyers, halls, or half-rooms.*
☐ 1 room   ☐ 6 rooms
☐ 2 rooms   ☐ 7 rooms
☐ 3 rooms   ☐ 8 rooms
☐ 4 rooms   ☐ 9 or more rooms
☐ 5 rooms

Form D-2
8

38 How many bedrooms do you have; that is, how many bedrooms would you list if this house, apartment, or mobile home were on the market for sale or rent?
☐ No bedroom
☐ 1 bedroom
☐ 2 bedrooms
☐ 3 bedrooms
☐ 4 bedrooms
☐ 5 or more bedrooms

39 Do you have COMPLETE plumbing facilities in this house, apartment, or mobile home; that is, 1) hot and cold piped water, 2) a flush toilet, and 3) a bathtub or shower?
☐ Yes, have all three facilities
☐ No

40 Do you have COMPLETE kitchen facilities in this house, apartment, or mobile home; that is, 1) a sink with piped water, 2) a range or stove, and 3) a refrigerator?
☐ Yes, have all three facilities
☐ No

41 Is there telephone service available in this house, apartment, or mobile home from which you can both make and receive calls?
☐ Yes
☐ No

42 Which FUEL is used MOST for heating this house, apartment, or mobile home?
☐ Gas: from underground pipes serving the neighborhood
☐ Gas: bottled, tank, or LP
☐ Electricity
☐ Fuel oil, kerosene, etc.
☐ Coal or coke
☐ Wood
☐ Solar energy
☐ Other fuel
☐ No fuel used

43 How many automobiles, vans, and trucks of one-ton capacity or less are kept at home for use by members of your household?
☐ None
☐ 1
☐ 2
☐ 3
☐ 4
☐ 5
☐ 6 or more

44 Answer ONLY if this is a ONE-FAMILY HOUSE OR MOBILE HOME — All others skip to 45.
a. Is there a business (such as a store or barber shop) or a medical office on this property?
☐ Yes
☐ No
b. How many acres is this house or mobile home on?
☐ Less than 1 acre → *Skip to 45*
☐ 1 to 9.9 acres
☐ 10 or more acres
c. In 1999, what were the actual sales of all agricultural products from this property?
☐ None   ☐ $2,500 to $4,999
☐ $1 to $999   ☐ $5,000 to $9,999
☐ $1,000 to $2,499   ☐ $10,000 or more

45 What are the annual costs of utilities and fuels for this house, apartment, or mobile home? *If you have lived here less than 1 year, estimate the annual cost.*
a. Electricity
Annual cost — *Dollars*
OR
☐ Included in rent or in condominium fee
☐ No charge or electricity not used
b. Gas
Annual cost — *Dollars*
OR
☐ Included in rent or in condominium fee
☐ No charge or gas not used
c. Water and sewer
Annual cost — *Dollars*
OR
☐ Included in rent or in condominium fee
☐ No charge
d. Oil, coal, kerosene, wood, etc.
Annual cost — *Dollars*
OR
☐ Included in rent or in condominium fee
☐ No charge or these fuels not used

2049

Form D-2
9

Appendix

275

Person 1 (continued)

46 Answer ONLY if you PAY RENT for this house, apartment, or mobile home — All others skip to 47.

a. What is the monthly rent?

Monthly amount — *Dollars*

$. 00

b. Does the monthly rent include any meals?

☐ Yes
☐ No

47 Answer questions 47a—53 if you or someone in this household owns or is buying this house, apartment, or mobile home; otherwise, skip to questions for Person 2.

a. Do you have a mortgage, deed of trust, contract to purchase, or similar debt on THIS property?

☐ Yes, mortgage, deed of trust, or similar debt
☐ Yes, contract to purchase
☐ No → *Skip to 48a*

b. How much is your regular monthly mortgage payment on THIS property? *Include payment only on first mortgage or contract to purchase.*

Monthly amount — *Dollars*

$. 00

OR

☐ No regular payment required → *Skip to 48a*

c. Does your regular monthly mortgage payment include payments for real estate taxes on THIS property?

☐ Yes, taxes included in mortgage payment
☐ No, taxes paid separately or taxes not required

d. Does your regular monthly mortgage payment include payments for fire, hazard, or flood insurance on THIS property?

☐ Yes, insurance included in mortgage payment
☐ No, insurance paid separately or no insurance

48 **a. Do you have a second mortgage or a home equity loan on THIS property?** *Mark ☒ all boxes that apply.*

☐ Yes, a second mortgage
☐ Yes, a home equity loan
☐ No → *Skip to 49*

b. How much is your regular monthly payment on all second or junior mortgages and all home equity loans on THIS property?

Monthly amount — *Dollars*

$. 00

OR

☐ No regular payment required

49 What were the real estate taxes on THIS property last year?

Yearly amount — *Dollars*

$. 00

OR

☐ None

50 What was the annual payment for fire, hazard, and flood insurance on THIS property?

Annual amount — *Dollars*

$. 00

OR

☐ None

51 What is the value of this property; that is, how much do you think this house and lot, apartment, or mobile home and lot would sell for if it were for sale?

☐ Less than $10,000
☐ $10,000 to $14,999
☐ $15,000 to $19,999
☐ $20,000 to $24,999
☐ $25,000 to $29,999
☐ $30,000 to $34,999
☐ $35,000 to $39,999
☐ $40,000 to $49,999
☐ $50,000 to $59,999
☐ $60,000 to $69,999
☐ $70,000 to $79,999
☐ $80,000 to $89,999

☐ $90,000 to $99,999
☐ $100,000 to $124,999
☐ $125,000 to $149,999
☐ $150,000 to $174,999
☐ $175,000 to $199,999
☐ $200,000 to $249,999
☐ $250,000 to $299,999
☐ $300,000 to $399,999
☐ $400,000 to $499,999
☐ $500,000 to $749,999
☐ $750,000 to $999,999
☐ $1,000,000 or more

52 Answer ONLY if this is a CONDOMINIUM —

What is the monthly condominium fee?

Monthly amount — *Dollars*

$. 00

53 Answer ONLY if this is a MOBILE HOME —

a. Do you have an installment loan or contract on THIS mobile home?

☐ Yes
☐ No

b. What was the total cost for installment loan payments, personal property taxes, site rent, registration fees, and license fees on THIS mobile home and its site last year? *Exclude real estate taxes.*

Yearly amount — *Dollars*

$. 00

➡ Are there more people living here? If yes, continue with Person 2.

Person 2

Census information helps your community get financial assistance for roads, hospitals, schools and more.

1 **What is this person's name?** *Print the name of Person 2 from page 2.*

Last Name

First Name   MI

2 **How is this person related to Person 1?** *Mark ☒ ONE box.*

☐ Husband/wife
☐ Natural-born son/daughter
☐ Adopted son/daughter
☐ Stepson/stepdaughter
☐ Brother/sister
☐ Father/mother
☐ Grandchild
☐ Parent-in-law
☐ Son-in-law/daughter-in-law
☐ Other relative — *Print exact relationship.*

If NOT RELATED to Person 1:

☐ Roomer, boarder
☐ Housemate, roommate
☐ Unmarried partner
☐ Foster child
☐ Other nonrelative

3 **What is this person's sex?** *Mark ☒ ONE box.*

☐ Male
☐ Female

4 **What is this person's age and what is this person's date of birth?**

Age on April 1, 2000

Print numbers in boxes.
Month   Day   Year of birth

➡ **NOTE: Please answer BOTH Questions 5 and 6.**

5 **Is this person Spanish/Hispanic/Latino?** *Mark ☒ the "No" box if not Spanish/Hispanic/Latino.*

☐ **No**, not Spanish/Hispanic/Latino
☐ Yes, Mexican, Mexican Am., Chicano
☐ Yes, Puerto Rican
☐ Yes, Cuban
☐ Yes, other Spanish/Hispanic/Latino — *Print group.* ↗

6 **What is this person's race?** *Mark ☒ one or more races to indicate what this person considers himself/herself to be.*

☐ White
☐ Black, African Am., or Negro
☐ American Indian or Alaska Native — *Print name of enrolled or principal tribe.* ↗

☐ Asian Indian
☐ Chinese
☐ Filipino
☐ Japanese
☐ Korean
☐ Vietnamese
☐ Other Asian — *Print race.* ↗

☐ Native Hawaiian
☐ Guamanian or Chamorro
☐ Samoan
☐ Other Pacific Islander — *Print race.* ↗

☐ Some other race — *Print race.* ↗

7 **What is this person's marital status?**

☐ Now married
☐ Widowed
☐ Divorced
☐ Separated
☐ Never married

8 a. **At any time since February 1, 2000, has this person attended regular school or college?** *Include only nursery school or preschool, kindergarten, elementary school, and schooling which leads to a high school diploma or a college degree.*

☐ No, has not attended since February 1 → *Skip to 9*
☐ Yes, public school, public college
☐ Yes, private school, private college

b. **What grade or level was this person attending?**
Mark ☒ ONE box.

☐ Nursery school, preschool
☐ Kindergarten
☐ Grade 1 to grade 4
☐ Grade 5 to grade 8
☐ Grade 9 to grade 12
☐ College undergraduate years (freshman to senior)
☐ Graduate or professional school *(for example: medical, dental, or law school)*

9 **What is the highest degree or level of school this person has COMPLETED?** *Mark ☒ ONE box. If currently enrolled, mark the previous grade or highest degree received.*

☐ No schooling completed
☐ Nursery school to 4th grade
☐ 5th grade or 6th grade
☐ 7th grade or 8th grade
☐ 9th grade
☐ 10th grade
☐ 11th grade
☐ 12th grade, **NO DIPLOMA**
☐ **HIGH SCHOOL GRADUATE** — high school DIPLOMA or the equivalent *(for example: GED)*
☐ Some college credit, but less than 1 year
☐ 1 or more years of college, no degree
☐ Associate degree *(for example: AA, AS)*
☐ Bachelor's degree *(for example: BA, AB, BS)*
☐ Master's degree *(for example: MA, MS, MEng, MEd, MSW, MBA)*
☐ Professional degree *(for example: MD, DDS, DVM, LLB, JD)*
☐ Doctorate degree *(for example: PhD, EdD)*

10 **What is this person's ancestry or ethnic origin?**

(For example: Italian, Jamaican, African Am., Cambodian, Cape Verdean, Norwegian, Dominican, French Canadian, Haitian, Korean, Lebanese, Polish, Nigerian, Mexican, Taiwanese, Ukrainian, and so on.)

11 a. **Does this person speak a language other than English at home?**

☐ Yes
☐ No → *Skip to 12*

b. **What is this language?**

(For example: Korean, Italian, Spanish, Vietnamese)

c. **How well does this person speak English?**

☐ Very well
☐ Well
☐ Not well
☐ Not at all

12 **Where was this person born?**

☐ In the United States — *Print name of state.*

☐ Outside the United States — *Print name of foreign country, or Puerto Rico, Guam, etc.*

13 **Is this person a CITIZEN of the United States?**

☐ Yes, born in the United States → *Skip to 15a*
☐ Yes, born in Puerto Rico, Guam, the U.S. Virgin Islands, or Northern Marianas
☐ Yes, born abroad of American parent or parents
☐ Yes, a U.S. citizen by naturalization
☐ No, not a citizen of the United States

14 **When did this person come to live in the United States?** *Print numbers in boxes.*
Year

15 a. **Did this person live in this house or apartment 5 years ago (on April 1, 1995)?**

☐ Person is under 5 years old → *Skip to 33*
☐ Yes, this house → *Skip to 16*
☐ No, outside the United States — *Print name of foreign country, or Puerto Rico, Guam, etc., below; then skip to 16.*

☐ No, different house in the United States

15 b. **Where did this person live 5 years ago?**
Name of city, town, or post office

Did this person live inside the limits of the city or town?

☐ Yes
☐ No, outside the city/town limits
Name of county

Name of state

ZIP Code

16 **Does this person have any of the following long-lasting conditions:**

	Yes	No
a. Blindness, deafness, or a severe vision or hearing impairment?	☐	☐
b. A condition that substantially limits one or more basic physical activities such as walking, climbing stairs, reaching, lifting, or carrying?	☐	☐

17 **Because of a physical, mental, or emotional condition lasting 6 months or more, does this person have any difficulty in doing any of the following activities:**

	Yes	No
a. Learning, remembering, or concentrating?	☐	☐
b. Dressing, bathing, or getting around inside the home?	☐	☐
c. (Answer if this person is 16 YEARS OLD OR OVER.) Going outside the home alone to shop or visit a doctor's office?	☐	☐
d. (Answer if this person is 16 YEARS OLD OR OVER.) Working at a job or business?	☐	☐

18 **Was this person under 15 years of age on April 1, 2000?**

☐ Yes → *Skip to 33*
☐ No

19 a. **Does this person have any of his/her own grandchildren under the age of 18 living in this house or apartment?**

☐ Yes
☐ No → *Skip to 20a*

b. **Is this grandparent currently responsible for most of the basic needs of any grandchild(ren) under the age of 18 who live(s) in this house or apartment?**

☐ Yes
☐ No → *Skip to 20a*

c. **How long has this grandparent been responsible for the(se) grandchild(ren)?** *If the grandparent is financially responsible for more than one grandchild, answer the question for the grandchild for whom the grandparent has been responsible for the longest period of time.*

☐ Less than 6 months
☐ 6 to 11 months
☐ 1 or 2 years
☐ 3 or 4 years
☐ 5 years or more

20 a. **Has this person ever served on active duty in the U.S. Armed Forces, military Reserves, or National Guard?** *Active duty does not include training for the Reserves or National Guard, but DOES include activation, for example, for the Persian Gulf War.*

☐ Yes, now on active duty
☐ Yes, on active duty in past, but not now
☐ No, training for Reserves or National Guard only → *Skip to 21*
☐ No, never served in the military → *Skip to 21*

b. **When did this person serve on active duty in the U.S. Armed Forces?** *Mark ☒ a box for EACH period in which this person served.*

☐ April 1995 or later
☐ August 1990 to March 1995 (including Persian Gulf War)
☐ September 1980 to July 1990
☐ May 1975 to August 1980
☐ Vietnam era (August 1964—April 1975)
☐ February 1955 to July 1964
☐ Korean conflict (June 1950—January 1955)
☐ World War II (September 1940—July 1947)
☐ Some other time

c. **In total, how many years of active-duty military service has this person had?**

☐ Less than 2 years
☐ 2 years or more

Person 2 (continued)

21 **LAST WEEK, did this person do ANY work for either pay or profit?** Mark ☒ the "Yes" box even if the person worked only 1 hour, or helped without pay in a family business or farm for 15 hours or more, or was on active duty in the Armed Forces.

☐ Yes
☐ No → Skip to 25a

22 **At what location did this person work LAST WEEK?** If this person worked at more than one location, print where he or she worked most last week.

a. **Address (Number and street name)**

(If the exact address is not known, give a description of the location such as the building name or the nearest street or intersection.)

b. **Name of city, town, or post office**

c. **Is the work location inside the limits of that city or town?**

☐ Yes
☐ No, outside the city/town limits

d. **Name of county**

e. **Name of U.S. state or foreign country**

f. **ZIP Code**

23 a. **How did this person usually get to work LAST WEEK?** If this person usually used more than one method of transportation during the trip, mark ☒ the box of the one used for most of the distance.

☐ Car, truck, or van
☐ Bus or trolley bus
☐ Streetcar or trolley car
☐ Subway or elevated
☐ Railroad
☐ Ferryboat
☐ Taxicab
☐ Motorcycle
☐ Bicycle
☐ Walked
☐ Worked at home → Skip to 27
☐ Other method

If "Car, truck, or van" is marked in 23a, go to 23b. Otherwise, skip to 24a.

23 b. **How many people, including this person, usually rode to work in the car, truck, or van LAST WEEK?**

☐ Drove alone
☐ 2 people
☐ 3 people
☐ 4 people
☐ 5 or 6 people
☐ 7 or more people

24 a. **What time did this person usually leave home to go to work LAST WEEK?**

☐ a.m. ☐ p.m.

b. **How many minutes did it usually take this person to get from home to work LAST WEEK?**

Minutes

Answer questions 25–26 for persons who did not work for pay or profit last week. Others skip to 27.

25 a. **LAST WEEK, was this person on layoff from a job?**

☐ Yes → Skip to 25c
☐ No

b. **LAST WEEK, was this person TEMPORARILY absent from a job or business?**

☐ Yes, on vacation, temporary illness, labor dispute, etc. → Skip to 26
☐ No → Skip to 25d

c. **Has this person been informed that he or she will be recalled to work within the next 6 months OR been given a date to return to work?**

☐ Yes → Skip to 25e
☐ No

d. **Has this person been looking for work during the last 4 weeks?**

☐ Yes
☐ No → Skip to 26

e. **LAST WEEK, could this person have started a job if offered one, or returned to work if recalled?**

☐ Yes, could have gone to work
☐ No, because of own temporary illness
☐ No, because of all other reasons (in school, etc.)

26 **When did this person last work, even for a few days?**

☐ 1995 to 2000
☐ 1994 or earlier, or never

Form D-2

14

Person 2 (continued)

27 **Industry or Employer** — Describe clearly this person's chief job activity or business last week. If this person had more than one job, describe the one at which this person worked the most hours. If this person had no job or business last week, give the information for his/her last job or business since 1995.

a. **For whom did this person work?** If now on active duty in the Armed Forces, mark ☒ this box → ☐ and print the branch of the Armed Forces.

Name of company, business, or other employer

b. **What kind of business or industry was this?** Describe the activity at location where employed. (For example: hospital, newspaper publishing, mail order house, auto repair shop, bank)

c. **Is this mainly** — Mark ☒ ONE box.

☐ Manufacturing?
☐ Wholesale trade?
☐ Retail trade?
☐ Other (agriculture, construction, service, government, etc.)?

28 **Occupation**

a. **What kind of work was this person doing?** (For example: registered nurse, personnel manager, supervisor of order department, auto mechanic, accountant)

b. **What were this person's most important activities or duties?** (For example: patient care, directing hiring policies, supervising order clerks, repairing automobiles, reconciling financial records)

29 **Was this person** — Mark ☒ ONE box.

☐ Employee of a PRIVATE-FOR-PROFIT company or business or of an individual, for wages, salary, or commissions
☐ Employee of a PRIVATE NOT-FOR-PROFIT, tax-exempt, or charitable organization
☐ Local GOVERNMENT employee (city, county, etc.)
☐ State GOVERNMENT employee
☐ Federal GOVERNMENT employee
☐ SELF-EMPLOYED in own NOT INCORPORATED business, professional practice, or farm
☐ SELF-EMPLOYED in own INCORPORATED business, professional practice, or farm
☐ Working WITHOUT PAY in family business or farm

30 a. **LAST YEAR, 1999, did this person work at a job or business at any time?**

☐ Yes
☐ No → Skip to 31

b. **How many weeks did this person work in 1999?** Count paid vacation, paid sick leave, and military service.

Weeks

c. **During the weeks WORKED in 1999, how many hours did this person usually work each WEEK?**

Usual hours worked each WEEK

31 **INCOME IN 1999** — Mark ☒ the "Yes" box for each income source received during 1999 and enter the total amount received during 1999 to a maximum of $999,999. Mark ☒ the "No" box if the income source was not received. If net income was a loss, enter the amount and mark ☒ the "Loss" box next to the dollar amount.

For income received jointly, report, if possible, the appropriate share for each person; otherwise, report the whole amount for only one person and mark ☒ the "No" box for the other person. If exact amount is not known, please give best estimate.

a. **Wages, salary, commissions, bonuses, or tips from all jobs** — Report amount before deductions for taxes, bonds, dues, or other items.

☐ Yes Annual amount — Dollars

☐ No

b. **Self-employment income from own nonfarm businesses or farm businesses, including proprietorships and partnerships** — Report NET income after business expenses.

☐ Yes Annual amount — Dollars

☐ No ☐ Loss

2055

Form D-2

15

Person 2 (continued)

31 **c. Interest, dividends, net rental income, royalty income, or income from estates and trusts** — *Report even small amounts credited to an account.*

☐ Yes   Annual amount — *Dollars*

☐ Loss

☐ No

d. Social Security or Railroad Retirement

☐ Yes   Annual amount — *Dollars*

☐ No

e. Supplemental Security Income (SSI)

☐ Yes   Annual amount — *Dollars*

☐ No

f. Any public assistance or welfare payments from the state or local welfare office

☐ Yes   Annual amount — *Dollars*

☐ No

g. Retirement, survivor, or disability pensions — *Do NOT include Social Security.*

☐ Yes   Annual amount — *Dollars*

☐ No

h. Any other sources of income received regularly such as Veterans' (VA) payments, unemployment compensation, child support, or alimony — *Do NOT include lump-sum payments such as money from an inheritance or sale of a home.*

☐ Yes   Annual amount — *Dollars*

☐ No

32 **What was this person's total income in 1999?** *Add entries in questions 31a—31h; subtract any losses. If net income was a loss, enter the amount and mark ☒ the "Loss" box next to the dollar amount.*

Annual amount — *Dollars*

☐ None   OR   ☐ Loss

33 **Are there more people living here? If yes, continue with Person 3.**

Form D-2

16

Person 3

1+1=2

Information about children helps your community plan for child care, education, and recreation.

1 **What is this person's name?** *Print the name of Person 3 from page 2.*

Last Name

First Name   MI

2 **How is this person related to Person 1?** *Mark ☒ ONE box.*

☐ Husband/wife
☐ Natural-born son/daughter
☐ Adopted son/daughter
☐ Stepson/stepdaughter
☐ Brother/sister
☐ Father/mother
☐ Grandchild
☐ Parent-in-law
☐ Son-in-law/daughter-in-law
☐ Other relative — *Print exact relationship.*

If NOT RELATED to Person 1:
☐ Roomer, boarder
☐ Housemate, roommate
☐ Unmarried partner
☐ Foster child
☐ Other nonrelative

3 **What is this person's sex?** *Mark ☒ ONE box.*

☐ Male
☐ Female

4 **What is this person's age and what is this person's date of birth?**

Age on April 1, 2000

Print numbers in boxes.
Month   Day   Year of birth

Person 3 (continued)

→ **NOTE: Please answer BOTH Questions 5 and 6.**

5 **Is this person Spanish/Hispanic/Latino?** *Mark ☒ the "No" box if not Spanish/Hispanic/Latino.*

☐ No, not Spanish/Hispanic/Latino
☐ Yes, Mexican, Mexican Am., Chicano
☐ Yes, Puerto Rican
☐ Yes, Cuban
☐ Yes, other Spanish/Hispanic/Latino — *Print group.*

6 **What is this person's race?** *Mark ☒ one or more races to indicate what this person considers himself/herself to be.*

☐ White
☐ Black, African Am., or Negro
☐ American Indian or Alaska Native — *Print name of enrolled or principal tribe.*

☐ Asian Indian   ☐ Native Hawaiian
☐ Chinese   ☐ Guamanian or Chamorro
☐ Filipino
☐ Japanese   ☐ Samoan
☐ Korean   ☐ Other Pacific Islander — *Print race.*
☐ Vietnamese
☐ Other Asian — *Print race.*

☐ Some other race — *Print race.*

7 **What is this person's marital status?**

☐ Now married
☐ Widowed
☐ Divorced
☐ Separated
☐ Never married

8 **a. At any time since February 1, 2000, has this person attended regular school or college?** *Include only nursery school or preschool, kindergarten, elementary school, and schooling which leads to a high school diploma or a college degree.*

☐ No, has not attended since February 1 → *Skip to 9*
☐ Yes, public school, public college
☐ Yes, private school, private college

b. What grade or level was this person attending? *Mark ☒ ONE box.*

☐ Nursery school, preschool
☐ Kindergarten
☐ Grade 1 to grade 4
☐ Grade 5 to grade 8
☐ Grade 9 to grade 12
☐ College undergraduate years (freshman to senior)
☐ Graduate or professional school (for example: medical, dental, or law school)

9 **What is the highest degree or level of school this person has COMPLETED?** *Mark ☒ ONE box. If currently enrolled, mark the previous grade or highest degree received.*

☐ No schooling completed
☐ Nursery school to 4th grade
☐ 5th grade or 6th grade
☐ 7th grade or 8th grade
☐ 9th grade
☐ 10th grade
☐ 11th grade
☐ 12th grade, **NO DIPLOMA**
☐ **HIGH SCHOOL GRADUATE** — high school DIPLOMA or the equivalent (for example: GED)
☐ Some college credit, but less than 1 year
☐ 1 or more years of college, no degree
☐ Associate degree (for example: AA, AS)
☐ Bachelor's degree (for example: BA, AB, BS)
☐ Master's degree (for example: MA, MS, MEng, MEd, MSW, MBA)
☐ Professional degree (for example: MD, DDS, DVM, LLB, JD)
☐ Doctorate degree (for example: PhD, EdD)

10 **What is this person's ancestry or ethnic origin?**

(For example: Italian, Jamaican, African Am., Cambodian, Cape Verdean, Norwegian, Dominican, French Canadian, Haitian, Korean, Lebanese, Polish, Nigerian, Mexican, Taiwanese, Ukrainian, and so on.)

2057

Form D-2

17

Unlocking the census with GIS

Person 3 (continued)

11 a. Does this person speak a language other than English at home?
- ☐ Yes
- ☐ No → Skip to 12

b. What is this language?

(For example: Korean, Italian, Spanish, Vietnamese)

c. How well does this person speak English?
- ☐ Very well
- ☐ Well
- ☐ Not well
- ☐ Not at all

12 Where was this person born?
- ☐ In the United States — Print name of state.

- ☐ Outside the United States — Print name of foreign country, or Puerto Rico, Guam, etc.

13 Is this person a CITIZEN of the United States?
- ☐ Yes, born in the United States → Skip to 15a
- ☐ Yes, born in Puerto Rico, Guam, the U.S. Virgin Islands, or Northern Marianas
- ☐ Yes, born abroad of American parent or parents
- ☐ Yes, a U.S. citizen by naturalization
- ☐ No, not a citizen of the United States

14 When did this person come to live in the United States? Print numbers in boxes.
Year

15 a. Did this person live in this house or apartment 5 years ago (on April 1, 1995)?
- ☐ Person is under 5 years old → Skip to 33
- ☐ Yes, this house → Skip to 16
- ☐ No, outside the United States — Print name of foreign country, or Puerto Rico, Guam, etc., below; then skip to 16.

- ☐ No, different house in the United States

15 b. Where did this person live 5 years ago?

Name of city, town, or post office

Did this person live inside the limits of the city or town?
- ☐ Yes
- ☐ No, outside the city/town limits

Name of county

Name of state

ZIP Code

16 Does this person have any of the following long-lasting conditions:

	Yes	No
a. Blindness, deafness, or a severe vision or hearing impairment?	☐	☐
b. A condition that substantially limits one or more basic physical activities such as walking, climbing stairs, reaching, lifting, or carrying?	☐	☐

17 Because of a physical, mental, or emotional condition lasting 6 months or more, does this person have any difficulty in doing any of the following activities:

	Yes	No
a. Learning, remembering, or concentrating?	☐	☐
b. Dressing, bathing, or getting around inside the home?	☐	☐
c. (Answer if this person is 16 YEARS OLD OR OVER.) Going outside the home alone to shop or visit a doctor's office?	☐	☐
d. (Answer if this person is 16 YEARS OLD OR OVER.) Working at a job or business?	☐	☐

18 Was this person under 15 years of age on April 1, 2000?
- ☐ Yes → Skip to 33
- ☐ No

Form D-2

Person 3 (continued)

19 a. Does this person have any of his/her own grandchildren under the age of 18 living in this house or apartment?
- ☐ Yes
- ☐ No → Skip to 20a

b. Is this grandparent currently responsible for most of the basic needs of any grandchild(ren) under the age of 18 who live(s) in this house or apartment?
- ☐ Yes
- ☐ No → Skip to 20a

c. How long has this grandparent been responsible for the(se) grandchild(ren)? _If the grandparent is financially responsible for more than one grandchild, answer the question for the grandchild for whom the grandparent has been responsible for the longest period of time._
- ☐ Less than 6 months
- ☐ 6 to 11 months
- ☐ 1 or 2 years
- ☐ 3 or 4 years
- ☐ 5 years or more

20 a. Has this person ever served on active duty in the U.S. Armed Forces, military Reserves, or National Guard? _Active duty does not include training for the Reserves or National Guard, but DOES include activation, for example, for the Persian Gulf War._
- ☐ Yes, now on active duty
- ☐ Yes, on active duty in past, but not now
- ☐ No, training for Reserves or National Guard only → Skip to 21
- ☐ No, never served in the military → Skip to 21

b. When did this person serve on active duty in the U.S. Armed Forces? Mark ☒ a box for EACH period in which this person served.
- ☐ April 1995 or later
- ☐ August 1990 to March 1995 (including Persian Gulf War)
- ☐ September 1980 to July 1990
- ☐ May 1975 to August 1980
- ☐ Vietnam era (August 1964—April 1975)
- ☐ February 1955 to July 1964
- ☐ Korean conflict (June 1950—January 1955)
- ☐ World War II (September 1940—July 1947)
- ☐ Some other time

c. In total, how many years of active-duty military service has this person had?
- ☐ Less than 2 years
- ☐ 2 years or more

21 LAST WEEK, did this person do ANY work for either pay or profit? Mark ☒ the "Yes" box even if the person worked only 1 hour, or helped without pay in a family business or farm for 15 hours or more, or was on active duty in the Armed Forces.
- ☐ Yes
- ☐ No → Skip to 25a

22 At what location did this person work LAST WEEK? If this person worked at more than one location, print where he or she worked most last week.

a. Address (Number and street name)

(If the exact address is not known, give a description of the location such as the building name or the nearest street or intersection.)

b. Name of city, town, or post office

c. Is the work location inside the limits of that city or town?
- ☐ Yes
- ☐ No, outside the city/town limits

d. Name of county

e. Name of U.S. state or foreign country

f. ZIP Code

23 a. How did this person usually get to work LAST WEEK? If this person usually used more than one method of transportation during the trip, mark ☒ the box of the one used for most of the distance.
- ☐ Car, truck, or van
- ☐ Bus or trolley bus
- ☐ Streetcar or trolley car
- ☐ Subway or elevated
- ☐ Railroad
- ☐ Ferryboat
- ☐ Taxicab
- ☐ Motorcycle
- ☐ Bicycle
- ☐ Walked
- ☐ Worked at home → Skip to 27
- ☐ Other method

2059

Form D-2

→ If "Car, truck, or van" is marked in 23a, go to 23b. Otherwise, skip to 24a.

23 b. How many people, including this person, usually rode to work in the car, truck, or van LAST WEEK?

☐ Drove alone
☐ 2 people
☐ 3 people
☐ 4 people
☐ 5 or 6 people
☐ 7 or more people

24 a. What time did this person usually leave home to go to work LAST WEEK?

☐ a.m. ☐ p.m.

b. How many minutes did it usually take this person to get from home to work LAST WEEK?
Minutes

→ Answer questions 25–26 for persons who did not work for pay or profit last week. Others skip to 27.

25 a. LAST WEEK, was this person on layoff from a job?

☐ Yes → Skip to 25c
☐ No

b. LAST WEEK, was this person TEMPORARILY absent from a job or business?

☐ Yes, on vacation, temporary illness, labor dispute, etc. → Skip to 26
☐ No → Skip to 25d

c. Has this person been informed that he or she will be recalled to work within the next 6 months OR been given a date to return to work?

☐ Yes → Skip to 25e
☐ No

d. Has this person been looking for work during the last 4 weeks?

☐ Yes
☐ No → Skip to 26

e. LAST WEEK, could this person have started a job if offered one, or returned to work if recalled?

☐ Yes, could have gone to work
☐ No, because of own temporary illness
☐ No, because of all other reasons (in school, etc.)

26 When did this person last work, even for a few days?

☐ 1995 to 2000
☐ 1994 or earlier, or never worked → Skip to 31

27 Industry or Employer — Describe clearly this person's chief job activity or business last week. If this person had more than one job, describe the one at which this person worked the most hours. If this person had no job or business last week, give the information for his/her last job or business since 1995.

a. For whom did this person work? If now on active duty in the Armed Forces, mark ☒ this box → ☐ and print the branch of the Armed Forces.

Name of company, business, or other employer

b. What kind of business or industry was this?
Describe the activity at location where employed. (For example: hospital, newspaper publishing, mail order house, auto repair shop, bank)

c. Is this mainly — Mark ☒ ONE box.

☐ Manufacturing?
☐ Wholesale trade?
☐ Retail trade?
☐ Other (agriculture, construction, service, government, etc.)?

28 Occupation

a. What kind of work was this person doing? (For example: registered nurse, personnel manager, supervisor of order department, auto mechanic, accountant)

b. What were this person's most important activities or duties? (For example: patient care, directing hiring policies, supervising order clerks, repairing automobiles, reconciling financial records)

Form D-2

20

---

29 Was this person — Mark ☒ ONE box.

☐ Employee of a PRIVATE-FOR-PROFIT company or business or of an individual, for wages, salary, or commissions
☐ Employee of a PRIVATE NOT-FOR-PROFIT, tax-exempt, or charitable organization
☐ Local GOVERNMENT employee (city, county, etc.)
☐ State GOVERNMENT employee
☐ Federal GOVERNMENT employee
☐ SELF-EMPLOYED in own NOT INCORPORATED business, professional practice, or farm
☐ SELF-EMPLOYED in own INCORPORATED business, professional practice, or farm
☐ Working WITHOUT PAY in family business or farm

30 a. LAST YEAR, 1999, did this person work at a job or business at any time?

☐ Yes
☐ No → Skip to 31

b. How many weeks did this person work in 1999? Count paid vacation, paid sick leave, and military service.
Weeks

c. During the weeks WORKED in 1999, how many hours did this person usually work each WEEK?
Usual hours worked each WEEK

31 INCOME IN 1999 — Mark ☒ the "Yes" box for each income source received during 1999 and enter the total amount received during 1999 to a maximum of $999,999. Mark ☒ the "No" box if the income source was not received. If net income was a loss, enter the amount and mark ☒ the "Loss" box next to the dollar amount.

For income received jointly, report, if possible, the appropriate share for each person; otherwise, report the whole amount for only one person and mark ☒ the "No" box for the other person. If exact amount is not known, please give best estimate.

a. Wages, salary, commissions, bonuses, or tips from all jobs — Report amount before deductions for taxes, bonds, dues, or other items.

☐ Yes Annual amount — Dollars

☐ No

b. Self-employment income from own nonfarm businesses or farm businesses, including proprietorships and partnerships — Report NET income after business expenses.

☐ Yes Annual amount — Dollars

☐ No   ☐ Loss

c. Interest, dividends, net rental income, royalty income, or income from estates and trusts — Report even small amounts credited to an account.

☐ Yes Annual amount — Dollars   ☐ Loss

☐ No

d. Social Security or Railroad Retirement

☐ Yes Annual amount — Dollars

☐ No

e. Supplemental Security Income (SSI)

☐ Yes Annual amount — Dollars

☐ No

f. Any public assistance or welfare payments from the state or local welfare office

☐ Yes Annual amount — Dollars

☐ No

g. Retirement, survivor, or disability pensions — Do NOT include Social Security.

☐ Yes Annual amount — Dollars

☐ No

h. Any other sources of income received regularly such as Veterans' (VA) payments, unemployment compensation, child support, or alimony — Do NOT include lump-sum payments such as money from an inheritance or sale of a home.

☐ Yes Annual amount — Dollars

☐ No

32 What was this person's total income in 1999? Add entries in questions 31a—31h; subtract any losses. If net income was a loss, enter the amount and mark ☒ the "Loss" box next to the dollar amount.

Annual amount — Dollars

☐ None OR   ☐ Loss

33 Are there more people living here? If yes, continue with Person 4.

2061

Form D-2

21

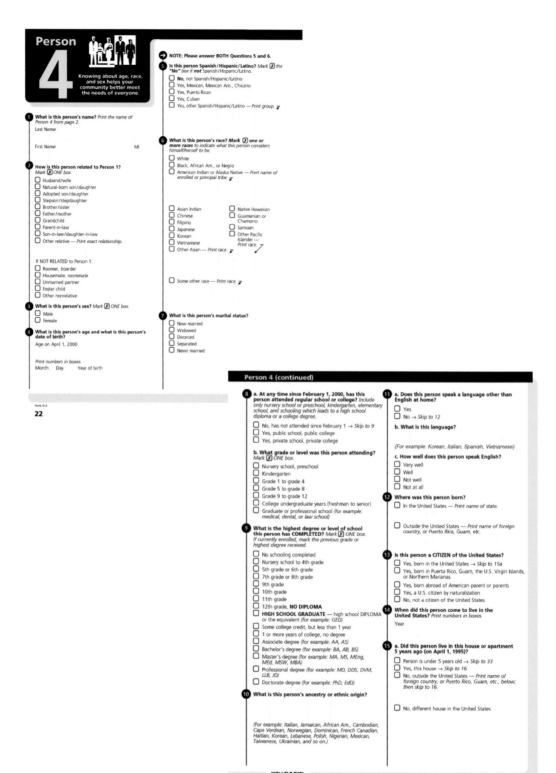

Person 4

Knowing about age, race, and sex helps your community better meet the needs of everyone.

➜ NOTE: Please answer BOTH Questions 5 and 6.

5. **Is this person Spanish/Hispanic/Latino?** Mark ☒ the **"No"** box if not Spanish/Hispanic/Latino.

☐ **No**, not Spanish/Hispanic/Latino
☐ Yes, Mexican, Mexican Am., Chicano
☐ Yes, Puerto Rican
☐ Yes, Cuban
☐ Yes, other Spanish/Hispanic/Latino — Print group. ↗

1. **What is this person's name?** Print the name of Person 4 from page 2.

Last Name

First Name   MI

2. **How is this person related to Person 1?** Mark ☒ ONE box.

☐ Husband/wife
☐ Natural-born son/daughter
☐ Adopted son/daughter
☐ Stepson/stepdaughter
☐ Brother/sister
☐ Father/mother
☐ Grandchild
☐ Parent-in-law
☐ Son-in-law/daughter-in-law
☐ Other relative — Print exact relationship.

IF NOT RELATED to Person 1:
☐ Roomer, boarder
☐ Housemate, roommate
☐ Unmarried partner
☐ Foster child
☐ Other nonrelative

6. **What is this person's race?** Mark ☒ one or **more races** to indicate what this person considers himself/herself to be.

☐ White
☐ Black, African Am., or Negro
☐ American Indian or Alaska Native — Print name of enrolled or principal tribe. ↗

☐ Asian Indian   ☐ Native Hawaiian
☐ Chinese   ☐ Guamanian or Chamorro
☐ Filipino   ☐ Samoan
☐ Japanese   ☐ Other Pacific Islander — Print race. ↗
☐ Korean
☐ Vietnamese
☐ Other Asian — Print race. ↗

☐ Some other race — Print race. ↗

3. **What is this person's sex?** Mark ☒ ONE box.

☐ Male
☐ Female

4. **What is this person's age and what is this person's date of birth?**

Age on April 1, 2000

Print numbers in boxes.
Month   Day   Year of birth

7. **What is this person's marital status?**

☐ Now married
☐ Widowed
☐ Divorced
☐ Separated
☐ Never married

Form D-2

22

Person 4 (continued)

8. a. **At any time since February 1, 2000, has this person attended regular school or college?** Include only nursery school or preschool, kindergarten, elementary school, and schooling which leads to a high school diploma or a college degree.

☐ No, has not attended since February 1 → Skip to 9
☐ Yes, public school, public college
☐ Yes, private school, private college

b. **What grade or level was this person attending?** Mark ☒ ONE box.

☐ Nursery school, preschool
☐ Kindergarten
☐ Grade 1 to grade 4
☐ Grade 5 to grade 8
☐ Grade 9 to grade 12
☐ College undergraduate years (freshman to senior)
☐ Graduate or professional school (for example: medical, dental, or law school)

9. **What is the highest degree or level of school this person has COMPLETED?** Mark ☒ ONE box. If currently enrolled, mark the previous grade or highest degree received.

☐ No schooling completed
☐ Nursery school to 4th grade
☐ 5th grade or 6th grade
☐ 7th grade or 8th grade
☐ 9th grade
☐ 10th grade
☐ 11th grade
☐ 12th grade, **NO DIPLOMA**
☐ **HIGH SCHOOL GRADUATE** — high school DIPLOMA or the equivalent (for example: GED)
☐ Some college credit, but less than 1 year
☐ 1 or more years of college, no degree
☐ Associate degree (for example: AA, AS)
☐ Bachelor's degree (for example: BA, AB, BS)
☐ Master's degree (for example: MA, MS, MEng, MEd, MSW, MBA)
☐ Professional degree (for example: MD, DDS, DVM, LLB, JD)
☐ Doctorate degree (for example: PhD, EdD)

10. **What is this person's ancestry or ethnic origin?**

(For example: Italian, Jamaican, African Am., Cambodian, Cape Verdean, Norwegian, Dominican, French Canadian, Haitian, Korean, Lebanese, Polish, Nigerian, Mexican, Taiwanese, Ukrainian, and so on.)

11. a. **Does this person speak a language other than English at home?**

☐ Yes
☐ No → Skip to 12

b. **What is this language?**

(For example: Korean, Italian, Spanish, Vietnamese)

c. **How well does this person speak English?**

☐ Very well
☐ Well
☐ Not well
☐ Not at all

12. **Where was this person born?**

☐ In the United States — Print name of state.

☐ Outside the United States — Print name of foreign country, or Puerto Rico, Guam, etc.

13. **Is this person a CITIZEN of the United States?**

☐ Yes, born in the United States → Skip to 15a
☐ Yes, born in Puerto Rico, Guam, the U.S. Virgin Islands, or Northern Marianas
☐ Yes, born abroad of American parent or parents
☐ Yes, a U.S. citizen by naturalization
☐ No, not a citizen of the United States

14. **When did this person come to live in the United States?** Print numbers in boxes.

Year

15. a. **Did this person live in this house or apartment 5 years ago (on April 1, 1995)?**

☐ Person is under 5 years old → Skip to 33
☐ Yes, this house → Skip to 16
☐ No, outside the United States — Print name of foreign country, or Puerto Rico, Guam, etc., below; then skip to 16.

☐ No, different house in the United States

2063

Form D-2

23

15 b. Where did this person live 5 years ago?
Name of city, town, or post office

Did this person live inside the limits of the city or town?
☐ Yes
☐ No, outside the city/town limits

Name of county

Name of state

ZIP Code

16 Does this person have any of the following long-lasting conditions?

	Yes	No
a. Blindness, deafness, or a severe vision or hearing impairment?	☐	☐
b. A condition that substantially limits one or more basic physical activities, such as walking, climbing stairs, reaching, lifting, or carrying?	☐	☐

17 Because of a physical, mental, or emotional condition lasting 6 months or more, does this person have any difficulty in doing any of the following activities?

	Yes	No
a. Learning, remembering, or concentrating?	☐	☐
b. Dressing, bathing, or getting around inside the home?	☐	☐
c. (Answer if this person is 16 YEARS OLD OR OVER.) Going outside the home alone to shop or visit a doctor's office?	☐	☐
d. (Answer if this person is 16 YEARS OLD OR OVER.) Working at a job or business?	☐	☐

18 Was this person under 15 years of age on April 1, 2000?
☐ Yes → Skip to 33
☐ No

19 a. Does this person have any of his/her own grandchildren under the age of 18 living in this house or apartment?
☐ Yes
☐ No → Skip to 20a

b. Is this grandparent currently responsible for most of the basic needs of any grandchild(ren) under the age of 18 who live(s) in this house or apartment?
☐ Yes
☐ No → Skip to 20a

c. How long has this grandparent been responsible for the(se) grandchild(ren)? If the grandparent is financially responsible for more than one grandchild, answer the question for the grandchild for whom the grandparent has been responsible for the longest period of time.
☐ Less than 6 months
☐ 6 to 11 months
☐ 1 or 2 years
☐ 3 or 4 years
☐ 5 years or more

20 a. Has this person ever served on active duty in the U.S. Armed Forces, military Reserves, or National Guard? Active duty does not include training for the Reserves or National Guard, but DOES include activation, for example, for the Persian Gulf War.
☐ Yes, now on active duty
☐ Yes, on active duty in past, but not now
☐ No, training for Reserves or National Guard only → Skip to 21
☐ No, never served in the military → Skip to 21

b. When did this person serve on active duty in the U.S. Armed Forces? Mark ☒ a box for EACH period in which this person served.
☐ April 1995 or later
☐ August 1990 to March 1995 (including Persian Gulf War)
☐ September 1980 to July 1990
☐ May 1975 to August 1980
☐ Vietnam era (August 1964—April 1975)
☐ February 1955 to July 1964
☐ Korean conflict (June 1950—January 1955)
☐ World War II (September 1940—July 1947)
☐ Some other time

c. In total, how many years of active-duty military service has this person had?
☐ Less than 2 years
☐ 2 years or more

21 LAST WEEK, did this person do ANY work for either pay or profit? Mark ☒ the "Yes" box even if the person worked only 1 hour, or helped without pay in a family business or farm for 15 hours or more, or was on active duty in the Armed Forces.
☐ Yes
☐ No → Skip to 25a

22 At what location did this person work LAST WEEK? If this person worked at more than one location, print where he or she worked most last week.
a. Address (Number and street name)

(If the exact address is not known, give a description of the location such as the building name or the nearest street or intersection.)

b. Name of city, town, or post office

c. Is the work location inside the limits of that city or town?
☐ Yes
☐ No, outside the city/town limits

d. Name of county

e. Name of U.S. state or foreign country

f. ZIP Code

23 a. How did this person usually get to work LAST WEEK? If this person usually used more than one method of transportation during the trip, mark ☒ the box of the one used for most of the distance.
☐ Car, truck, or van
☐ Bus or trolley bus
☐ Streetcar or trolley car
☐ Subway or elevated
☐ Railroad
☐ Ferryboat
☐ Taxicab
☐ Motorcycle
☐ Bicycle
☐ Walked
☐ Worked at home → Skip to 27
☐ Other method

→ If "Car, truck, or van" is marked in 23a, go to 23b. Otherwise, skip to 24a.

b. How many people, including this person, usually rode to work in the car, truck, or van LAST WEEK?
☐ Drove alone
☐ 2 people
☐ 3 people
☐ 4 people
☐ 5 or 6 people
☐ 7 or more people

24 a. What time did this person usually leave home to go to work LAST WEEK?
☐ a.m. ☐ p.m.

b. How many minutes did it usually take this person to get from home to work LAST WEEK?
Minutes

→ Answer questions 25–26 for persons who did not work for pay or profit last week. Others skip to 27.

25 a. LAST WEEK, was this person on layoff from a job?
☐ Yes → Skip to 25c
☐ No

b. LAST WEEK, was this person TEMPORARILY absent from a job or business?
☐ Yes, on vacation, temporary illness, labor dispute, etc. → Skip to 26
☐ No → Skip to 25d

c. Has this person been informed that he or she will be recalled to work within the next 6 months OR been given a date to return to work?
☐ Yes → Skip to 25e
☐ No

d. Has this person been looking for work during the last 4 weeks?
☐ Yes
☐ No → Skip to 26

e. LAST WEEK, could this person have started a job if offered one, or returned to work if recalled?
☐ Yes, could have gone to work
☐ No, because of own temporary illness
☐ No, because of all other reasons (in school, etc.)

26 When did this person last work, even for a few days?
☐ 1995 to 2000
☐ 1994 or earlier, or never worked → Skip to 31

Person 4 (continued)

27 Industry or Employer — *Describe clearly this person's chief job activity or business last week. If this person had more than one job, describe the one at which this person worked the most hours. If this person had no job or business last week, give the information for his/her last job or business since 1995.*

a. For whom did this person work? *If now on active duty in the Armed Forces, mark [X] this box →* ☐ *and print the branch of the Armed Forces.*

Name of company, business, or other employer

b. What kind of business or industry was this? *Describe the activity at location where employed. (For example: hospital, newspaper publishing, mail order house, auto repair shop, bank)*

c. Is this mainly — *Mark [X] ONE box.*
☐ Manufacturing?
☐ Wholesale trade?
☐ Retail trade?
☐ Other (agriculture, construction, service, government, etc.)?

28 Occupation

a. What kind of work was this person doing? *(For example: registered nurse, personnel manager, supervisor of order department, auto mechanic, accountant)*

b. What were this person's most important activities or duties? *(For example: patient care, directing hiring policies, supervising order clerks, repairing automobiles, reconciling financial records)*

29 Was this person — *Mark [X] ONE box.*
☐ Employee of a PRIVATE-FOR-PROFIT company or business or of an individual, for wages, salary, or commissions
☐ Employee of a PRIVATE NOT-FOR-PROFIT, tax-exempt, or charitable organization
☐ Local GOVERNMENT employee (city, county, etc.)
☐ State GOVERNMENT employee
☐ Federal GOVERNMENT employee
☐ SELF-EMPLOYED in own NOT INCORPORATED business, professional practice, or farm
☐ SELF-EMPLOYED in own INCORPORATED business, professional practice, or farm
☐ Working WITHOUT PAY in family business or farm

30 a. LAST YEAR, 1999, did this person work at a job or business at any time?
☐ Yes
☐ No → *Skip to 31*

b. How many weeks did this person work in 1999? *Count paid vacation, paid sick leave, and military service.*
Weeks

c. During the weeks WORKED in 1999, how many hours did this person usually work each WEEK?
Usual hours worked each WEEK

31 INCOME IN 1999 — *Mark [X] the "Yes" box for each income source received during 1999 and enter the total amount received during 1999 to a maximum of $999,999. Mark [X] the "No" box if the income source was not received. If net income was a loss, enter the amount and mark [X] the "Loss" box next to the dollar amount.*

For income received jointly, report, if possible, the appropriate share for each person; otherwise, report the whole amount for only one person and mark [X] the "No" box for the other person. If exact amount is not known, please give best estimate.

a. Wages, salary, commissions, bonuses, or tips from all jobs — *Report amount before deductions for taxes, bonds, dues, or other items.*
☐ Yes   Annual amount — Dollars

☐ No

b. Self-employment income from own nonfarm businesses or farm businesses, including proprietorships and partnerships — *Report NET income after business expenses.*
☐ Yes   Annual amount — Dollars

☐ No   ☐ Loss

Person 4 (continued)

31 c. Interest, dividends, net rental income, royalty income, or income from estates and trusts — *Report even small amounts credited to an account.*
☐ Yes   Annual amount — Dollars

☐ No   ☐ Loss

d. Social Security or Railroad Retirement
☐ Yes   Annual amount — Dollars

☐ No

e. Supplemental Security Income (SSI)
☐ Yes   Annual amount — Dollars

☐ No

f. Any public assistance or welfare payments from the state or local welfare office
☐ Yes   Annual amount — Dollars

☐ No

g. Retirement, survivor, or disability pensions — *Do NOT include Social Security.*
☐ Yes   Annual amount — Dollars

☐ No

h. Any other sources of income received regularly such as Veterans' (VA) payments, unemployment compensation, child support, or alimony — *Do NOT include lump-sum payments such as money from an inheritance or sale of a home.*
☐ Yes   Annual amount — Dollars

☐ No

32 What was this person's total income in 1999? *Add entries in questions 31a—31h; subtract any losses. If net income was a loss, enter the amount and mark [X] the "Loss" box next to the dollar amount.*

Annual amount — Dollars
☐ None   OR   ☐ Loss

33 Are there more people living here? If yes, continue with Person 5.

Person 5

Your answers help your community plan for the future.

1 What is this person's name? *Print the name of Person 5 from page 2.*
Last Name

First Name   MI

2 How is this person related to Person 1? *Mark [X] ONE box.*
☐ Husband/wife
☐ Natural-born son/daughter
☐ Adopted son/daughter
☐ Stepson/stepdaughter
☐ Brother/sister
☐ Father/mother
☐ Grandchild
☐ Parent-in-law
☐ Son-in-law/daughter-in-law
☐ Other relative — *Print exact relationship.*

If NOT RELATED to Person 1:
☐ Roomer, boarder
☐ Housemate, roommate
☐ Unmarried partner
☐ Foster child
☐ Other nonrelative

3 What is this person's sex? *Mark [X] ONE box.*
☐ Male
☐ Female

4 What is this person's age and what is this person's date of birth?
Age on April 1, 2000

Print numbers in boxes.
Month   Day   Year of birth

→ NOTE: Please answer BOTH Questions 5 and 6.

5 Is this person Spanish/Hispanic/Latino? Mark ☒ the **"No"** box if **not** Spanish/Hispanic/Latino.

☐ **No**, not Spanish/Hispanic/Latino
☐ Yes, Mexican, Mexican Am., Chicano
☐ Yes, Puerto Rican
☐ Yes, Cuban
☐ Yes, other Spanish/Hispanic/Latino — Print group. ↗

6 What is this person's race? Mark ☒ one or more races to indicate what this person considers himself/herself to be.

☐ White
☐ Black, African Am., or Negro
☐ American Indian or Alaska Native — Print name of enrolled or principal tribe. ↗

☐ Asian Indian　　☐ Native Hawaiian
☐ Chinese　　　　☐ Guamanian or Chamorro
☐ Filipino
☐ Japanese　　　　☐ Samoan
☐ Korean　　　　☐ Other Pacific Islander —
☐ Vietnamese　　　　Print race. ↗
☐ Other Asian — Print race. ↗

☐ Some other race — Print race. ↗

7 What is this person's marital status?
☐ Now married
☐ Widowed
☐ Divorced
☐ Separated
☐ Never married

8 a. At any time since February 1, 2000, has this person attended regular school or college? Include only nursery school or preschool, kindergarten, elementary school, and schooling which leads to a high school diploma or a college degree.

☐ No, has not attended since February 1 → Skip to 9
☐ Yes, public school, public college
☐ Yes, private school, private college

b. What grade or level was this person attending? Mark ☒ ONE box.

☐ Nursery school, preschool
☐ Kindergarten
☐ Grade 1 to grade 4
☐ Grade 5 to grade 8
☐ Grade 9 to grade 12
☐ College undergraduate years (freshman to senior)
☐ Graduate or professional school (for example: medical, dental, or law school)

9 What is the highest degree or level of school this person has COMPLETED? Mark ☒ ONE box. If currently enrolled, mark the previous grade or highest degree received.

☐ No schooling completed
☐ Nursery school to 4th grade
☐ 5th grade or 6th grade
☐ 7th grade or 8th grade
☐ 9th grade
☐ 10th grade
☐ 11th grade
☐ 12th grade, NO DIPLOMA
☐ HIGH SCHOOL GRADUATE — high school DIPLOMA or the equivalent (for example: GED)
☐ Some college credit, but less than 1 year
☐ 1 or more years of college, no degree
☐ Associate degree (for example: AA, AS)
☐ Bachelor's degree (for example: BA, AB, BS)
☐ Master's degree (for example: MA, MS, MEng, MEd, MSW, MBA)
☐ Professional degree (for example: MD, DDS, DVM, LLB, JD)
☐ Doctorate degree (for example: PhD, EdD)

10 What is this person's ancestry or ethnic origin?

(For example: Italian, Jamaican, African Am., Cambodian, Cape Verdean, Norwegian, Dominican, French Canadian, Haitian, Korean, Lebanese, Polish, Nigerian, Mexican, Taiwanese, Ukrainian, and so on.)

---

11 a. Does this person speak a language other than English at home?
☐ Yes
☐ No → Skip to 12

b. What is this language?

(For example: Korean, Italian, Spanish, Vietnamese)

c. How well does this person speak English?
☐ Very well
☐ Well
☐ Not well
☐ Not at all

12 Where was this person born?
☐ In the United States — Print name of state.

☐ Outside the United States — Print name of foreign country, or Puerto Rico, Guam, etc.

13 Is this person a CITIZEN of the United States?
☐ Yes, born in the United States → Skip to 15a
☐ Yes, born in Puerto Rico, Guam, the U.S. Virgin Islands, or Northern Marianas
☐ Yes, born abroad of American parent or parents
☐ Yes, a U.S. citizen by naturalization
☐ No, not a citizen of the United States

14 When did this person come to live in the United States? Print numbers in boxes.
Year

15 a. Did this person live in this house or apartment 5 years ago (on April 1, 1995)?
☐ Person is under 5 years old → Skip to 33
☐ Yes, this house → Skip to 16
☐ No, outside the United States — Print name of foreign country, or Puerto Rico, Guam, etc., below; then skip to 16.

☐ No, different house in the United States

b. Where did this person live 5 years ago?

Name of city, town, or post office

Did this person live inside the limits of the city or town?
☐ Yes
☐ No, outside the city/town limits

Name of county

Name of state

ZIP Code

16 Does this person have any of the following long-lasting conditions:

	Yes	No
a. Blindness, deafness, or a severe vision or hearing impairment?	☐	☐
b. A condition that substantially limits one or more basic physical activities such as walking, climbing stairs, reaching, lifting, or carrying?	☐	☐

17 Because of a physical, mental, or emotional condition lasting 6 months or more, does this person have any difficulty in doing any of the following activities:

	Yes	No
a. Learning, remembering, or concentrating?	☐	☐
b. Dressing, bathing, or getting around inside the home?	☐	☐
c. (Answer if this person is 16 YEARS OLD OR OVER.) Going outside the home alone to shop or visit a doctor's office?	☐	☐
d. (Answer if this person is 16 YEARS OLD OR OVER.) Working at a job or business?	☐	☐

18 Was this person under 15 years of age on April 1, 2000?
☐ Yes → Skip to 33
☐ No

Person 5 (continued)

19 a. Does this person have any of his/her own grandchildren under the age of 18 living in this house or apartment?

☐ Yes
☐ No → Skip to 20a

b. Is this grandparent currently responsible for most of the basic needs of any grandchild(ren) under the age of 18 who live(s) in this house or apartment?

☐ Yes
☐ No → Skip to 20a

c. How long has this grandparent been responsible for the(se) grandchild(ren)? If the grandparent is financially responsible for more than one grandchild, answer the question for the grandchild for whom the grandparent has been responsible for the longest period of time.

☐ Less than 6 months
☐ 6 to 11 months
☐ 1 or 2 years
☐ 3 or 4 years
☐ 5 years or more

20 a. Has this person ever served on active duty in the U.S. Armed Forces, military Reserves, or National Guard? Active duty does not include training for the Reserves or National Guard, but DOES include activation, for example, for the Persian Gulf War.

☐ Yes, now on active duty
☐ Yes, on active duty in past, but not now
☐ No, training for Reserves or National Guard only → Skip to 21
☐ No, never served in the military → Skip to 21

b. When did this person serve on active duty in the U.S. Armed Forces? Mark ☒ a box for EACH period in which this person served.

☐ April 1995 or later
☐ August 1990 to March 1995 (including Persian Gulf War)
☐ September 1980 to July 1990
☐ May 1975 to August 1980
☐ Vietnam era (August 1964—April 1975)
☐ February 1955 to July 1964
☐ Korean conflict (June 1950—January 1955)
☐ World War II (September 1940—July 1947)
☐ Some other time

c. In total, how many years of active-duty military service has this person had?

☐ Less than 2 years
☐ 2 years or more

21 LAST WEEK, did this person do ANY work for either pay or profit? Mark ☒ the 'Yes' box even if the person worked only 1 hour, or helped without pay in a family business or farm for 15 hours or more, or was on active duty in the Armed Forces.

☐ Yes
☐ No → Skip to 25a

22 At what location did this person work LAST WEEK? If this person worked at more than one location, print where he or she worked most last week.

a. Address (Number and street name)

(If the exact address is not known, give a description of the location such as the building name or the nearest street or intersection.)

b. Name of city, town, or post office

c. Is the work location inside the limits of that city or town?

☐ Yes
☐ No, outside the city/town limits

d. Name of county

e. Name of U.S. state or foreign country

f. ZIP Code

23 a. How did this person usually get to work LAST WEEK? If this person usually used more than one method of transportation during the trip, mark ☒ the box of the one used for most of the distance.

☐ Car, truck, or van
☐ Bus or trolley bus
☐ Streetcar or trolley car
☐ Subway or elevated
☐ Railroad
☐ Ferryboat
☐ Taxicab
☐ Motorcycle
☐ Bicycle
☐ Walked
☐ Worked at home → Skip to 27
☐ Other method

Person 5 (continued)

→ **If "Car, truck, or van" is marked in 23a, go to 23b. Otherwise, skip to 24a.**

23 b. How many people, including this person, usually rode to work in the car, truck, or van LAST WEEK?

☐ Drove alone
☐ 2 people
☐ 3 people
☐ 4 people
☐ 5 or 6 people
☐ 7 or more people

24 a. What time did this person usually leave home to go to work LAST WEEK?

☐ a.m.   ☐ p.m.

b. How many minutes did it usually take this person to get from home to work LAST WEEK?

Minutes

→ **Answer questions 25–26 for persons who did not work for pay or profit last week. Others skip to 27.**

25 a. LAST WEEK, was this person on layoff from a job?

☐ Yes → Skip to 25c
☐ No

b. LAST WEEK, was this person TEMPORARILY absent from a job or business?

☐ Yes, on vacation, temporary illness, labor dispute, etc. → Skip to 26
☐ No → Skip to 25d

c. Has this person been informed that he or she will be recalled to work within the next 6 months OR been given a date to return to work?

☐ Yes → Skip to 25e
☐ No

d. Has this person been looking for work during the last 4 weeks?

☐ Yes
☐ No → Skip to 26

e. LAST WEEK, could this person have started a job if offered one, or returned to work if recalled?

☐ Yes, could have gone to work
☐ No, because of own temporary illness
☐ No, because of all other reasons (in school, etc.)

26 When did this person last work, even for a few days?

☐ 1995 to 2000
☐ 1994 or earlier, or never worked → Skip to 31

27 Industry or Employer — Describe clearly this person's chief job activity or business last week. If this person had more than one job, describe the one at which this person worked the most hours. If this person had no job or business last week, give the information for his/her last job or business since 1995.

a. For whom did this person work? If now on active duty in the Armed Forces, mark ☒ this box → ☐ and print the branch of the Armed Forces.

Name of company, business, or other employer

b. What kind of business or industry was this? Describe the activity at location where employed. (For example: hospital, newspaper publishing, mail order house, auto repair shop, bank)

c. Is this mainly — Mark ☒ ONE box.

☐ Manufacturing?
☐ Wholesale trade?
☐ Retail trade?
☐ Other (agriculture, construction, service, government, etc.)?

28 Occupation

a. What kind of work was this person doing? (For example: registered nurse, personnel manager, supervisor of order department, auto mechanic, accountant)

b. What were this person's most important activities or duties? (For example: patient care, directing hiring policies, supervising order clerks, repairing automobiles, reconciling financial records)

Person 5 (continued)

29 Was this person — *Mark ☒ ONE box.*
☐ Employee of a PRIVATE-FOR-PROFIT company or business or of an individual, for wages, salary, or commissions
☐ Employee of a PRIVATE NOT-FOR-PROFIT, tax-exempt, or charitable organization
☐ Local GOVERNMENT employee *(city, county, etc.)*
☐ State GOVERNMENT employee
☐ Federal GOVERNMENT employee
☐ SELF-EMPLOYED in own NOT INCORPORATED business, professional practice, or farm
☐ SELF-EMPLOYED in own INCORPORATED business, professional practice, or farm
☐ Working WITHOUT PAY in family business or farm

30 a. LAST YEAR, 1999, did this person work at a job or business at any time?
☐ Yes
☐ No → *Skip to 31*

b. How many weeks did this person work in 1999? *Count paid vacation, paid sick leave, and military service.*
Weeks

c. During the weeks WORKED in 1999, how many hours did this person usually work each WEEK?
Usual hours worked each WEEK

31 INCOME IN 1999 — *Mark ☒ the "Yes" box for each income source received during 1999 and enter the total amount received during 1999 to a maximum of $999,999. Mark ☒ the "No" box if the income source was not received. If net income was a loss, enter the amount and mark ☒ the "Loss" box next to the dollar amount.*

For income received jointly, report, if possible, the appropriate share for each person; otherwise, report the whole amount for only one person and mark ☒ the "No" box for the other person. If exact amount is not known, please give best estimate.

a. Wages, salary, commissions, bonuses, or tips from all jobs — *Report amount before deductions for taxes, bonds, dues, or other items.*
☐ Yes   Annual amount — *Dollars*

☐ No

b. Self-employment income from own nonfarm businesses or farm businesses, including proprietorships and partnerships — *Report NET income after business expenses.*
☐ Yes   Annual amount — *Dollars*
☐ Loss
☐ No

31 c. Interest, dividends, net rental income, royalty income, or income from estates and trusts — *Report even small amounts credited to an account.*
☐ Yes   Annual amount — *Dollars*
☐ Loss
☐ No

d. Social Security or Railroad Retirement
☐ Yes   Annual amount — *Dollars*
☐ No

e. Supplemental Security Income (SSI)
☐ Yes   Annual amount — *Dollars*
☐ No

f. Any public assistance or welfare payments from the state or local welfare office
☐ Yes   Annual amount — *Dollars*
☐ No

g. Retirement, survivor, or disability pensions — *Do NOT include Social Security.*
☐ Yes   Annual amount — *Dollars*
☐ No

h. Any other sources of income received regularly such as Veterans' (VA) payments, unemployment compensation, child support, or alimony — *Do NOT include lump-sum payments such as money from an inheritance or sale of a home.*
☐ Yes   Annual amount — *Dollars*
☐ No

32 What was this person's total income in 1999? *Add entries in questions 31a—31h; subtract any losses. If net income was a loss, enter the amount and mark ☒ the "Loss" box next to the dollar amount.*
Annual amount — *Dollars*
☐ None   OR
☐ Loss

33 Are there more people living here? If yes, continue with Person 6.

Form D-2

32

Person 6

Housing information helps your community plan for police and fire protection.

1 What is this person's name? *Print the name of Person 6 from page 2.*
Last Name

First Name   MI

2 How is this person related to Person 1? *Mark ☒ ONE box.*
☐ Husband/wife
☐ Natural-born son/daughter
☐ Adopted son/daughter
☐ Stepson/stepdaughter
☐ Brother/sister
☐ Father/mother
☐ Grandchild
☐ Parent-in-law
☐ Son-in-law/daughter-in-law
☐ Other relative — *Print exact relationship.*

If NOT RELATED to Person 1:
☐ Roomer, boarder
☐ Housemate, roommate
☐ Unmarried partner
☐ Foster child
☐ Other nonrelative

3 What is this person's sex? *Mark ☒ ONE box.*
☐ Male
☐ Female

4 What is this person's age and what is this person's date of birth?
Age on April 1, 2000

Print numbers in boxes.
Month   Day   Year of birth

➡ NOTE: Please answer BOTH Questions 5 and 6.

5 Is this person Spanish/Hispanic/Latino? *Mark ☒ the "No" box if not Spanish/Hispanic/Latino.*
☐ No, not Spanish/Hispanic/Latino
☐ Yes, Mexican, Mexican Am., Chicano
☐ Yes, Puerto Rican
☐ Yes, Cuban
☐ Yes, other Spanish/Hispanic/Latino — *Print group.*

6 What is this person's race? *Mark ☒ one or more races to indicate what this person considers himself/herself to be.*
☐ White
☐ Black, African Am., or Negro
☐ American Indian or Alaska Native — *Print name of enrolled or principal tribe.*

☐ Asian Indian   ☐ Native Hawaiian
☐ Chinese   ☐ Guamanian or Chamorro
☐ Filipino
☐ Japanese   ☐ Samoan
☐ Korean   ☐ Other Pacific Islander — *Print race.*
☐ Vietnamese
☐ Other Asian — *Print race.*

☐ Some other race — *Print race.*

7 What is this person's marital status?
☐ Now married
☐ Widowed
☐ Divorced
☐ Separated
☐ Never married

2073

Form D-2

33

Person 6 (continued)

8 a. At any time since February 1, 2000, has this person attended regular school or college? *Include only nursery school or preschool, kindergarten, elementary school, and schooling which leads to a high school diploma or a college degree.*

- ☐ No, has not attended since February 1 → *Skip to 9*
- ☐ Yes, public school, public college
- ☐ Yes, private school, private college

b. What grade or level was this person attending? *Mark ☒ ONE box.*

- ☐ Nursery school, preschool
- ☐ Kindergarten
- ☐ Grade 1 to grade 4
- ☐ Grade 5 to grade 8
- ☐ Grade 9 to grade 12
- ☐ College undergraduate years (freshman to senior)
- ☐ Graduate or professional school *(for example: medical, dental, or law school)*

9 What is the highest degree or level of school this person has COMPLETED? *Mark ☒ ONE box. If currently enrolled, mark the previous grade or highest degree received.*

- ☐ No schooling completed
- ☐ Nursery school to 4th grade
- ☐ 5th grade or 6th grade
- ☐ 7th grade or 8th grade
- ☐ 9th grade
- ☐ 10th grade
- ☐ 11th grade
- ☐ 12th grade, **NO DIPLOMA**
- ☐ **HIGH SCHOOL GRADUATE** — high school DIPLOMA or the equivalent *(for example: GED)*
- ☐ Some college credit, but less than 1 year
- ☐ 1 or more years of college, no degree
- ☐ Associate degree *(for example: AA, AS)*
- ☐ Bachelor's degree *(for example: BA, AB, BS)*
- ☐ Master's degree *(for example: MA, MS, MEng, MEd, MSW, MBA)*
- ☐ Professional degree *(for example: MD, DDS, DVM, LLB, JD)*
- ☐ Doctorate degree *(for example: PhD, EdD)*

10 What is this person's ancestry or ethnic origin?

(For example: Italian, Jamaican, African Am., Cambodian, Cape Verdean, Norwegian, Dominican, French Canadian, Haitian, Korean, Lebanese, Polish, Nigerian, Mexican, Taiwanese, Ukrainian, and so on.)

11 a. Does this person speak a language other than English at home?

- ☐ Yes
- ☐ No → *Skip to 12*

b. What is this language?

(For example: Korean, Italian, Spanish, Vietnamese)

c. How well does this person speak English?

- ☐ Very well
- ☐ Well
- ☐ Not well
- ☐ Not at all

12 Where was this person born?

- ☐ In the United States — *Print name of state.*

- ☐ Outside the United States — *Print name of foreign country, or Puerto Rico, Guam, etc.*

13 Is this person a CITIZEN of the United States?

- ☐ Yes, born in the United States → *Skip to 15a*
- ☐ Yes, born in Puerto Rico, Guam, the U.S. Virgin Islands, or Northern Marianas
- ☐ Yes, born abroad of American parent or parents
- ☐ Yes, a U.S. citizen by naturalization
- ☐ No, not a citizen of the United States

14 When did this person come to live in the United States? *Print numbers in boxes.*
Year

15 a. Did this person live in this house or apartment 5 years ago (on April 1, 1995)?

- ☐ Person is under 5 years old → *Skip to 33*
- ☐ Yes, this house → *Skip to 16*
- ☐ No, outside the United States — *Print name of foreign country, or Puerto Rico, Guam, etc., below; then skip to 16.*

- ☐ No, different house in the United States

Person 6 (continued)

15 b. Where did this person live 5 years ago?
Name of city, town, or post office

Did this person live inside the limits of the city or town?

- ☐ Yes
- ☐ No, outside the city/town limits

Name of county

Name of state

ZIP Code

16 Does this person have any of the following long-lasting conditions:

	Yes	No
a. Blindness, deafness, or a severe vision or hearing impairment?	☐	☐
b. A condition that substantially limits one or more basic physical activities such as walking, climbing stairs, reaching, lifting, or carrying?	☐	☐

17 Because of a physical, mental, or emotional condition lasting 6 months or more, does this person have any difficulty in doing any of the following activities:

	Yes	No
a. Learning, remembering, or concentrating?	☐	☐
b. Dressing, bathing, or getting around inside the home?	☐	☐
c. (Answer if this person is 16 YEARS OLD OR OVER.) Going outside the home alone to shop or visit a doctor's office?	☐	☐
d. (Answer if this person is 16 YEARS OLD OR OVER.) Working at a job or business?	☐	☐

18 Was this person under 15 years of age on April 1, 2000?

- ☐ Yes → *Skip to 33*
- ☐ No

19 a. Does this person have any of his/her own grandchildren under the age of 18 living in this house or apartment?

- ☐ Yes
- ☐ No → *Skip to 20a*

b. Is this grandparent currently responsible for most of the basic needs of any grandchild(ren) under the age of 18 who live(s) in this house or apartment?

- ☐ Yes
- ☐ No → *Skip to 20a*

c. How long has this grandparent been responsible for the(se) grandchild(ren)? *If the grandparent is financially responsible for more than one grandchild, answer the question for the grandchild for whom the grandparent has been responsible for the longest period of time.*

- ☐ Less than 6 months
- ☐ 6 to 11 months
- ☐ 1 or 2 years
- ☐ 3 or 4 years
- ☐ 5 years or more

20 a. Has this person ever served on active duty in the U.S. Armed Forces, military Reserves, or National Guard? *Active duty does not include training for the Reserves or National Guard, but DOES include activation, for example, for the Persian Gulf War.*

- ☐ Yes, now on active duty
- ☐ Yes, on active duty in past, but not now
- ☐ No, training for Reserves or National Guard only → *Skip to 21*
- ☐ No, never served in the military → *Skip to 21*

b. When did this person serve on active duty in the U.S. Armed Forces? *Mark ☒ a box for EACH period in which this person served.*

- ☐ April 1995 or later
- ☐ August 1990 to March 1995 (including Persian Gulf War)
- ☐ September 1980 to July 1990
- ☐ May 1975 to August 1980
- ☐ Vietnam era (August 1964—April 1975)
- ☐ February 1955 to July 1964
- ☐ Korean conflict (June 1950—January 1955)
- ☐ World War II (September 1940—July 1947)
- ☐ Some other time

c. In total, how many years of active-duty military service has this person had?

- ☐ Less than 2 years
- ☐ 2 years or more

21 LAST WEEK, did this person do ANY work for either pay or profit? Mark ☒ the "Yes" box even if the person worked only 1 hour, or helped without pay in a family business or farm for 15 hours or more, or was on active duty in the Armed Forces.

☐ Yes
☐ No → Skip to 25a

22 At what location did this person work LAST WEEK? If this person worked at more than one location, print where he or she worked most last week.

a. Address (Number and street name)

(If the exact address is not known, give a description of the location such as the building name or the nearest street or intersection.)

b. Name of city, town, or post office

c. Is the work location inside the limits of that city or town?
☐ Yes
☐ No, outside the city/town limits

d. Name of county

e. Name of U.S. state or foreign country

f. ZIP Code

23 a. How did this person usually get to work LAST WEEK? If this person usually used more than one method of transportation during the trip, mark ☒ the box of the one used for most of the distance.

☐ Car, truck, or van
☐ Bus or trolley bus
☐ Streetcar or trolley car
☐ Subway or elevated
☐ Railroad
☐ Ferryboat
☐ Taxicab
☐ Motorcycle
☐ Bicycle
☐ Walked
☐ Worked at home → Skip to 27
☐ Other method

→ If "Car, truck, or van" is marked in 23a, go to 23b. Otherwise, skip to 24a.

b. How many people, including this person, usually rode to work in the car, truck, or van LAST WEEK?
☐ Drove alone
☐ 2 people
☐ 3 people
☐ 4 people
☐ 5 or 6 people
☐ 7 or more people

24 a. What time did this person usually leave home to go to work LAST WEEK?

☐ a.m. ☐ p.m.

b. How many minutes did it usually take this person to get from home to work LAST WEEK?
Minutes

→ Answer questions 25–26 for persons who did not work for pay or profit last week. Others skip to 27.

25 a. LAST WEEK, was this person on layoff from a job?
☐ Yes → Skip to 25c
☐ No

b. LAST WEEK, was this person TEMPORARILY absent from a job or business?
☐ Yes, on vacation, temporary illness, labor dispute, etc. → Skip to 26
☐ No → Skip to 25d

c. Has this person been informed that he or she will be recalled to work within the next 6 months OR been given a date to return to work?
☐ Yes → Skip to 25e
☐ No

d. Has this person been looking for work during the last 4 weeks?
☐ Yes
☐ No → Skip to 26

e. LAST WEEK, could this person have started a job if offered one, or returned to work if recalled?
☐ Yes, could have gone to work
☐ No, because of own temporary illness
☐ No, because of all other reasons (in school, etc.)

26 When did this person last work, even for a few days?
☐ 1995 to 2000
☐ 1994 or earlier, or never

Form D-2

36

---

27 Industry or Employer — Describe clearly this person's chief job activity or business last week. If this person had more than one job, describe the one at which this person worked the most hours. If this person had no job or business last week, give the information for his/her last job or business since 1995.

a. For whom did this person work? If now on active duty in the Armed Forces, mark ☒ this box → ☐ and print the branch of the Armed Forces.

Name of company, business, or other employer

b. What kind of business or industry was this? Describe the activity at location where employed. (For example: hospital, newspaper publishing, mail order house, auto repair shop, bank)

c. Is this mainly — Mark ☒ ONE box.
☐ Manufacturing?
☐ Wholesale trade?
☐ Retail trade?
☐ Other (agriculture, construction, service, government, etc.)?

28 Occupation

a. What kind of work was this person doing? (For example: registered nurse, personnel manager, supervisor of order department, auto mechanic, accountant)

b. What were this person's most important activities or duties? (For example: patient care, directing hiring policies, supervising order clerks, repairing automobiles, reconciling financial records)

29 Was this person — Mark ☒ ONE box.
☐ Employee of a PRIVATE-FOR-PROFIT company or business or of an individual, for wages, salary, or commissions
☐ Employee of a PRIVATE NOT-FOR-PROFIT, tax-exempt, or charitable organization
☐ Local GOVERNMENT employee (city, county, etc.)
☐ State GOVERNMENT employee
☐ Federal GOVERNMENT employee
☐ SELF-EMPLOYED in own NOT INCORPORATED business, professional practice, or farm
☐ SELF-EMPLOYED in own INCORPORATED business, professional practice, or farm
☐ Working WITHOUT PAY in family business or farm

30 a. LAST YEAR, 1999, did this person work at a job or business at any time?
☐ Yes
☐ No → Skip to 31

b. How many weeks did this person work in 1999? Count paid vacation, paid sick leave, and military service.
Weeks

c. During the weeks WORKED in 1999, how many hours did this person usually work each WEEK?
Usual hours worked each WEEK

31 INCOME IN 1999 — Mark ☒ the "Yes" box for each income source received during 1999 and enter the total amount received during 1999 to a maximum of $999,999. Mark ☒ the "No" box if the income source was not received. If net income was a loss, enter the amount and mark ☒ the "Loss" box next to the dollar amount.

For income received jointly, report, if possible, the appropriate share for each person; otherwise, report the whole amount for only one person and mark ☒ the "No" box for the other person. If exact amount is not known, please give best estimate.

a. Wages, salary, commissions, bonuses, or tips from all jobs — Report amount before deductions for taxes, bonds, dues, or other items.
☐ Yes   Annual amount — Dollars
   $
☐ No

b. Self-employment income from own nonfarm businesses or farm businesses, including proprietorships and partnerships — Report NET income after business expenses.
☐ Yes   Annual amount — Dollars
   $ ☐ Loss
☐ No

2077

Form D-2

37

Person 6 (continued)

31 c. Interest, dividends, net rental income, royalty income, or income from estates and trusts — *Report even small amounts credited to an account.*

☐ Yes   Annual amount — *Dollars*

☐ Loss

☐ No

d. Social Security or Railroad Retirement

☐ Yes   Annual amount — *Dollars*

☐ No

e. Supplemental Security Income (SSI)

☐ Yes   Annual amount — *Dollars*

☐ No

f. Any public assistance or welfare payments from the state or local welfare office

☐ Yes   Annual amount — *Dollars*

☐ No

g. Retirement, survivor, or disability pensions — *Do NOT include Social Security.*

☐ Yes   Annual amount — *Dollars*

☐ No

h. Any other sources of income received regularly such as Veterans' (VA) payments, unemployment compensation, child support, or alimony — *Do NOT include lump-sum payments such as money from an inheritance or sale of a home.*

☐ Yes   Annual amount — *Dollars*

☐ No

32 What was this person's total income in 1999? *Add entries in questions 31a—31h; subtract any losses. If net income was a loss, enter the amount and mark ☒ the "Loss" box next to the dollar amount.*

Annual amount — *Dollars*

☐ None   OR

☐ Loss

33 Thank you for completing your official U.S. Census form. If there are more than six people at this address, the Census Bureau may contact you for the same information about these people.

Form D-2

38

References

Bennefield, R., and R. Bonnette. 2003. *Structural and occupancy characteristics of housing: 2000.* Census 2000 Brief C2KBR-32. Washington, D.C.: U.S. Department of Commerce, U.S. Census Bureau.

Bonnette, R. 2003. *Housing costs of homeowners: 2000.* Census 2000 Brief C2KBR-27. Washington, D.C.: U.S. Department of Commerce, U.S. Census Bureau.

Canada.com 2003. Some 20,000 Canadians worship at the altar of Yoda. May 13, 2003. *www.canada.com/national/features/census/story.html?id=a4623A62-5195-4B57-B40B-087D8F38Cf6F* (accessed May 7, 2004).

Cantwell, P., H. Hogan, and K. Styles. 2003. *The use of statistical methods in the U.S. Census: Utah vs. Evans.* Research Report Series #2003-05. Washington, D.C.: U.S. Bureau of the Census, Statistical Research Division.

Conlin, M. 2003. Unmarried America. *BusinessWeek* (October 20): 106–116.

Davis, H. C. 1990. *Regional economic impact analysis and project evaluation.* Vancouver: University of British Columbia Press.

Day, J. C., and E. C. Newburger. 2002. *The big payoff: Educational attainment and synthetic estimates of work-life earnings.* Current Population Reports P23-210. Washington, D.C.: U.S. Department of Commerce, U.S. Census Bureau.

Dent, B. 1999. *Cartography: Thematic map design.* Boston: WCB/McGraw–Hill.

Fisher, G. M. 1997. *The development of the Orshansky Poverty Thresholds and their subsequent history as the official U.S. poverty measure.* U.S. Department of Health and Human Services. www.census.gov/hhes/poverty/povmeas/papers/orshansky.html#C3 (accessed November 3, 2003).

Franklin, R. S. 2003. *Migration of the young, single, and college-educated: 1995 to 2000.* Census 2000 Special Reports CENSR-12. Washington, D.C.: U.S. Department of Commerce, U.S. Census Bureau.

Griffin, D. H., and S. M. Obenski. 2002. *Meeting 21st century demographic data needs— Implementing the American Community Survey: May 2002.* Washington, D.C.: U.S. Department of Commerce, U.S. Census Bureau.

Harder, C. 1998. *Serving maps on the Internet.* Redlands, Calif: ESRI.

Hobbs, F., and N. Stoops. 2002. *Demographic trends in the 20th century.* Census Special Reports CENSR-4. Washington, D.C.: U.S. Department of Commerce, U.S. Census Bureau.

Hovland, M. A., J. G. Gauthier, and W. F. Micarelli. 2000. *History of the 1997 Economic Census.* Washington, D.C.: U.S. Department of Commerce.

Jones, N., and A. Symens Smith. 2001. *The two or more races population: 2000.* Census 2000 Brief C2KBR/01-6. Washington, D.C.: U.S. Department of Commerce, U.S. Census Bureau.

Kain, J. F. 1992. The spatial mismatch hypothesis: Three decades later. *Housing Policy Debate* 3: 2, 371–460.

Kaufman, J. E., and J. E. Rosenbaum. 1992. The education and employment of low-income black youth in white suburbs. *Education Evaluation and Policy Analysis* 14: 3, 229–240.

Kingsley, G. T. 1998. *Neighborhood indicators: Taking advantage of the new potential.* National Neighborhood Indicators Partnership Report. Washington D.C.: The Urban Institute.

Kingsley, G. T., ed. 1999. *Building and operating neighborhood indicator systems: A guidebook.* National Neighborhood Indicators Partnership Report. Washington, D.C.: The Urban Institute.

Klosterman, R. 1990. *Community analysis and planning techniques.* Savage, Md.: Rowman and Littlefield Publishers.

Kreider, R. M., and T. Simmons. 2003. *Marital status: 2000.* Census 2000 Brief C2KBR-30. Washington, D.C.: U.S. Department of Commerce, U.S. Census Bureau.

Lavin, M. 1996. *Understanding the census: A guide for marketers, planners, grant writers and other data users.* Kenmore, N.Y.: Epoch Books.

Malone, N., K. F. Baluja, J. M. Costanza, and C. J. David. 2003. *The foreign-born population: 2000.* Census 2000 Brief C2KBR-34. Washington, D.C.: U.S. Department of Commerce, U.S. Census Bureau.

McGranahan, D. 1999. *Natural amenities drive rural population change.* Agricultural Economic Report no. 781. Washington, D.C.: U.S. Department of Agriculture, Economic Research Service. www.ers.usda.gov/Publications/AER781 (accessed October 13, 2003).

Monmonier, M. 1996. *How to lie with maps.* Chicago, Ill.: University of Chicago Press.

Myers, D. 1992. *Analysis with local census data: Portraits of change.* Boston, Mass.: Academic Press.

Perry, M. J. 2003. *State-to-state migration flows: 1995 to 2000.* Census 2000 Special Reports CENSR-8. Washington, D.C.: U.S. Department of Commerce, U.S. Census Bureau.

Peterman, W. 2000. *Neighborhood planning and community-based development: The potential and limits of grassroots action.* Thousand Oaks, Calif.: Sage Publications.

Pitcoff, W. 1997. Redefining community development, part I. *Shelterforce* 96.

Richman, N., and Y. Kawano. 2000. Neighborhood information is not just for the experts. *Shelterforce* 113.

Robinson, G., B. Ahmed, P. Das Gupta, and K. Woodrow. 1993. Estimation of population coverage in the 1990 United States Census based on demographic analysis. *Journal of the American Statistical Association* 88 (423): 1061–1071.

Rosenbaum, J. E. 1996. Changing the geography of opportunity by expanding residential choice: Lessons from the Gautreaux Program. *Housing Policy Debate* 6: 1, 231–269.

Sanoff, H. 2000. *Community participation methods in design and planning.* New York: John Wiley and Sons, Inc.

Shin, H. B., with R. Bruno. 2003. *Language use and English-speaking ability: 2000.* Census 2000 Brief C2KBR-29. Washington, D.C.: U.S. Department of Commerce, U.S. Census Bureau.

Simmons, T., and G. O'Neill. 2001. *Households and families: 2000.* Census 2000 Brief C2KBR/01-8.

Simmons, T., and J. Lawler Dye. 2003. *Grandparents living with grandchildren: 2000.* Census 2000 Brief C2KBR-31. Washington, D.C.: U.S. Department of Commerce, U.S. Census Bureau.

Srinivasan, N., and E. Christopher. 2001. Moving the 1990 Census transportation planning package to a GIS platform. www.fhwa.dot.gov/ctpp/1990note2.pdf (accessed December 19, 2003).

Tatian, P. 2003. *Using information for community change: The national neighborhood indicators partnership.* Presentation at the National Conference of the American Planning Association, April 1. Denver, Colorado.

U.S. Bureau of Economic Analysis. 1997. *Regional multipliers: A user handbook for the regional input-output modeling system (RIMS II).* 3rd ed. Washington, D.C.: U.S. Department of Commerce, U.S. Bureau of Economic Analysis.

U.S. Census Bureau. 2003a. *2000 Census of Population and Housing, Summary File 3, Technical Documentation, SF3/11(RV).* Washington, D.C.: U.S. Department of Commerce, U.S. Census Bureau.

U.S. Census Bureau. 2003b. *Technical assessment of ACE Revision II.* Washington, D.C.: U.S. Department of Commerce, U.S. Census Bureau.

U.S. Census Bureau. 2003c. *DSSD ACE Revision II Memorandum Series #PP-60.* Washington, D.C.: U.S. Department of Commerce, U.S. Census Bureau.

U.S. Census Bureau. 2003d. *TIGER/Line Files, 2002, Technical Documentation.* Washington, D.C.: U.S. Department of Commerce, Census Bureau.

U.S. Census Bureau. 2003e. *American Community Survey operations plan.* (Release 1: March) Washington, D.C.: U.S. Department of Commerce, U.S. Census Bureau.

U.S. Census Bureau. 2003f. *2000 Census of Population and Housing, Public Use Microdata Sample, United States: Technical documentation.* Washington, D.C.: U.S. Department of Commerce, U.S. Census Bureau.

U.S. Census Bureau. 2002a. *Measuring America: The decennial census from 1790 to 2000, POL/02-MA(RV).* Washington, D.C.: U.S. Department of Commerce, U.S. Census Bureau.

U.S. Census Bureau. 2002b. *Census 2000 Basics, MSO/02-C2KB.* Washington, D.C.: U.S. Department of Commerce, U.S. Census Bureau.

U.S. Census Bureau. 2002c. *Comparison of ACE Revision II results with demographic analysis.* DSSD ACE Revision II Estimates Memorandum Series #PP. Washington, D.C.: U.S. Department of Commerce, U.S. Census Bureau.

U.S. Census Bureau. 2002d. *ACE Revisions II results: Further study of person duplication.* Washington, D.C.: U.S. Department of Commerce, U.S. Census Bureau.

U.S. Census Bureau. 2002e. *Census transportation planning package 2000 (CTPP2000): Definition of Subject Characteristics.* Washington, D.C.: U.S. Department of Commerce, U.S. Census Bureau.

U.S. Census Bureau. 2001. *ESCAP II: Demographic analysis results,* ACE Policy II, Report no. 1 (October 13). Washington, D.C.: U.S. Department of Commerce, U.S. Census Bureau.

U.S. Census Bureau. 2000a. *Census 2000 operational plan.* Washington, D.C.: U.S. Department of Commerce, U.S. Census Bureau.

U.S. Census Bureau. 2000b. *PUMS accuracy of the data(2000).* www.census.gov/acs/www/ Downloads/C2SS/AccuracyPUMS.pdf (accessed December 19, 2003).

U.S. Census Bureau. 1997. *Census 2000: Participant statistical areas program guidelines.* Washington, D.C.: U.S. Department of Commerce, U.S. Census Bureau.

U.S. Department of Housing and Urban Development. 2002a. *The American Community Survey: Challenges and opportunities for HUD.* Washington, D.C.: U.S. Department of Housing and Urban Development.

U.S. Department of Housing and Urban Development. 2002b. *Guide to PD&R data sets.* Washington, D.C.: U.S. Department of Housing and Urban Development. www.huduser. org/Datasets/datasets.pdf (accessed July 15, 2003).

U.S. Department of Housing and Urban Development. 1999. Research on fair market rents. *U.S. Housing Market Conditions,* May. www.huduser.org/periodicals/ushmc/spring99/ summary-2.html (accessed July 15, 2003).

U.S. Department of Housing and Urban Development. 1995. *National Survey of lead-based paint in housing.* Washington, D.C.: U.S. Department of Housing and Urban Development.

U.S. Department of Labor, Bureau of Labor Statistics, and U.S. Census Bureau. 2002. *Current population survey: Design and methodology.* Technical Paper 63RV. Washington, D.C.: U.S. Department of Labor, Bureau of Labor Statistics, and U.S. Department of Commerce, U.S. Census Bureau.

U.S. Department of Transportation, Bureau of Transportation Statistics. 2003a. *NHTS 2001 Highlights Report, BTS03-05.* Washington, D.C.: U.S. Department of Transportation, Bureau of Transportation Statistics.

U.S. Department of Transportation, Bureau of Transportation Statistics. 2003b. *Commuting expenses: Disparity for the working poor.* BTS Issue Brief 1. Washington, D.C.: U.S. Department of Transportation, Bureau of Transportation Statistics.

U.S. Department of Transportation, Bureau of Transportation Statistics. 2003c. *Transportation difficulties keep over half a million disabled at home.* BTS Issue Brief 3. Washington, D.C.: U.S. Department of Transportation, Bureau of Transportation Statistics.

U.S. Department of Transportation, Bureau of Transportation Statistics. 2003d. *OmniStats.* Washington, D.C.: U.S. Department of Transportation, Bureau of Transportation Statistics. October 3, 4.

U.S. Department of Transportation, Bureau of Transportation Statistics. 2002a. *National transportation statistics, BTS 02-08.* Washington, D.C.: U.S. Department of Transportation, Bureau of Transportation Statistics.

U.S. Department of Transportation, Bureau of Transportation Statistics. 2002b. *Transportation statistics annual report 2001, BTS02-07.* Washington, D.C.: U.S. Department of Transportation, Bureau of Transportation Statistics.

U.S. General Accounting Office. 2003a. *2000 Census redistributes federal funding among states.* GAO-03-178. Washington, D.C.: U.S. General Accounting Office.

U.S. General Accounting Office. 2003b. *Decennial census: Methods for collecting and reporting data on the homeless and others without conventional housing need refinement.* GAO-03-227. Washington, D.C.: U.S. General Accounting Office.

U.S. General Accounting Office. 2002a. *2000 Census: Best practices and lessons learned for more cost-effective nonresponse follow-up.* GAO-02-196. Washington, D.C.: U.S. General Accounting Office.

U.S. General Accounting Office. 2002b. *2000 Census: Coverage evaluation matching implemented as planned, but Census Bureau should evaluate lessons learned.* GAO-02-297. Washington, D.C.: U.S. General Accounting Office.

U.S. General Accounting Office. 2002c. *2000 Census: Refinements to Full Count Review Program could improve future data quality.* GAO-02-562. Washington, D.C.: U.S. General Accounting Office.

U.S. General Accounting Office. 2000. *Short- and long-form response rates.* GAO/GGD-00-127R. Washington, D.C.: U.S. General Accounting Office.

U.S. General Accounting Office. 1999. *2000 Census: Contingency planning needed to address risks that pose a threat to a successful census.* GAO/GGD-00-6. Washington, D.C.: U.S. General Accounting Office.

U.S. General Accounting Office. 1998. *Decennial census: Overview of historical census issues.* GAO/GGD-98-103. Washington, D.C.: U.S. General Accounting Office.

U.S. General Accounting Office. 1991. *1990 Census: Limitations in methods and procedures to include the homeless.* GGD-92-1. Washington, D.C.: U.S. General Accounting Office.

U.S. Office of Management and Budget. 2000. *Standard occupational classification (SOC) Manual: 2000.* Washington, D.C.: Office of Management and Budget.

U.S. Office of Management and Budget. 1998. *North American industry classification system, United States 1997.* Washington, D.C.: Office of Management and Budget.

U.S. Office of Management and Budget. 1987. *Standard industrial classification manual 1987.* Washington, D.C.: Office of Management and Budget.

Weinberg, D.H., V. J. Huggins, R. A. Kominski, and C. T. Nelson. 1997. A survey of program dynamics for evaluating welfare reform. Paper prepared for Statistics Symposium XIV, "New Directions in Surveys and Censuses," November. www.sipp.census.gov/spd/spdove-1.htm (accessed October 23, 2003).

Woodward, J., and B. Damon. 2001. *Housing characteristics: 2000.* Census 2000 Brief C2KBR/01-13. Washington, D.C.: U.S. Department of Commerce, U.S. Census Bureau.

Index

A

Accuracy and Coverage Evaluation (ACE), 19–21
    ACE Revision II, 19–21
aerial photography, 74–80
See also orthophotographs
American Community Survey (ACS), 2–3, 11–14, 60, 86, 88, 108, 183, 187, 208–210, 214, 264
American FactFinder, 53–61, 62, 64, 67–68, 144, 147, 149
American Housing Survey (AHS), 83, 192, 203–204, 207–209, 224
Annual Survey of Manufactures (ASM), 152
    related surveys, 152

B

blocks, 21-22
block groups, 21-23
Bureau of Economic Analysis (BEA), 130, 158, 172
    economic data and analysis, 158
    gross state product, 158
    Regional Input-Output Multipliers (RIMS II), 158
    state and local personal income, 158
Bureau of Labor Statistics (BLS), 150, 153, 154, 155–158, 173, 208
    Covered Employment and Wages (ES202), 153, 155–156, 173
    Current Employment Statistics (CES) survey, 86, 133, 150, 156
    Injuries, Illnesses, and Fatalities (IIF), 157–158
    Local Area Unemployment Statistics (LAUS), 157
    major employment and related data series, 155–158
    Mass Layoff Statistics (MLS), 157

Unlocking the Census with GIS
Cover design, book design, image editing, and production by Savitri Brant
Copyediting and proofreading by Tiffany Wilkerson
Cartographic review by Edith M. Punt
Printing coordination by Cliff Crabbe

DATE DUE